Contributing Authors

JAMES KERN
Ph.D., The Ohio State University
Professor of Psychology
University of Texas

NATHAN BRODY
Ph.D., University of Michigan
Associate Professor of Psychology
New School for Social Research

ALBERT HUNT
Ph.D., Cornell University
Research Professor of Psychology
University of Illinois

HAROLD M. SCHRODER
Ph.D., The University of London
Professor of Psychology
Princeton University

PHILIP R STONE
Ph.D., Harvard University
Associate Professor of Social Relations
Harvard University

PETER SUEDFELD
Ph.D., Princeton University
Associate Professor of Psychology
Rutgers University

RICHARD TOMLINS
Ph.D., University of Pennsylvania
Professor of Psychology
Rutgers—The State University

Contributing Authors

JAMES BIERI
Ph.D., The Ohio State University
Professor of Psychology
University of Texas

NATHAN BRODY
Ph.D., University of Michigan
Associate Professor of Psychology
New School for Social Research

J. McV. HUNT
Ph.D., Cornell University
Research Professor of Psychology
University of Illinois

HAROLD M. SCHRODER
Ph.D., The Ohio State University
Professor of Psychology
Princeton University

PHILIP J. STONE
Ph.D., Harvard University
Associate Professor of Social Relations
Harvard University

PETER SUEDFELD
Ph.D., Princeton University
Associate Professor of Psychology
Rutgers—The State University

SILVAN TOMKINS
Ph.D., University of Pennsylvania
Professor of Psychology
Rutgers—The State University

PERSONALITY THEORY
AND
INFORMATION PROCESSING

Edited by

HAROLD M. SCHRODER
PRINCETON UNIVERSITY

PETER SUEDFELD
RUTGERS—THE STATE UNIVERSITY

THE RONALD PRESS COMPANY · NEW YORK

Library of Congress Catalog Card Number: 77–123053
PRINTED IN THE UNITED STATES OF AMERICA

Preface

Students of psychology typically find personality to be one of the most intriguing topics within the discipline. Part of the fascination lies in the relevance of the subject: man is the proper study of mankind. All of human behavior is built on the foundation of personality, so that the compleat theorist must advance explanations for individual consistency and variety in perception, cognition, motivation, development, social relations . . . in fact, in all of those topics which are represented by chapters in textbooks of general psychology.

This book is concerned with one broad category of theories, a category which has become prominent in recent years. Information processing—the characteristic ways in which an individual selects, organizes, stores, and uses information in adapting to various aspects of his world—is the basis of a number of explanatory formulations. The specific theories exhibit the same diversity as does personality theory generally, although there is more agreement on basic concepts.

Because of the overwhelming abundance of established theories and its own relative novelty, the information processing model has been ignored by textbook writers. There is no personality text which covers this category of theory, although a few of the more recent books have mentioned one or two specific formulations. For the working psychologist, it provides an easily available compendium of a number of approaches which are not brought together in any other single publication.

The contributing authors were selected on the basis of their scholarship in the field and the diversity of their views. Most major theories are presented in some detail, although there is no attempt to devote a chapter to every one. A further consideration has been to bring together in one concise volume views which have hitherto been available either in incomplete form or only by tracking down and integrating a great number of partial expositions.

In all, the chapters represent a diversity of approaches and opinions in the area. At the present time, no one viewpoint has either gained or deserved predominance; the mixed nature of the sample presented here is thus a faithful reflection of the mixed population. The major ideas and methods have been included, and it is hoped that their presence in one book may lead to their closer association in the work of interested psychologists. Such an association seems necessary if the information processing approach is to provide more than just another set of competing formulations to a field which is already overcrowded with theories.

HAROLD M. SCHRODER
PETER SUEDFELD

Princeton, New Jersey
New Brunswick, New Jersey
October, 1970

Contents

Contents

PERSONALITY THEORY
AND
INFORMATION PROCESSING

1

Information Processing as a Personality Model

PETER SUEDFELD

Many theorists who are concerned with the ways in which man adapts to his environment have recently taken the term "information processing" as their trademark. From the information processing viewpoint, the essence of the organism's interaction with the world is the identification and acquisition of potentially useful stimuli, the translation and transformation of the information received into meaningful patterns, and the use of these patterns in choosing an optimal response. Obviously, the major interest is in cognitive processes, the "black box" so fatally forbidding to some theorists and so fatally attractive to others.

This approach has become one of the dominant theoretical movements of contemporary experimental psychology. It has contributed new ideas to every subfield. To mention a few of its applications, Garner (1962) has used it to formulate problems in perception and cognition; Berlyne (1960, 1965) and Broadbent (1958), among others, have considered the nature of thinking and problem solving from this point of view; G. A. Miller (1956) pioneered its use in the study of memory; Hebb (1955) based his model of neurophysiology upon it; it is the hallmark of the "new look" in motivation theory (e.g., Haber, 1966); Heider (1958), Festinger (1957), and other consistency theorists have built it into their explications of attitude change and interpersonal attraction. Relatively recently, it has gained support among personality theorists who have translated both development and adult functioning into information processing terms. They use the parameters of information acquisition, transformation, and utilization to explain general behavorial tendencies as well as individual differences. Since the incorporation of this view into personology is relatively new, a number of theories, presumably overlapping to some extent, compete for prominence; this book presents the major formulations, with different emphases, most of which are not available in any other single publication.*

EARLY PRECURSORS

Interest in information processing has a long history. The precursors of modern psychology were deeply involved in the study of memory, thought, and perception—not only in the stimulus and the response, as became the vogue later, but primarily in the covert processes which intervene between the two. Epistemology, from naive realism to logical positivism, has explored the ways in which knowledge is built up from the bricks provided by the external world. In the transition from philosophy to psychology, associationists and faculty psychologists began to formulate models which would eventually lead to the experimental investigation of cognitive processes. Early psychologists—Galton, Wundt, James, Titchener—often in disagreement with each other, were all vitally interested in intellectual functioning, while Müller, Donders, and Münsterberg investigated the physiological substrata of thinking and perceiving. The functionalists, with James, Külpe, Dewey, and their followers, emphasized the adaptive behavior of the organism; the Würzburg school centered its interest on the activity of the mind, the actual processing of information (see, e.g., Murphy, 1949).

All of these lines of interest may be counted among the early origins of information processing theories. More recently, the Gestalt school has emphasized the transforming and organizing functions of the perceptual and cognitive mechanisms. Here, however, stimulus characteristics are still considered to be crucial in affecting the subsequent central activity. The major intervening construct is the now discredited neurological isomorphism. Lewin's (1935, 1936) field theory, with its emphasis on the nature of the psychological processing structures themselves, was a further step toward the current point of view and may be its most direct ancestor.

* A recent volume, *Readings for a cognitive theory of personality* (edited by J. C. Mancuso; Holt, Rinehart & Winston, 1970), contains brief reprinted articles and excerpts from the available literature, with commentary by the editor.

RECENT DEVELOPMENTS

A major source of impetus was the development of electronic computers and the use of computer programs to simulate intelligence. The use of models analogous to contemporary mechanical devices is not unusual in psychology: Freud's closed system of psychic energy has been likened to the steam engine, while early S–R theory viewed the brain as a telephone switchboard. Information processing theory borrowed many concepts from electronic data processing, including the idea of programs, vital to the explanation of personality from this viewpoint. Computers provide one more great advantage: they can be programmed to simulate human cognitive behavior, and thus to test theoretical constructs in observable operation. This is a benefit of striking value, making possible much better tests of the theory and also making the analogy more useful; as Reitman (1965) points out, complex cognitive systems seem to require complex theoretical explanations which in turn necessitate complex representational languages and demonstrations. The computer provides these last better than any symbolic tool previously available (see Tomkins and Messick, 1963; Loehlin, 1968).

The first major contribution which explicitly emphasized the information processing basis of behavior was Hebb's *The Organization of Behavior* (1949). Hebb's emphasis on the central processes which intervene between external stimulus and overt response, and the insistence on conceiving of the organism as active rather than merely reactive, aroused the interest of a wide variety of psychologists. The concept of cell assemblies and phase sequences, which has been termed "probably the most seminal theory to appear in the postwar era" (Reitman, 1965, p. 6), provided a persuasive alternative to the brain-as-switchboard model. A great outpouring of work followed, centered on the study of cognition and related processes (attention, expectancy, etc.). Workers who had found no satisfying theoretical structure for their investigations of problem solving, thinking, perception, concept formation, and the like, helped to fill in this attractive new framework (e.g., Allport, 1955; Berlyne, 1965; Broadbent, 1958; Harper et al., 1964; Hunt, 1962; G. A. Miller et al., 1960; Newell and Simon, 1961; Reitman, 1959; Selfridge, 1955).

As it has developed, the new approach has strong ties to field theory (Lewin, 1935, 1936). It has a relatively small number of basic concepts, which are relevant to a great number of specific problems and situations. Some of these variables are identical to ones handled by field theorists and, later, by general-systems theorists (Berrien, 1969; J. G. Miller, 1955). For example, the nature of the interchanges between systems and the information load which can be handled effectively are central concerns in all of these theories.

CURRENT CONCERNS

Soon after the integration of the approach into the study of cognition, theorists began to appreciate its implications for concepts of personality (see Blake and Ramsey, 1951). Intelligence is probably the oldest focus of interest combining the two areas; now, rather than using mere cognitive ability or aptitude as a relevant variable, transformational structures were hypothesized to be important to the personologist's concerns. Perhaps the distinctive characteristic of information processing theorists of personality is their concern with the structure, rather than the content, of relevant cognitive mechanisms. For instance, whereas Adorno et al. (1950), in *The Authoritarian Personality*, had foreshadowed much later work on rigidity and simplistic information handling, their formulations were content-bound and thus of relatively restricted scope. The more recent approaches in this field have made significant contributions toward a much wider range of behavioral, attitudinal, and intellectual contexts.

An examination of the theories based on the cognitive approach reveals several common interests. Many writers, for example, concern themselves with questions of input flow—in Lewinian terms, the permeability of boundaries. This is an old issue, dealt with in the past through such concepts as the defense mechanisms of avoidance and denial (A. Freud, 1936; Hartmann, 1939) and, from a somewhat different theoretical standpoint, perceptual defense (McGinnies, 1949). It is also treated in a great deal of work on attitude change, in relation to source and message credibility, information search, etc. (e.g., Festinger, 1957; Hovland and Janis, 1959; Insko, 1967). Piaget's (1936) discussion of assimilation and accommodation is likewise relevant to the understanding of how and why certain information is processed while other information is rejected or "unnoticed." The work of Stroop (1935), followed by others (see Jensen & Rohwer, 1966), has emphasized individual differences in keeping out irrelevant information—i.e., proneness to interference. Satiability, the amount of information which can be processed before the boundary hardens, has also been used as a personality variable (Petrie et al., 1958; Wertheimer, 1955).

Once information does enter the system, it is subject to various transformations. There are two major ways of dealing with transforming mechanisms as personality characteristics: one is to classify them according to their general ability to differentiate and integrate information, the other is to emphasize specific structural tendencies. The first of these approaches is typified by theories which deal with information processing complexity. How well the individual can discriminate along and across stimulus dimensions (Berkowitz, 1957; Bruner & Tajfel, 1961; Fillenbaum, 1959; Gardner, 1953; Gardner et al., 1959; Marrs, 1955; Pettigrew, 1958; Tajfel et al., 1964), and/or how rich he is in ways of organizing and patterning information (Barron, 1953; Bieri, 1961; Harvey et al., 1961; Kelly, 1955; Schroder et al., 1967), is viewed as a basic aspect of personality. Among the second group of theories are those which distinguish field- and body-orientation (Witkin et al., 1954, elaborated into a complexity-type theory by Witkin et al., 1962), constriction and flexibility (Klein, 1954), internal and external locus of control (Rotter et al., 1962), leveling and sharpening (Gardner et al., 1959; Holzman, 1954), repression and sensitization (Byrne, 1961), focusing and scanning (Gardner et al., 1959; Holzman, 1966; Schlesinger, 1954), and various "conceptual styles" (Kagan et al., 1963). The relationships among these variables, crucial to an understanding of information processing structures, are yet to be intensively investigated.

Another common focus is on rigidity. The ease with which cognitive organization can be altered appears to be one of basic dimensions used by contemporary personality theorists. As usual, Lewin (1935) anticipated this interest three decades ago, in the proposition that psychological restructuring is affected by the firmness of boundaries and the fluidity of regions. Piaget (1936) and Bruner (1966) have traced the development of a child's cognitive behavior from rigidity to increasing flexibility. Rigidity was a central concept in the theories of Adorno et al. (1950), Fenichel (1945), Frenkel-Brunswik (1949), and Rokeach (1960) and is, of course, linked to the psychoanalytic consideration of perseveration and fixation.

EVALUATION

Obviously, there are many differences among these theories both in substance and in emphasis. However, their approaches are sufficiently related that some generalizations can be made. If one looks at the cognitive personality theories in the light of some of Hall and Lindzey's (1957, pp. 19–27) attributes, the following conclusions can be drawn.

Formal Attributes

Clarity and Explicitness. Like most theories in psychology, those under consideration here leave something to be desired. As usual, there is an inverse relationship between the fraction of the relevant phenomena with which a given framework attempts to deal and the explicitness of that framework. The use of mathematical (e.g., information theory) language and of computer simulation (Tomkins & Messick, 1963) provides aids to clarity; but the diversity and richness of some of the theories have forced many writers into either pseudo-operational or only peripherally operational explications. At the descriptive level, some theorists (e.g., Piaget) are admirably clear, but even they tend to muddle things when they reach the explanation stage. Others can only improve, even from the very basic phenomenal stages, but usually fail to take advantage of the opportunity.

Relation to Empirical Phenomena. Obviously, these theories do describe and at least plausibly account for many kinds of behavior. In fact, too many; it has become clear that the level of information processing complexity, for instance, depends upon which of the tests currently in use is being considered, and that different tests of "complexity" measure widely different things (Suedfeld et al., 1969; Vannoy, 1965). The dubious quality of some of the tests adds to this problem. Validity and reliability data are scarce; norms are almost nonexistent, with nongeneralizable median or quartile splits being the most common method for categorizing samples. Scoring is often tedious and scoring rules sometimes have a vagueness approaching the level of literary criticism. Some tests overlap, and for all we know may essentially duplicate, measures of intelligence (Guilford, 1956). All in all, the psychometric aspect of this research, on which most of the individual-difference conclusions rest, is an insecure foundation. (See Scott, 1963, for further discussion of these problems.)

The theories can also be used to explain events which did not happen —e.g., the explanation of Harvey et al. (1961) of the lack of resistance of American prisoners of war in Korea (Biderman, 1963). In general, a criticism made of Lewin's field theory may also be applied to these, its heirs: the theory may be impressive and the studies may be elegant, but the connections between the two are often tenuous at best.

Research Generated by the Theory. Here again, Lewin's offspring bear the family resemblance. The information processing approaches have been extraordinarily fruitful in generating empirical research, both in the field and in the laboratory. This is in part due to the unusually interesting quality of the theoretical concepts and in part to the energy and ingenuity of the theorists. Certainly people like Piaget, Kelly, and Witkin—to name only a few of the leaders—not only illuminate large areas of investigation but also strike a spark among colleagues and students to extend the light even further. Almost no recent book on personality, learning, development, or motivation has been without at least one chapter or contribution dealing with cognitive theory, and the number of books and articles centered on this topic is becoming staggering.

Substantive Attributes

Teleology. As befits cognitively oriented theorists, most of the major writers in the group take purposiveness for granted. It is not really a central aspect in any of the formulations; as Hall and Lindzey remark about contemporary personality theory in general, "Most personality theorists seem to conceive of man as a purposive creature but even where this is not taken for granted it does not seem to be a matter of hot dispute" (1957, p. 539).

Unconscious Determinants. Even those members of the group who started with a psychoanalytic orientation (e.g., Adorno et al., 1950; Hartmann, 1939; Rapaport, 1958) have emphasized the conscious aspects of information processing. For them, the cognitive variables may be dimensions which can be looked at separately from the unconscious processes, although of course in the ongoing personality the two interact. Still, while the functionings of the ego are affected by unconscious urges, it is the secondary process that is of interest. For example, the defense mechanisms of the ego are shaped largely by the stresses of the unconscious; but the "ego psychologists" concentrate on how the defenses—once shaped—influence the thinking process (see, e.g., Rapaport, 1951). Those theorists who have no analytic predilection generally ignore the question of unconscious determinants. For example, the word "unconscious" does not appear in the indices of Harvey et al. (1961), Kelly (1955), Flavell's (1963) summary of Piaget, nor even Rokeach (1960). To introduce such concepts would add a great amount of noise to an already noisy system; although the black box may contain an even blacker one, to proceed on this assumption would lead to chaos.

Reinforcement and Association. The cognitive theorists focus on the reward value of information processing efficiency. First, the appropriate use of cognitive ability tends to lead to goal attainment; second, such a use is rewarding in itself (see, e.g., Hartmann, 1939; White, 1959). The latter idea, that the processing of information is intrinsically rewarding, is a central one in the "new motivation theory" (see Fiske & Maddi, 1961) and has played an equally important role in the "new personality theory." In fact, it has been hypothesized that otherwise rewarding consequences may be aversive if they hinder the processing of information (Schroder et al., 1967).

The Learning Process vs. Acquisitions of Personality. Here, the cognitive personality theorists show a variety of emphases. Some are primarily concerned with the gradual development of the cognitive structures (Piaget, Bruner), whereas others devote their attention to the finally acquired structures themselves (Kelly, Bieri, Rokeach, Tomkins). The majority apply themselves to both, preferring to explain how the system develops as well as how it functions (J. McV. Hunt, Harvey et al., Witkin).

Genetic Factors. Hereditary differences in information processing characteristics or capabilities are generally ignored in favor of environmental explanations. Piaget describes a partly invariant biologically programmed developmental sequence. Development involves the interplay between assimilation of new information and accommodation of the existing cognitive structure to the new input, leading to increased complexity and abstractness first in the sensory-motor and then in the conceptual realm (see Flavell, 1963). Sugerman and Haronian (1964) imply a link between field independence and somatotype. As a rule, however, nurture is given much more attention than nature, partly on implicit philosophical grounds. Genetic determinism is, first of all, deplorably illiberal: it asserts that all men are not created equal. This is particularly bothersome because value judgments are at least implicit in many theories. Who can deny that it is bad to be authoritarian, rigid, dogmatic, cognitively simple, etc? Not only that, but such an hypothesis is also shockingly un-American, since it posits a state of affairs which we cannot control. At least on the human level, heredity is not open to experimental techniques. Thus, the predilection of most psychologists—including the cognitive personality theorists—for environmental explanations is unlikely to undergo rapid change. J. McV. Hunt (1961) has been especially prominent in analyzing the relatively secondary role of hereditary factors even in such supposedly fixed traits as intelligence.

Early Development. Few of the information processing theorists concentrate on the effects of early childhood, although J. McV. Hunt considers the first few years crucial for optimal cognitive development. Other writers (e.g., Harvey et al., 1961), while stressing the need for appropriate encounters and experiences in childhood, tend to be more liberal in their time spans. It is interesting that there has been so little attempt to incorporate the literature on sensory and motor restriction into personality theory (but see Rapaport, 1951). In general, always excepting Piaget, Bruner, and Hunt, the researchers in this area are much more interested in contemporary than in past environmental characteristics.

Continuity of Development. Those workers who address themselves to development in a more than perfunctory way usually deal with this question indirectly. They tend to discuss the developmental process and the functioning of the adult system separately, with but little attempt to relate the ongoing activities of the latter to the course of the former. Stages, if any (Piaget, Harvey et al.), are seen as coming in a fixed sequence, but whether each depends causally upon the previous one is not demonstrated empirically.

Holism. The most influential of the theories are holistic, although in practice some emphasize specific traits. Witkin's is one example of a theory which developed into a holistic formulation gradually. Beginning with an ingenious line of theorizing about field dependence as a trait affecting perceptual information processing, Witkin et al. (1954) went on to show that the trait generalizes to (or has a counterpart in) some cognitive behaviors. Eventually, Witkin and his coworkers (1962) arrived at the concept of psychological differentiation as a basic personality variable in the handling of informational inputs. The structural emphasis of the approach facilitates a macroscopic view, since structure presumably represents a much more general tendency than does the content of any given stimulus-response sequence. Thus, organismic holism is often assumed by definition. In practice, however, researchers tend to abstract environmental variables of interest and manipulate them in interaction with a specific structural level or style—a recognition that, no matter how holistic the theory, most experiments deal with an artificial microcosm (e.g., Schroder et al., 1967). Exceptions to this rule, in the form of field research, do exist but are fairly rare (Piaget—see Flavell, 1963; Schroder et al., 1965; Suedfeld, 1967). Operationally, what holistic emphasis remains tends to be field- rather than organism-oriented.

Uniqueness. Cognitive personality formulations are generally nomothetic rather than idiographic (for an exception, see Broverman, 1962). While the total individual may be unique, his particular cognitive style, conceptual level, etc., are shared by many others. Since it is these characteristics which are of primary interest, the theorist will concentrate on similarities and differences between groups rather than between individuals.

The Psychological Environment. One of the major concerns is the relationship between the external world and the phenomenal world. Thus, while the psychological reality is one central factor, the objective reality is equally central. Here, contemporary theorists depart from Lewin's exclusive interest in the psychological environment.

The remaining Hall and Lindzey dimensions are either not very rele-

vant or have already been dealt with under other headings. It is notice-
able that the theories under consideration show great degrees of similarity on many of these dimensions.

GENERAL COMMENTS

Information processing is certainly a lively, and probably a useful,
approach to personality. Given the ubiquity of communicative and
problem-solving acts in daily life, any set of theories which has the
promise of accurate categorization and prediction of such behaviors is
bound to play a large role in the personology of the future. The empirical orientation of most adherents to the cognitive view is another
strong point.

On the other hand, there is no doubt that the approach is not a
panacea. Conceptually, it is "cold psychology": except for Tomkins, the
theorists tend to ignore the emotions—and logically so, since the preferred model is the unemotional computer (a point to ponder for those
of us who tend to look at theories as clues to the theorist's own personality). Problems of interpersonal relations, commitment, morality,
ideology, and the like, obviously vital aspects of personality, are pushed
aside by most of the writers (Piaget and Rokeach are notable exceptions). Formally, the theories tend to be so complex that they are
difficult to evaluate. The definitions are often vague and/or circular
and the derivations of hypotheses are not strongly logical. Operationally, variables are often confounded, experimenter bias and subject expectation uncontrolled, and psychometric instruments unproven.

Actually, all of these problems are interwoven. Operational definitions of a variable such as integrative ability are offered in terms of
particular tests. The tests themselves correlate to a greater or lesser
degree. Are the writers dealing with different kinds of integrations, or
with measures which differ in efficiency, or with different traits, some
of which—or, in fact, all of which—might be called by a more appropriate term? Starting with this unresolved confusion, experimenters
apply their manipulations. These may interact with the measured personality variable, whatever it is. They may also interact with other
unmeasured variables; or perhaps only with others. Suppose that behavioral differences are found. To what can they be ascribed? Usually,
the original personality test is claimed as having "construct validity"—
i.e., experimenters had used it before and obtained predicted results. It
is then concluded that, indeed, integrative ability made the difference
here. In some cases hypothesis derivation is so loose that any outcome
can be logically postdicted. Seldom is there an attempt to apply critical

tests to the central concepts of a given theory, and never a systematic line of research aimed at elucidating the differences, similarities, and redundancies between sets of theories, or at pitting one theory against another.

The remedying of these faults and the investigation of relationships among the theories and between these and noncognitive theories, is important work for the future. We may now be approaching the point where the continued use of a given theoretical construct in one situation after another is giving us diminishing returns; the time may be ripe for linking up along the entire front.

Plan of the Book

The first chapter having served as a brief introduction to the information processing point of view, the next two deal with areas of both historical and current relevance. Mathematical information theory has been a crucial component in cybernetics and in the application of mathematical models to psychological problems. It has also been confused with information processing theory, leading to frustration and misunderstanding. Brody's discussion of information "theory" (a misnomer as he points out) provides a personological counterpart of such influential treatments in other realms of psychology as those of Garner (1962) and Reitman (1965). The clarity and elegance of information theory as a language can help greatly to improve the internal consistency and general rigor of cognitive personality theories.

As has been indicated, the development of electronic computers was one of the crucial steps in the formation of the theories with which we are concerned. The computer is not only the basic model from which theoretical descriptions have been constructed, but also a unique device for testing those descriptions and their implications. Incidentally, the use of the term "information processing" to describe computer functions has been another source of semantic confusions. The chapter by Stone examines some of the ways in which electronic hardware and its related software have been used by personality theorists, and points to future applications in theory building and research. Stone's chapter acts as a transition from the narrowly limited mathematical definition of information to the more wide-ranging and less strict usages favored by the personologists discussed in the later chapters. The loosening of the bonds is visible in the simulation of "hot cognition" and other dynamic processes which forms the core of the review.

J. McV. Hunt then discusses the motivational aspects of information processing. Motivation is an integral part of the study of personality, as it is of the study of learning. Hunt provides a thorough exposition of the new look in motivation theory, relating and contrasting it to the classical propositions popular among earlier personologists. This overview, like several other chapters, calls for the inclusion of varied sources of data and hypotheses, from physiological psychology to sociology. As has been indicated, the next chapter is also by Hunt, and deals with developmental sequences in information processing. Here again the reader will find that classical theories of personality development are at best incomplete. The reward value of information and of information processing tie this chapter to the previous discussion of motivational factors. The implications of this work, both theoretical and as applicable to child-rearing and education, are revolutionary in developmental psychology.

James Bieri then presents a general overview of several information processing theories of personality, with an emphasis on the cognitive styles approach. Individual differences in cognitive style have been used, like traits in more traditional models, to categorize and characterize members within populations. Styles can be looked upon as stable information processing structures—programs, cognitive maps—which control behavior across many contexts. Bieri's own work on cognitive complexity is not only an important part of this movement, but also serves as a comparison with other prominent systems.

The chapter by Tomkins summarizes perhaps the richest, most diverse viewpoint in the field. His emphasis on the "warmth" of personaltiy is unique among contributors to cognitive personology. Tomkins applies himself to almost everything: computer simulation, neurophysiology, history, social change—it is no wonder that the complete and detailed exposition of his theory is a multi-volume work (Tomkins, 1962 ff.) which is still largely unpublished. The application of information processing principles to an explanation of affective functioning is a particularly interesting and original feature of the theory.

Having presented his conceptual systems theory in two books (Harvey et al., 1961; Schroder et al., 1967), Schroder in his chapter concentrates on the implications of this framework for social psychology. The study of group behavior and social judgment has been a special interest of conceptual systems researchers for some time, and has been pursued in situations ranging from internation simulations through Peace Corps training sites to sensory deprivation chambers. The experimental induction of conceptual complexity, of which this chapter is the first comprehensive review, is a novel contribution to the study of information processing as a personality variable.

2

Information Theory, Motivation, and Personality

NATHAN BRODY

This chapter deals with several topics in the area of personality and motivation which are amenable to an information theoretic analysis. For the purpose of this discussion the term "information theory" is an unfortunate misnomer for two reasons. First, the word "theory" as it is ordinarily understood refers to a set of concepts which can be used to predict and explain empirical phenomena. Information theory, as it has been used in psychology, is not a theory in this sense at all. Rather, it is a technique for the measurement and conceptualization of certain quantities which may be empirically meaningful. Second, in common with many mathematical representations of concepts which are used in ordinary discourse, information theory assigns a limited and technical meaning to the concept of information. Moreover, most of the uses of information theory to be discussed here deal with something which is at most tangentially related to what is ordinarily called information.

UNCERTAINTY AND ITS MEASUREMENT

If information theory is not a theory and does not deal in any simple sense with information, then what is it? Information theory grew out of problems in the area of communication involving electrical signals, e.g., telegraphy. The classic formulation of this theory was published in 1948 by Claude Shannon (Shannon & Weaver, 1949). Shannon's paper presented a quantification of the concept of information and a general mathematical treatment of information transmission. Shannon's ideas rapidly influenced psychological research, particularly in the areas of psycholinguistics, perception, and cognition (for general reviews of this work, see Attneave, 1959; Garner, 1962; G. A. Miller, 1953).

What follows is a brief nontechnical introduction to some of the concepts of information theory. Imagine two people in a communication situation in which one person is giving some information to a second person who is receiving that information. How do we measure the amount of information that has been received by the second person? The amount of information transmitted by the first person to the second depends on the extent of ignorance of the second person. Imagine that the first person is required to send a message about which day of the week it is. He says, "Today is Wednesday." If the second person was certain that today is Wednesday, he has received no information. We can assume that he could have predicted that Person 1 would have said Wednesday in this situation. Suppose, however, that person 2 has been lost at sea for several days and is totally *uncertain* about which day of the week it is. The communication about the day of the week from Person 1 could, in this instance, mention with equal probability any one of the seven days. In this latter case, after receiving the communication the second person has received information from the first person since the communication served to reduce this uncertainty about the day of the week. This example indicates three important aspects about the quantification of information. First, the amount of information is not a function of a specific message but depends rather on the total set of messages that might have been sent. Second, information is something which reduces uncertainty about which of several alternative messages or events will occur. Third, uncertainty refers to a situation in which there is a set of alternative events, each of which has some probability of occurrence.

It is intuitively reasonable that the uncertainty (conventionally symbolized as H and measured by a unit of measure called a "bit") increases as the number of equally likely alternatives increases. If H is to have a value greater than zero, there must be at least two possible alternative events which can occur. Given two equally likely events (think of the toss of an unbiased coin), the H value of this set of alternative events is 1 bit. H is conventionally defined by the following equation:

$$H \text{ in bits} = \log_2 A$$

where A = the number of alternative events.

The formula given above is valid only in the special case where each alternative event has an equal probability of occurrence. Since H is defined in terms of logarithms to the base 2, each doubling of the number of alternative events adds 1 bit of H. Consequently, a bit of information can be thought of as that amount of information which reduces the number of equally likely alternative events by half.

The H value of a set of events depends not only on the number of alternatives but also on the probabilities of occurrence of each of the alternative events. It is intuitively clear that H should have its maximum value where each of the events is equally likely to occur. The general formula for H deals with a *weighted average* of the H of each of the events in the set. Suppose that there are two possible alternatives with probabilities of occurrence of .9 and .1, respectively. The amount of information conveyed by the event whose probability of occurrence is .1 is greater than the amount of information conveyed by the event whose probability of occurrence is .9. The uncertainty of a single event with known probability is called the surprisal value and is given by the formula:

$$h = \log_2 1/p$$

where h = the uncertainty of an individual event and p is the probability of occurrence of that event. However, repeated over a long series of random trials the event whose probability of occurrence is .9 will occur nine times more often than the event whose probability of occurrence is .1. Thus, the contribution of each event to the uncertainty of the total set of events is given by the formula:

$$h = p \log_2 1/p$$

If we obtain a sum of the contribution to the total H of each of the alternative events, we get the formula:

$$H = \Sigma p_i \log_2 1/p$$

which by the laws of logarithms is equivalent to:

$$H = - \Sigma p_i \log_2 p_i$$

To summarize, the formula for H given above represents the basic definitional formula of information theory. It is a weighted average which increases as the number of alternative events increases, and it assumes its maximum value for any given number of alternative events when the probability of occurrence of each of the events is equal.

We are now in a better position to understand why the H formula gives us a definition which is only tangentially relevant to some of our ordinary conceptions of information. First, the measure applies only in those situations in which it is possible to specify a set of alternative events and assign to each of them a probability of occurrence. Second, the measure tells us nothing about the value of the information received. A bit of information may have very different value to a person in different circumstances. Finally, it has been argued that information theory does not deal with meaning (Bar-Hillel, 1955).

H AS A MEASURE OF VARIABILITY

For our purposes, initially, we can think of H as a measure of the variability of a set of events. Typically, when we think of variability in a quantitative way we think about the variance, a measure of the degree to which a set of numbers is "spread out" or dispersed about the mean (arithmetic average). In order to think about the variance of a collection of numbers we must have a situation which permits the assignment of numbers to objects such that the number assigned is a linear function of the hypothetical true value of the object on the scale. Such a numerical scale is called an interval scale (Stevens, 1951). Suppose, however, that we have a situation in which we cannot assign numbers to objects in any meaningful way; that is, we have nominal scale data, which permits us to assign objects to different classes, but there is no quantitative relation among the classes. If numbers were assigned to such a class, one could think of the number as being merely a name for the class but not as indicating any quantitative characteristic of the class. What could be meant by a measure of the variance of such data? We can think of H as such a measure. Given nominal scale data and the requirement of selecting an element at random and guessing in which subclass it will be assigned, our accuracy in guessing will be a function of the H value of that set of events. Similarly, if we are to guess at the numerical value of an element chosen at random which can be assigned a value on an interval scale, our errors in prediction will be a function of the variance of the distribution. Our best prediction will always be the mean of the distribution. Errors of prediction will depend on the variance, which depends on the degree of dispersal of the scores about the mean. Thus, where we have quantitative data, the variance provides us with a measure of the unpredictability of a set of scores. Where we have nonquantitative data, H provides us with a measure of unpredictability which is quite analogous to the variance. McGill (1954) has explored this analogy and has shown that many of the properties of the variance are shared by H. For example, one can partition H quite analogously to the partitioning of variance in the analysis of variance. The critical difference between these two measures of variability stems from differences in the type of data for which each is an appropriate measure. The variance, being a measure appropriate for quantitative data, indicates the *magnitude* of each error in prediction whereas H, being a measure of variance appropriate for nonquantitative data, provides a measure for which there is no meaning to the concept of the magnitude of an error in prediction.

STUDIES DEALING WITH RESPONSE UNCERTAINTY

If a subject is asked to respond in a situation several times, an H value can be computed by partitioning his responses into discrete classes and noting the probability of occurrence of each response class. H here represents a measure of the intrasubject variability of the subjects' responses. What generalizations can be made about such a measure of intrasubject variability? It has been argued that the intrasubject variability of responses decreases under conditions of high motivation (Carlton, 1962; DeValois, 1954).

An experiment by Eriksen and Wechsler (1955) is relevant. In their study, subjects were presented with a psychophysical task in which they had to state which of eleven different sized squares was being presented to them on any given trial. By examining the probabilities of occurrence for each subject for each of the eleven possible responses and computing H, we have an index of a subject's intrasubject response variability. It should be noted that there is less than perfect discrimination in such a task. If all subjects were able perfectly to discriminate the eleven squares, then the subject's response on each trial would be perfectly correlated with the stimulus. Consequently, the H values of each subject's set of responses would be identical. Eriksen and Wechsler had two groups of subjects in their study. The experimental group received electric shocks at random intervals during the course of the experiment. The control group did not receive shocks. The investigators found that the H values of the experimental group's responses were significantly lower than the H values of the control group's responses. Thus, these results indicate that intrasubject response variability, as indexed by H, decreases under conditions of high motivation.

Extending these results to a situation in which response uncertainty was measured in a different way, Brody (1964) attempted to study the effects of motivation on response uncertainty when the influence of the stimulus was removed. In his experiment, subjects were required to state whether a circle or a square had been shown to them. Subjects were told that the stimulus would be presented subliminally (that is, the stimulus would be projected on a screen for a duration which was too short to permit conscious identification). Actually, no stimuli were presented at all. The instructions served as a ruse to get subjects interested and involved in the tasks. Each subject was required to respond to the stimuli 200 times. The subjects in this experiment were divided into two groups on the basis of scores on the Taylor scale, an individual difference measure of anxiety. Subjects who scored high on the Taylor scale could be assumed to have performed the task under conditions of higher motivation than subjects who scored low on the Taylor scale.

It was possible to determine for each subject the probability of occurrence of each of the two possible responses, circle and square. By applying the formula for H to these probabilities, the uncertainty of each subject's response sequence could be determined. However, such an analysis was superficial since it neglected the sequential character of the responses.

Consider the two following sequences:

1. $A B B B A B A A A B$

2. $A B A B A B A B A B$

Although both sequences have an equal number of A's and B's, it is clear that sequence 1 is in some sense more variable than sequence 2. In the case of sequence 1, knowledge of the preceding letter (A or B) does not reduce the uncertainty about which letter will follow. A and B are both equally probable following an A or a B. In the case of the second sequence, knowledge of the preceding letter completely removes any uncertainty about the following letter. It is possible to understand the greater variability of sequence 1 in another way. We can infer that sequence 2 is generated by the principle of alternation. Given two elements, A and B, there are only two possible sequences of length 10 that can be generated which conform to the principle of alternation. An examination of sequence 1 permits us to infer that it is random. There are 2^{10} possible sequences of length 10 that can be a random combination of the elements A and B. Thus, sequence 1 can be considered one of a large class of possible sequences which could have occurred, and consequently the population of sequences from which it is assumed to derive has a higher H value than the population from which sequence 2 is assumed to derive. It is possible to analyze the average uncertainty remaining in a sequence given knowledge of 1, 2, 3, . . . n previous responses. This is called a sequential redundancy analysis (Attneave, 1959). Brody applied a fourth-order sequential redundancy analysis (consideration of the effect of three previous responses on the following response) to each subject's response sequence. He found that subjects who scored high on the Taylor scale tended to generate response sequences whose H value was significantly higher than the response sequences generated by low-anxiety subjects.

Brody's results on the effect of anxiety on response uncertainty are not in agreement with those of Eriksen and Wechsler. Therefore, the generalization that response uncertainty is decreased under conditions of high motivation is not universally valid. It is not clear how these conflicting effects of motivation on response uncertainty can be reconciled within a common theoretical framework. It is possible to suggest an interpretation based on Hull's theory (1943). Hull's central equation is:

$$D \times sHr = sEr$$

where D = Drive, a variable that represents an overall level of motivation

sHr = the set of all habit tendencies present in any given situation

sEr = performance

This formula implies that increases in drive can have two contradictory effects on response uncertainty. First, if some habits (or response tendencies) are stronger than others, then increases in drive (or motivation) will tend to increase the response strength of these dominant responses relative to other responses which are present. This in turn results in an increase in the probability of occurrence of these responses relative to others. In this way, increases in drive can result in a decrease in response uncertainty by leading to a departure from an equiprobable distribution of response probabilities. It is also the case that increases in drive can lead to an *increase* in response uncertainty. This can happen in situations in which there are a number of responses below a hypothetical threshold of response evocation. Increases in drive lead to increases in the response strength of all available responses. Consequently, the number of responses above a threshold for response evocation can increase when drive is increased. The increase in number of responses with probability of occurrence greater than zero would lead to an increase in response uncertainty.

In the Eriksen and Wechsler experiment there were only eleven possible responses, each of which was clearly above threshold (subjects tended to use all eleven responses but not with equal probability). Eriksen and Wechsler assume that there are number biases and that the response strengths associated with the numbers 1–11 are not equal for any given subject. Therefore, in this situation, high drive could lead to an increase in the probability of occurrence of dominant responses. However, since all responses are above threshold, increases in drive could not theoretically lead to increases in response uncertainty.

In the Brody experiment, it is *possible* that certain combinations of the response sequences of circles and squares have response strengths below the hypothetical value of response evocation. For example, for a particular subject the response strength associated with the occurrence of a sequence in which a fourth circle follows three previous circles may be below threshold. Thus, there is some possibility that high drive states could serve to increase response uncertainty by increasing the response strengths associated with unusual response sequences such that the response strengths were above the value required for response evocation.

This interpretation is at least tangentially supported by the results of a study by Brody et al. (1967) in which subjects were required to respond several times to a list of word associates. Subjects high in anxiety tended to respond with different words on each repetition of the stimulus word. Also, d-amphetamine, a drug which serves to activate the organism and which is considered as a source of drive, had the same effect as anxiety as measured by the Taylor scale—an increase in the variability of word associates. In the word-associate study it is quite clear that there is at least the theoretical possibility that remote, below-threshold responses are energized into behavior by increases in drive level.

We can summarize this line of theoretical reasoning as follows: The effect of motivation on response uncertainty depends on other variables. In particular, states of high motivation will tend to result in decreases in response uncertainty where all responses are above the threshold of response evocation and where some responses have response strengths which are greater than others. Where these two conditions do not prevail, states of high motivation can theoretically lead to an increase in response uncertainty.[1]

In the experiments we have considered, subjects' responses have been categorized by the experimenter and the H value of each subject's re-

---

[1] For a different explanation of increases in response variability under conditions of high motivation, see Broen and Storms (1961) and the discussion of the application of their theoretical ideas to response variability in Brody *et al.* (1967).

sponse sequences has then been computed. The experiment is not presented to a subject as a study of the variability of responses, even though the experimeter intends to analyze this aspect of the subject's data. Further, the number of response categories which a subject is permitted to use is fixed by the experimenter in the experiments we have discussed by Brody and by Eriksen and Wechsler. A subject can be presented with a large number of stimuli and asked to place them into categories using any number of categories he wishes. With this procedure, the task is more or less explicitly presented to the subject as a study of categorizing behavior.

Glixman (1965) has used H and related measures in such a study. Glixman asked his subjects to sort sets of statements into groups or categories. A subject could use any number of categories he wanted. Three sets of statements were used dealing respectively with the self, war, and objects. By assigning probabilities based on the number of statements assigned by each subject to each category used by him, Glixman was able to compute the uncertainty of each subject's categories for each of the three sets of statements. He found significant correlations among the H values assigned to the different categories of statements. Thus, subjects behave consistently with respect to the variability of their categorizing behavior across different topical domains. Glixman also found that the mean H values were highest for the description of objects, next highest for the statements about war, and lowest for the statements about self. Glixman concludes from these data that the uncertainty of categorizing behavior is a function of the degree of personal relevance of the stimuli being categorized. Statements referring to self are taken to have greater personal relevance than statements referring to objects.

Glixman also used another information theory measure, H/Hmax, to summarize subjects' categorizing behavior. Hmax is obtained by $\log_2 N$ where N equals the number of categories used by a subject for a particular domain. If the subject used all of his categories with equal probability, H/Hmax would equal 1. This ratio declined as the frequencies with which the subject used his categories became more unequal. Glixman found that the mean H/Hmax values were lowest for the statements referring to self, indicating, in his interpretation, that the domains of greatest personal relevance will have a more unequal distribution of categories than other domains.

Glixman's conclusions about interdomain differences in categorizing behavior must be accepted cautiously. The H and H/Hmax values assigned to the categorization of a set of statements are undoubtedly influenced by many characteristics of the statements other than their degree of personal relevance to the subject. The number of statements in the domain as well as differences among the statements will no doubt influence the number of categories and the distribution of statements over categories. For any set of statements, differences in categorizing behavior between subjects are clearly meaningful. However, generalizations about the effects of different sets of statements on categorizing behavior are much more risky. Before accepting Glixman's interpretations we should find out whether the particular relations he found to hold among different sets of statements would hold for other sets of statements from these domains. It might be possible to find a collection of statements about the self whose mean H value would differ significantly from the mean H value obtained by the set used by Glixman in his study.

STUDIES DEALING WITH INFORMATION TRANSMISSION

The experiments we have discussed have focused on response uncertainty. Little or no attention has been given to the role of the stimulus. Information theory can be used in a more general way to specify the relationship between stimuli and responses. Here the focus of attention is on what is called information transmission. Let us return to the Eriksen and Wechsler experiment to illustrate the meaning of information transmission. In this experiment, the experimenter repeatedly presents the subject with one of several different sized squares, and the subject states which square he believes is being presented to him. Information transmission refers to the degree of relationship between stimuli and responses. If information transmission is perfect, knowing the stimuli, it is possible to predict the response and vice versa. T, the measure of information transmission, is thus analogous to a coefficient of correlation, which indicates the degree of predictability between pairs of scores. T is computed as follows. Given a matrix of stimuli and responses in which the probability of occurrence of each response to each stimulus is noted, the stimulus uncertainty is computed by obtaining the probability of occurrence of each stimulus, and then the H formula is applied to these probabilities:

$$H(s) = - \Sigma p \, \log_2 \, p_i$$

The response uncertainty is obtained by an analogous procedure whereby the H formula is applied to each of the summed response probabilities:

$$H(r) = - \Sigma p_j \, \log_2 \, p_j$$

The amount of information transmitted (T (s,r)) is defined as follows:

$$T(s,r) = H_{(s)} + H_{(r)} - H_{(s,r)}$$

where the $H_{(s,r)}$ represents the joint uncertainty and is obtained by applying the H formula to the joint probabilities of responding with a particular response to a particular stimulus:

$$H(s,r) = - \Sigma \Sigma p_{ij} \log_2 p_{ij}$$

Perfect information transmission would occur where $H(s) = H(r) = H(s,r)$. In such a case there would be a unique response for each stimulus and $T(s,r)$ and $H(s)$ would be equal. This conceptual definition has led to a number of studies which have indicated that the amount of information which human beings can transmit about unidimensional stimuli (stimuli which vary on one dimension such as the size of a square) tends in general to be limited to about 2.8 bits or roughly 7 differentiations (G. A. Miller, 1953).

We have considered the effect of motivation on $H(r)$. What is the effect of motivation on $T(s,r)$? In the Eriksen and Wechsler study, $T(s,r)$ measures were obtained for each subject. They found that the shock group did not differ significantly from the nonshock group in mean $T(s,r)$. $H(r)$, of course, sets an upper limit on $T(s,r)$. The reduction in $H(r)$ for the shock group was not sufficient to produce a decrement in $T(s,r)$. The Eriksen and Wechsler finding is particularly interesting because it bears directly on a theoretical generalization advanced by Easterbrook (1959). Easterbrook has summarized a large body of research which fits the following generalization: high drive acts to reduce the range of cues that an organism uses. We can get a feeling for the meaning of Easterbrook's generalization by discussing one of the experiments he cites.

In a study by Bursill (1958) the subject was required to keep a pointer superimposed upon another pointer which was in motion. The subject was also simultaneously assigned the task of responding, by pressing appropriate keys, to the occasional illumination of one of six lights that were arranged in a semicircle. Drive was manipulated by changing the temperature of the room in which the task was performed. Under conditions of high temperature, peripheral signals of greater eccentricity were not responded to.

Easterbrook states that high drive leads to a funneling or concentration of attention. The reduction in cue utilization is seen by Easterbrook as an index of what Tolman referred to as a decrease in width of the cognitive map under conditions of high motivation (Bruner et al.,

1955). Easterbrook points out that his generalization can be given a more precise formulation by the use of information theory as follows: The total amount of information transferred by the behavior of an organism is reduced under conditions of high drive. We can appreciate the way in which this generalization applies to data by returning to the Bursill experiment. Under conditions of low drive (moderate temperature) there is, in at least one sense, greater information transmission. From an examination of the subject's responses one could infer more accurately the nature of the stimulus presented than from an examination of the subject's responses under high drive (high temperature) conditions.

However, the information theory formulation of Easterbrook's generalization is open to criticism. First, there is only one study known to the writer in which $T(s,r)$ values were actually computed—the previously mentioned Eriksen and Wechsler study. Recall that in their study high drive did *not* decrease information transmission. Thus, the experiment of clearest relevance to the generalization does not support it.

Second, the information theory form of the generalization, although specifically giving a more precise formulation of the original generalization about cue utilization, actually misses a significant aspect of the original meaning of the generalization. Easterbrook points out that the probability of cue utilization under high drive varies inversely as a function of the degree to which the cue is, in some sense, peripheral. Thus, in Bursill's experiment the probability of reporting a cue under conditions of high drive varied inversely with the eccentricity of the cue. Since information theory measures are inherently measures appropriate for the nominal scale, any concept of order is simply not defined. Consequently, the arrangement of categories is completely arbitrary. Because of this, one cannot express with information theory the idea that the cues which are not responded to are those which are peripheral rather than central.

Third, the data cited by Easterbrook are not precisely related to the information theoretic form of his generalization. This imprecision stems from Easterbrook's definition of a cue as a characteristic of the environment which can be shown to have some effect on an organism's responses. Thus, a cue is not an independently specified characteristic of the environment but can only be inferred from an examination of the organism's responses. Since a cue is inferred from responses, a reduction in the variability of responses could lead to the inference of a reduction in cue utilization. The procedure involved in the computation of $T(s,r)$ allows for the analytic separation of "perceptual" from response effects. Easterbrook's procedure of inferring cue utilization or perceptual effects from responses does not permit this separation. Thus, it is not clear whether the evidence cited by Easterbrook supports the generalization that response variability is reduced under high drive or the generalization advanced by him.

The problem involved here is analogous to the one faced in studies which show an elevated threshold for the recognition of tachistoscopically presented taboo words. Before saying that taboo words are perceived less readily than ordinary words, one must establish that the effect is not attributable to changes in the responses by which one infers perceptual recognition. That is, the subject may hesitate to inform the experimenter that the word presented to him is a socially taboo one until he is absolutely certain that he has correctly identified the word. In such a case, taboo words would affect characteristics of responding but not perceptual capacity *per se*.

A final comment on Easterbrook's work concerns some distinctions about information transmission which help to clarify his generalization. In most of the experiments cited by Easterbrook, at any given moment the subject has presented to him a stimulus array of some complexity containing many potential "cues." In the Eriksen and Wechsler experiment the stimulus presented to the subject is quite simple, a square. The subject's task is not one of successfully selecting and responding to several different aspects of the stimulus. $T(s,r)$ values obtained in experiments like Eriksen and Wechsler's refer to the ability of an individual to differentiate a unidimensional stimulus continuum (size). The experiments dealt with by Easterbrook are concerned with multidimensional stimuli and deal with the subject's ability to "notice" several aspects of a stimulus presented to him. The usual information transmission study deals with a task which emphasizes a *successive* comparison —that is, the comparison of a particular stimulus with other stimuli that have been presented. The experiments cited by Easterbrook deal more with a task that emphasizes simultaneous perceptual capacity. The stimulus presented to the subject contains sufficient complexity for the focus of investigation to be on the subject's capacity to "notice" several characteristics of the stimulus. This analysis suggests that Eriksen and Wechsler's study is not really concerned with the issue dealt with by Easterbrook.

It is possible to design an experiment which involves the actual computation of $T(s,r)$ and deals with an information processing task that is more analogous to those dealt with by Easterbrook. The relevant experiment would involve the computation of ability to transmit information about multidimensional stimuli under different motivational conditions. A relevant experimental design is provided by a study by Klemmer and Frick (1953). In their study they measured ability to transmit information about a dot in a plane. A dot in a plane is a two-dimensional stimulus since, in order correctly to identify its position, one must know its location on each of two dimensions. Klemmer and Frick also measured ability to transmit information about four dots presented simultaneously on a 3 × 3 grid. Here the stimulus can be considered as an eight-dimensional stimulus since its correct identification involves the proper assignment of a locus on each of two dimensions to each of four dots. With a multidimensional stimulus, the task presented to a subject appears to be more analogous to the tasks dealt with by Easterbrook, involving the ability to deal simultaneously with several aspects of a complex stimulus. It is possible to analyze the data from an experiment involving such a stimulus array in a manner exactly equivalent to that used to compute $T(s,r)$ with a unidimensional stimulus. In summary, the above analysis suggests that it might be correct to translate Easterbrook's generalization as follows: increases in drive lead to decreases in ability to transmit information where the stimulus is multidimensional.

INFORMATION THEORY AND CLINICAL JUDGMENT

Bieri and his associates have used information theory as a basis for studying clinical judgments (Bieri et al., 1966). Miller and Bieri (1963) have analyzed the agreement among a group of clinicians (experienced social workers). In their study, subjects were presented with a series of vignettes about a person which could include information about each of three dimensions: developmental history, current behavior, and interview material. Seven conditions of judgment were formed by giving subjects vignettes involving each of these dimensions in isolation and in all combinations. In those cases in which subjects received vignettes containing information about two or more dimensions, the information from the separate dimensions was independently judged to indicate comparable levels of psychopathology. All groups of subjects judged each vignette on one of three dimensions—object relations, defenses, and clinical judgment. Each of these dimensions contained eight separate response classifications for each dimension of judgment. Miller and Bieri computed $H(r)$ and $T(s,r)$ measures for these data. Each subject responded once to each vignette judged by him. Thus, the $T(s,r)$ and $H(r)$ measures obtained by Miller and Bieri refer to the intersubject consistency of judgment with respect to the vignettes.

Twenty-one different $H(r)$ and $T(s,r)$ measures were obtained by separately analyzing the judgments for each of the seven stimulus conditions on each of the three response dimensions. The group $H(r)$ values varied from 2.77 to 2.98 bits, indicating that the subjects tended to use all eight categories of responses on each dimension with relatively equal frequency. Note that with eight response categories the maximum value $H(r)$ could have is 3 bits. The $T(s,r)$ values ranged from .88 to 1.49 bits with most of the values grouped slightly above 1 bit. Thus, the judgments made by different subjects are not in agreement. These values indicate that different subjects, *under the condition of this experiment*, had considerable disagreement among themselves in the assignment of the fictitious persons described by the vignettes to the response categories provided by Miller and Bieri.

In a second study of clinical judgment, Tripodi and Bieri (1964) extended the earlier work reported by Miller and Bieri. Tripodi and Bieri presented to groups of subjects acting as judges three types of information consisting of statements about aggression, body anxiety, and social withdrawal. Within each dimension, items were selected to cover a wide range of pathology. There were eight statements for the body anxiety and social withdrawal dimensions and three sets of eight statements for the aggression dimension. Statements from the stimulus dimensions were combined in several ways to form descriptive vignettes of people to be judged. Each group of subjects making judgments was required to go through the judgment task twice with a period of one week intervening between judgments. Thus, it was possible to study the intrajudge consistency as well as the interjudge consistency.

The intrajudge $T(s,r)$ values for each of the stimulus dimensions were all approximately 2 bits. Tripodi and Bieri did not report the $H(r)$ values but the maximum $H(r)$ would be 3 bits. Thus, the judges were relatively consistent among themselves.

Tripodi and Bieri also found that when the vignettes were formed by combining information from different stimulus dimensions where the statements drawn from each of the dimensions indicated roughly comparable degrees of maladjustment, there was little or no increase in intrasubjects $T(s,r)$ over the values obtained by examining vignettes made up of a statement drawn from a single stimulus dimension. However, where vignettes were formed by combining statements from two separate dimensions where the statements were negatively correlated with respect to the degree of maladjustment that they were previously judged to indicate, the intrajudge $T(s,r)$ values decreased. For example, the $T(s,r)$ for vignette dealing with aggression was 1.98 bits; the $T(s,r)$ for vignettes formed by combining statements about aggression with statements indicating a different degree of maladjustment about withdrawal was 1.65 bits. When a judge is given inconsistent information from different dimensions, he becomes less consistent in his judgments.

In addition to an analysis of intrajudge consistency, Tripodi and Bieri also obtained interjudge group $T(s,r)$ rates. This data analysis is comparable to the analysis in the Miller and Bieri study. The interjudge $T(s,r)$ values obtained for unidimensional vignettes and those formed by a combination of stimulus dimensions where the statements drawn from separate dimensions agreed with respect to maladjustment ranged from .78 to 1.13 bits. There were no significant differences in interjudge $T(s,r)$ values between the unidimensional and multidimensional vignettes of this type. However, the interjudge $T(s,r)$ values obtained for vignettes formed by combining statements from different stimulus dimensions which were in disagreement were significantly lower and dropped to values as low as .18 bits. Thus, where the vignette to be judged contained contradictory information, agreement among judges largely disappeared.

It is instructive to point out certain crucial differences between the experiments of Bieri and his associates and the more traditional information transmission studies using stimuli which can be rigorously specified in physical terms. The traditional studies have not focused on group $T(s,r)$ but rather on $T(s,r)$ computed by an examination of the repeated responses of an individual. Even where $T(s,r)$ is computed on the basis of p values obtained by combining the responses of different subjects, the $T(s,r)$ values obtained are usually comparable to those obtained by obtaining the mean $T(s,r)$ for $T(s,r)$ values computed separately for each individual. In a psychophysical study there is usually a "correct" answer. For example, if a subject is required to indicate where a vertical line crosses a horizontal line, the existence of a correct answer tends to produce a situation in which perfect intrasubject $T(s,r)$ tends to lead to perfect intersubject $T(s,r)$. This is, of course, not a logically necessary fact. However, it would be quite unusual if each subject were consistent in his classification of such a stimulus but subjects differed radically among themselves in the classification of a stimulus with a physically specifiable correct answer. In the case of clinical judgment where there is no "correct" answer it is, of course, quite possible that different judges will consistently classify a particular vignette in different ways. This is why group and individual $T(s,r)$ values can be radically different.

The information theory analysis of clinical judgment appears more suitable for the computation of interjudge $T(s,r)$ than for intrajudge $T(s,r)$. Tripodi and Bieri's measurement of intrajudge $T(s,r)$ was deficient in that they used only two replications. This is hardly enough to obtain meaningful estimates of the probability of classifying a particular vignette in a particular way. Also, the intrajudge $T(s,r)$ values are probably very unstable, depending on such things as the length of time intervening between judgments (one week in this case) and the instructions given to the subjects. It is probably the case that, given enough time to learn the material, the intrajudge $T(s,r)$ rates would be substantially higher. This experimental situation can be thought of as analogous to learning a paired-associate list in which the subject is required to learn a particular response for each stimulus (vignette). Given enough practice with the material, intrajudge $T(s,r)$ values that are substantially higher than those reported by Tripodi and Bieri can be obtained. This prediction should be contrasted with studies which show only limited improvement in $T(s,r)$ rates after extended practice in psychophysical tasks (see Hartman, 1954). The reason for this difference probably lies in the complexity of the stimulus. Given stimuli which are complex enough to differ from one another on several discriminably different dimensions, it should be possible to learn to identify them accurately and to differentiate among a large set of them.

This analysis also serves to explain why there is little or no effect of increasing the stimulus dimensionality of the vignette in Bieri's studies. The vignettes probably contain so many respects in which they differ from one another that they are sufficiently discriminable from each other. In the psychophysical experiments dealing with a unidimensional stimulus continuum there is one and only one respect in which the stimuli differ. In such a case making the stimulus multidimensional has a clearcut effect on $T(s,r)$.

There is one respect in which Bieri failed to make full use of information theory measurement. One of the interesting questions about clinical judgment is the extent to which it is patterned or configurated. Think of a statement such as: "In making a clinical judgment the clinician considers the meaning and significance of a particular characteristic of the person in the light of the total personality of the person." Such a statement implies, minimally, that the relationship between a characteristic of a person (considered as a stimulus) and the response category assigned to that person on the basis of the characteristic depends on other characteristics of that person. This occurrence of such a pattern of judgments can be taken as reflecting a limited concept of the organization of personality. It is interesting to note that such a conception can provide great difficulties for such methods of studying personality as factor analysis. This assertion can be exemplified by a consideration of what is sometimes called a "moderator" variable. A moderator variable is a variable that moderates the relationship between two other variables such that the correlation between variables X and Y can change for different values of variable Z. Consider the following extreme example: $r_{xy} = +1.00$ for subjects above the median on variable Z whereas $r_{xy} = -1.00$ for subjects below the median on variable Z. In such a case Z may be said to moderate the relationship between X and Y. Since factor analysis is conventionally based on matrices of correlations between variables, where the correlations are computed by dealing with the population of subjects as a whole, a factor analysis would simply begin with a data reduction which precludes the discovery and elucidation of such moderator relations. Consequently, to the extent to which personality is organized as described above, conventional factor analysis can be considered an inadequate technique for the description of personality organization (see Kogan and Wallach, 1964).

This digression into moderator variables is prompted by the fact that one can measure relations among variables on the nominal scale which are quite analogous to moderator effects by use of multivariate information theory measures (Attneave, 1959; McGill, 1954). Consider a situation in which there are three variables—one response variable and two stimulus variables. The total predictable uncertainty in C (the response variable) from a knowledge of the stimulus variables can be represented as $T(c,ab)$ and partitioned into three components: $T(c,a)$, the amount of information transmitted between C and A where A is considered in isolation; $T(c,b)$, the amount of information transmitted between C and B where B is considered in isolation; $T(c,\overline{ab})$, the amount of information predicted about C from knowledge of the interaction of A and B. $T(c,\overline{ab})$ is analogous to an interaction term in the analysis of variance. The total predictable uncertainty of C, $T(c,ab)$, may be contained in any one or any combination of these three quantities. Consider the example in Table 2–1, where $T(c,ab)$ is composed entirely of $T(c,\overline{ab})$.

TABLE 2–1

A Matrix of Probabilities in which $T(c,ab)$ Is Composed
Entirely of $T(c,\overline{ab})$

	a_1b_1	a_2b_1	a_1b_2	a_2b_2
c_1	.25	.00	.00	.25
c_2	.00	.25	.25	.00

Note that in the example presented in the table the prediction of anything about C requires knowledge about both values of A and B. In order to obtain the interaction uncertainty, it is necessary to have what is analogous to a "factorial design." That is, it is necessary to consider all possible combinations of the A and B variables in order to discover the way in which they interact with one another. Note further that the existence of such interactions is analogous to the existence of moderator effects on the interval scale. Where there is interaction uncertainty, it is appropriate to say that the relationship between a pair of variables is moderated by position on a third variable. Such interaction and "moderation" can, of course, be extended to cases where there are four or more variables composed of three or more predictor stimulus variables and a response variable.

This discussion of multivariate information measures points to a possible inadequacy in the work of Bieri in that his subjects are not presented with all possible combinations of the stimulus categories. Bieri does combine all of his stimulus *dimensions,* but he does so in a limited way (by pairing items from two different dimensions which are either positively or negatively correlated). Bieri does not present to his judges the 49 possible combinations of stimulus conditions formed by factorially combining all of the items from one dimension with all of the items from a second dimension. Consequently, it is impossible to measure precisely the interaction uncertainty. It seems that one of the more interesting empirical questions that can be raised about clinical judgment is the extent to which judgments about a person on the basis of one kind of characteristic depend on the other characteristics of the person. Future investigations of the problem of clinical judgment within the context of information theory should permit the computation of interaction effects in order to study this problem.

NEED FOR INFORMATION AND INFORMATION THEORY

It has been suggested that information theory may be useful in helping to explain exploratory and curiosity behavior (Berlyne, 1960, 1963; Jones, 1966). This section presents a theoretical conception of the need for information (N_I). By the need for information is meant a motivational state which predisposes an individual to engage in activity that is instrumental to the acquisition of information.

Under what conditions is the need for information aroused? Deprivation is at least a sufficient condition (although perhaps not a necessary condition) for the arousal of many motive states. A. Jones and his collaborators have investigated the effects of information deprivation on what is here called N_I. Jones et al. (1961) placed subjects in a light-proof and partially soundproof chamber similar to those used in sensory deprivation experiments. They contend that the environment in such a chamber is completely devoid of information. In one of their experiments the subject was permitted to select by means of a "cafeteria switch" the uncertainty of a set of 24 flashes of red and green lights he could receive by making an appropriate instrumental response. They varied the uncertainty of the sequence of lights by varying the proportion of randomly determined lights. They found that subjects placed in the information deprivation environment develop a preference for sequences whose uncertainty value is high. Also, subjects deprived of access to the manipulandum which controlled the presentation of the stimulus sequence had higher eventual response rates than subjects not deprived of access to the manipulandum.

The study by Jones et al. indicates that subjects who are deprived of information will choose to perform an instrumental response which leads to the acquisition of information. Subjects acquire information in this situation since a sequence containing random lights is at least partially unpredictable. Consequently, the subject's observation of the red or green light provides information to him. The experiment indicates that deprivation is at least a sufficient condition for the arousal of the need for information. Also, the degree of arousal of the need for information depends on the amount of information deprivation.

It is not clear from our discussion of the above experiment whether the acquisition of information is the critical incentive which produces the instrumental responses. Perhaps there is some other aspect of the stimulus sequence which is confounded with its ability to transmit information to a subject. Jones (1964) addressed himself to this question by noting that three variables are confounded in any sequence which can transmit information. They are called by him:

1. Information—the degree to which a subject can predict the sequential occurrence of the stimuli in the sequence
2. Complexity—the degree to which the sequence is physically random
3. Fluctuation—the degree to which the stimulus categories alternate

These variables stand in a transitive relation such that information implies complexity and fluctuation (but not the converse) and complexity implies fluctuation (but not the converse). Jones created experimental conditions which separated these variables. A condition involving complexity without randomness was created by repeatedly presenting a subject with the same random sequence of lights. Such a sequence, although physically random, contains no information since the subject is eventually able to predict the sequential occurrence of the stimuli. A condition containing fluctuation without complexity and without information was created by presenting a subject with alternating sequences, that is, red, green, red, green, etc. Such a sequence contains maximal stimulus change and fluctuation without being random or unpredictable. In a series of studies Jones (1964) was able to show that the critical characteristic of the stimulus sequences he dealt with was their information value, not their complexity or fluctuation. He found that, given a choice between sequences differing in complexity and information, subjects developed a preference for series which contained information as opposed to series which contained complexity without information. Of the three stimulus characteristics dealt with, only information produced a linear increase in response probabilities as a function of deprivation.

Jones and his colleagues have also explored the effects of satiation and of deprivation on the need for information. Jones and McGill (1967) exposed subjects to one or five hours of a random sequence of two different tones at the rate of one per second. After this "information satiation" procedure, subjects were given an opportunity to select sequences of tones differing in the amount of information (degree of randomness) they contained. They found that in the initial hour following satiation, the subjects in the five-hour group, relative to the one-hour satiation group, demonstrated a preference for sequences of tones with zero information, that is, for alternating sequences of tones which were perfectly predictable.

In another study, Thornton and Jones (1965) were able to show that the satiation effect was not specific to sensory modalities. Information satiation in the auditory modality led to a decreased preference for sequences containing information in the visual modality. The Jones experiments have clearly shown that the need for information can be manipulated by deprivation and satiation conditions. Before these results can be accepted as perfectly valid, they should be extended to other types of stimuli which differ in their capacity to transmit information.

It can be argued that a stimulus which contains uncertainty arouses the need for information to reduce the uncertainty. The concept of the uncertainty of a stimulus appears, at first impression, to be a paradoxical notion since uncertainty refers to a set of possible events. A single event is usually taken to have zero uncertainty. However, a single stimulus can be considered as being one of a set of possible stimuli. By referring to implicit populations of stimuli which can vary with respect to the number of different kinds of stimuli contained in the population, it is possible to speak of a stimulus as having a higher stimulus uncertainty than another. In order to make a statement about the uncertainty of a single stimulus, it is necessary to make inferences about the population of stimuli to which it is assumed to belong. The uncertainty of the stimulus with which we are concerned really refers to the uncertainty of the person who is perceiving the stimulus. When stimulus A is said to have more uncertainty than stimulus B, we mean that it is less predictable by a subject. Consequently, when stimuli A and B have been appropriately perceived and/or categorized, the subject may be said to have received more information from A than from B. Stimuli which arouse uncertainty in a person are then assumed to arouse the need for information in that person. The arousal is not completely generalized in that the person does not seek information about any stimulus. Rather the person is motivated to receive information about the stimulus which has a significant amount of uncertainty.

Berlyne has performed a number of experiments which demonstrate the arousal of the need for information by stimuli which are high in uncertainty. Berlyne (1958a) exposed subjects to pairs of figures and noted the amount of time the subject fixated on each figure. Each pair of figures contained one regular and one irregular arrangement of the same elements (see Fig. 2–1a). It is possible to argue that the

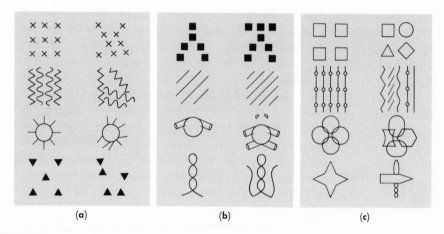

(a)   (b)   (c)

Fig. 2–1. Stimuli used by Berlyne. (a) Irregularity of arrangement. (b) Amount of material. (c) Heterogeneity of elements.

irregular stimulus arrangement has more uncertainty than the regular stimulus. The simplest way of applying information theory concepts to such a stimulus is to note that there are fewer possible stimuli which can be created by the regular arrangement than by an irregular arrangement of the same number of elements. Consequently, the regular stimulus transmits less information to a subject than the irregular stimulus. Berlyne found that subjects spent more time looking at the irregular stimulus member of the pair of stimuli. Or, to put it in a somewhat more theoretical way, given a choice between two stimuli which differ in the amount of information they transmit, subjects prefer to look at that stimulus which transmits more information.

Berlyne also compared pairs of stimuli which differed in the number of similar elements contained in the stimulus (see Fig. 2–1b). Here again, it can be argued that a stimulus composed of six slanted lines transmits more information than a stimulus composed of four slanted lines. This argument assumes that the stimulus containing more elements is a member of a larger subset of possible stimuli than the stimulus containing fewer elements; that is, specifying the same constraints for permissible permutations of the elements, one can construct a larger set of stimuli given a larger set of elements. Berlyne found that subjects spent more time looking at the stimulus containing a greater number of elements.

Berlyne in addition compared stimuli which differed with respect to the heterogeneity of the elements out of which they were constructed (see Fig. 2–1c). Again it can be argued that stimuli composed of heterogeneous elements transmit more information than stimuli composed of homogeneous elements. Given similar constraints, we can arrange heterogeneous elements into a greater number of possible stimuli than homogeneous elements. Again Berlyne found that subjects spent more time looking at the stimulus which was composed of heterogeneous elements than at the stimulus composed of homogeneous elements.

Berlyne varied a number of other characteristics of the stimulus pair presented to a subject. In each case a plausible argument can be made that the stimulus which transmitted more information was looked at for a longer period of time than the stimulus member which contained less information. Berlyne's experiment leads to the conclusion that subjects will prefer to look at stimuli which transmit more information. It can be argued that any stimulus which potentially transmits information arouses the need for information. Stimuli which contain more information can be considered to arouse more need for information and consequently subjects spend more time looking at them.

In another experiment Berlyne (1963) presented subjects with a series of quotations each of which was followed by the names of two or three possible authors. The percentage of teachers choosing each author was supplied. The students were asked to choose the quotation for which they preferred to know the correct author. Berlyne found that subjects chose quotations followed by three authors more than those followed by two authors. They also chose quotations with equi-probable percentage distribution of teacher's responses more than questions with skewed response distributions. Thus subjects chose those quotations where the answer would transmit to them the greatest amount of information.

These experiments by Berlyne, as well as many others reviewed by him, indicate that stimuli which potentially transmit information tend to produce instrumental activity (looking, choosing, etc.) which provides information that then reduces the subject's uncertainty about the stimulus. These experiments make no attempt to deprive subjects of information prior to the introduction of a stimulus that arouses uncertainty. Consequently, we can conclude that deprivation is not a necessary condition for the arousal of the need for information.

INDIVIDUAL DIFFERENCES

There are two recent experiments which indicate that there may be individual differences in the need for information. Houston and Mednick (1963) studied two groups of subjects who scored high and low respectively on Mednick's R.A.T. test of creativity (see Mednick, 1962). Subjects were presented with series of word pairs consisting of a noun and a non-noun member. Each time a subject chose the non-noun member of the pair, the experimenter responded with an improbable word associate to that word; each time the subject chose a noun, a highly probable word associate to that word was presented by the experimenter. Subjects who scored high on the R.A.T. showed an increasing tendency to choose the non-noun member of the pair, whereas subjects who scored low on the R.A.T. showed an increasing tendency to choose the noun member of the pair. The Houston and Mednick study indicates that subjects who scored high on a test for creativity, given a choice between two instrumental responses (choosing a noun or a non-noun member of a pair) which differ with respect to the amount of information they lead to, will tend to choose the response that produces more information. The greater information value of the improbable associate follows from the fact that the set of all improbable associates of any word is undoubtedly larger than the set of all probable associates of a word.

A recent experiment by Levin and Brody (1966) was designed to clarify the relationship between creativity as measured by the R.A.T. and the need for information. In their study, subjects who were either high or low in creativity (as measured by R.A.T.) were placed in an information deprivation environment for either one or five hours, at the end of which they were given access to a button which produced random sequences of lights. Highly creative subjects in the one-hour deprivation condition had a mean frequency of 8 information responses for the first hour following deprivation, whereas low creative subjects had a mean frequency of less than 1 response. In the five-hour deprivation condition the mean frequency of information responses for the first hour following deprivation was approximately 8 for the high creative subjects and approximately 7 for the low creative subjects. These results suggest that deprivation, at least within the limits used in this study, is totally irrelevant for the high creative subjects. On the other hand, deprivation is a relevant condition for the arousal of the need for information for the low creative subjects who are presumably low in the need for information.

How does the amount of potential information transmitted by a stimulus event affect the incentive value of that stimulus? The Jones studies suggest that the incentive values of stimuli differing in their capacity to transmit information are a function of a subject's prior satiation or deprivation of information, with the former condition increasing the incentive values of stimuli with low potential to transmit information and the latter condition increasing the incentive value of stimuli with a relatively high capacity to transmit information. Of course, these results hold for only a relatively restricted range of potential information values. The Houston and Mednick study suggests that the incentive value of stimuli which differ in ability to transmit information is dependent upon an individual's creativity. Munsinger and Kessen (1964, 1966) have reported a number of studies in which subjects were asked to state their preferences for stimuli which were randomly constructed figures differing with respect to the number of independent turns they contained. The greater the number of turns, the greater the amount of potential information transmitted by the stimulus since the number of different stimuli contained in a population of stimuli from which a given random figure is constructed increases with the number of independent turns contained in the stimulus. Subjects tended to prefer stimuli of intermediate number of turns.

The results of Munsinger and Kessen's studies appear paradoxical when considered in conjunction with the studies of Berlyne. Berlyne's results lead to the generalization that the capacity of a stimulus to arouse the need for information is a monotonically increasing function of its capacity to transmit information. However, individuals tend to prefer stimuli of intermediate capacity to transmit information. Considered together, these results may be taken to imply that there are situations in which an individual faced with a stimulus with high uncertainty can be in a state of conflict. On the one hand, such an individual may have a high need for information about that specific stimulus. On the other hand, for this particular individual, the stimulus may be above the optimum uncertainty value and thus have a negative incentive value. Such an individual would then be faced with an approach–avoidance conflict.

The studies reviewed in this section on the need for information suggest that information theoretic concepts provide a useful way of conceptualizing a common characteristic of diverse stimuli, viz., their uncertainty and capacity to transmit information. This characteristic of stimuli, in turn, has important motivational characteristics. The precise effect of a stimulus with the capacity to transmit information depends on a number of other variables, including prior exposure to other such stimuli, the uncertainty of the stimulus, and the personality of the individual exposed to the stimulus. It is possible to point to a particular study which illustrates the significance of each of these variables, but the possible relations and interactions among them have not been studied. Consequently, there appears to be a need for studies involving factorial designs in which these variables may be jointly examined.

3

Computer Models of
Information Processing*

PHILIP J. STONE

This chapter describes applications of computer information processing models to human information processing procedures. Rather than discuss problems in the abstract, several applications concerning problem solving are discussed in detail, illustrating how a "higher order" computer language enables concise, explicit formulations and testing of alternative models. The topics of "hot cognition" and "belief structures" are discussed, with special attention given to the problems of representing human natural language processing in computer models.

The chapter does not assume any previous experience with modeling or computers, but is written in the hope that the reader will be tolerant in considering what may be a new and unfamiliar approach. Since a mystique is often attributed to computer simulations, a main point is to demonstrate that there is little mystery involved and that a notation in program form can be a useful vehicle for communicating not only with a computer, but with fellow scientists.

* The author is grateful to Kenneth Colby, E. B. Hunt, Herbert Simon, and Peter Suedfeld for their comments on an earlier draft of this chapter. The present chapter benefits greatly from their suggestions. An earlier draft was also used in a seminar at the Center for Advanced Study in the Behavioral Sciences. The members of the seminar, Norman Anderson, John Crook, Tjalling Koopmans, J. Michael Montias, Robert R. Sears, John Van de Geer, and Morris Zelditch, were especially helpful in giving a close examination of the examples and offering the viewpoints of non-specialists regarding the presentation of computing procedures. The author is also grateful to Jan Smedslund, University of Oslo and Fellow at the Center, for his introduction to the intriguing characteristics of his experiment.

TWO KINDS OF INFORMATION PROCESSING

In the preceding chapter, Brody has discussed information process-ing from the point of view of information theory. He shows, for ex-ample, how Claude Shannon's classical formulation of Uncertainty (H) being related to the $\log_2$ of alternatives can be applied to measuring the complexity of a task from the alternatives available. The theory can be used directly to evaluate intersubject and intrasubject differences in performance.

In this chapter, information processing will be used to refer to the broad class of symbol manipulation procedures that can be represented on a "stored program" information processing machine, originally de-scribed by Von Neumann, and today represented by the electronic com-puter. If we are to take the position suggested in a later chapter by Schroder, that an information processing approach to personality in-volves "the way a person selects, organizes, and stores information in adapting to particular aspects of his world," then the computer models may very well have their place.

Both kinds of information processing assume that the different pieces of information used to represent a situation can be clearly identified and precisely stated. But while one emphasizes the capacities of informa-tion processing and the amount of information transmitted, the other emphasizes a modeling of the mechanisms by which the transmission or organization of information takes place.

Both kinds of information formulations, with their speculations about what is going on inside the mind, are avenues of reaction against stim-ulus–response behaviorism, in which speculations about the mechanisms within the "black box" were discouraged as being irrelevant and distract-ing from the task of science. The major figures discussed in the other chapters—Lewin, Witkin, Kelly, Piaget, and others—refused to so limit themselves.

At first, the inference of such processes might be regarded as in a tradition of philosophical speculation as to the mechanisms of the mind. However, rather than assume unnecessary givens or only speculate as to what "must be" the processes of the mind, the psychologist is con-cerned with developing models based on inferences grounded in careful research and demonstrations.[1]

There is always, of course, a tempting delight in fabricating models of the mind's processes in much the same manner as utopian writers use

---

[1] The lack of avenues to evidence proved to be a recurrent stumbling block. Hegel marshalled his German rhetoric to convince himself that the royal road must be phrenology!

everyday knowledge to envision the operation of an ideal society. Such efforts can be ingeniously creative and an excellent source of research ideas.

The topic here, however, is the development of computer program representations in the day-to-day work of the social scientist. A comprehensive model of information processing procedures in personality is not presented because our knowledge and research are still many years from such a synthesis. Instead, the discussion is necessarily of human information processing models in limited research situations, and of somewhat more general modeling problems and data gathering challenges to be tackled next. While our detailed examples are highly cognitive, we end with some consideration of such additional factors as defense mechanisms, motivations, emotions, natural language, and social influence.

Given these goals, we cannot at the same time pretend to review the literature. Our examples are selected to illustrate points. In most cases, there exist other excellent examples that could have been used instead. For a literature review, the reader is referred to Loehlin's (1968) lucid little book and to Abelson's (1968a) chapter on simulation in the revised *Handbook of Social Psychology*. Similarly, this chapter cannot be a "compleat guide" to all the tricks in computer modeling of human information processes. Again we have been selective and attempted to focus on basic processes and some of the more salient issues.

MODELING THE PSYCHOLOGICAL EXPERIMENT

Inasmuch as so much of our information in psychology comes from the experiment, we begin by modeling that situation. It is useful to represent it not with one model, but three. One model is a representation of the design of the experiment—the "rules of the game" as formulated in the instructions for the experimenter and the subject before the task is to begin. The second is the model of the experimenter, that is, what he actually does within the framework of the rules. The third is the performance of the subject.

The model of the experiment governs the interaction between the experimenter and the subject. It makes assignments so that the experimenter and the subject are "taking turns" in a sequence specified by the rules of the experiment. It also keeps a record of what has happened, deciding when the experiment is to be terminated and what outcome is to be reported. In many ways, it can be considered similar to an umpire governing the interaction between two teams and keeping official score.

The model of the experimenter is often quite simple, such as merely reading stimuli from a list. In other cases, such as when the next stimulus depends on the past responses from the subject, it may be considerably more complex. It is the subject, of course, whose personality is to be modeled and studied. The models for representing the subject's performance will be the focus of our concern here.

The computer may be used to represent only one or two models, not all three. If instead of a model of a subject we have a real subject sitting at a computer terminal, then we have a computer-run experiment. Instead of a computer model of the experimenter, we might have a trainee experimenter at the computer terminal, or the model builder may want to take over the experimenter role himself to see if he can design sequences of stimuli that will display weaknesses in the computer model of the subject. All these alternatives tend to go hand in hand.

A simulation of an experiment can be run many times under many different conditions. In some designs, the experimental variable will be a change in the rules of the experiment or the stimuli presented. In other designs, the experimental variable will be the personality type of the subject, with two types of subjects run to show their differences in performance.

This general paradigm can be extended to a variety of situations other than the standard psychological experiment. Instead of an experimenter and a subject, we may have two subjects of known personality types being modeled in a bargaining game situation. We may have a subject and a group, such as in modeling the conformity experiments of Asch (1951), or behavior in a communication net as studied by Bavelas (1950). Rather than have a subject and other subjects, we may have a nation and other nations, such as some of the inter-nation models of Guetzkow (1963).[2] Much of what we have to say here about the relatively simple problem solving situations also has direct applications to modeling these situations.

In constructing a representation of an experiment, one may find that the subject model has in fact few feasible alternatives open to it, and that the outcomes are mainly determined by constraints imposed by the models of the experiment and the experimenter. A psychological experiment is best designed to infer which of several possible clearly defined psychological mechanisms is operating. This is what Platt (1966) would call a case of "strong inference." Building a model forces the investigator to consider whether the experiment allows viable alternative processes on the part of the subject, and to specify how each process works.

[2] In this case, the work of the nations is divided into external and internal decision maker roles, which are then carried out by people simulating the nations.

Sometimes two experimental designs will appear to be very similar, such that they should elicit the same problem solving processes from the subject. Making a model often forces a close examination of the details as to whether the constraints on the subject are indeed really the same. Two apparently similar designs may have features that lead to vastly different information processing in most subjects.

TYPES OF MODELS

Models in general are selective imitations. Our concern in this chapter is with a specific type, "information processing models," and we should note the implications.

When an architect builds a model of a building, he is usually concerned with the form of the structure and how it fits into the setting for which it is intended. Since it is unimportant how strong the model is, he usually makes it out of soft wood or heavy paper rather than the brick and concrete to be used in the actual building. Once completed, the model can be used to study the perspectives offered from different angles. It can also be used to experiment with changes in the shape of the building. A building is a static object and the architect has constructed a static model to represent its shape and color.

In contrast to the static building, behavior and the hypothesized mechanisms that control it are dynamic. While it is possible to make a static model of a process (a flow diagram of a computer program is just that), it is much more advantageous to have a model that is itself dynamic, that is, capable of being put through its paces or "exercised." Thus information *processing* models are quite different from the static models of the architect.

A further stricture centers on the word "information." A wind tunnel offers a dynamic model of air movement. In this case, the stuff in the model (air) is the same stuff that occurs in the real event. In contrast, an information processing model represents certain aspects of the situation with symbols. The processes are then represented by procedures for making transformations on the symbols.

For some scientists, the very act of representing some of the contents of the "black box" with symbols is an intolerable first step. The symbol is not the same thing to the computer as the real thing is to the subject. Until computers have similar sensations and awarenesses (the kinds of essences studied by Wundt and the later introspectionists) they are really not suitable for modeling human processes. Yet, these same scientists might be quite content to acknowledge that the trajectory information of missiles can be successfully produced by a computer model without the computer experiencing the heat of the jet blasts or the pressure of acceleration. Computer information processing models are but one selective way of explanation and should therefore be approached with care, caution, and humility rather than either overconfidence in their potentials or an emotional denial that they have any relevance at all.

In this writer's view, models are but tools for representing a level or stage of thinking in a long-term process of detective work called science. If a model is so seductive in its elegance that it stops further thinking, then it has defeated its own purpose in existing. Instead, the demands of clarity and explicitness in building a model should highlight where thinking is incomplete or awkward, and thereby lead to better and more elegant reconceptualization. A good model contributes to its own obsolescence. Given this view, the issue of whether a model is "correct" or "adequate" becomes largely irrelevant. It is rather considered as the best we can do at our current stage of thinking. As Tukey (1968) points out, there is a strong tendency to engage in all sorts of statistical exercises to "sanctify" a model at hand rather than get on with the further detective work.

If we are to use the computer to represent the information processing abilities of humans, then we make the curious assumption examined by Turing (1959), that human information processing abilities can be represented as a subset of computer information processing capabilities. This fact should aid in emphasizing the selectivity in focusing on the information processing aspects of the mind. At present, we have much better knowledge about the limitations of what is "computable" than the limitations of what is "thinkable." In addition to the limitation of scope, there is also the limitation of magnitude: the vast storehouse of both relevant and irrelevant experience with which any human approaches a problem is of a much greater order of information magnitude than any computer model known today.

Given any phenomena being studied, an investigator may wish to make several different kinds of data representations to further his understanding. First, he may ask how well is the variance of one variable accounted for by the variances of other measured variables and he might employ a multivariate statistical analysis procedure, such as step-wise multiple regression, to produce a model that tests this. Second, he may wish to show a path of causal dependency among the variables being measured.[3] Third, he may use a form of mathematics such as simultaneous equations, rather than an information processing computer model, to describe the relationships being observed.

---

[3] See, for example, the paper on path analysis applications in sociology by Duncan (1966).

This writer takes the view that all these resources are valuable and should be used as needed. There is little point in trying to establish that one is better than another. Nevertheless, differences in purpose should be kept clearly in mind. A model generated to account for variances has a different purpose than a model developed to represent one's thinking about a process. A model developed to identify dependency relationships is different from one that attempts to put forth the process mechanisms that explain dependency relationships. One kind of model often can and should lead to another.

Some investigators, instead of giving their main concern to the question, "What are the cognitive processes of people?" have focused on "How do computers function better than people?" and have built their models to study this question. Actually, such work in artificial intelligence tends to go hand in hand with studies of human processes. Today there is considerable interest in computers as being "intelligence amplifiers," using the combined abilities of the human and the machine to produce new intellectual capabilities.[4] In the examples that follow, we present several cases where a machine can solve a simple problem in direct ways while people tend to be more roundabout in their preferred processes. Such contrasts tend to further our understanding of both man and the machine.

IMPLEMENTING A COMPUTER INFORMATION PROCESSING MODEL

During the past decade, the computer languages geared to handling numerical processing (such as FORTRAN and ALGOL) have been quite different and separate from the "list processing" languages (such as IPL-V and LISP) used for many information processing models in the behavioral sciences. Which kind of computer language a person chose often had considerable bearing on how he would go about solving his problem. The existence of multiple languages furthermore hampered communication among scientists. It was difficult for a colleague to understand a notation if he was used to a different one. The notations of the early list processing languages, in particular, tended to be lengthy for people to follow.

The logic of list information processing languages has been explained several times in the literature, including an excellent exposition by Reit-

---

[4] In another article (Stone et al., 1970), the author discusses the kinds of everyday information services a computer may offer in time-shared consoles of a rather simple design. Taken together, the variety of uses indicates their being a standard facility of the school, office, and at least middle-class home of the future.

man (1965). Numerous manuals are available that discuss the numerical processing languages in detail. Each language tends to have its forte. Unfortunately, much effort has gone into arguing whether one is better than another rather than into building comprehensive ones that would satisfy everyone. This is partly because computers were not yet equal in size and scope to the task of integration.

Several years ago, Weizenbaum (1963) designed procedures to provide list processing capabilities within a numerical language, thus combining the advantages of both approaches. This marriage by necessity had a certain amount of awkwardness and so did not satisfactorily solve the communication problem. More recently, a new language called "Programming Language I" (PL/I) was developed to incorporate many features of past languages. While any sophisticated programmer will find much to complain about in PL/I, the merging of basic string and numerical capabilities, combined with a concise, readable syntax (plus the fact that it has been backed by the IBM Corporation) will probably result in its being an influential programming language for modeling purposes for the next several years. In this chapter, our examples will be in PL/I code. We will start with some simple examples and then move to more complex ones, explaining the different aspects of the code as they occur. With a little care, the reader without programming experience should be able to follow all the examples.

In the past, the complexities and amount of detail work involved in programming and debugging have often caused investigators to hire programmers to carry out their work for them. Problems in communication between the programmer and the investigator, together with inevitably long time delays in getting runs through the computer, often caused frustrations that more than offset any gains to be made from having a computer model. Several investigators have reported in print that it was not worth it, while others have not acknowledged past costs and have persisted onward more committed than ever.

In contrast, the models in this chapter were written by the author in leisure hours from a typewriter terminal[5] at the Center for Advanced Study in the Behavioral Sciences connected by regular telephone line to a nearby commercial time-shared computer service that offers a version of PL/I language.[6] The models were developed, tested, revised, and retested in a short amount of time. All of the models presented

[5] A portable Datel selectric typewriter is connected by an acoustic coupler to an ordinary telephone. The computer connection is obtained by dialing a number on the telephone.

[6] See Bates and Douglas (1967) for a description of PL/I. The version used here is called RUSH and is made available on a time-shared system by the Allen Babcock Corp., Los Angeles, one of more than seventy time-sharing commercial computing services now being offered.

here involve less than two pages of typewritten PL/I code. The computer charge for debugging and testing a model was in the tens, rather than hundreds of dollars.[7] In short, although computers have now been available at universities for more than a decade, recent developments in commercially available time-shared services have dramatically changed the situation with regard to modeling.

TWO REPRESENTATIONS OF THE SMEDSLUND EXPERIMENT

Our first example is a simple task developed by Smedslund in Norway (1968) for studying mental processing involved in rapid logical reasoning. The example has been selected because although it does not require the subject to carry a heavy cognitive load to solve it, the more natural solution from the point of view of artificial intelligence is quite different from the way people handle it. Smedslund has used reaction time information to indicate which of several different possible information processing mechanisms people use to solve the task.

The instructions, here somewhat condensed, run as follows:

> This is a study of thinking. In front of you on a piece of paper you see a V on the left and an H on the right. [The Norwegian words for left and right are "vestre" and "høyre."] V and H represent two quantities which at the beginning of each task are equal. Remember that each new task begins with V = H. "Plus" (+) means that a unit is added to one of the quantities and "minus" (−) means that a unit is subtracted from one of the quantities. "Plus V" means that a unit is added to V, "minus H" means that a unit is subtracted from H, and so on.

> Each task starts with V = H and includes three "plus" or "minus" operations. You are to state which of the quantities is largest at the end [another version of the experiment asks which is smallest] by saying "V" or "H" as soon as you know the answer. It is important that you answer as fast as possible.

The instructions then include several examples. For instance, if the experimenter says "plus H, plus V, minus V" (+ H + V − V) then the answer is that more H remains and the subject should say "H." The first ten test items used by Smedslund are shown in Fig. 3–1. The reader may wish to try them out on himself to see how he solves the problem. Smedslund has the experimenter read the three operations aloud and

[7] The computer company charges only for the amount of central processor time used rather than the length of time hooked to the machine. The rate of charge depends on how much of memory is needed when it is processing. The Smedslund model, described below, took about five hours of work at the console to build, test, and make numerous revisions, costing about $25 in all for computer charges. The connection to the computer was an unmetered local phone call.

1. $+V+H-V$	6. $-H-V+H$
2. $-V+V+V$	7. $+V-V+V$
3. $+H+H+V$	8. $+H-V-H$
4. $-H+V+H$	9. $-H+H-V$
5. $-H-H-V$	10. $+V+V-V$

Fig. 3–1. First ten items in Smedslund experiment.

then starts a stopwatch. To be exact, then, the reader should have each item read aloud to him.

Model of the Experiment

The model of the experiment was designed to allow for several different modes of control. It begins by asking the person sitting at the typewriter three questions: (1) "Is the task to say which is > or which is <?" The user of the program responds by typing in a ">" or a "<" sign indicating which instruction set is to be assumed. (2) "Do you wish to be the experimenter?" If the answer is "Yes," the model will wait at each trial for the experimenter to type in the three operations to be used on that trial. If the answer is "No," the model will call on an experimenter model for the operations. The experimenter model is currently set to generate three operations randomly. (3) "Which model of the subject shall we use?" The different models have been assigned numbers and the person using the simulation types in the number of the model he wants.

Upon receiving answers to these questions, the model of the experiment goes into operation, supervising the successive trials and keeping records. The model of the subject may have procedures for measuring how much "work" was involved in arriving at a solution, depending on the number of program rules executed in the process and an assignment of difficulty that was made for each rule. The solution, plus the total amount of work involved, is reported back after each trial on the typewriter terminal.

The Ways Humans Solve It

From Smedslund's reaction time data and from our own experience with the problem, it appears that most subjects first look for a pair of V's or H's. If both members of the pair have the same sign, then that quality predominates and is used to produce an answer. Thus, for example, the third stimulus in Fig. 3–1 shows a pair of H's, both with a plus sign. If the instruction is to say which is larger, the answer of course is "*H*." If the instruction is to say which is smaller, then an additional step has to be made of making a reversal and saying "*V*."

In cases where the pair of letters has like signs, we would expect the following factors to affect reaction time:

1. The time taken to locate the pair. If it is the first two of the three operations, this time should be lowest. If the pair is the second and third operations, it may be longer. If it is the first and third operations, with the opposite letter occurring in between, it is longest. As we shall see, if all three operations instead of just two use the same letter, this seems to cause some confusion and slows down the reaction time.
2. The necessity for a "reversal" in order to produce the desired answer. Smedslund's data quite clearly indicate that this delays reaction time.

Note that if the pair is the first two operations and they are of like sign, then the answer can be given without waiting for the third operation. If the operations are randomly produced, this should occur on 25 per cent of the trials. In fact, the subjects almost always waited for the third operation to be presented.

If the pair has opposite rather than like signs, then the pair is canceled and it is the remaining third operation that contains the clue to the solution. Thus, in the first item in Fig. 3–1, the two *V*'s cancel and the "+*H*" remaining indicates that *H* is the larger amount. It would seem that making reference to the third operation, after finding a pair that cancels, would take a little extra work. Otherwise, the steps to solution, including occasionally a "reversal" step at the end in order to produce the answer required by the instructions, are the same.

An Artificial Intelligence Solution

The most direct solution does not involve searching for pairs at all. Using this strategy, the answer can be produced before the third operation is given 50 per cent of the time. The procedure for the direct solution is presented in PL/I notation in Fig. 3–2. This model of the subject is begun when the experiment program transfers control to it by a command "CALL ModelS."[8] The first line of the code indicates that "ModelS" is a procedure (i.e., a routine) using variables "*a*, *A*, task, and Result." The next line declares that "*a*" is subscripted to contain three values and each value is a single character string; "*A*" is similarly

---

[8] Note that this system distinguishes between small and capital letters. The words Model, MODEL, and model, for example, are three different symbols to the computer. Inasmuch as PL/I words such as IF, CALL, THEN, ELSE, GO TO, etc. are always reported in capitals, it is useful to make variables in small letters, or in mixed capital–small-letter combinations for ease in later reading.

```
ModelS:   PROCEDURE (a,A,task,Result);
          DECLARE a(3) CHARACTER (1), A(3) CHARACTER (1),
             Result CHARACTER (1), task CHARACTER (1);

Start:    tally=0;

Test:     IF a(1)="+" & A(1)="H" | a(1)="—" & A(1)="V"
             THEN tally=tally+1;
             ELSE  tally=tally—1;

          IF a(2)="+" & A(2)="H" | a(2)="—" & A(2)="V"
             THEN tally=tally+1;
             ELSE  tally=tally—1;

          IF ABS(tally)=2 THEN GO TO Decide;

          IF a(3)="+" & A(3)="H" | a(3)="—" & A(3)="V"
             THEN tally=tally+1;
             ELSE  tally=tally—1;

Decide:   IF task=">" & tally>0 | task="<" & tally<0
             THEN Result="H";
             ELSE  Result="V";

          RETURN;
          END ModelS;
```

Fig. 3–2. Artificial intelligence model of subject behavior in the Smedslund experiment.

subscripted. "Result" and "task" are declared unsubscripted strings of one character.

The experiment program transfers the item for that trial (whether entered from the console or generated by the experimenter program) to subject model by the six characters in the format $a(1)$, $A(1)$, $a(2)$, $A(2)$; $a(3)$, $A(3)$ so that the small a's represent the signs and the large A's represent the letters. If the task is to say which is largest, the variable "task" will have been set to ">." If the task is to say which is smallest, then "task" is set to "<." The model of the subject is to report back to the experiment program that the "Result" is the character V or the character H.

The actual instructions to be executed begin at the next line labeled "Start:," the label being indicated by the use of a colon. This line sets a new variable, used internally by the routine and called "tally," to zero. Control then proceeds down through the following statements until the RETURN statement is reached, at which time control passes back to the experiment.

In order to read the notation in this routine, the following symbols must be known:

"1" means "or"
"&" means "and"
"ABS" means "absolute value of"
"=" in an IF test statement signifies equality as in algebra; otherwise it means "set equal to" as when we set "tally" equal to zero
">" means "greater than"
"<" means "less than"

The heart of the subject model is a test phase which is repeated up to three times, once for each of the sign–letter combinations in the order they are presented. The variable "tally" is used to keep track of the score for each pass of the loop. When an IF statement finds the sign–letter combination being tested is either $+H$ or $-V$, then a score is added to "tally" in favor of H being greater. Otherwise (that is, if it is $-H$ or $+V$) a score is subtracted from tally in favor of V being greater. If, after the second test, tally is equal to either plus or minus two, then no more sign–letter combinations need be tested and control passes (by means of a GO TO instruction) to the statement labeled "Decide:."

The IF statement labeled "Decide:" determines whether one of two sets of conditions exists: either the Task = ">" and tally was greater than zero, or the Task = "<" and tally was less than zero. If either set holds, the Result is set equal to H. Otherwise, Result is set equal to V. RETURN then transfers control back to the experiment program.

Using this approach, a stimulus can be one of two levels of difficulty: either it can be solved after the second sign–letter combination is present or the decision must wait for the third sign–letter combination. Otherwise, according to this strategy, all stimuli are alike in the kind and amount of work needed for solving them.

Model of a Human Solution

A computer simulation of a search-for-pairs strategy is shown in Fig. 3–3. The same information is transmitted by the experiment model as before and the same kind of response information is expected back. Thus, the first two lines are the same as Fig. 3–2, except we have called this routine "ModelH" to distinguish it from the previous model.

The search for a pair is in the section beginning with the line labeled "Start:." These lines present a series of IF tests for each pair of letters. The first-and-second-letter pair is tested first. If these are found to be

```
ModelH:  PROCEDURE (a,A,task,Result);
         DECLARE a(3) CHARACTER (1), A(3) CHARACTER (1),
         Result CHARACTER (1), task CHARACTER (1);

Start:   IF  A(1) = A(2)
              THEN IF a(1) = a(2) THEN point = 1;
                                  ELSE  point = 3;

              ELSE IF A(2) = A(3)
                   THEN IF a(2) = a(3) THEN point = 2;
                                       ELSE  point = 1;

              ELSE IF A(1) = A(3)
                   THEN IF a(1) = a(3) THEN point = 1;
                                       ELSE  point = 2;

              ELSE STOP;

Decide:  IF task=">" & a(point)="+" I task="<" & a(point)="—"

         THEN Result = A(point);

         ELSE IF A(point) = "V" THEN Result = "H";
                                ELSE  Result = "V";

         RETURN;

         END ModelH;
```

Fig. 3–3. Model of human subject behavior in the Smedslund experiment.

alike, then their signs are tested. If they have the same sign, then, as discussed above, the pair determines the answer. Therefore the variable "point" is assigned to 1, indicating that sign–letter combination predominates (it could just as well have been set to 2, in that it is the same sign–letter). If the letters in the pair have opposite signs, then, as we have discussed, they cancel each other out and the remaining sign–letter combination is the clue to the answer. In the case where the pair is the first and second letters, the remaining letter is the third letter, so "point" is accordingly set to 3.

If the first and second letters are found to be not the same [i.e., $A(1) \neq A(2)$], the program next tests whether the second and third letters are the same. If this is not the case, it tests whether the first and third letters are the same. If even this fails, then the item must have an illegal letter (there are only two legal letters and three positions to be filled) so a STOP instruction is given to halt execution. The computer will automatically tell the line number at which the stop occurs.

For any pair of like letters, the further processing is the same. The signs of that pair are tested. If they are the same, then "point" is set to the number of the first member of the pair. If not, then "point" is set to indicate the letter that is not involved in the pair.

Figure 3–3 has laid out the IF tests in a manner which will hopefully make them easy to follow (the machine would just as well accept them crowded together on one line). As soon as the testing reaches a semicolon, transfer is to the statement labeled "Decide:." This series of IF tests could also be represented by a tree structure, as shown in Fig. 3–4.

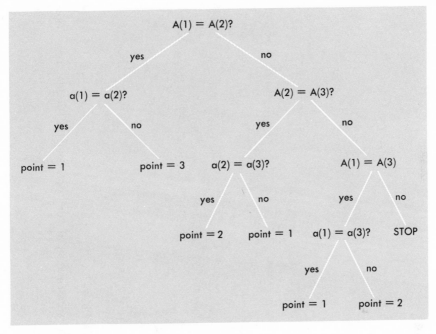

Fig. 3–4. "IF" test structure contained in Fig. 3–3, beginning with line labeled "Start."

The statement labeled "Decide:" uses the sign–letter combination indicated by "point" to produce the result. If the task is ">," then, if the sign indicated by "point" is "+," the answer is the letter indicated by "point." Otherwise a reversal must be made and the opposite letter used. Similarly, if the task is "<" and the sign indicated by "point" is "−," then the result is the letter indicated by "point." Otherwise, it is the opposite letter.

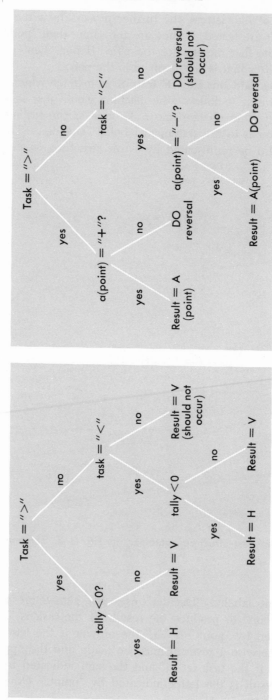

Decide rule, Fig. 3-3

Decide rule, Fig. 3-2

Fig. 3–5. Tree representation of "or" statements in "decide" rules (Figs. 3–2 and 3–3).

The setting to the opposite letter is done by testing to see if the letter pointed to is a V and if so making the result an H. Otherwise, the letter must be an H so the result is V.

Comparison of the Two Models

As can be seen, both the artificial intelligence model and the human simulation can be rather tersely stated. Why then is the solution humans prefer different? The answer this writer suggests is that the process represented by the "or" signs in the tests in Fig. 3-2 would require that the person create a disjunctive category and count its occurrences. If, for example, the task is to determine which is greater, then the user would consider either $+H$ or $-V$ as members of the category that H is greater. As soon as there are two instances of that category, it is certain that H is greater.

We know, however, from Bruner et al.'s exposition of 14 years ago (1956) that such handling of disjunctive categories is difficult for most people. Except for such concepts as a baseball strike (scored whenever a ball is swung at and missed *or* whenever a ball passes successfully over the plate *or* whenever a foul ball is hit but not caught and there are less than two strikes already) our skills at counting occurrences of disjunctive categories usually do not get much practice. While indeed the disjunctive concept in the Smedslund experiment is no more complicated than that of a baseball strike, the idea of using it did not occur to many people. People apparently can use disjunctive categories that exist in our culture, but they do not tend to invent them readily.

The difference between the "or" specification in the "Test:" section of Fig. 3-2 and the occurrences of "or" elsewhere in Figs. 3-2 and 3-3 brings up a point that is occasionally overlooked in discussing disjunctions, but which seems to be important to understanding how humans select information processing strategies. In the other occurrences, as shown in Fig. 3-5, the "or" specification serves as a shorthand for tree directions. The user need not create the disjunctive category, but instead can follow out the trees. In Fig. 3-2, on the other hand, the equivalence of $+H$ and $-V$ must be recognized in incrementing or decrementing "tally" as many times as necessary. The processes represented by a tree format are no longer adequate. This kind of disjunction causes people problems so that they often will select a strategy that allows them to avoid it.

Both models would predict that some responses would occur before the third item is read, although this would occur twice as often if the artificial intelligence strategy is being used. Smedslund speculates that subjects might be holding back, thinking they are not allowed to respond until the presentation is finished. Only one subject of the three studied intensively (each given 16 repetitions of the 32 items used) produced zero reaction times. The first occurred on the 11th repetition for a case where the first two letters and signs were identical $(+H \ +H \ -H)$. Thereafter, the zero reaction time occurred in 95 per cent of such items. On the 14th repetition, a zero reaction time appeared to the item $- H + V + H$, indicating that the subject had finally switched over to the artificial intelligence strategy at least some of the time. Thereafter, zero reaction times occurred for 79 per cent of such items.

It would be interesting to see what would happen if subjects were explicitly instructed to see if they can respond before the third item is presented. Our models would lead us to predict that many subjects, if put to the task, could come out with a response when the first two letters are identical, especially if the series were read at a slower speed than Smedslund used. Only a few subjects, we would predict, would exhibit the disjunctive category model at work and even they might switch back to the apparent use of the pair-search strategy because it is easier to handle.

Predicting Reaction Times

If we assume that the human using a particular information processing strategy on a particular item will go through a similar number of steps as used by the computer model, then the number of steps used by the model should be an index of amount of cognitive "work" used and may be related to the average reaction time for that item. In the case of the disjunctive category model, as we have seen, the amount of work is a function of whether two or three tests need be made. In the pair-search model, however, the amount of work is dependent on several variables. First, we can assume that if the pair is the first two letters, this is more quickly found than if it is the second two letters, which in turn is more quickly found than if it is the first and third letters.

Let us assign work loads 1, 2, and 3 respectively to each of these cases, although in fact the split pair (first and third letters) may cause such additional difficulty that an additional work load point should be assigned to it. If the signs associated with the pair are identical, then the solution is readily forthcoming and only one additional work load point might be assigned. If the signs are opposite so that the pair cancels itself, then a reference must be made to the third letter (which at least involves an additional shifting of attention), so that at least two more work load points are appropriate. Finally, the generation of an answer may involve still additional work if the reversal is needed at the end, that is, the naming of the opposite letter. The total work, then, for any one item could vary from 2 units for $+ H + H - V$ (where the task is to say which is greater) to 7 units for $+ H - V - H$ (where again the task is to say which is greater).

In fact, the predicted scores correlated quite highly (+.57) with the rank orderings of reaction times found by Smedslund. When the reaction times were plotted against the predicted scores, an examination of deviant cases indicated one important additional factor previously overlooked, namely that the processing of items where all three letters were the same but the signs varied took longer than expected. It would seem that the handling of three identical letters, when the strategy is to look for pairs, takes a little extra time unless all three signs are also the same.

Still other strategies than the two presented here are possible. For example, it is evident that the pairing strategy could search for pairs of signs rather than pairs of letters. The computer simulation would be quite parallel to that shown in Fig. 3–3, yet the pattern of predicted reaction times would be remarkably different. In this case, for example, $+ H - H + V$ would take longer to solve, but $+ H + V - H$ would be solved more quickly.

Further experimentation might reveal that people have characteristic skills in handling even so simple a matter as the different steps in the pair-search strategy. Some may skim over the letters rapidly for pairs, but lag in shifting attention to the third sign–letter combination when the letter pair signs cancel. Others may quickly shift attention, but be awkward at doing the reversal manipulation when it is needed. Understanding human information processing involves the identification of component procedures and the extent to which they reflect particular mental abilities, socially conditioned general styles of operation, or skills that are easily learned for the particular task. In addition to the study of component procedures, such an understanding also involves studying the flexibility and effectiveness with which the components can be put together to form strategies.

THE GREGG–SIMON MODEL OF THE
BOWER–TRABASSO EXPERIMENT

For the Smedslund experiment, the specification of alternative models and the process of inferring from the data which one is probably being used by the subject is relatively straightforward. This is partly because the alternative models are very different and lead to the expectations of quite different performance. Lest we appear unduly optimistic, a second example is presented illustrating how the task can become more complicated, not because of computer programming difficulties, but because more alternatives can be stated and it is harder to distinguish between them in the data. This is true especially if the subject is likely to change strategies during the course of the experiment.

Gregg and Simon (1967) have developed a series of information processing models to describe behaviors of subjects in some experiments performed by Bower and Trabasso (1964). They then compare these models in detail with the stochastic, noncontinuity, mathematical models that Bower and Trabasso developed to characterize the performances of subjects in their experiments. To simplify discussion, we here consider a straightforward version of the experiment:

The subject is given a series of stimuli. Each stimulus can vary on several dimensions from the others. Let us here say that the color can be red or blue, that the size can be large or small, and that the shape can be a diamond or a triangle. Each stimulus is said to belong to one of two groups; let us say the names of the groups are "Ruk" and "Jom." The subject is to say which group the stimulus belongs to when it is presented. He will then be told whether he is right or wrong. The experiment ends when the subject is able to name correctly the group for each of ten stimuli in a row. Membership in groups "Ruk" or "Jom" is determined, respectively, by the presence or absence of one of the attributes. Assignment on the basis of conjunctive or disjunctive combinations of attributes is not used.

Both Gregg and Simon as well as Bower and Trabasso chose to assume that until the subject "knows" the correct concept, he may make correct responses with certain probabilities, but after "learning" takes place (which comes as an event, rather than being acquired gradually) a correct response will be made to all stimuli presented thereafter. The subject maintains an overall probability of correct response until this event takes place. For Gregg and Simon, however, the probability of a correct response on any particular trial very much depends on the presumed information processing that is going on in the subject at that moment.

Gregg and Simon build their formal process models from the informal process model put forth by Bower and Trabasso (1964, p. 39, which in turn stems from Restle, 1962):

The subject in a concept-identification experiment is viewed as testing out various hypotheses (strategies) about a solution of the problem. Each problem defines for the subject a population of hypotheses. The subject samples one of these hypotheses at random and makes the responses dictated by the hypothesis. If his responses are correct, he continues to use that hypothesis on the next trial.

In the models put forth by Gregg and Simon (as well as by Bower & Trabasso) the assumption is made that the subject only entertains and tests one hypothesis at a time. It is assumed *no* work is being done on backup hypotheses. This assumption in at least some cases is probably not true. However, as we will see, the alternatives are already many and difficult enough to test even when this limiting assumption is made. If the assumption is dropped, the complexity of the models multiplies greatly.

A COMPUTER SIMULATION

A computer model of the experiment again allocates moves to the experimenter and the subject and keeps score. This model begins by asking the person at the console how many dimensions are to be used and what are their different values. It also asks what is the "correct" value, that is, the one used to classify the stimulus as being a "Ruk" or a "Jom."

The different values are represented in the models by a string of characters, in which each character stands for a different value. In our example, we have six values: red, blue, large, small, diamond, and triangle. We represent them by the six letters "rbLSdt" with the alternation of small and capital letters to remind us that there are three dimensions. Let us say that the triangle ("t") is the property that identifies "Ruks"; all stimuli that do not have this property are "Joms."

The experiment model also asks if the role of the experimenter is to be manually performed from the typewriter terminal. If so, it will pause at each trial to receive a new stimulus from the terminal. If not, it uses an experimenter model to generate stimuli. The experimenter model randomly generates in this case one color, one size, and one shape for each trial. Whether typed in from the console or generated by the experimenter model, the stimulus is in the form of the three-letter string. For example "rLd" would stand for "red, large, diamond."

In this simulation, the dimension-value relation only plays a role in the experimenter model. None of the subject models in fact pay any attention to it. Instead, the subject models all consider a list of possible values and regard any stimulus as a sublist of values taken from this list.[9]

Gregg and Simon present four alternative models, to which we have added a fifth.

[9] In certain variations of the experiment discussed by Gregg and Simon, the "correct" value was changed in the midst of the experiment to its opposite value on that dimension. At this point, of course, the attribute membership of a value again becomes important.

Replacement Model

Imagine the possible hypotheses represented by buttons well stirred in a pot. The subject begins by picking a hypothesis out of the pot at random. He then uses that hypothesis in evaluating stimuli until he is told he is wrong. At that point, he again returns to the pot to pick out a hypothesis. Each time he takes out a button to read his new hypothesis, he immediately puts the button back in the pot; thus the idea of "replacement." He may sample the same button again in the future.

To consider further what happens in the experiment, let us say the subject picks out the hypothesis that "b" indicates "Ruk"; the correct hypothesis is "t"; and that the experimenter presents the stimulus "rSd." Since the stimulus does not contain a "b," the subject says "Jom." Since, however, the stimulus also does not contain a "t," the experimenter says "right." Thus the subject is right for the wrong reasons but doesn't know it. According to our model, he will keep the hypothesis for the next trial. Let us say the next stimulus is "bSt." The subject now says "Ruk" because the stimulus contains a "b," but the experimenter says "right" because the stimulus also contains a "t." Again, the subject is right for the wrong reason. The next stimulus, let us say, is "bLd." The subject says "Ruk" and the experimenter says "wrong," because the stimulus does not contain a "t." The subject now goes back to the list of letters representing possible hypotheses and samples a new one. This process continues until the subject has ten correct responses in a row, at which point the experiment is over.

The computer model for the subject is quite simple. From the information supplied at the beginning of the experiment, we know there are N possible values and these are represented by a string of letters. A routine labeled NEWHYP generates an initial new hypothesis by getting a random number "C" between 1 and N and then selecting the "Cth" operation from the string of letters. This item is then used as the current hypothesis "CH" against which each successive stimulus is evaluated until it is disconfirmed and routine NEWHYP is used again to generate another CH.

The PL/I programming language has two built-in functions that are very useful for handling character string representations. One is called INDEX and has two arguments, the first being the name of the string being searched and the second being the pattern that is being searched. If the pattern is found, the value of INDEX will be the number of the character position in the string at which the pattern was first found to begin. If the pattern is not found, then the function returns the value zero. The other function is called SUBSTR and has three arguments. This function is used to pick out or make replacements on a substring within a string. The first argument is the name of the string. The second argument is the character position in the string (which may have been found by a previous INDEX operation) at which the pattern is said to start. The third argument gives the number of characters which the substring is said to contain. If the third argument is a one, the substring is only one character long. If the third argument is missing, the substring is assumed to continue to the end of the string.

For example, if our string "HYP" were "rbLSdt" and we said

$$X = INDEX(HYP,"t")$$

the computer would set X equal to 6, because "t" is the sixth item in the string. If we wanted to then replace a "t" we have found with a "Z," we would write

$$SUBSTR(HYP,X,1) = "Z"$$

which then sets the Xth item (which we have just set to 6) to be a "Z." If we wanted to set string Y to be the substring of two letters preceding a "t" we would write

$$Y = SUBSTR(HYP,X-2,2)$$

which would then set Y equal to the two-letter string "Sd." [10]

The INDEX function can also be used in IF statements. Should the value of INDEX be zero, the test is considered to have failed. If it is greater than zero, it is passed. For example, in the following statement, Y is set equal to Z if the substring "pm" is found on string K. Otherwise Y is set equal to S.

IF INDEX(K,"pm") THEN Y=Z;
ELSE Y=S

With this brief excursion into PL/I string functions, we can describe the key statements in the simulation. Picking out the randomly generated Cth item from the string HYP representing possible hypotheses in order to select a new current hypothesis is done by one statement:

$$CH = SUBSTR(HYP,C,1)$$

---

[10] PL/I string functions also can be nested for rather powerful search procedures. For example, the following four-rule loop would count the number (n) occurrences of "tx" in a string HYP:

```
        n=0;
        m=1;
loop:   X=INDEX(SUBSTR(HYP,m), "tx");
        IF X=0 THEN GO TO exit; ELSE n=n+1;
        m=X+m;
        GO TO loop
```

What is the correct value?
t
How many values are there?
6
Give the values as a string of letters in quotes.
"rbLSdt"
How many values are on each stimulus?
3
Which strategy do you wish the subject to use?
1
Do you want to be the experimenter?
yes

rLD
1. b Jom 1.
bSd
2. b Ruk 0.
rSd
3. L Jom 1.
rLt
4. L Ruk 2.
bLt
5. L Ruk 3.
rSd
6. L Jom 4.
rLd
7. L Ruk 0.
rSt
8. d Jom 0.
bLd
9. b Ruk 0. (samples hypothesis "b" again)
rSd
10. t Jom 1. (gets correct hypothesis)
rLt
11. t Ruk 2.

bSt
12. t Ruk 3.
bLt
13. t Ruk 4.
rSd
14. t Jom 5.
bSd
15. t Jom 6.
bLd
16. t Jom 7.
rLt
17. t Ruk 8.
rSt
18. t Ruk 9.
bSt
19. t Ruk 10.

END OF EXPERIMENT, TOTAL OF 19 TRIALS USED.

Fig. 3-6. Sample run, replacement model.

Once the subject has a *CH*, he can use this to test stimuli. The *CH* is tested against the three-letter string called STIM representing the stimulus:

IF INDEX(STIM,*CH*) THEN says="Ruk";
    ELSE says="Jom"

Similarly, only a short statement is needed by the experiment model to test whether indeed the correct hypothesis (here called VERITAS) is on the stimulus string STIM and accordingly evaluate the response made by the subject:

IF INDEX(STIM,VERITAS)
    THEN IF says="Ruk" THEN reply="right";
                ELSE reply="wrong";
    ELSE IF says="Jom" THEN reply="right";
                ELSE reply="wrong"

For each trial, the computer prints out the trial number, the current hypothesis *CH*, the response of the subject to the stimulus, the reply from the experiment model, and a tally of how many correct responses have now been made in a row. If the stimulus was generated by the experimenter program instead of being entered from the console, it is also printed. An example run using this replacement model is shown in Fig. 3–6.

Non-Replacement Model

This is the same as the replacement model except for the following changes. First, after the *C*th item is taken from string HYP, it is checked to see if it is a blank. If a blank is found, control transfers back to get a new hypothesis again:

IF *CH* = " " then go to NEWHYP

Otherwise, the *CH* is accepted and the *C*th position is set to blank so it will not be used again.

SUBSTR(HYP,*C*,1) = " "

In terms of our buttons-in-the-pot model, this is equivalent to having only one button for each alternative hypothesis and not replacing the button once it is drawn.

Models one and two represent two extremes of perfect memory of past hypotheses vs. no memory at all. Some sort of decaying memory function, in which the button has a certain probability at any move of getting back in would perhaps be more realistic, and could easily be added with a few more lines of program. However, in terms of over-all number of trials to completion, it is very hard to distinguish between models one and two, and the performance of a decaying memory model would fall in between.

In order to decide between two models, we generally need more in-formation than just how many trials were taken to completion. One important addition is the list of responses (not the *CH*) made for each stimulus. In distinguishing between models one and two, however, this would still not help much, although there are situations that should not arise if model two in fact is in operation.

Simon and his associates have long advocated having the subject relate what is on his mind as the experiment proceeds. At the simplest level, we can have him tell us his *CH* at each trial. We could also ask him to tell us what factors were involved in picking a new *CH* every time he does so. These additions would greatly simplify the task of distinguishing between two models.

Local Non-Replacement

Gregg and Simon present a model intermediate to models one and two, in which the new button picked is compared with the last button and if they are the same another draw is made. This corresponds then to a special immediate recall memory that only lasts until a new hy-pothesis is selected. Instead of creating *CH* directly from the string HYP of possible alternatives, we will create a new hypothesis *NH* which we will compare with the last hypothesis *CH*. If they are the same, we will sample again; otherwise *CH* is set equal to *NH*. In PL/I notation this reads:

$$NH=SUBSTR(HYP,C,1);$$
$$\text{IF } CH=NH \text{ GO TO NEWHYP};$$
$$\text{ELSE } CH=NH$$

This model might be considered a minimum improvement over model one, for it will not select the hypothesis it has just discarded.

Local Consistency

Gregg and Simon propose another model in which a check is made to see if the new hypothesis is a member of the previous stimulus STIM. If so, the model is made to sample again for another new hypothesis.

If indeed, the subject has just said "Ruk" and the reply is "wrong," then the subject can eliminate not only the current hypothesis, but also the other values on the stimulus from the list of candidates in selecting a new hypothesis. However, if the subject said "Jom" and was told "wrong," then he knows that the correct hypothesis is one of the attributes on that stimulus.

Gregg and Simon in their article accidentally omit this second situation. Indeed, their local consistency strategy, as reported, would be inappropriate for this situation.

A more appropriate local consistency model then is represented by the following code to be used when the subject has been told "wrong" and he now considers a new hypothesis candidate *NH*.

```
IF  INDEX(STIM,NH)
     THEN IF  says="Ruk" THEN GO TO NEWHYP;
                    ELSE CH=NH;
     ELSE IF  says="Jom" THEN GO TO NEWHYP;
                    ELSE CH=NH
```

This says that if the subject has been told "wrong" for saying "Ruk" and the new hypothesis being considered was on the last stimulus, he should get another new hypothesis; on the other hand, if he had been told "wrong" for saying "Jom" and the new hypothesis is not on the last stimulus, then he should get a new hypothesis. Otherwise, he accepts the new hypothesis and makes it the current hypothesis.

Global Consistency: The Perfect Performance

Gregg and Simon propose an additional model in which after being told "wrong" all the values on the stimulus are removed from the list of possible alternatives. Again, this would be appropriate only for those cases where the subject said "Ruk" and was told "wrong."

In fact, a perfect consistency solution requires consideration of four situations:

1. The subject has said "Ruk" and is told "wrong." In this case, the subject can remove all of the values on the stimulus as candidates for future new hypotheses.
2. The subject has said "Jom" and is told "wrong." In this case, the subject can replace his list of possible hypotheses with just those values that were on his list and were also part of the stimulus.
3. The subject says "Ruk" and is told "right." In addition to keeping the current hypothesis, he can remove from the list of future candidates all those not on the stimulus.
4. The subject says "Jom" and is told "right." In addition to keeping the current hypothesis, he can remove from the list of future possibilities all those values occurring on the stimulus.

The routines for accomplishing this are quite straightforward, drawing on the mechanism of a DO loop. At the beginning of the session, the user is asked how many attributes will occur on the stimulus (that is, how many characters will be on the string STIM). This is stored as variable "nSTIM."

For situations one and four:

```
loop1: DO r=1 by 1 to nSTIM;
       m=INDEX(HYP,SUBSTR(STIM,r,1));
       IF m > 0 THEN SUBSTR(HYP,m,1) = " ";
       END loop1
```

The first line says that the instructions between the line labeled "loop1" and the line "END loop1" are executed once for each value of "r," starting at 1 and going up to the value of "nSTIM." The second line tests whether the rth item on the string STIM can be found on the current string HYP of possible hypotheses. This is done by making the second argument of INDEX the function SUBSTR, which picks off the rth item of STIM. If the rth item on STIM is indeed found in HYP (that is, $m>0$), then line three changes that character of string HYP to a blank.

For situations two and three, it might be thought that we could just replace the contents of string HYP with the contents of STIM. Before doing this, we must remove from STIM those values that are absent from HYP so we do not put values back on HYP that are already discarded.

For situations two and three:

```
loop2: DO r = 1 by 1 to nSTIM;
       IF INDEX(HYP,SUBSTR(STIM,r,1))=0
          THEN SUBSTR(STIM,r,1) = " ";
       END loop2;
       HYP=STIM
```

The loop tests each value on list STIM to see if it is on the list of possible hypotheses, HYP. If not, a blank is set to this position of STIM. After the loop has been done for each value on STIM, then HYP is replaced by STIM.[11]

It should be noted that our concern has been with alternative psychological models and that we have not discussed alternative computer representations of any one model. Even within one programming lan-

---

[11] Note that the string STIM can be shorter than the string HYP. This is made possible by declaring HYP as having a variable length at the beginning of the program. The last operation, in this case, would reduce the length of HYP to three characters.

guage, a particular model usually may be communicated in different ways, just as different words and sentence structures can be used to communicate the same idea in English. In our examples, the use of DO loops or a particular choice of nesting IF statements vs. using OR specifications are conveniences that we chose to use. Exactly the same information processes could have been represented with a different design of statements. The choice between different forms of stating instructions to a computer, if much computer processing is to be done, is usually made on the basis of which will be executed most quickly. In our case, since the amount of computer processing is rather trivial given the power of modern computers, our concern has been on the conciseness of the procedures and the ease in describing them to the reader.

PASSING TURING'S TEST

The data gathered by Bower and Trabasso would indicate that people are much less than perfect information processors in this kind of experiment. They have imperfect memories and they tend not to take advantage of all available information.

Let us remember that we have only considered models for the situation in which the subject is entertaining one hypothesis at a time (although in the perfect consistency model this no longer makes a difference). There also is no reason to assume that a subject is constant in his strategy. Assuming that a perfect consistency strategy represents too big a cognitive load, he may use one partial strategy for a while and then shift to another, for example, perhaps trading off for a while using a simpler strategy for keeping a better memory.

To demonstrate the complexity of the problem, instead of setting the subject model at the beginning to use a particular strategy, let us add a random routine so that every so many moves the current strategy changes. Let us also assign stimulus presentation at each trial to the person at the console, so he can present stimuli designed as best he can to make the model of the subject reveal its current strategy. To make the situation more like that advocated by Gregg and Simon, let us also have the computer not only print out the subject model's response but also report its current hypothesis. Now, with all these advantages, how well can an expert at the typewriter console follow what strategy is being used with what information remembered? In fact, the computer model can give a remarkably human performance. Except for the fact that the computer types back a response faster than most people would, the person at the terminal may be unable to distinguish whether he has a real person or the computer model at the other end. When this is the case, the computer model is said to have passed what is known as "Turing's test" (1950).

Even if a model passes Turing's test, the understanding of the phenomena being modeled may be far from complete. In our model, we still have two random components to represent processes that we have not attempted to understand. One is picking a new hypothesis from the list of possible hypotheses. Assuming there are several alternatives still available, how do we know which one is selected? We don't, so the model essentially flips a coin to choose one. In so doing, we are saying that this choice is governed by factors outside the concern of our experiment which, in terms of running the experiment on many subjects, act in a random way on the data. One subject, for example, may have a liking for blue as a color so chooses that whenever possible. Another subject may be form- rather than color-dominant and thus be more sensitive to size attributes. At any time, we could redefine the domain of our concern and replace this random function with a procedure; for example, we might perhaps give subjects a color–form dominance test and a color preference test before the experiment and use the resulting information in our model to predict which hypothesis will be considered first.

A second random mechanism represents oscillation between different available strategies. In this experiment, the subject may, at different times, use several of the strategies and pieces of information available to him, although to take in all information with a perfect memory for the entire experiment would be quite a cognitive feat. At present, neither we nor the person at the console has information as to which strategies should be preferred at a particular point in the experiment. Until then, Turing's test is passed with our present models.

THE GREGG AND SIMON POSITION

The Gregg and Simon paper, to this writer's knowledge, is the first comparison paper of its type and is highly recommended. Gregg and Simon quote Bower and Trabasso to show that Bower and Trabasso do indeed have an informal information processing model in mind that they use to develop their stochastic mathematical formalization. They then show that their process model has all the advantages of a mathematical model, except, of course, the advantage of being able to make mathematical derivations. In trade, the process model has the additional advantages of more closely representing the procedure used by the subjects in coming to a solution. The Bower–Trabasso mathematical approach is presented as closing off further investigation while the process model is seen as fostering a closer examination of the subjects' information processing procedures.

Rather than argue the superiority of stochastic theory models vs. process models, why not use both? Trabasso and Bower (1968) have continued using mathematics to many good ends, even if it perhaps has led them to look at problems different from those emphasized by process models. A two-way street of exchange probably exists. Gregg and Simon have learned from Bower and Trabasso's work. Batchelder (1968) has in turn argued convincingly that a formal process model may be very useful in aiding the derivation of a formal axiomatic mathematical model.

EVALUATING THE UTILITY OF AN EXPERIMENT

Given the purposes considered here, one basis for evaluating an experiment is the leverage it offers in getting the subject to reveal his preferred information processing procedures. When the design of an experiment is such that a particular pattern of responses could have been produced by a variety of different processes, then we are not in a strong position to make inferences. The Smedslund experiment is more satisfactory because, although simpler, it offers tighter information as to which alternatives the subject was using.

Use of Process Models To Relate Different Experiments

Once alternative process models have been studied and tested for one experiment, a base is formed for branching out and relating that knowledge to processes in other experiments. For example, the pioneering concept attainment study of Bruner et al. (1956) also asked the subject to guess the concept which the investigator had in mind on the basis of feedback as to whether each stimulus was a member of that concept. The experiment differed in that the subject was allowed to choose the test stimulus for the next trial from the cards available. How then does this change in the experimental procedure change the psychological information processing models used by the subject?

If we assume a model similar to the basic one developed for the previous experiment, then the subject should form a hypothesis and select cards that are instances of that hypothesis until he is told he is wrong, at which time he would select another hypothesis and test those cards. Thus if the hypothesis is "red" he should select cards containing "red" [12] until he is told he is wrong. This indeed is what Bruner et al. described as the strategy of "Successive Scanning."

The other extreme of making as perfect a solution as possible, which Bruner et al. call "Simultaneous Scanning," would correspond to our fourth model. At each step, the subject uses all the information in the card to eliminate possible hypotheses. The selection of a new card would be based on the remaining list of possible hypotheses at that trial. This added selection routine would be designed to eliminate as many of the remaining hypotheses on the trial as possible.

Bruner et al. pose two additional strategies quite different from anything we have considered so far. In these approaches, the subject presents different cards until he finds one that the experimenter says is an instance of the concept. He then uses this card as a reference in selecting other cards that differ only in certain features until he has narrowed the different alternatives down to what must be the basis of the concept. These strategies are called "Conservative Focusing" (where only one attribute is changed per trial) and "Focused Gambling" (in which more than one attribute is varied at a time). These strategies then are almost completely a result of the subject being able to submit tests centered around what is known to be a positive instance. It lacks a parallel in the Bower and Trabasso kind of experiment.

The Bruner et al. experiments thus permitted the identification of very different information processing strategies for handling a particular problem. No elaborate process model was needed to aid in the identification and separation of the different strategies. They stood out by themselves. One reason was that in having the subject select a card from among many the burden of choice was put more on the subject and he played a more active role in the experiment, thus revealing much more about his strategies. Often the desire for experimental rigor has resulted in the subjects being unnecessarily passive, with a resulting low yield of information about the strategies they are using.

Given that some of the Bruner et al. strategies involved considering a number of hypotheses at once and narrowing them down, it is curious that some later investigators have assumed that subjects consider only one hypothesis at a time. Appropriately designed experiments, together with more intensive data analysis of the choices made at each trial, should provide clear information as to what kinds of people use what kinds of strategies in what situations. The assumption of the single hypothesis is a parsimonious explanation that often does quite well in explaining overall learning curves. Our goal is not, however, to

---

[12] In the Bruner experiment, each attribute has three values. Thus there is no single "opposite" as there was in both the Smedslund and the Gregg and Simon situations.

explain away data but to infer as much as possible how human information processing procedures operate.

Another procedural difference in the Bruner et al. experiments was to use complex concepts involving the conjunction and disjunction of attributes. Thus the concept might be "red triangles" or "all cards that are either red or are a triangle." Additional comparison experiments would allow us to investigate the question: How do subjects' preferences between alternative information processing models change as the complexity of the problem is increased in different ways?

The development of process models for attaining complex concepts has since been explored by E. B. Hunt (1962) and E. B. Hunt et al. (1966). Rather than consider a series of alternative strategies, one major representation was created and run under a series of alternative conditions, such as a restricted memory. As with much pioneering work, the initial concern was not whether we could develop alternative models, but whether we could make any feasible representation at all for solving the problem. Hunt's "Concept Learner" model was quite successful in the task of attaining concepts. Indeed, it could solve problems that were nearly impossible for humans. With limitations put on its abilities, it could be tempered to produce a fairly human-like performance. Most problems that were difficult for humans would also take longer for the Concept Learner model. In these ways and others, information processing models will relate different experiments and facilitate a systematic, cumulative development of experimental knowledge, much as the existence of models in psychophysics has organized the development of knowledge in that field.

Major Past Developments in Computer Information Processing Models in Psychology

Almost every science has its major concepts and techniques, and past computer modeling of human information processes has not been an exception. We here consider two such techniques: tree building and difference reduction.

Tree Building. Information trees have been extensively used to represent both structures of information to be referenced by a computer model (e.g., a kinship tree) and the sequences by which tests are to be made (e.g., Fig. 3-4). A computer model may create an information tree in storing pieces of information and mapping their subcategory and supracategory relationships. It also may create a tree as a list of directions to be consulted later, i.e., a plan.

The early list processing languages were essential in making complex tree representations feasible on the computer. The general importance of information trees has come to be widely recognized, such that the more recent general-purpose language PL/I has rudimentary "structure" facilities and operations for allocating computer memory for such structures during the execution of the program as a basic part of the language.

The list processing languages not only have supplied procedures for building tree structures, but also included tools for using the resulting structure. A system of operations involving pointers is made available to search the tree structure for information. Additional operations permit the changing, discarding, or insertion of information in the existing tree structure. Indeed it has been the facility of making alterations in an existing tree structure that makes the program management problems in designing list computer languages particularly complex.

Two kinds of search commands are used in connection with trees. One is the search for a particular item. For example, in referring to a kinship structure, we might ask: "Is there someone on the Jones kinship tree named 'Alice'?" Other searches may be based on a contextual specification: "Who are Alice's first cousins?"

Once procedures were worked out, a computer could be used to build trees in a variety of sizes and shapes. This raised the question: "Do people have such trees in their head?" If indeed trees are used to represent short-term memory, long-term memory, plans, and the like, what are the constraints in each case that the tree would have? It also raised such questions as: "Do people search through a tree like a computer?" and "In what ways are trees inappropriate and when are other forms of information structuring used?"

Trees can vary in a number of ways. Perhaps most studied has been the constraint of "depth," that is, the number of nodes between the origin of the tree and the furthest end point. Yngve (1960), for example, has shown that if sentence construction is represented by a tree, then certain rules limiting the depth of the trees can be identified; people do not tend to form syntactic structures that violate these depth rules. Other constraints relate to the number of branches at any node and to the overall breadth of the tree. Still other questions relate to whether a tree can re-enter itself, that is, whether a branch at one node can lead back to a node higher up on the tree.

Psychologists interested in how people play games have recognized that it would be impossible for a person to examine the full tree of contingencies that would follow from a particular move, so that they only develop a partial tree of implications in planning their strategy. The heuristic rules used in making such selective considerations in planning have received considerable attention by a number of researchers.

Difference Reduction. For over a decade, several of the strongest proponents of computer modeling have given considerable attention to the processes by which a problem is broken down into its components and then the steps needed to achieve the desired goals are reformulated into a series of subtasks that together represent a solution to the problem. G. A. Miller et al. (1960) gave an early review of this approach emphasizing the importance of continuing feedback in making such formulations and showing how this approach could be used to explain a variety of different types of problems in the behavioral sciences. This little book, which has since been translated into several languages including Russian, was an important attack against "black box" behaviorism and popularized the legitimacy of considering information organization in the study of behavior. The writing of this book stemmed from thinking at the RAND Corporation under the influence of Simon, Newell, and others, which was developed into a set of computer programs called the General Problem Solver. A summary of the work done with these programs over an entire decade has recently been reported in length by Ernst and Newell (1967).

While earlier reports on the General Problem Solver (GPS) emphasized the general process of finding steps that would reduce differences between the present state and the desired goal, the more recent presentation by Ernst and Newell gives considerable attention to the process of conceptualizing the problem in such a way that difference reduction can take place. Hitting upon a workable representation of the problem would seem to be a necessary prerequisite to solving a task, no matter how good one is at reducing differences once a representation is found. Most representations tend to be suggested by the terms in which the problem is stated. The difficulty of many puzzles hinges on the versatility of the subject in developing a different representation. As Polya demonstrated in *How To Solve It* (1944), a basic strategy is to note similarities between a current problem and another problem for which a representation is known and then apply that representation to the new problem.

Relations of Well-Structured Problem Solving to Everyday Thought Processes

Problem solving experiments such as we have examined are usually highly artificial situations. The problem is usually abstract, with little reference to the myriad of thoughts that concern the subject in his ordinary daily life. The alternatives are unusually clearcut. The decision making becomes unusually crisp. Indeed, is there any relation to the processes that go into how an adolescent decides what school to go to or what job to take, how an adult decides whom he will vote for, or even how a housewife decides what she will have for dinner?

One well recognized difference is that decisions made in everyday life are influenced by social pressures. Case studies of decision making in government and business clearly show decisions as a result of social processes and not just lining up facts. The personality of the decision maker generally makes him more accepting of some styles of influence than others, and he will heed the advice of some kinds of people more than others.

Given the amount of theory and research on influence, there exists an extensive basis for the development of computer models. The most well-known formulations have been the balance, consistency, and congruity models, which have recently been interrelated in a sourcebook by Abelson et al. (1968). Kelman (1958) has explored and related compliance, identification, and internalization as three forms of influence. Schneidman (1961) has inventoried what he calls "psycho-logic" mechanisms by which people influence each other. Osgood (1963) has proposed three universal dimensions by which people regard each other. Simon and Guetzkow (1955) have formalized processes toward uniformity in groups, as has Cohen (1963). Other important work has been done in small group research, reference group theory, and organization theory, to cite but a few topics.

Two factors come to bear on the modeling of personality in social situations. One is that the situation must be replicable or naturally recur so that the effects of changes in different factors can be observed. A second is that the more numerous the avenues of social influence in a situation, the more complex will be any comprehensive analysis. Several situations, such as the Asch experiment and the Guetzkow game cited earlier, have been quite suitable for studying the influence of personality characteristics, national character, social training, and the like. Barber (1966) is an example where real government groups, in which the members know each other well and the patterns of influence are well established, are brought into a standard laboratory situation for detailed study.

Information Models of Motivation and Emotion

So far our discussion has emphasized the way people think about problems and decide their behavior. In this way, it is easy to consider personality differences in tolerance for complexity, perseverance, openness to influence from external sources vs. the tendency to think for oneself, flexibility in changing strategies, amount of completion before one is satisfied and stops, speed of processing, etc.

Given this base, it is a relatively simple matter to add more components to the model representing motivation and emotion. Simon (1967) has discussed at length how such motivational and emotional controls can fit into an information processing theory.

In some cases, an emotion will cut off work on a task. Let us say, for example, that each time a subject is wrong, that adds one unit of frustration but that each time he is correct, his frustration drops two units. Let us say further that if his frustration reaches 20 units, he displays anger and goes home. Thus, for when there is failure, we add a program step that increases a variable we will call "Frus":

$$Frus=Frus+1$$

and when there is success, we decrease this variable by 2:

$$Frus=Frus-2$$

At the end of each trial, the current level of frustration is tested to see if the subject still wants to continue:

$$IF\ Frus\ >\ =\ 20\ THEN\ STOP$$

Similarly, if a subject has many successes, such that Frus becomes a large negative number, then he may regard the problem as conquered (even though the experimenter is not satisfied) and lose interest in continuing. The rates at which frustration increases or decreases, as well as the cutoff points at which new behavior will appear, are then aspects of the subject's personality.

Motivations can be handled in a similar way. The buildup of a motive past a certain threshold may cause the current activity to be interrupted and set aside so that action can be taken to reduce the motivation. Thus, I stopped my typing when I got thirsty, got a glass of water, and drank it before I resumed typing. If it had been inconvenient for me to get the water, I probably would have let my thirst build up further.

Whether a motive will interrupt depends on such conditions as how easily it can be satisfied and how much urgency there is in completing the current activity. If a person perseveres at a task under conflicting motivations, various factors in his cognitive performance may be affected. How a physiological state is interpreted may depend on the past history of information processing. Research has shown that people will vary widely in how they interpret an emotional arousal produced by drug infusion.

"Hot Cognition"

Abelson (1963) coined the term "hot cognition" to contrast with the relatively cold cognition of the problem solving experiment. His model first tested whether an incoming proposition was credible in terms of existing propositions representing the current belief system. If so, the proposition could be accepted and stored. If not, then the belief system could be changed, the interpretation of the incoming proposition could be changed, or the incoming proposition itself may not be challenged as much as the credibility of the person who said it.

Colby (1963, 1967) at Stanford has joined Abelson in his concern for modeling hot cognition processes, in this case focusing on beliefs of a psychoneurotic patient. Beliefs, values, etc., obtained from the patient are to be stored in memory banks and used as a reference in processing new information. Tesler et al. (1967) proposed using a directed graph representation for the computer simulation of belief systems.

In the Tesler et al. system, a "belief . . . is an attitude toward a proposition about concepts." Propositions may have both a level of credibility (from 0 to 100) and a level of foundation. The two are not the same, thus "There is a man behind that wall" might have little foundation but be credible. They further state that

$$\text{cred}(p) + \text{cred}(\bar{p}) \geqq 100$$
$$\text{found}(p) + \text{found}(\bar{p}) \leqq 100$$

The first statement says that both a statement and its opposite may be credible. They could not both be incredible, for if (p) is incredible, then we must accept $(\bar{p})$. Both a proposition and its negation could be unfounded, but if one is founded, it distracts the likelihood of its opposite being founded. In addition, Tesler et al. postulate that each proposition is associated with an intensity with which it is believed. The intensity of (p) and $(\bar{p})$ will be the same.

Concepts in general are described in the Tesler et al. system as having a level of importance, a longevity of time since they were formed, and a level of inhibition against being considered.

In this Tesler et al. system, beliefs are related to each other as nodes in a directed graph. The arcs between nodes are different types, including that of membership, being a subset, being a consequence, belonging, suggesting that, or having a property. It is not only the existence of concepts and their attributes, but the relationship between concepts that is used to evaluate incoming information.

Mapping Information Structures

In general, while early work tended to emphasize modeling the information processing mechanisms of thought, recently there has been more emphasis on the challenge of mapping the information structures used by these mechanisms. The number of items stored in such structures is probably equaled by the number of cards in a large library catalog. However, the extent of what Schroder et al. (1967) call "integration" between the different items exceeds any information system man has built. Most large man-made systems, such as the Library of Congress library index system and the world's telephone system, by comparison have relatively simple hierarchical interconnections.

The everyday decisions of any adult may draw on such an oversized, cluttered attic full of past ideas, experiences, beliefs, values, constructs, plans, attitudes, or what have you, all interconnected and available for reference at a variety of conscious and subconscious levels that in many cases the mapping may seem to be more effort than it is worth. Just a simple decision, such as going to see a movie one has been told about, may draw on information from all corners of this attic.

To what extent, then, can we represent in a computer the integrated complex information structures humans use? The procedures suggested by Colby and Abelson seem to have considerable promise if applied to more limited topic spheres within the individual's total information structure. While everything within the total information structure is interconnected, if only indirectly, there are many sections that tend to form subclusters. The loss caused by temporarily ignoring ties with the larger structure may be offset by having a more workable unit for study, much in the way that organs like the liver, heart, and kidney may for some purposes be profitably studied apart from their relation to the rest of the body.

Many miscellaneous spheres within the total information structure are hardly worth mapping. On the other hand, there may be considerable value in mapping the information spheres associated with deciding to use a radically new household product, or "making up one's mind" about an unusual political candidate, or forming a political ideology in college. A number of relevant propositions and a very useful model have been developed by Stefflre (1965) for studying the processes by which people relate to new concepts.

The same principles used to study an individual's information sphere and the processes he uses to assimilate new information in that sphere can be extended to the study of how an entire electorate will perceive new issues. To the extent that the assumption holds true that people of similar home backgrounds, education, etc., tend to think alike, then demographic variables become useful in identifying groups in which known proportions will think about an issue in a certain way. For example, in 1960, Pool et al. (1964) on a contract with the Democratic Party, investigated whether Kennedy's religion, as a campaign issue, would win or cost him votes. The citizenry of the country was divided into 480 model types, based on region of the country, party preference, religion, sex, socioeconomic status, and city size. Within each group, predictions were made from past poll data as to how many people would be influenced by this factor, either to change their vote or to stay home on election day. Without detailed knowledge of the processes by which information about Kennedy as a Democrat-Catholic would be assimilated, the authors had to make a number of educated guesses about the proportions, coming to a particular outcome in each of these groups. An excellent state-by-state prediction was made of the actual voting pattern.

It is likely that future data banks not only will contain information about what proportion of persons in a certain year preferred a certain candidate, but also will contain basic information about what proportions of people have certain kinds of information spheres and what proportions use certain information processes in assimilating new information. In such a case, the reaction of the electorate to a proposal or event could be well anticipated in advance. As discussed elsewhere (Stone, 1970), major changes could result in our political processes.

A number of techniques are available to get at an information sphere held by a person. Several classic investigations of particular spheres, such as Smith et al.'s (1956) investigation of attitude structures toward Russia, or Lane's (1962) study of political ideologies, have relied heavily on depth interviewing. Other techniques include sentence completion, word association, the semantic differential, Kelly's REP test, the TAT test, and content analysis of past communications. As Leary (1957) points out, each tool tends to be appropriate to a particular level of information structuring.

Opinion Molecules

Abelson (1968b) has proposed that many processing mechanisms may be specific to a domain of information. For any domain, a person has a set of propositions or processing "molecules," as Abelson calls them, for handling new information and developing expectations.

An example of a molecule shared in a culture should illustrate how these sphere-specific processes operate. Country and western music exhibits stable expectation molecules about love triads. If A, who is married to B, comes to love C, then A should feel guilty, B should have a broken heart, and C should be suspicious and worry about C's relationship with B, etc. Given the identification of who is doing the singing (A, B, or C) and a statement of the situation in the first lines of the lyrics, country and western music listeners can limit the alternatives of what may occur in the next lines. These predictions are guided by a shared opinion molecule particular to this sphere. Country and western music is a classic case of what Fiske and Maddi (1961) describe as interest maintained through moderate sized, controlled doses of novelty. The molecule provides a context for assimilating the new information.

Processes of Selecting Information

For any average piece of incoming information, people apply only a small part of their relevant information processing powers. Everyday thought is hard to predict because relatively brief and simple processing draws upon highly integrated complex information structures.

Yet man is continually bombarded with so much information that he has to be selective in what information he processes and he has to economize in his processing allocations. Each time he takes a new fixation with his eyes, many bits of information usually present themselves for attention and consideration. In communicating with a person, there are not only the words, but many paralinguistic events to absorb. Neisser (1967) has brought together data indicating that the information gained at each glance remains in relatively complete form for a short time in what he calls "iconic storage." However, the evidence from short-term and long-term memory research indicates that the details of information quickly fade and that what is remembered becomes schematized, with irregularities of the original event replaced by regularities.

Freud (1900) presented the thesis that the process of assimilating information also carries over to dreaming. Conscious attention may focus on processing that is relatively logical and well conceptualized. Subconscious processing and later dreaming may be more focused on metaphorical or allegorical assimilation into a highly integrated information structure. Dreaming may involve some special processing that is incompatible with our normal daytime activity. Zarcone et al. (1968) have indicated that certain forms of schizophrenia are characterized by an inability to confine such processing to the period of sleep.

Representation of Language in Information Processing Models

The models of problem solving experiments generally have the advantage that the role of language can be ignored. Language is used to communicate the rules of the experiment to the subject. But all three information processing models—the experiment, the experimenter, and the subject—usually can be represented without reference to language processes.

In mapping belief systems and in modeling the processing of belief information, language comes to have a much more important role. Most beliefs are stated as propositions in natural language, although some investigators have come to use a simplified language structure in order to avoid unnecessary complications. No matter what simplifications are made, the model builder is still confronted with syntactic, semantic, and pragmatic language problems (Morris, 1946).

Abelson uses a three-term language for stating propositions in a noun–verb–noun format in which either of the nouns in turn can be replaced with another proposition. New information is fed into the model in this format.

Colby, on the other hand, sees little relevant information coming from linguistics so long as it is heavily occupied with transformational grammars and has taken a structuralist approach in working directly on semantic and pragmatic problems. It may be that the requirements for building models may lead to the solution of linguistic problems that would otherwise go largely ignored.

Any single sentence usually provides a number of pieces of information that must be unraveled and compared against the existing belief structure. Osgood et al. (1956) has described a technique, "evaluative assertion analysis," in which one step is to derive all the possible basic propositions from a sentence. Once basic propositions are identified, they become the initial grist for information processing. Computer aided content analysis procedures can be used to relate the terms of the proposition to the categories of the existing information structure which is then used to test the credibility of the statement.

A more complete analysis, however, does not stop with the analysis of basic propositions. It looks at the interconnection between propositions in the incoming information, that is, the development of themes and arguments. It then relates them to existing information molecules. Little has yet been done at this level of complexity.

If a model uses natural language, this usually implies that the model should have available to it a large amount of information common to users of the language. Abelson and Carroll (1965), for example, found in modeling the beliefs of a well known conservative politician that a large proportion of the information put into the model was hardly unique to a person with a conservative point of view, but was information common to speakers of the language. Most of this kind of information, propositions such as "China is an Asian country," "The GOP is an American political party," etc., can be found in an ordinary abridged dictionary.

One of the first needed steps in belief system modeling, then, would be to develop a model of all information contained in an ordinary desk dictionary. This might serve as a basic reference to which the belief structures of a particular personality in regard to a particular topic could be added.

An extensive attempt to represent the information contained in a dictionary has been undertaken by Quillian (1967). This has required a rather thorough analysis of our everyday assumptions about what a dictionary is and how it accomplishes its task. A special tree system, involving a distinction between "type" and "token" nodes, with connections across a series of planes, is used to represent basic dictionary information. The words used in a definition can in turn be looked up. Rather than uncover an irreducible set of primitive terms, "everything is defined" in Quillian's system, "in terms of some ordered configuration of other things in the memory." Applying this procedure to the concepts people carry in their head, Quillian illustrates the magnitude of the task with an example:

Suppose . . . that a subject were asked to state everything he knows about the concept "machine." Each statement he makes in answer is recorded and when he decides he is finished, he is asked to elaborate further on each thing he has said. As he does so, these statements in turn are recorded and upon his "completion" he is asked if he cannot elaborate further on each of these. In this way, the subject can clearly be kept talking for several days, if not months, producing a voluminous body of information. This information will start off with the more "compelling" facts about machines, such as that they are usually man-made, involve moving parts, and so on and will proceed "down" to less and less inclusive facts, such as that typewriters are machines and then eventually get to much more remote information about machines, such as the fact that a typewriter has a stop which prevents its carriage from flying off each time it is returned. We are suggesting that this information can all be usefully viewed as part of the subject's concept of "machine."

Quillian's model is at present only able to perform rudimentary comparisons between the definition structures for different concepts and to make quasi-English sentences about the similarities it finds. Like the Tesler and Colby model, it is an initial step in a direction in which much work remains to be done.

Meanwhile, basic problems of getting the computer to identify the different senses of common words are just being solved (cf. Stone et al., 1969). While some might take the view that models employing representations of natural language are just as far in the future as highly competent mechanical translations from one language to another, this writer proposes that inroads to using natural language in belief system models can be made in a series of steps, and can grow along with computer language handling abilities.

Both the representation of very large integrated information structures and the handling of natural language in computer models have hinged on the availability of large random-access computer memories. If the computer is to get to a piece of information it must be able to do so in a reasonable amount of time. While a large amount of data can be stored on magnetic tape, it takes the computer a long time to spin down the tape and retrieve the information it wants. The recent availability, at low cost, of large random-access storage devices, including disks and data cells with their capabilities of retrieving any piece of information in less than a second, now for once provides a means for beginning to handle this problem.[13]

SUMMARY

In describing the application of computer information processing models, we have attempted to show how the relatively simple models of logical problem solving demonstrate the potentials for eventual modeling of complex belief systems. The more limited problem solving models have the advantages of (1) being easier to program, (2) usually having well-defined data gathered under a variety of experimental conditions, (3) exhibiting the impact of fewer personality variables at a time, (4) avoiding most of the problems inherent in handling language, (5) allowing for "strong inference," that is, the formulation of clearly defined alternatives and testing between them. They also offer a number of significant questions and challenges to understanding human information processing.

The modeling of belief systems, on the other hand, as yet offers none of these advantages. One cannot help reading even such a thoughtful review as Loehlin's (1968) treatment of Abelson's, Colby's, Gullihorn's, and his own ALDOUS personality models without being bothered by the continuing lack of supportive data and the haunting question of whether any attempt to work on belief system models is not mostly still just idle speculation. Yet the understanding of man's everyday "hot cognition" processes and his highly integrated belief structures is too important, especially in a modern democratic society, just to shelve as being too complex a problem for this century. More scholars are needed to respond to the challenge, both in constructing models and in the systematic gathering of data.

[13] Recent developments have greatly reduced the costs of such random-access storage. In the Allen–Babcock system, for example, a very large amount of information can be stored and the cost for data cell storage (with one data cell containing over 400,000,000 characters) is under $5 per month per 100,000 characters.

4

Intrinsic Motivation: Information and Circumstance*

J. McV. HUNT

In the theory of motivation which has been dominant in both academic psychology and psychoanalysis for the past half-century, organisms are driven. *Motivation* and *drive* are both modern terms; as introduction, let us sketch their short histories.

The term *motivation* has its roots in the Latin word *movere*, meaning "to move" or "to move an animal or person to a course of action." Until Descartes (1649) attempted to explain the behavior of animals in terms of mechanistic principles, it was generally assumed that men are moved by their souls, and the problems of human motivation were discussed under such rubrics as conation, decision, desire, and volition. These problems, moreover, were typically discussed in discourses on aesthetics, ethics, and politics, rather than in discourses on psychology. Descartes accepted the tradition of man's soul, but some of his contemporaries and successors extended the application of mechanistic principles to the actions of human beings as well as lower animals. In England, Thomas Hobbes (1588–1679), David Hartley (1704–1757), and Joseph Priestley (1733–1804) carried on the mechanistic tradition. In France, Julien de

* This chapter is a revision of the review of evidence and of the argument presented earlier (J. McV. Hunt, 1963b, 1965a).

la Mettrie (1709–1751) explicitly applied mechanical principles to the behavior of man in *L'Homme Machine* (1784), and in the following century Claude Bernard (1859) discovered the internal environment and the phenomena of physiological regulation, which Walter B. Cannon (1915) then described in *Bodily Changes in Pain, Hunger, Fear, and Rage*. In Germany, in the nineteenth century, Ernst Brücke, Hermann von Helmholtz, Jacques Loeb, and Karl Ludwig built upon the mechanistic tradition, and Loeb (1890, 1899) began teaching his tropistic, comparative psychology in America in 1901. It was partially in the tradition of such thinkers and partially in the romantic revolt against the tradition of conscious control that Freud formulated his theories in which *Trieb* and the unconscious were central.

Woodworth introduced the term *drive* into the lexicon of American psychology by his distinction between the "machine" and the drive or power that makes the machine go. Gradually, from the writings of Freud (e.g., 1905, 1915), from the investigations of hunger (Cannon & Washburn, 1912) and thirst (Cannon, 1918), and from the theorizing of such psychologists as Carr (1925), Dashiell (1925), Freeman (1934), Guthrie (1938), Holt (1931), Hull (1943), Melton (1941), Miller and Dollard (1941), Mowrer (1950), Thorndike (1913), and Warden (1931), emerged the dominant view of motivation that all animals, including human beings, are driven to action by painful stimulation, homeostatic needs—which produce drive when unmet—and/or sex, or by originally neutral stimuli associated with these so-called primary drives.

The terms *motivation* and *drive* were combined with somewhat unfortunate consequences. Apparently it was Freud who popularized the proposition that "all behavior is motivated." But when this relatively meaningless phrase is modified, as it came to be, by the addition of "by painful stimuli, homeostatic needs, and sex [the primary drives], or by the acquired drives based upon these," it appears to be wrong. The burden of this chapter is to show why, to introduce the conception of intrinsic motivation—a system of motivation inherent in information processing and action—and to summarize the evidence for the existence of such a system.

MOTIVATION QUESTIONS AND THEIR TRADITIONAL ANSWERS

Although motivation has recently been conceived chiefly in terms of drives, motivation theory has been far from simple. It contains a number of questions with their theoretical answers. A first question asks what instigates organisms to action and what stops their action. In the traditionally dominant theory, the instigators are the drives based on painful stimuli, such homeostatic needs as hunger and thirst, and sex. Beyond these primary drives are the acquired drives, originally innocuous stimuli which have been associated with the three kinds of primary drives and become conditional stimuli for the same emotional responses, thereby becoming able to instigate action. Whenever either primary or acquired drives cease to operate, the theory holds, organisms stop their action and become quiescent.

A second motivational question asks what energizes activity and controls vigor. The traditionally dominant answer has been found in the intensity of the painful stimulation, in the degree of homeostatic need or of sex drive, and in the intensity of the acquired drives, those emotional responses originally part of the total response to the primary drive stimuli. Although this statement of the relationship between vigor of action and strength of drive has been widely accepted, the acceptance actually came before relevant empirical data were available; the relationship proved so imperfect that Hull (1943, see chap. 14) considered the vigor and the likelihood of response to be a multiplicative function of the strengths of drive and of habit.

A third issue concerns the direction of behavior and its hedonic value. According to the traditionally dominant view, organisms withdraw from and avoid situations which will increase the level of their drive or excitement and, contrariwise, approach and seek situations which will reduce the level of their drive. In organisms without speech, withdrawal and avoidance have typically been conceived to be the equivalents of negative hedonic value, and approach and search to be the equivalents of positive hedonic value. From this standpoint, all motivation is considered to be aversive in character.

A fourth issue concerns the factors accounting for emotional attachment, or cathexis, or love. According to the traditionally dominant view, organisms are presumed to develop emotional attachments for those objects, places, and persons associated with drive reduction or leading to anticipation of drive reduction. Thus, the human infant is presumed to become attached to his mother because she serves to reduce the anxieties aroused by the infant's hunger and other discomforts (Freud, 1926). Similarly, the "secondary reinforcements" of behavior theory are innocuous stimuli which, having been associated with drive reduction, are presumed to signal relief from either primary drives or anxiety (see, e.g., Mowrer, 1960).

A fifth issue concerns the factors controlling choice of response. Choice of response has traditionally been seen as a matter of the kind of drive stimulus operating and of the nature of the organism's past experience with it. Each drive stimulus has been presumed to give rise to a hierarchy of responses, and that response which has served effectively to reduce drive in such situations in the past has been presumed to occur as the dominant response at any given time (Hull, 1943; Miller & Dollard, 1941).

A sixth question asks what controls the choice of goals. Since Freud (1915) termed drive reduction to be the "aim of behavior," and since Hull (1943) and others have seen goal responses to be drive reducers, the goal-choice question became equivalent in the short run to the first, instigation question and was given the same answer. In the long run, however, the goal-choice question concerns those relatively distant objectives especially characteristic of human action. Inasmuch as most of the evidence upon which the dominant theory of motivation is based has come either from the observations of human beings in psychotherapy or from experiments on such laboratory animals as rats, the answers to the long-run goal-choice questions have been either indirect or extrapolative. Extrapolative answers have come largely in terms of the notion of acquired drives (see, e.g., Dollard & Miller, 1950; N. E. Miller, 1951), but such extrapolations of acquired drives pose quandaries, as J. S. Brown (1953) has pointed out.

A seventh issue concerns the factors which institute behavioral change or learning. Learning is as large a topic in psychology as motivation. When learning is the focus of attention, motivation is typically but a chapter. On the other hand, when motivation is the focus of attention, learning is but a chapter. In the traditionally dominant motivation theory of the recent past, learning has been seen to result from frustration (Hull, 1943; Melton, 1941; Miller & Dollard, 1941). Once any given mode of response ceases to reduce the drive, that response is thought weakened relative to others in the hierarchy, and these others are then tried out until one serves to reduce the drive.

An eighth question asks what accounts for the persistence of a given response or a given goal-seeking behavior in the face of frustration. The dominant answer has been given in terms of the number of times the action has previously succeeded in reducing the drive (Hull, 1943, pp. 102–12). But the fact that those responses of laboratory animals which have infrequently brought success persist longer than those responses which have regularly brought successful drive reduction belies this nicely succinct answer (see Humphreys, 1939a; and the review by Jenkins & Stanley, 1950). Pathological persistence in the form of the "repetition compulsion," moreover, suggested to Freud (1920), late in his career, a basis for motivation "beyond the pleasure principle." It was partially to account for the repetition compulsion that he posited his concept of the "death instinct" and the aggressive drive.

PAIN AVOIDANCE AND THE INCENTIVE SYSTEMS

The succinct answers to the motivation questions provided by the traditionally dominant theory have given it a high degree of elegance. Moreover, an extensive body of experimental evidence has lent these accounts a bulwark of empirical support. The theory *is* essentially true for that innately outlined system of motivation that one may call "pain avoidance." On the other hand, it is untrue in various essentials for such innately outlined systems of motivation as the homeostatic needs, sex, and, one should add, sleep. Moreover, it gives no account of activities which occur in the absence of these motive systems, activities which constitute one line of evidence for a motive system inherent in the organism's informational interaction with its circumstances.

Believers in exciting and pleasurable incentives have not been wanting even during the period in which the conceptual scheme outlined above has been dominant (see Bühler, 1918, 1928; Crespi, 1942; McClelland et al., 1953; McDougall, 1923; Spence, 1956; Thorndike, 1913; Tolman, 1925; and Young, 1936, 1961). As mentioned above, however, the dominant theoretical position has been that pleasure in merely a matter of drive reduction (Hull, 1943; Dollard & Miller, 1950; N. E. Miller, 1951; Miller & Dollard, 1941) or of the anticipation of drive reduction (Mowrer, 1960). Freud (1905) wrote of the pleasures deriving from the stimulation of the erogenous zones in his *Three Contributions to the Theory of Sex,* but as a more formal theorist (1915) he explicitly made pleasure a matter of reducing excitation from the physiological stimuli. From the investigations using implanted electrodes, it appears that systems of motivation innately outlined within the subcortical neuroanatomy exist both for pain avoidance (Delgado, 1955; Delgado et al., 1956) and for pleasure giving (Olds, 1955, 1960; Olds & Milner, 1954). In the case of the latter, on the contrary, organisms approach those objects or situations which either prolong and increase electrode stimulation of the relevant structures or increase arousal. These are the defining operations which distinguish the pain-avoidance systems from the pleasure-giving systems. Pain reduction may indeed be relatively pleasurable while the painful stimulation is active. Those cues signaling reduction of pain, moreover, may be reinforcing for behaviors as long as the organism is exposed to painful stimulation. Those same cues, however, may also fail to acquire secondary reinforcing value that will hold when the organism is no longer exposed to painful conditions (see Beck, 1961).

The pleasure-giving systems of motivation innately outlined in the subcortical neuroanatomy appear to be of more than one kind. The central nervous system of vertebrates appears to be built "from the inside out" (Pribram, 1960): the internal core of the brain stem consists of the structures in the "old brain," structures present in reptiles and amphibia before the "new" cortical structures made their evolutionary appearance. These "old" structures mediate the regulation of visceral activities, the investigation of which began with the work of Claude Bernard (1859) and was continued in the work of Karplus (1910, 1912) and of Karplus and Kreidl (1909). It was such work which led Cannon (1915) to formulate the conception of homeostasis and of such homeostatic needs as hunger, thirst, the maintenance of body temperature, and respiratory regulation. Electrical stimulation of these structures with implanted electrodes not only instigates (or inhibits) eating and drinking, but it also has reinforcement value: an organism will persist in activities which lead to such stimulation of these structures. Thus, although such stimulation is exciting, it has incentive value. This incentive value probably corresponds to that excitement associated with the consummatory activities gratifying such needs as hunger and thirst. Just such an incentive motivational factor has been assumed by Spence (1947) and later incorporated by Hull (1951) in his theory of behavior.

The contention here is that these homeostatic need systems constitute a separate category of motivating systems quite distinct from the pain-avoidance system, from the sex system, and from that system of motivation inherent in the organism's informational interaction with circumstances. Although this is not the place to elaborate the evidence, it is worth noting that the studies of conflict by N. E. Miller (1944) pitted the anticipatory satisfaction of hunger against the anticipation of painful stimulation. From the fact that investigations using implanted electrodes have uncovered negative reinforcement values for stimulation of certain structures and positive reinforcement values for stimulation of other structures related to the homeostatic needs, and from the fact that evidences of behavioral conflict appear when anticipations of pain are pitted against exciting anticipations of gratification for homeostatic needs, it seems unlikely that Freud (1915) correctly considered all motivation aversive or that Hull (1951, 1952) correctly considered the excitement from drive stimuli (D) and excitement from anticipation of gratification (K) equivalent in their multiplicative interaction with habit strength. It seems rather that there are separate systems in which cues that have led to painful stimulation acquire drive value and are avoided, while cues that have led to gratification of homeostatic needs acquire incentive value and are approached and sought.

Sex appears to comprise another motivating system, one quite distinct from pain avoidance and from homeostatic need. Like the homeostatic need systems, and despite Freud's (1915) later account to the contrary, sex is positive in that the organism approaches the sources of input that are exciting. As shown by N. E. Miller (1958) in rats, and by Dua and MacLean (1964) in male monkeys, stimulation of certain structures in the limbic system of the subcortical forebrain has strong reinforcement value. Moreover, in the work on male monkeys by Dua and MacLean, stimulation of these structures through implanted electrodes resulted in erection of the penis and even in ejaculation. As has often been noted, an individual organism can survive without sexual stimulation or gratification, but not without hunger and thirst gratification or temperature regulation.

Recent investigations, then, clearly indicate that pain avoidance, the homeostatic needs, and sex are highly important motivational systems, that they are quite distinct, although they influence one another, and that whereas organisms withdraw from and avoid objects associated with and leading to painful stimulation, they approach and seek objects leading either to the consummatory acts of eating and drinking in the case of hunger and thirst, or to the consummatory act of copulation in the case of sex.

Although the three systems of motivation above differ in various respects, they are alike in that while operant they keep organisms active. Sleep, which also has a stucture stimulable with implanted electrodes (see Lindsley, 1957), appears, on the contrary, to deactivate organisms and to cut them off from receptor inputs.

While the information on all these systems is extensive and tremendously important, the main task of this chapter is to show that these systems are not the whole story.

EVIDENCE OF ACTIVITY IN THE ABSENCE OF DRIVE OR NEED

Implicit in the commonly made assertion that "all behavior is motivated" is the additional notion that organisms become quiescent in the absence of painful stimulation, homeostatic need, and sex, or of the acquired drives based upon them (Freud, 1915; Hull, 1943). Not so. Since World War II, a number of studies have found that young animals do indeed play, manipulate things, explore new regions, and seek new sources of perceptual input in the absence of these primary drives and acquired drives (see J. McV. Hunt, 1963a, 1965a). In 1945, Beach surveyed the studies of play in young animals and came to the further conclusion that the playful activity is most likely to occur in the absence of the motives traditionally considered essential. Even more recently, Harlow et al. (1950) reported that monkeys would learn to disassemble a three-device puzzle "with no other 'drive' and no other 'reward' than the privilege of unassembling it." Two well-fed and well-watered monkeys worked repeatedly for Harlow (1950) at disassembling a six-device puzzle, once working at this for ten consecutive hours despite their freedom from painful stimulation, hunger, and thirst, and still showing "enthusiasm for their work" at the tenth hour of testing.

In an extensive program of investigation beginning in 1950, Berlyne (1960) discovered that rats will explore new areas if only given an opportunity and that the more varied the objects in the region to be explored, the more persistent the rats' explorations. Berlyne also found that variations in innocuous receptor inputs will instigate and sustain looking or listening and that novelty, incongruity, and complexity will reinforce behavior in human beings (Berlyne, 1957a, 1957b, 1957c, 1958a, 1958b).

In another extended series of investigations, Montgomery (1952) demonstrated—by having his animals start alternately at the opposite ends of a double-T maze or +maze—that the spontaneous tendency of rats to go alternately to the goal boxes at the opposite ends of the T is no matter of fatigue of a given turning response, as Hull (1943) had contended. Rather it is a matter of avoiding the place that the animals have most recently encountered—a matter, in other words, of choice favoring the less familiar of two alternatives (Montgomery, 1953). Montgomery and Segall (1955) noted that rats will learn merely to get an opportunity to explore an unfamiliar area.

Similarly, Butler (1953) reported that monkeys will learn discriminations merely to obtain the privilege of peeking through a window in the opaque walls of their cages or (Butler, 1958) of listening to tape-recorded sounds. Finally, at McGill University a series of studies indicated that human beings will scarcely tolerate homogeneity of input for more than three days (Bexton et al., 1954; Heron et al., 1956): undergraduates were well fed, free of pain and strong stimulation of any kind, and even without the ubiquitous allusions to sex, but although paid twenty dollars a day, they would seldom remain quiescent more than three days in a room where the stimulus variation was so carefully minimized.

Evidence of this kind was not entirely absent before World War II. Appleton (1910), Bühler (1928), and Groos (1896) had noted that play was common in the absence of hunger, thirst, and fear or pain. Nissen (1930) had repeatedly objected to traditional drive theory on the basis of his finding that rats would leave their familiar nests and cross an electrified grid to get to a Dashiell maze filled with fresh and novel objects. The long neglect of such evidence was probably motivated by what Festinger (1957) has termed "cognitive dissonance": such contentions and such evidence were simply too dissonant with the traditionally dominant drive theory to be credible. Since World War II, however, dissonant evidence has accumulated in such quantities as to demand recognition.

Modes of Theoretical Recognition

This accumulation of evidence dissonant with the traditionally dominant theory has resulted in several modes of theoretical recognition. One is "drive naming." Beach (1945) wrote of an instinct—the equivalent of a drive—to play, but later (1955) he questioned the usefulness of instincts as explanation. Nissen (1930), Mote and Finger (1942), Montgomery (1954), and others have written of an "exploratory drive." Harlow et al. (1950), Harlow and McClearn (1954), and others have written of a "manipulative drive." Butler (1953) has called for a drive for "visual exploration." Recently, Berlyne (1950, 1960), and earlier, Dashiell (1925), Romanes (1883), and Thorndike (1913) have written of a "curiosity drive" and used it to explain both exploratory and manipulative behavior. Erikson (1950) has postulated an "urge for contact," and both he and Mittelmann (1954) have proposed an "urge for locomotion." Finally, Nissen (1930, 1954) and Glanzer (1953a, 1953b) have mentioned a "need for stimulation," Nissen (1954) claiming that the brain needs stimulation just as the stomach needs food.

Although drive names may be useful as rubrics indicating topical areas, drive naming is a theoretical blind alley. It appears to revisit the instinct naming of McDougall (1908), and just as this went down under the criticism of Bernard (1924), Dunlap (1919), Watson (1924), and Woodworth (1928) for being but pseudo-explanation, so should drive naming be dropped today for the same reasons. When the drive names become accepted as explanations, they are logical shuttles tending to delay the thought and investigation which, ultimately, should lead to genuine explanation and understanding. Actually, of course, not all of those who have named drives have been satisfied with just that: Beach (1955), Berlyne (1960), Harlow (1950), and Montgomery (1953) have all been concerned with the nature of the mechanisms underlying these activities. Moreover, Harlow (1950) was among the first to use the term "intrinsic motivation," the term used here for that system of motivation conceived to inhere within organisms' informational interaction with their circumstances.

A second mode of theoretical acknowledgment of activities in the absence of painful stimulation, homeostatic need, and sex is "telic-significance naming." The joy which children appear to take in new-found accomplishments has led Hendrick (1943), for instance, to postulate an "urge to mastery." In his splendid discussions of this evidence, White (1959, 1960) has attributed such activities to "competence motivation." Although such terms of telic significance may also be helpful as classificatory and mnemonic devices, they provide no handles for developing hypotheses about antecedent–consequent relationships. Moreover, if accepted as explanations, they too tend to delay the thought and investigation that lead to understanding.

A third mode of theoretical recognition of this evidence is the postulation of "spontaneous activity." It has been said that "to be alive is to be active," and Hebb (1949) has argued that since the electroencephalogram appears to indicate that brain cells are always active, the instigation question requires no answer. J. McV. Hunt (1960), G. A. Miller et al. (1960), and Taylor (1960) have all postulated "spontaneous activity" in their theoretical writings. It was L. I. O'Kelly (personal communication) who pointed out that this notion of "spontaneous activity" is just as defective in explanatory power as the notions of instinct and drive, and for precisely the same reasons.

These modes of theoretical recognition fail, then, to explain the evidence. Further, since organisms do not become quiescent in the absence of painful stimulation, homeostatic need, and sex, or in the absence of the acquired drives based upon these, a mechanism of motivation must inhere within the informational interaction of organisms with their environments. There must be systems of motivation inherent in information reception through the ears and eyes, information processing, and action. These systems of motivation, one in information processing per se, and another in action, may be termed "intrinsic motivation."

INTRINSIC MOTIVATION AND THE INSTIGATION QUESTION

Intrinsic motivation, if so defined, must be considered essentially a cognitive theory of motivation such as Tolman (1938, 1945) proposed. Although such cognitive theories contained much that was attractive, they stumbled badly on the instigation question. Drive theory answered this question easily: a given pattern of activity starts with the onset of the drive stimulus and stops with the cessation of this stimulus. Recently, however, the change in the theoretical notion of the functional unit of the nervous system from the reflex arc to the feedback loop has smoothed the path for a theory of intrinsic motivation to answer the instigation question.

From Reflex Arcs to Feedback Loops

The conception of the reflex arc has its historical bases in Descartes' (1649) conviction that the bodies of animals are machines energized by forces of the external world and in the notion of involuntary movements as stimuli-forced (Willis, 1672). The conception has its neuroanatomical foundations in the discoveries that spinal nerves have separate ventral and dorsal roots (Bell, 1811) and that dorsal roots have sensory functions while ventral roots have motor functions (Magendie, 1822). Marshall Hall (1843) formulated the principle of the reflex, identifying it with the neuroanatomical conception of the reflex arc; and Sechenov (1863) then extrapolated this conception to brain function, thereby preparing the way for Pavlov's (1928) conditioned reflexes. Even so, the concept of the reflex arc was largely established by Sherrington's work beginning before 1890 and culminating in 1906 with *The Integrative Action of the Nervous System*. Although Sherrington recognized that the reflex arc was a logical construct, his writing combined with the simplicity of the notion to establish it so well that, in spite of Dewey's (1896) stringent criticism, the reflex is considered even today to exist as an organic entity, and it is generally forgotten that Sherrington worked chiefly with spinal preparations in which the brain did not participate. While the concept of reflexive action clearly answers the instigation question, its inability to handle the matter of set or attention has always been a serious defect. As William James (1890) noted, the relatively loud, persistent ticking of a clock may completely escape notice until it stops. Conversely, the faint sound of a child's distant cry may bring a mother up sharply, despite louder noises, so long as that cry is not completely masked. Such obvious facts have always implied that the instigation of activities cannot be merely a matter of the onset of stimulation.

Recently, neurophysiologists have been demonstrating that the Bell–Magendie Law, that dorsal roots have spinal nerves and ventral roots have motor nerves, was overgeneralized. They have shown that efferent impulses from the brain feed back through fiber tracts previously thought to be completely sensory and that these impulses serve to regulate the rate of firing in the sensory nerves at points close to the peripheral receptors. The evidence of central regulation of afferent inputs has been reviewed by Granit (1955) and by Lindsley (1956). Its importance for the instigation question is perhaps best dramatized in a study recording the cochlear responses to tones through electrodes implanted within the cochlear nuclei of cats (Hernandez-Peon et al., 1956), a study in which the electrical evidence of cochlear responses to a tone was markedly reduced whenever the cats were exposed to such other stimuli as the sight of mice in a bell jar or to the odor of fish. Although the interpretation of this investigation has been questioned, there is other functional evidence that the anatomical equipment for such feedback loops exists for other systems. In the case of vision, for instance, Walker and Weaver (1940) have found that eye movements can be elicited by stimulating portions of the visual receptor center in the occipital lobes of monkeys.

Correspondingly, in the control of the force of muscular action, sensory fibers pass through what have traditionally been considered to be motor tracts and nerves to influence the rate of firing in central motor centers. For instance, fibers from the thalamus that connect with other fibers originating in the receptors of muscle and skin also connect upward to the precentral gyrus of the motor cortex (Pribram, 1958, 1960). Apparently these connections permit feedback from the stretch receptors in contracting muscles to influence the rate of firing of the pyramidal cells in the motor centers, and thereby to modulate the force of muscle contraction. Such evidence of direct feedback control—through what have traditionally been considered either solely sensory or solely motor nerves—indicates the inadequacy of the notion of the reflex arc as the basic functional unit of the nervous system.

The TOTE Unit and Incongruity as Instigator

G. A. Miller et al. (1960) have generalized the concept of the feedback loop as the "test-operate-test-exit (TOTE) unit" and suggested this unit as successor to the reflex as the functional unit of the nervous system (see Fig. 4–1). To illustrate, one of the most familiar feedback

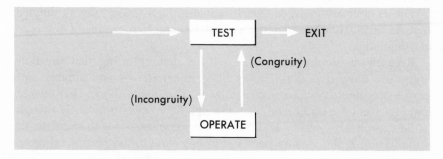

Fig. 4–1. Representation of the TOTE unit, a successor to the concept of the reflex (after Miller, Galanter, & Pribram, 1950, p. 26).

mechanisms is the home thermostat. In this device, the standard, which serves as the *test*, is the setting on the thermometer. When the temperature falls below the standard for which the thermometer is set, the electrical circuit which operates the furnace is closed. The furnace then *operates* until the temperature rises to the standard—the thermostat setting. When this occurs, that is, when the *test* is met, the mechanism breaks the circuit, and the system makes its *exit*.

Similarly, when conditions in a living being match its prevailing motivational standard, the organism is freed for other activities. In this TOTE sequence, the testing device may be said to instigate the operation when there is an *incongruity* between prevailing conditions (comparable to room temperature in the illustration) and some organismic standard (comparable to the temperature setting of the thermostat). The operation continues until, as so tested, there is *congruity* between the condition and the standard. As thus conceived, incongruity becomes the basis for starting the organism on some given operation or activity, and return to congruity becomes the basis for stopping the organism's operation. As generic constructs, then, *incongruity* and *congruity* provide an answer to the instigation question.

Elaboration of the TOTE Unit with Various Kinds of Standards

Again, when this motivational principle of the TOTE unit is generalized broadly, *incongruity* becomes a kind of generic instigator. Miller et al. (1960) suggest that the arrows in their TOTE-unit diagram may represent three levels of abstraction: energy in the form of nervous impulses, information, and control. At the level of energy, the arrows represent nervous impulses, and the standard is a threshold. At the level of information, the arrows represent information flowing from one place to another, and the test is based on some informational standard. At the level of control, the arrows represent such a list of instructions as might comprise the program for an electronic computer, and the standard may be a goal, a plan, or even an ideal.

Various kinds of standards may be conceived. One might be the "comfort" standard, based on a threshold for pain. Perhaps the notion of the TOTE unit would never have been invented to account for pain avoidance, but the concept of a "comfort" standard serves to bring the facts of pain avoidance into a consonant relationship with the TOTE unit. As Schneirla (1959, 1964) has pointed out, receptor inputs of excessively low intensities may be unattractive if not painful, and intensities too high for the comfort standard become not only unattractive but disagreeable and painful. In either case, incongruities with the comfort standard may be seen to occasion action, and congruities to occasion stopping action.

A second kind of standard may be found in what Pribram (1960) has termed the "biased homeostats of the hypothalamus." Such a homeostatic standard is the concentration of blood sugar, which, when falling below a certain standard level, activates the on-going receptors along the third ventricle to release glycogen from the liver and to prime the distance receptors for attention and excited approach to signs of food.

Under conditions of such incongruity, the organism is said to be hungry. Another such homeostatic standard is the concentration of sodium ions in the blood stream and spinal fluid, which, when rising above a standard level, activates processes involved in the regulation of water balance and primes the organism to perceive and avidly to follow signs of water. Under conditions of incongruity with this sodium ion standard, we say that the organism is thirsty.

Although humoral factors figure in sexual motivation, it is not easy to make the various facts of sex nicely consonant with the conception of a humoral standard. The facts of sex behavior appear to fit better the ethologists' conception of a "specific-action-potential" (see Lorenz, 1937; or Thorpe, 1951). In the case of sex there seems to be a buildup of a special kind of sexual readiness to which both internal conditions and exciting perceptual inputs contribute. This increased tension lowers the threshold for the stimuli effective in releasing the action pattern, and even the "overflow activity" (*Leerlaufreaktion*) is exemplified in sexual dreams with or without orgasm. Orgasm does, at least temporarily, stop the action, but then the buildup through internal humoral factors and external receptor inputs begins again (Beach, 1956).

Within the domain of the organism's informational interaction with circumstances several kinds of standards appear. Perhaps the most primitive consists in the central processes controlled by on-going receptor inputs. Whenever there is a change from this standard, the organism exhibits what the Russians have termed the "orienting reflex," consisting of attention to the source of the changed input and of arousal (Berlyne, 1960; J. McV. Hunt, 1963a; Razran, 1961; Sokolov, 1963). It is just this kind of phenomenon to which William James called attention in noting that one hears the loud ticking of a grandfather's clock only when it stops.

A second, also relatively primitive, kind of informational standard is the hypothetical template, or central representative process, which has derived from repeated encounters with the patterns of input change associated with specific objects, persons, and places. It is apparently such a standard which permits the recognition of objects and supplies the basis for the expectations with which later inputs can be incongruous.

Central in psychological development appears to be an epigenesis of standards within the human infant's informational interaction with circumstances (see Chapter 5). In the course of this development, action becomes differentiated from information processing. This differentiation appears to begin when infants recognize a number of different objects. Emerging recognition appears to supply a basis for attractiveness, and a series of recognitions appears to lead to a kind of "learning set" that "things should be recognizable." With this learning set emerges the goal of recognition that Woodworth (1947) considered to reinforce perception (Hunt, 1963a, 1965a). Somewhat further on in the course of psychological development, intentional actions emerge, actions in which any of the infant's schemata may become a goal or be used as a means to a goal. In this domain of action, the standard is a goal, and incongruity becomes operationally equivalent to frustration. In the domain of information processing, however, the standards take the form of adaptation levels (Helson, 1964), of expectations of conceptions, and of theories.

Separation of Action from Information Processing

This separation of action from information processing gets support from recent neurophysiological investigations of and theorizing about brain function. When the reflex-analogous view of brain function emerged, the telephone switchboard was the dramatic new instrument providing a mechanical model for the connections between stimulus and response. Association was conceived to take place across the cortex, and the telephone switchboard model, which replaced the model of the "neural groove" (James, 1890), provided both a conception of how various receptor inputs could be connected with various motor outputs and a conception of how one reflex might be connected to another in chain fashion to account for complex activity. This switchboard model was so attractive and teachable that it persisted in spite of the fact that evidence had already rendered it untenable when it was adopted. The model was entirely too simple to fit the neuroanatomical evidence from the work of Ramón y Cajal (1904) and the theory of evolutionary levels of central neural organization formulated by Hughlings-Jackson (1884). Moreover, the theory of chaining persisted as an account of complex action despite Lashley's (1917) point that the speed of the nervous impulse is too slow to permit one movement of a pianist's finger to be the stimulation for the motion of his next finger in a cadenza. Even as late as World War II, nevertheless, Hull (1943) considered it self-evident that the brain "acts as a kind of automatic switchboard" (pp. 18, 384). Perhaps it is only with the advent of the electronic computer—that dramatic mechanical model of the mid-twentieth century—that the notion of the switchboard can be displaced by the notion of active information processes. This replacement illustrates Conant's (1951) principle that "a theory is only overthrown by a better theory, never merely by contradictory facts" (p. 48).

At any rate, when electronic computers were developed, Wiener (1948) and others were immediately struck by the analogy between computer processes and human thought. Programming these computers to

solve logical problems, moreover, has led to generalized consideration of
the processes that must go on within the brain to permit animals and
human beings to do what they obviously can do. Newell et al. (1958)
have suggested that the process involved must have the following components:

1. A control system consisting of a number of memories, which contain
   symbolized information, and which are interconnected by various ordering relations . . .
2. A number of primitive information processes which operate on the information in the memories. (Each primitive process is a perfectly
   definite operation for which no physical mechanisms exist.) . . .
3. A perfectly definite set of these processes [organized] into whole *programs* of processing.

That such components are required for solving logical problems suggested to certain neuropsychologists the task of looking for counterparts
within mammalian brains. Analogs of these computer components may
reside, as Pribram (1958, 1960) has suggested, within what Rose and
Woolsey (1949) have termed the "intrinsic portions of the cerebrum."
Rose and Woolsey have separated the cerebrum into an extrinsic portion
and two intrinsic portions (see Fig. 4-2). The one portion is extrinsic
because it connects directly to receptors and to affectors. It is composed
of the ventral and geniculate nuclei of the thalamus, the sensory regions
of the cortex receiving thalamic relay-fibers from the eyes, the ears, the
various receptors of the skin, etc., and those portions of the cerebral
cortex giving rise to the motor tracts to the muscles and glands (see
Fig. 4-2).

The second, or intrinsic, portion has itself two sectors, a division
which lends support to the hypothetical separation of action from information processing. The frontal intrinsic sector consists of the dorso-
medial nucleus of the thalamus, of the frontal association areas of the
cerebral cortex, and of the limbic system, with its connections to the
centers of homeostatic need around the internal core of the brain and
in the hypothalamus. It appears to be especially involved in action because interrupting the tracts leading to the cortex from the medial
nucleus of the thalamus and the structures near the core of the brain
disrupts executive function (see Fig. 4-2). Such lesions have been
found to disorganize delayed reaction and double alternation in primates
(Jacobsen et al., 1935) and in a human patient (Nichols & Hunt, 1940).
Human patients with such lesions may have normal memory for events
prior to surgery and readily recall a series of digits or instructions immediately after given, but they cannot carry out a sequence of actions
or develop plans. From such evidence, Pribram (1960, pp. 12, 22) has
suggested that here, perhaps, are the hierarchical arrangements of TOTE-

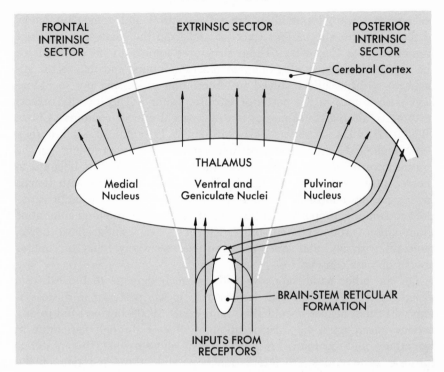

Fig. 4–2. Diagrammatic representation of the division of the cerebrum into an extrinsic sector and two intrinsic sectors based on the presence or absence, respectively, of peripheral connections. The extrinsic sector consists of the geniculate and ventral nuclei of the thalamus. These receive direct afferents from peripheral receptor systems, and of the various sensory regions of the cortex (auditory, somesthetic, visual, etc.), to which they send inputs, and also of such motor centers of the cortex as the precentral gyrus, from which the pyramidal tracts originate and descend to the cells in the ventral gray portions of the spinal cord. The frontal intrinsic sector consists of those portions of the frontal lobes that do not give rise to direct motor fibers, the dorso-medial nucleus of the thalamus, and the hypothalamus. The posterior intrinsic sector includes those portions of the parietal and temporal lobes receiving no direct receptor inputs and their connections with the brain-stem reticular formation (after Pribram, 1958, with modifications).

unit mediating intentions and plans, especially those in which the interconnections among the "biased homeostats of the brain-stem core" participate.

The posterior intrinsic sector is composed of the pulvinar nucleus of the thalamus, those portions of the parietal and temporal lobes which receive no sensory-input fibers from the ventral and geniculate nuclei of the thalamus, and various tracts to and from the brain-stem reticular formation (see Fig. 4–2). These structures appear to be essential for the recognition and intelligibility of receptor inputs, and this sector appears to be especially involved in information processing per se. Monkeys with lesions in the posterior intrinsic sector fail to identify objects or to make alternative responses to differing patterns or contours (Chow, 1951, 1952, 1954; Mishkin, 1954; Mishkin & Pribram, 1954), but they show none of the impairments of function associated with lesions (in the frontal intrinsic sector) of those fiber tracts leading from the thalamus to the receptive centers in the cortex. Furthermore, monkeys with lesions in this posterior intrinsic sector respond indiscriminately to large variations in stimulus properties; in the case of vision, only the total amount of illumination is differentiated, and as Klüver's (1941) studies have shown, monkeys with occipital lobes removed are essentially blind to contour and brightness contrast.

On the other hand, monkeys with no such damage to the extrinsic visual input system and with lesions only in the posterior intrinsic system will catch a gnat in mid-air (Blum et al., 1950) but will fail in any actions based upon the identification of objects through variations in brightness and contour. Pribram (1960) suggests that this posterior intrinsic system must, therefore, make possible the separation of the invariant properties characterizing objects, places, and persons from those properties varying with point of view, distance, etc. This could be accomplished if some coded representation of the invariants were stored in the posterior intrinsic system. Thus, this posterior system might contain hierarchically arranged stores of coded representations of the invariant properties of receptor inputs from objects, persons, and places viewed from various angles and distances. Such stores would correspond functionally with what Hebb (1949) has called the "cell assemblies" and conceived to derive from early "primary learning." Here these stores can be referred to generically as "the storage" for coded representations of past inputs from the receptors, especially from the eyes and the ears. It is thus that this posterior intrinsic system appears to be especially important for recognitive and intelligibility functions.

The standard of the test component of the TOTE unit must have special properties in the case of information processing. Whereas past experience appears to have a relatively small role in establishing standards for blood sugar and for sodium ion concentration (in hunger and thirst), only a momentary role in the establishment of the standard for on-going receptor inputs, and only a partial role in the establishment of the comfort standard (see Salama & Hunt, 1964), the role of experience looms very large in establishing the standards for information processing. If an investigator either knew or could control an organism's perceptual encounters with a given category of objects, it should be possible to specify quantitatively the characteristics of the standard, and to define the motivating informational incongruities in terms of the discrepancy between those which the organism has previously encountered and those of his present encounter. When only the various dimensions of the energies delivered at the subject's receptors are involved, the standard can be defined in the terms of Helson's (1947, 1964) *adaptation level* as the weighted log-mean of, for instance, the intensities of input having been encountered, and the motivating incongruity can be defined as the discrepancy between a measure of present input and this measure of the standard.

When the motivating incongruity involves information, the problem is more complicated. It may become possible to quantify such motivating incongruities in the terms of information theory (see Attneave, 1954, 1959; Shannon & Weaver, 1949). Yet the very fact that informational standards are in a continuous process of change with experience complicates such measurement. It is further complicated by the fact that experience appears to change even the nature of the units [see Bruner's (1957) work on perceptual readiness and evidence of the effects of experience on perception by Mackworth & Bruner (1965), Munsinger & Kessen (1964), and Munsinger et al. (1964)]. Perhaps these units undergo an epigenetic transformation with the acquisition of each new learning set in psychological development.

Once a learning set that things should be recognizable has been acquired, for instance (see Chapter 5), the incongruity between present inputs and the standard based on the constancies of past perceptual encounters appears to start operations of search for additional information. Such search is illustrated in the adjustment of receptors to achieve clearer recognition (Woodworth, 1947) and in the continued scrutiny of novel objects to which Berlyne (1960) has applied the term "curiosity." The search, which may be conceived to be the operational phase of the TOTE unit, can be said to make its exit from the motivational stage when there has become available in the storage some representation consonant with the inputs of the moment—when the object scrutinized has been recognized and identified. To quote Pribram (1960, p. 22), "the organism is satisfied when it is fully informed." As will be seen when the role of motivation in the direction of behavior is considered, this task-like recognitive function of information is but one aspect of the motivational role of an organism's informational interaction with circumstances.

INTRINSIC MOTIVATION AND THE ENERGIZATION QUESTION

Cognitive theories of behavioral control have made little place for emotion or for energetics. They have been notoriously "cold." Although G. A. Miller et al. (1960) also said little about emotion, they did note that "in any situation where a successful plan suddenly becomes useless, the reluctant desertion of the plan is accompanied by strong emotions" (p. 98). They also noted that "the more or less sudden realization that an enduring plan must be changed at a strategic level is accompanied by a great deal of emotion and excitation" (p. 116). On the topic of energetics, they noted only that "what we call an 'effort of will' seems to be in large measure a kind of emphatic inner speech" (p. 71). Considerable evidence indicates, however, that action and information processing provide important bases for emotion and energization.

Emotional Arousal from Frustration

In the case of action, the standard which provides the test for incongruity or congruity is the goal or plan, generically considered. In the case of pain avoidance, the plans appear to reside within the incongruity between the comfort standard and the intensity of receptor input. In the case of homeostatic needs, the plans appear to derive from discrepancies between existing conditions of the internal environment and the biases of the "homeostats of the brain-stem core." In the case of intrinsic motivation, primordial plans apparently arise when an infant attempts to maintain or regain perceptual contact with a newly recognized object; his "learning set" that "things should be perceptually recognizable" establishes a kind of habitual task to achieve recognitive clarity and identification (see Woodworth, 1947; Mackworth & Bruner, 1965). Interference with activity toward goals or with plans is frustrating, and frustration is commonly recognized as a basis for distress. Dewey (1894) formulated a frustrative theory of emotional distress, as did Freud (1917, p. 335) in his early theory of anxiety as a "souring" of unsatisfied libido. Insofar as frustrative distress energizes the organism, these conceptions are also theories of energetics.

Only recently have such formulations been tested empirically. In a series of studies by Amsel (1958) and his collaborators, hungry rats were trained to run down a straight alley-maze into a goal-box for food and then to leave this first goal-box and run down another alley into a second goal-box with perceptual characteristics quite different from the first (Amsel & Roussel, 1952). When the time the rats took to run from goal-box I to goal-box II had achieved an asymptotic stable minimum, they were frustrated by omission of food in the first goal-box on intermittent trials. Thus frustrated, the rats ran faster through maze II than they did on trials when food was present in goal-box I. They also ran faster on the average than did their unfrustrated controls. Similarly hinting arousal from frustration, in one of the few investigations using physiological indicators of emotional arousal on frustrated subjects, Yoshii and Tsukiyama (1952) found increased frequency and decreased amplitude of rats' EEG waves when their food was unexpectedly absent in the goal-box of their maze.

Unfortunately, it is not at all certain that such arousal derives merely from interference with plans. From the standpoint of drive-reduction theory, the activity interfered with is serving to diminish the primary drive of hunger; either omission of the goal object or interfering with an instrumental activity like running toward the goal-box can thus be interpreted as merely reinstating the original hunger drive. Such an interpretation is quite tenable for the results of both kinds of experiments just cited because both are dependent upon homeostatic need as a source of motivation.

Demonstrations of arousal from the incongruity of frustrating a plan have come from other sources. Such arousal appears to be implied by the tendency of human subjects to resume uncompleted tasks (Zeigarnik, 1927) and to recall uncompleted tasks (Rickers-Ovsiankina, 1928) more frequently than completed tasks. Unfortunately, these studies contain neither direct physiological evidence of emotional arousal nor a clear index of energy in the action.

Emotional Arousal from Information Incongruity

In information processing, the case for emotional arousal from incongruity is clearer. Any arousal that may occur with incongruous inputs can hardly be attributed to the return of drive-stimuli. Especially is this true when, as with the clock which one hears only when it stops ticking (James, 1890), the incongruity consists of a reduction in the intensity of input. The already mentioned work of the Russian investigators on the orienting reflex is relevant. The orienting response consists of such relatively overt changes in the sense organs as dilation of the pupil, photochemical changes in the retina, changes in such skeletal muscles as those directing the sense organs, arrests of on-going actions, and increased muscle tonus. Along with these are such relatively covert evidence of arousal as increased palmar conductance (GSR), vascular changes measured with the plethysmograph, changed heart rate (EKG), and changes in brain waves (EEG) (see Berlyne, 1960; Maltzman &

Raskin, 1965; Razran, 1961; Sokolov, 1963). In the orienting reflex, central processes based on the on-going input constitute the standard, and incongruity consists in a change of one or more of the various characteristics of the input. Important for the argument that such incongruity causes emotional arousal is the fact that all of the covert aspects of the orienting reflex have long been classified as physiological or "expressive" indicators of emotion. The studies of Sokolov (1963), moreover, show that orienting responses to changing auditory characteristics may result in increased sensitivity to visual inputs, thus indicating that orienting responses to one input may facilitate its becoming a conditional stimulus for other responses (see also Maltzman & Raskin, 1965).

The perceptual adaptation apparently involved in the orienting reflex provides a basis for even more dramatic evidence of emotional arousal from incongruity. Perceptual adaptation is one name for the fact that continuing perceptual contact with a given source of input leads gradually to a decrease in arousal and a withdrawal of attention. Repeated perceptual encounters with a given input have a similar effect, for which Thompson and Spencer (1966) have used the term *habituation*. The operations required to investigate such habituation are the same as those employed to establish what Helson (1964) has called the "adaptation level."

Two experiments will demonstrate that arousal results from incongruity between inputs and "expectations," that is, standards based on repeated perceptual encounters. In one of these experiments Sharpless and Jasper (1956) repeatedly presented loud sounds for some three seconds to cats with needle electrodes, connected to an electroencephalogram, implanted in their brains. At first, each presentation evoked a burst of the irregular, high-frequency EEG waves of low magnitude commonly associated with either anxiety or great effort. With successive presentations, the EEG arousal-reactions became shorter, and the changes in frequency and magnitude became less in degree. After some thirty presentations, the cats' arousal-reactions had essentially disappeared. When the presentations were repeated day after day, the arousal-reactions tended to recover each day, but the habituation became more and more rapid. Following habituation, a change in *any characteristic* of the sounds brought back the fast EEG waves of low magnitude: a reduction in loudness was as effective in restoring the arousal-reactions as an increase in loudness, and changed pitch was as effective as changed loudness.

A second, even more dramatic, experiment supplies evidence of arousal from incongruity, evidence which, unlike that derived from frustrating hungry animals, is hardly attributable to any return of a drive stimulus. This is the work of Vinogradova (1958) as reported by Berlyne (1960) and Razran (1961). According to these secondary reports, Vinogradova repeatedly presented a tone, wired in sequence with an electric shock, to human subjects and plethysmographically measured their vascular changes. The presentations constitute a typical sequence for classical conditioning: presumably, large vascular responses occurred chiefly to the electric shock, then began to respond to the tone. But the vascular response to the whole sequence decreased with repeated presentations and was finally extinguished; then, by omitting the shock, which in traditional drive theory would be considered the noxious portion of the stimulus complex, the tone alone brought the return of the vascular arousal response. It is exceedingly difficult to see how such a return of the vascular indication of arousal when the accustomed painful shock was omitted can be anything except evidence of arousal evoked solely by incongruity between the tone alone and a standard based upon the sequential organization of tone followed by shock. In this context, the tendency of organisms to adapt to any particular change of input constitutes one very important basis for the standards determining the incongruity or congruity of the new input. This is the basis for the *adaptation level* of which Helson (1964) has made so much in psychological theory.

It is worth recalling also that two clinically based theories of anxiety are consonant with the notion that emotional arousal has one source in the incongruity between circumstances encountered and standards based on past experience. In Rogers' (1951) theory of anxiety, "psychological tension" or "maladjustment," the source is an "inconsistency" between the self-concept and various concrete perceptions. Rogers' idea of the self-concept corresponds to what is here called a "standard"; it is a standard based upon information about the self already in the storage. Presumably, this information derives both from idiosyncratic perceptual interaction with circumstances, physical and social, and from communicated evaluation "taken over from others, and perceived in distorted fashion as if [it] had been experienced directly" (Rogers, 1951, p. 498). Rogers' operational definition of "inconsistency" is the discrepancy between the self and the ideal self, each described with inventories or adjective check lists. Such operations make this "inconsistency" a special case of what is here termed "incongruity."

The second of these formulations comes from Kelly (1955). The standards here are what Kelly calls "personal constructs," presumably derived from an individual's creative efforts to make sense out of his observations and out of what he is taught in the course of communication with others. Thus, an individual may be led by communications from others to so construe the world that the information coming from his perceptions is highly incongruous with his constructions. Kelly considers such incongruity to be the major basis for emotional distress or anxiety.

This line of conceptualization has still largely unexamined implications for personality dynamics (Hunt, 1965b). Both Sigmund Freud (1926) and Anna Freud (1936) conceived of the mechanisms of defense as serving to protect an individual from anxiety. Sigmund Freud, at least in his later days when he came to see repression as a consequence of anxiety rather than its source, saw anxiety originating out of such painful experiences as castration threats, Oedipal anxiety, and other overwhelmingly intense emotions. The fact that Festinger (1957) and his students have found human subjects utilizing various strategies to avoid information dissonant (incongruous) with their beliefs and commitments suggests that these mechanisms of defense probably function as much to protect individuals from information incongruous with their experience-based, informational or plan standards as from anxiety per se. Perhaps the most important category of stored information in this context is that concerning the self, a very important kind of standard (see Hilgard, 1949).

In any case, this evidence indicates that a cognitive, information processing theory of motivation need not be "cold."

INTRINSIC MOTIVATION AND THE DIRECTION-HEDONIC QUESTION

Intrinsic motivation's answer to the direction-hedonic question is both interesting and problematic. It is interesting because it promises to help explain the motivational phenomena called "spontaneous interest in learning," "growth motivation," "thirst for knowledge," and "self-actualization." It is problematic because, operationally, incongruity is still a very slippery notion. Measurement operations that will yield successive approximations of clarification are hard to devise, particularly since incongruity appears to be a source both of withdrawal or avoidance and of approach or seeking.

Consider first withdrawal and avoidance. In his theory of cognitive dissonance, Festinger (1957) has said "the basic hypotheses I wish to state are as follows: (1) The existence of dissonance, being psychologically uncomfortable, will motivate a person to try to reduce the dissonance and achieve consonance. (2) When dissonance is present, in addition to trying to reduce it, the person will actively avoid the situations and information which would likely increase the dissonance" (p. 3). Here, dissonance belongs within the domain of the generic notion of incongruity. Withdrawal, avoidance, and a negative hedonic evaluation of incongruity have been illustrated in the experiments of Hebb and Riesen (1943) and Hebb (1946). Fearful withdrawal responses occurred in the chimpanzees of the Yerkes Primate Laboratory when Hebb (1946) presented them with a sculpture head of a chimpanzee (the expected remainder of the body was absent) or with an anesthetized infant chimpanzee (the customary posture and motions absent). Since these chimpanzees had been reared under known conditions where it was impossible for such perceptions to have become associated with painful stimulation, the fearful withdrawal could not be attributed to pain. Near panic could also be induced in young chimpanzees merely by having the friendly experimenter appear wearing a Halloween mask or the coat of the also-familiar animal keeper. Such fearful withdrawal cannot be explained by the conditioning theory of fear illustrated by the studies of Watson and Raynor (1920).

Jones and Jones (1928) had already noted that children will withdraw in fear from objects with which they have had no experience. Such fears tend to appear only after a certain age, so the Joneses, and Jersild and Holmes (1935) as well, attributed them to maturation. Hebb and Riesen (1943) noted that infant chimpanzees also come to fear strangers only after they are several months old, and then under conditions in which they cannot possibly have suffered from contacts with strangers. Evidence that this delay in fearful withdrawal from strangers is no mere unfolding of fear responses with maturation, however, came from rearing chimpanzee infants in the dark. Riesen (1947) found the dark-reared chimpanzees to be without such fear at the customary age of its appearance, but they too came to fear strangers after they had repeated visual encounters with experimenters and keepers after being brought into the light. Hebb (1949) argued from this that fearful withdrawal is an unlearned response to the "familiar in an unfamiliar guise." Familiarity is based on the stored residues of past perceptual encounters, and it may be seen to constitute the standard of a TOTE unit with which new encounters are compared.

Many puzzling fear-like disturbances in both children and pets become understandable in these terms. Fears of the dark and of solitude in the human child puzzled Freud (1926), and such fears in the chimpanzee puzzled Köhler (1959). Such disturbances can readily be seen as the consequence of the incongruity resulting from marked changes in the accustomed receptor inputs within any familiar context. Related examples are the pet dog that barks excitedly and whines when his young master walks on his hands; the cat that loves to be petted by his child-mistress and by a familiar neighbor in whose house he was raised, but runs frantically to hide when he sees the neighbor carrying the child on his shoulders; and the young child who becomes disturbed when familiar nursery rhymes are altered in the reading. Moreover, Piaget (1936) noted that his children showed emotional distress at their encountering altered versions of things they had come to recognize. In the domain of esthetics, furthermore, the dissonances of some modern music and the absence of familiar forms in some modern painting and in some statuary often repel if not frighten beholders brought up on more standard fare. Such observations are consonant with Festinger's (1957) formulation of dissonance, or incongruity, as a source of hedonic discomfort and withdrawal.

On the other hand, a variety of observations indicates that sources of incongruous inputs may also elicit approach responses and provide pleasure. These observations come from those same studies cited to show that organisms do not become quiescent in the absence of primary and acquired drives. Recall that Berlyne (1960) found that both rats and human beings will remain longer oriented to and close to novel (incongruous) objects than to objects already highly familiar. Recall that Montgomery found that spontaneous alternation of rats in a T maze is basically a matter of their choosing the relatively more novel goal-box, and that Butler's (1954) monkeys learned to open a door in their opaque cages and to make various discriminations merely for the opportunity to get a look at the changing scene outside. Remember also that once human beings have been faced for some considerable time with homogeneous, unchanging, and therefore almost completely congruous circumstances, they actively seek the relative incongruity of new situations of almost any kind (Bexton et al., 1954; Heron et al., 1956). The strong incentive value of incongruity under such circumstances has been dramatized by the behavior of a young man of "high-brow" musical tastes who, during his third afternoon within the stimulus-deprivation chamber at McGill, repeatedly pressed a key to get some two minutes of "country music" from a scratchy record (Hebb, personal communication).

The Hypothesis of Optimal Incongruity

The fact that sources of incongruous perceptual input are sometimes repelling and displeasing and at other times attractive and pleasing has been puzzling. One way through the puzzle is to conceive that there must be an optimal level of incongruity. This optimal level of incongruity appears to comprise another kind of standard, which, under any given set of circumstances at any given time and at any given stage of development, provides a source of hedonic pleasure and attraction. Either too little or too much incongruity, on the other hand, is hypothetically a source of hedonic irritation and is repelling. Various forms of an optimum hypothesis have been suggested by a number of theorists, with each one seeing the nature of what is optimal in somewhat different fashion.

The optimum hypothesis was implicit in Hebb's (1949) discussions of pleasure and fear. Later, Hebb and Thompson (1954) made the optimum hypothesis explicit. Their optimum was one of "fear and frustration" (p. 51). This formulation has had limited usefulness as a guide to investigation, however, because "fear and frustration" are already products of an organism's interaction with its circumstances.

McClelland et al. (1953) have formulated the more readily tested notion of an optimal discrepancy between the organism's adaptation level (Helson, 1947, 1959, 1964) and the receptor input as the basis for positive affective arousal. Inputs showing too little discrepancy presumably go unnoticed and are hedonically neutral in this formulation; inputs too discrepant with the adaptation level are a source of negative affect. It will be recalled that Helson's adaptation level for any characteristic of any receptor input is generally that level for which the subject has been habituated. Recall also that the adaptation level is a kind of standard, one which has the measured value of the weighted log-mean of the intensities of input previously encountered, where intensity is the characteristic of input concerned. This formulation has led Haber (1958) to postulate a symmetrical butterfly curve to describe the hypothetical relation between affective value and the discrepancy of the level of an input presented with a subject's adaptation level for that particular input characteristic (see Fig. 4–3). Moreover, Haber (1958) has shown that this hypothetical relationship holds for paired comparisons of the hedonic values of water temperatures that deviate from 1 to 15 degrees from the adaptation level for temperature which comes

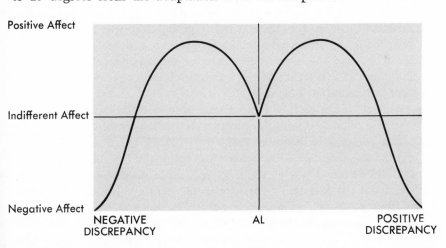

Fig. 4–3. Affective value as a theoretical function of discrepancy of level of stimulation from the adaptation level (AL) (after Haber, 1958).

with continued immersion of a part of the body in water of a given temperature till it yields "no temperature sensation." In this interesting pioneering experiment, the hypothetical symmetrical relationship was shown to hold, however, only for adaptation levels not very different from normal skin temperature; no attempt was made to test both wings of the curve for adaptation levels well above or below normal skin temperature.

Perhaps the largest body of experimental evidence relevant to the McClelland et al. (1953) version of the optimum hypothesis is to be found in the investigations of the reinforcing effects of light upon barpressing. In his review of these studies, Lockard (1963) came to the conclusion that changes in the intensity of light could not account for these reinforcing effects, and that the effects must be found directly in the intensity characteristics of the light stimulation. Since Lockard's review, Kiernan (1964) has noted that the investigations of Leaton et al. (1963) show that when the ongoing intensity is the standard, changes in the intensity of light do have reinforcing effects and that decrements as well as increments of intensity have positive reinforcing value. Still more recently, McCall (1965, 1966) has devised ingenious experiments to measure levels of intensity antecedent and consequent to the barpress. He has found a highly significant interaction between the antecedent level or standard of intensity and the consequent levels of intensity. Of this interaction variance, 86 per cent can be attributed to stimulus change, and decrements of intensity have reinforcing value approximately equivalent to increments of equal amount. No evidence of negative reinforcing effects from larger discrepancies, however, has been found in this work.

This version of the optimum hypothesis appears to have several serious limitations. First, various kinds of receptor input appear to have innate hedonic values. Evidence for innately negative hedonic values derives from the fact that the bitter taste of sucrose octaacetate (SOA) (Warren & Pfaffmann, 1958), flicker in the intensity of light (Meier et al., 1960), and contact vibration (Hunt & Quay, 1961) fail to become positive or even neutral with a lifetime of continual encounters unless they become sequentially organized with the pleasurable excitement of consummatory acts, as in the case of Pavlov's (1927) use of shock to signal coming food or of Lipsitt and Kaye's (1965) use of an originally rejected tube-nipple to give dextrose and water. Evidence for innate positive hedonic values derives from the fact that human neonates who get positive reinforcement from dextrose and water change their rejection of a tube-nipple to acceptance (Lipsitt & Kaye, 1965), and from the fact that very young chicks (Fantz, 1957) and neonates prefer looking at certain patterns (Fantz, 1963) and colors (Staples, 1932; Stirnimann, 1944).

Innate differences in other aspects of the motivational value of receptor inputs are attested by species differences in habituation to various qualities of auditory and visual input. For instance, the orienting response to the rustling sound of grass rubbing grass is extremely persistent in the rabbit, but it extinguishes readily in the dog (Razran, 1961). Such species differences suggest that genotypic differences in motivational values for various characteristics of inputs may well exist for individuals as well as for species. Maltzman and Raskin (1965) have indeed found individual differences in the orienting responses of adult human beings, but whether these have any genotypic roots has not been determined. Nevertheless, the existence of such innate hedonic values for some kinds of inputs puts a serious limitation on this form of the optimum hypothesis.

The second limitation lies in the absence of any place for context in the McClelland–Haber formulation. Hebb (1949), at least implicitly, alluded to a factor of context in his statement that "those sensory conditions are called pleasant, then, which contribute to the *current* development in the cerebrum [and motivate] the preoccupation with what is new and not too new" (pp. 232–33; italics added). The crucial importance of context has been noted in the studies of Berlyne (1957b), Dember (1956), and Kivy et al. (1956).

A third limitation resides in lack of generality. A separate formulation is required for each input characteristic of each receptor modality. While the specifics can be individually investigated, they seem less efficient a lead to the generality that—hopefully—can be obtained by dealing directly with informational characteristics of input.

Optimal Arousal or Optimal Incongruity

Other interpreters of the existing evidence have considered the optimum to exist as a level of arousal (Hebb, 1955; Leuba, 1955) or as a level of something like incongruity, e.g., "arousal potential" (Berlyne, 1960), complexity (Walker, 1964), or "uncertainty" (Munsinger & Kessen, 1964). In a combination of these, McClelland et al. (1953) explicitly made affective arousal the crucial factor in their motivation theory, but they also made affective arousal consequent to the discrepancy between the input of the moment and the adaptation level (AL) for that input characteristic.

Hebb's (1949) seminal formulation that "those sensory conditions are called pleasant . . . which contribute to the current development of the cerebrum . . . [and motivate] the preoccupation with what is new and not too new" (p. 323) implied the existence of something like an optimum of incongruity. Despite this earlier formulation, Hebb (1955) later explicitly postulated an optimum of arousal based on the indications that efficiency of "cue function" is maximal at a moderately high level of arousal (see Fig. 4-4). From the facts that optimal reaction time (Lansing et al., 1956), minimal discrimination time (Fuster, 1957), and the capacity of the cortex to discriminate pairs of light flashes with

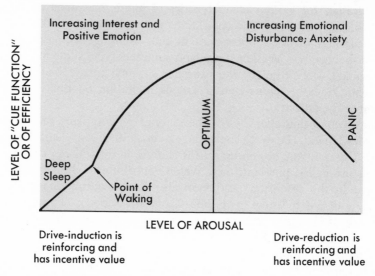

Fig. 4-4. The level of "cue function" and efficiency as functions of the level of arousal, with theoretical implications for incentive or reinforcement value (after Hebb, 1955, with modifications).

minimal intervals between them (Lindsley, 1957, p. 86) all occur at intermediate levels of arousal, as these levels are measured by the EEG and other physiological indicators, Hebb apparently inferred that an optimal level of arousal for "cue function" must also divide withdrawal from approach and the displeasure of boredom and fear from pleasure. Thus, he assumed that the unwillingness of the subjects of Bexton et al. (1954) to remain for more than three days in an unchanging environment must result from their inability to tolerate the aversiveness of low levels of arousal. Such an interpretation got some empirical support from the fact that EEG records of these subjects indicated an abnormally low average level of arousal in conjunction with their avid desire for variations in stimulation.

Leuba (1955) has proposed a similar formulation from somewhat different facts. Leuba noted what appears to be a curvilinear relationship between the efficiency of such executive operations as reaction time

(Freeman, 1940) or pursuit-performance (Schlosberg & Stanley, 1953) and the degree of arousal (see again Fig. 4-4). Thus, maximal efficiency of executive functioning, represented with level of "cue functions" on the ordinate of Fig. 4-4, comes with moderately high levels of arousal, as represented on the abscissa. Like Hebb, Leuba generalized from such evidence of an optimal level of arousal for executive efficiency to an optimal level of arousal for the direction of behavior and hedonic value. Thus, he assumed that levels of arousal below the optimum resulted in such stimulation seeking as that in the peeking behavior of Butler's (1953) monkeys and that levels of arousal above the optimum were the basis for withdrawal from stimulation. Leuba's term "stimulation" apparently meant intensity of input, and other characteristics of input did not figure in his formulation.

The curvilinear relationship of either level of cue function or level of efficiency with level of arousal carries no necessary implication that an optimal level of arousal exists below which situations that increase arousal have incentive value and above which situations that reduce arousal have incentive value. The finding of EEG waves of lower than average frequency and of larger than average amplitude in the records of the students encountering nearly homogeneous inputs in the McGill experiments would seem to support such an interpretation, but Berlyne (1960) offers an alternative view of this evidence.

Berlyne's interpretation was suggested by a formulation made originally by Myers and Miller. When Myers and Miller (1954) found that satiated and presumably comfortable rats would press a bar or turn a wheel for an opportunity to explore the differently colored opposite ends of a Miller–Mowrer box, they assumed from drive theory that homogeneous inputs produce a monotony or "boredom drive." Such a drive, they assumed further, could be reduced by obtaining such variation of receptor inputs (incongruity) as a rat can get by changing its position in exploratory behavior. Berlyne (1960, pp. 188 ff) has also made the assumption that homogeneous input produces a "boredom drive," thereby increasing arousal. Berlyne was apparently led to his version of the optimum hypothesis by assuming what he calls an optimum of "arousal potential." Figure 4-5, drawn to depict both the Berlyne conception and the writer's, differs from Fig. 4-4. Whereas in Fig. 4-4 the ordinate represents efficiency and the abscissa represents arousal, in Fig. 4-5 the ordinate represents arousal and the abscissa represents either "arousal potential" or incongruity.

According to Berlyne, "arousal potential" inheres in the "collative variables" ("stimulus change," "novelty," "incongruity," and "complexity") deriving from the relationship between receptor inputs of the moment and residues of past experience. Although Berlyne (1960,

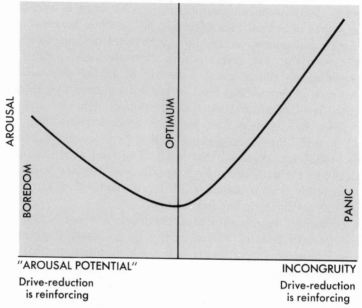

Fig. 4–5. Arousal as a theoretical function of "arousal potential" (Berlyne, 1960) or "incongruity" (after Hunt, 1963b).

chaps. 7 and 8) holds that these collative variables are in some degree of conflict, defined as competition for the final common path, this is but a matter of opinion. In any event, his definition of "arousal potential" puts it in the domain of informational interaction and makes it a special case, if not the equivalent, of what is here generically termed *incongruity*. Thus, the abscissa of the graph in Fig. 4–5 may properly be said to represent "incongruity" as well as "arousal potential."

In his defense of the conception that homogeneity of input produces a boredom drive, Berlyne, like Hebb, has appealed to the results of the McGill studies of Bexton et al. (1954) and Heron et al. (1956). While Hebb accepted the low average frequency of EEG waves with their high average amplitude as evidence of lower than optimum arousal during homogeneous input, Berlyne (1960) argued that the low averages may not have been the basis for the withdrawal of the McGill students from the situation. Berlyne cites personal correspondence with Heron to the effect that at times the subjects of this experiment showed irritation and fear, and he suggests that their withdrawal may well have been instigated by momentarily heightened arousal of an irritating boredom drive. Still another intrepretation of this evidence can be made. Since Heron et al. (1956) report that their subjects experienced hallucinations and showed fear during the third day of the homogeneous input, it may be suggested that the fearful implications of discovering oneself to be hallucinating instigated the withdrawal of those students from the experiment.

It is somewhat ironic that Hebb (1955), who was the first to formulate at least an implicit version of the incongruity hypothesis (Hebb, 1946, 1949), should be led by these studies of stimulus deprivation to abrogate this hypothesis in favor of one that makes arousal rather than incongruity the essential factor in answers to the direction question. It is perhaps even more ironic that Myers and Miller (1954) and Berlyne (1960), who have been concerned to preserve the drive-reduction theory, have proposed a formulation that makes incongruity in informational interaction the center of the causal relationships.

The Hebb–Leuba arousal theories and the Berlyne or incongruity formulations have quite different empirical implications. First is the matter of level of physiologically indexed arousal associated with the times that an organism seeks stimulus change. If the Hebb–Leuba theory is correct and an optimum of arousal does determine the direction of behavior with respect to the source of input and an arousal level below the optimal standard is aversive, then monkeys in a Butler-type experiment should show levels of arousal below average when they open the window of the cage to peep at things outside. Contrariwise, if Berlyne's formulation is correct and it is homogeneous input that produces a boredom drive, the monkeys should time their peeping behavior with higher than average levels of arousal. Although prompted by other theoretical considerations, a series of experiments by Fox (1962) is relevant. Fox placed monkeys in darkened cages so equipped that a bar-press illuminated a 60-watt lamp overhead for 0.5 second, and he kept continuous EEG recordings from implanted electrodes within the monkeys' brains. As the monkeys remained in the dark and did not press the bar, the EEG recordings showed increasing predominance of the slow waves of high amplitude implying reduced arousal. Whenever these slow waves of high amplitude came to occupy 80–95 per cent of the total record for as long as 20 seconds, Fox reported that a burst of bar-pressing for light could safely be predicted to occur within the following 20 seconds. These results favor the Hebb–Leuba notion that arousal levels below the optimum are aversive and motivate an organism to seek change of receptor input. Fox himself, however, interpreted his results to mean that the monkeys needed light to maintain an optimum level of arousal in the brain-stem reticular formation. But rats will press a bar for decrements as well as increments of light intensity (McCall, 1965, 1966), which suggests the Fox's monkeys might also have pressed for decrements as well as increments if his experiment had been designed to permit such a possibility. The fact that Fox's results are congruent with an interpretation of a need for light may well be an artifact of his experimental design.

Second, the Hebb–Leuba and the Berlyne formulations imply quite different effects of exciting and tranquilizing drugs on preferences for presentations affording high and low levels of incongruity. Moreover, the notion that the main cause of the direction of preferences resides in the cognitive domain of an optimum of incongruity implies still other effects of such drugs. If the Hebb–Leuba theory that there is an optimal level of arousal which the organism attempts to maintain is correct, pharmacological exciters should reduce preference for novel, highly incongruous presentations, and pharmacological tranquilizers should increase preference for novel presentations. If the Berlyne hypothesis that arousal determines direction toward the goal of minimal arousal is correct, pharmacological exciters should (as above) reduce preference for novel presentations, but pharmacological tranquilizers should increase acceptance of either novel or boringly homogeneous inputs. If the notion that an optimum of incongruity within the cognitive domain determines direction is correct, neither pharmacological exciters nor tranquilizers should influence preferences for novel over banal presentations.

So far, it is the last of these three possibilities that has received empirical support. In a comparison of the effects of injections of epinephrine and of sterile isotonic saline on novelty preference, Haywood and Hunt (1963) found no effect whatever. The theoretical significance of this finding was marred, however, by failure of the injection of epinephrine to increase palmar sweat, for palmar sweat is the physiological indicator of arousal most consistently manifest in encounters with incongruous input (Haywood, 1961, 1962). In perhaps the clearest of studies showing this, Haywood (1963) has found that delayed auditory feedback, a nice example of incongruity, produces marked increases in palmar sweating without altering either heart rate or pulse pressure. In another study of the effects of pharmacological agents upon preference for high and low levels of incongruity, Schulte (1964) compared the effects of injections of metamphetamine, which should increase arousal, with the effects of sodium amytal, which should decrease arousal, and with the effect of sterile isotonic saline, which should not alter arousal. As the measure of preference for differing levels of incongruity, Schulte employed the Munsinger–Kessen (1964) set of random shapes containing figures of 5, 6, 8, 10, 13, 20, 31, and 40 independent turns. Although Munsinger and Kessen (1966) found that repeated encounters with shapes of many turns increase preference for those with many turns and reduce preference for those with fewer turns, Schulte found that these pharmacological agents had no effect whatever. This absence of effect on preference by pharmacological exciters and tranquilizers suggests, at least tentatively, that arousal may have no effect upon preference for various levels of incongruity in perceptual inputs, and that the association of arousal with incongruity may be a one-way affair from the side of perceptual to central energizing processes, and then from central energizers to motor functions.

Such a one-way relationship may explain some of the results of pharmacological exciters on the rate of bar-pressing with and without perceptual reinforcement. When Fox (1962) measured rates of bar-pressing for light in monkeys before and after injections of amphetamine, he found markedly increased rates of responding. Yet, when no flash of light resulted from pressing the bar, the result was but a slight increase during the first hour of testing, and then a decline to a very low level of responding. Such results are puzzling when considered in conjunction with amphetamine's lack of effect on preference, until one considers also some findings of Schachter and his collaborators with human subjects. In a study by Schachter and Singer (1962), injections of epinephrine, especially when unexplained, markedly increased the vigor of either hostile or whimsical behavior, which behavior depending upon the actions of a stooge in the situation. In a study by Schachter and Wheeler (1962), injections of epinephrine increased both frequency and vigor of laughs at a slap-stick comic movie over such behavior following injections of sterile isotonic saline. These studies suggest that the arousal induced by such pharmacological agents may affect the vigor of any motor system, even bar-pressing, without altering inputs with varying levels of incongruity. Thus, in Fox's study (1962), so long as bar-pressing brought changes in intensity, the amphetamine energized the bar-pressing instigated by them, but when these contingent changes in light intensity were absent, the amphetamine had little or no effect.

Were it not for the fact that cue function—as indexed by such measures as threshold for flicker-fusion and time between paired flashes of light (Lindsley, 1957)—is maximal with intermediate levels of arousal, one might say with some confidence that the chain of effect is from perception of incongruity to arousal to energization of motor action. One might also say that pharmacologically induced increases and decreases of arousal affect motor action without affecting preference for incongruity. So far, however, this issue is far from settled.

ROLE OF INTRINSIC MOTIVATION IN THE
ANSWERS TO OTHER QUESTIONS

It should be understood from the foregoing that the motivation inherent in informational interaction is not the only kind involved in instigation, in energization, or in determining the direction of behavior. Painful stimulation, homeostatic need, sex, and various acquired drives generally participate with the motivation intrinsic to informational interaction. In what follows, an attempt will be made to sketch, very briefly and synoptically, intrinsic motivation's answers to other motivational questions.

Intrinsic Motivation and Cathexis

Several lines of evidence suggest that recognitive familiarity has an important role in the development of cathexis or of emotional attachments to objects, persons, and places. One of these derives from the phenomena which the ethologists have investigated under the term *imprinting*. For centuries, one presumes, poultry raisers have taken for granted and utilized the fact that young birds of one species will become attached to the female of another species that has hatched the eggs and been within view of the infant birds in their first hours after hatching. Nearly a century ago, Spalding (1873) observed that chicks hatched in an incubator will follow the first moving object they encounter. This phenomenon of "imprinting," as Lorenz (1937) has called it, consists, then, of a young bird's perceptual encounter with an object and later proneness to follow that object, to approach it in preference to other objects, to utter cries of distress as the imprinted object escapes view, and to utter sounds of contentment as perceptual or preferably actual contact with it is established. In a series of splendid laboratory experiments, Hess (1959, 1962) has considered following the object, the model, to be part of the imprinting process and has limited the criteria of imprinting to various measures of the strength of preference for the model employed. From his findings he has concluded that the strength of imprinting is a function of the amount of effort spent by the young bird to keep the model within perceptual range during the imprinting encounter. On the other hand, various investigators, including Hess, have observed independently that merely visual and auditory contact with the model will later lead to following and to such other behavioral items in Lorenz's defining list as distress cries if the model threatens to escape from view, and as preference for the model over objects not previously encountered (Hess, 1959; H. James, 1959; Jaynes, 1956, 1957, 1958; and Moltz, 1960). The generality of this phenomenon across species is attested by its description in buffalo and zebra by Hediger (1950), in sheep by Grabowski (1941), and J. P. Scott (1945), and in deer by Darling (1938).

A second line of evidence comes from Piaget's observations of his own children, and it suggests that recognitive familiarity plays a role not unlike imprinting in the early attachments of human infants. Piaget (1936) describes the beginnings of intention as attempts to retain or to regain perceptual contact with "interesting spectacles." When one examines the nature of these spectacles, one finds they are typically repeatedly encountered objects or happenings (Hunt, 1963b). At first, perceptual encounters with these spectacles elicit no such effort, but they come to elicit it apparently as a consequence of repeated perceptual encounters (see Chapter 5, p. 153 ff.). At this point, the encounter is likely to bring a smile. Spitz (1946) has contended that the smile is the basic social response, but smiling at the appearance of a human being may be but a special case of the smile of recognition. Piaget (1936) reports his infant children smiling at other repeatedly encountered objects such as a newspaper on the cover of the infant's bassinet, and even the appearance of the infant's own hand. Piaget's observations also suggest that once the smile of recognition has appeared, the infant manifests actions to retain perceptual contact with the "interesting spectacle" as it threatens to withdraw.

A third line of related evidence derives from the observations of separation anxiety and fear of the strange. Neither of these forms of distress appears in very young primates (Hebb and Riesen, 1943) or very young human infants (A. Freud & Burlingham, 1944). "Separation anxiety," like homesickness, appears to arise with loss of perceptual contact with familiar objects, persons, and places. It might, perhaps, be better called "separation grief." Such emotional disturbance does not appear during the first three or four months following birth, in chimpanzees reared under the controlled conditions of the Yerkes Primate Laboratory (Hebb & Riesen, 1943). Nor did "separation anxiety" occur in infants less than seven or eight months old when they were removed from their families during the London blitz of World War II (A. Freud & Burlingham, 1944). One may look upon such distress as corresponding to that manifested by birds when the imprinted model is escaping or has escaped from hearing and view. The fact that such kinds of distress make their appearance in chimpanzees reared in darkness only after they have lived in the light for several weeks (see Riesen, 1947) suggests that recognitive familiarity underlies the emotional attachment which, when broken, produces the separation distress.

A fourth line of evidence derives from experiments conducted specifically to test the hypothesis that recognitive familiarity is a basis for cathexis. When, in an exploratory study (Hunt and Uzgiris, 1968), infants a month old were exposed for some four weeks to visual displays over their cribs and were then tested for their looking-preference for the familiar pattern or a simultaneously presented strange one, they preferred the familiar pattern. Following exposure to the visual display for another four weeks, the same children preferred the unfamiliar display in a similar test. Subsequent findings with this method have been less clear than the exploratory findings; whether the hypothesis will be confirmed experimentally remains to be seen (Uzgiris & Hunt, 1965). In another experiment (Sheldon, 1967) rats in an unfamiliar Y runway preferred the goal-box containing an object that had been in their nest-cage over the other goal-box containing a novel object. This preference proved to be a function of the unfamiliarity of the total situation, for, as the Y runway became familiar, the preference of the rats shifted to the goal-box containing the novel object.

Intrinsic Motivation and the Choice Questions

For a good many motivational theorists the choice questions are central (see Bindra, 1959; Hebb, 1949; Maslow, 1954; Miller et al., 1960; Taylor, 1960). These questions are difficult, and it is only candid to admit that fully satisfactory answers do not exist. In a sense, the answer to the goal-choice question determines the answer to the question of choice of activities, for when goals are present, activities are the means to achieve them.

Although the organism's information processing and action undoubtedly make a major contribution to the choice of goals, other categories of motivation certainly participate too. The conception of the hierarchy of needs, such as Maslow (1943, 1954) proposed, has considerable validity. In Maslow's conceptualization, a strong need prescribes the goal for an organism's action; those needs high in the hierarchy of prepotency must be satisfied before those lower in the hierarchy can appear. Thus, when basic homeostatic needs are gratified, safety needs emerge; when these are gratified, the needs for love and esteem appear; and when these are gratified, the needs for self-actualization and the desire-to-know appear. One can agree that such a hierarchy of motives exists without agreeing with either the categories of need or their order in the hierarchy.

In the conceptual scheme proposed here, the highest level of prepotency should probably go to escape from pain. Animals threatened by encountering perceptual inputs which have led previously to painful stimulation (acquired fear drives) will starve themselves to death (Masserman, 1943). The anticipated intensity of painful input, of course, is a major factor determining the prepotency of the pain-avoidance system. In the absence of strong pain, homeostatic needs become dominant, and strong hunger and thirst will dominate many other kinds of motives and overcome many scruples. Hungry and thirsty animals do not play (Beach, 1945), for instance. Hunger has made cannibals of decent civilized Americans. The case of the Donner party that got caught in the snows in the Sierra Nevadas on their way to the gold rush in California is pertinent: after weeks with only enough food to live, women who had earlier been concerned to get their nice furniture to their destination, fed their children and themselves on human flesh. Strong hunger and thirst will dominate and repress sex. On the other hand, as may be observed in any college, sexual motivation can and often does interfere with both long-term educational goals and the more short-term plans instrumental to achieving such goals. Among goal-plans are hierarchies both of importance and prepotency and of organizational subsidiation. In certain goal-plans, e.g., getting a professional education, all the various motive systems considered here may participate (see Cattell, 1950, p. 158). These goal-plans also undergo a change in nature and structure with psychological development (see Chapter 5). Typically the pursuit of planned goals tends to predominate over concern with incongruity, positive or negative.

On the other hand, the typical order does not hold in all cases. Some men endure hunger and thirst and considerable pain to achieve artistic goals which have little relationship to these needs. Moreover, martyrdom is a fact. Some men endure intense agony rather than behave in fashions too dissonant with their self-concepts, especially when they feel that their behavior affects the trust of others. It is upon such loyalty that much of military discipline depends (Grinker and Spiegel, 1945).

The attitudes, beliefs, and values acquired during socialization supply the basis for the choice of many goals. They dictate what things it is important to do. At any given stage of life, the attitudes, beliefs, and values already established presumably supply the standards whereby the choices of goals are made (see Taylor, 1960). These attitudes, beliefs, and values appear to be typically acquired through the process of communicative corrections a child encounters in his contact with parents and others. Cultures vary in the kinds of corrections they supply, and thus cross-cultural variations in values reside in what Sherif (1936) has called "social norms," in what Sumner (1906) has called "folkways," and in what W. I. Thomas (see Volkart, 1951) has called the "definitions of situations."

There is another side to this question on the choice of goals. Just as attitudes, beliefs, and values of the members of a group or a culture supply standards against which each individual measures his own tentative goals in the process of choosing among them, these same attitudes, beliefs, and values supply a standard against which the individual weighs the behavior of others in all kinds of situations. When their behavior differs from the cultural standard enough to produce distressful incongruity, it becomes a basis for disapproval, even hostile disapproval.

Thus, the internalized standards of the group become also a basis for an individual's judgment of the goal choices and behavior of others. Even from such a sketchy consideration of this issue, perhaps it can readily be seen that the motivation inherent in informational interaction with circumstances integrates nicely with the role theory of social psychologists stemming from the thought of George Herbert Mead (1934a), and that intrinsic motivation is probably one of the major bases for most of the pressures for social conformity.

Inasmuch as the choice of an action or response is typically a choice of means to achieve a given goal, the choice of goal limits the relevant actions. Within these limits, the individual's choice is probably in part a function of the motive system operative and in part a function of habit, as Hull (1943) and Miller and Dollard (1941) have contended, and in part a matter of the individual's conceptual grasp of the operative casual relationships. It is in this latter part that information processing, or thought, has its role in the choice of action.

Intrinsic Motivation and Behavioral Change

The hypothesis of an optimal level of incongruity suggests a basis for behavioral and conceptual change, or learning, which differs markedly from those traditional in learning theory.

In the traditionally dominant theory of drive reduction, behavior changes have been seen to be motivated by frustration (Freud, 1932, p. 166; Melton, 1941) or by fatigue (Hull, 1943; Miller & Dollard, 1941). In such problem situations as those proposed by Thorndike's (1898) puzzle box, when the animals' ready-made responses failed to achieve the goal of escaping the enclosure to get to the food outside, they typically manifested a variety of actions. These actions constitute what Hull (1943) later called the "response hierarchy," according to which the unrewarded repetition of a response at the top of the hierarchy was conceived gradually to weaken that response and to permit the appearance of others originally below it in the hierarchy. Such response substitution was supposed to continue until a response or a combination of responses appeared which by leading to the reward, survived at the fittest for the situation. While hundreds, perhaps thousands, of studies of animal learning attest that behavior will change in this fashion, the weakening of dominant responses in a hierarchy by means of frustration or fatigue constitutes neither an efficient way to control behavior nor the only motivation for behavioral change. As far as efficiency is concerned, Skinner (1953b) and his colleagues have demonstrated that response patterns can be obtained much more quickly by progressive shaping with reinforcement. With his bias against theory (Skinner,

1950), Skinner (1953a, 1958) has defined reinforcement as any stimulus event that will change the frequency of a selected response of a given organism in a given situation. Although this definition of reinforcement includes informational inputs, for the most part Skinner and his followers have actually used extrinsic rewards, such as food for hungry animals. The result has been a highly efficient technology for controlling behavior and getting animals to do what a trainer wants them to do.

In the case of behavioral change from frustration and from shaping with reward, the change comes via the fate of an action with respect to its goal. Changes in attitude and in belief have been produced in quite a different fashion, by means of the input of information through the receptor systems. When an individual encounters information dissonant with his attitudes or beliefs, he either changes beliefs (Hovland et al., 1957; Rosenberg et al., 1960) or somehow discounts the credibility of the information encountered (Festinger, 1957); insofar as actions are a function of beliefs held, the input of information through the perceptual system thus produces behavioral change quite independent of the fate of any action. Since such studies come historically out of social psychology and the study of attitudes, they are seldom considered under the rubric of learning; but such behavioral change would appear to be as much learning as is that which occurs as a consequence of frustration or shaping with reward.

The hypothesis of an optimal incongruity supplies yet another motivational basis for behavioral change inherent within the organism's auditory and visual interaction with circumstances. As has already been noted, repeated encounters with given patterns of input lead to adaptation, or the extinction of attentional and arousal reactions. The principle of adaptation applies to sequential organizations of input as well as to repeated encounters with fixed levels of intensity or static patterns. As Hebb (1949) put the matter, "the phase sequence continually needs new content to maintain its organization and persistence [p. 227] . . . the thoroughly familiar arouses a well organized phase sequence; the very fact that it is well organized means that it runs its course promptly, leaving the field for less well-established sequences: even so, from this theoretical point of view, one would find behavior dominated always by the thought process that is not *fully* organized—one that is achieving new organization or one in which synaptic decay makes it necessary that organization be reachieved" (p. 229). Whether such psychoneurologizing be ultimately correct or not, it does acknowledge and dramatize the principle of adaptation or habituation so evident psychologically in the process of a person's informational interaction with sequentially organized circumstances. Behavior change is presumably an inevitable byproduct of this process.

Experimental demonstrations of intrinsically motivated behavior change are very few. One line of evidence exists in the interests children and various animals show in the incongruity of changing or novel circumstances. A study by Charlesworth (1964) shows that children repeat "games" with surprising outcomes more often than "games" with expected outcomes. While hardly evidence of behavioral change, this preference for the more complex (increasing incongruity) appears to underlie the tendency for children to progress, for instance, from buttoning large buttons to buttoning smaller and smaller ones among the Montessori materials (see Fisher, 1912). Such a preference may explain why children of ages 10–12, given block-design problems, tend to spend more and more time with the more complex problems (Earl, 1957). Such a principle may account for what Hendrick (1943) has called the "urge to mastery" and what White (1959, 1960) has termed "competence motivation" (see Chapter 5).

An experiment by Dember et al. (1957) in which rats were presented with a choice between two levels of visual complexity in a figure-8 maze apparently illustrates the same principle. In one part of this experiment, the walls of one loop were painted solidly black or white, and the walls of the other loop in black and white horizontal stripes. In the second part, the walls of one loop were painted in horizontal stripes, the walls of the other in vertical stripes. (Horizontal stripes are almost by definition more complex than solid colors in the sense that the eye encounters more changes in the level of illumination per unit of time in the striped setting than in the one of solid color; similarly, vertical stripes are more complex than horizontal stripes.) Theorizing from grounds somewhat similar to those presented here, Dember et al. did not predict which loop any animal would prefer on its first encounter, because they did not know the complexity to which the animal was adapted, but they did predict that those animals changing their loop preference (defined as spending more time in one loop than in the other) from one encounter to a second of the same duration would change from the less to the more complex one. Of a total of 13 animals making spontaneous changes of preference in the course of successive encounters with the two pairs of mazes, 12 were in the predicted direction.

The aesthetic domain affords many illustrations of similar psychological growth. That which determines the consonance or dissonance of tonal combinations has long been at issue: Benjamin Franklin commented on the matter in his autobiography. Helmholtz saw consonance as continuous tonal sensation and dissonance as intermittent sensation, but Stumpf noted that dissonance would appear in the absence of beat-like intermittents and offered the interpretation that consonance is a matter of fusion, while dissonance is a matter of failure of tones to fuse. Whether or not tones fuse seems to be a matter of their vibration ratios (see Lundin, 1953, pp. 83 ff.). It was Moore (1914) who offered the view that consonance was a matter of fusion with repeated encounters or hearings. Thus, he noted that a rise in both consonance and pleasantness of combined tones with a given vibration interval occurs with repeated hearing, but that the pleasantness later declines with further hearings. Moore noted also that the octave, the most consonant of intervals, is typically not the most pleasant: the fifth gives way to the third, and the third to the fourth with repeated hearings. He suggested, furthermore, that with frequent hearing, the minor seventh may well ultimately rank as the most pleasurable of all intervals because "it makes more demands upon the mind than any other."

This same principle is manifest in the case of sequential organizations of music. Simple melodies without orchestration lose their appeal with fewer hearings than do those same melodies with orchestration. Moreover, on first hearing, complex melodies may be less appealing than simple melodies but, with repeated hearings, gain pleasantness and retain it through a larger number of hearings (based on an informal experiment by D. H. Whittier, personal communication).

The hypothesis of an optimal standard of incongruity, when combined with at least illustrative experimental evidence and with observational evidence from sources as diverse as psychological development and aesthetics, attests to the existence and suggests the gross outlines of a mechanism for such a "growth motivation" as has been assumed, for instance, by Froebel (1826), Maslow (1954), and Montessori (1909) (see Chapter 5).

Intrinsic Motivation and Persistence

Persistence may characterize several aspects of psychological functioning. When persistence characterizes goal-striving against momentary obstacles and defeats, it is called courage and considered desirable. When persistence involves a person's pursuit of an impossible goal, it may take on the tragic character epitomized by Captain Ahab's quest of the great white whale in Herman Melville's *Moby Dick*. When persistence characterizes an animal's or person's use of behavioral patterns repeatedly and regularly leading to frustration, it is considered pathological. It was noting such fixed persistence of various habits leading to distress which prompted Freud (1920) to postulate, in *Beyond the Pleasure Principle*, a "repetition compulsion" he assumed to be motivated by a "death instinct." When persistence characterizes attitudes and beliefs despite evidence to the contrary, it is termed rigidity and considered irrational. The basic laws underlying persistence of these various aspects of functioning may be less separate and distinct than the terms used to name them or the values placed upon them, but even though the established empirical facts are few, some things may be said about persistence.

The traditional answer to the persistence question was formulated in terms of response strength, one measure of which was resistance to extinction. Thus defined, persistence was thought proportional to the number of times an action had been reinforced by a reduction of drive (Hull, 1943, pp. 102, 112; Miller & Dollard, 1941; Williams, 1938). Such a relationship was already contrary to some evidence when it was proposed. As Jenkins and Stanley (1950) have pointed out, Pavlov (1927) explicitly recognized the importance of partial or intermittent reinforcement and indicated that it involved "some further condition which has up to the present been overlooked" (p. 386), Skinner (1933) found "periodic reinforcement" a source of increased resistance to extinction, and Tolman and Brunswik (1935) considered the same phenomenon under "equivocality in means–end relationships"—even before Hull (1943) definitively formulated the principle that resistance to extinction is proportional to the number of reinforcements. Moreover, Humphreys has found that the persistence of conditioned eye blinks (1939a), verbal expectations (1939b), conditioned galvanic skin responses (1940), and instrumental acts (1943) tends to be greater with relatively few reinforcements randomly mixed with non-reinforcements, than with a greater number of regular reinforcements; this finding Hull later termed a "Humphreys paradox."

According to the incongruity principle one would expect that a consistent absence of reinforcement would be less incongruous with a background standard based upon an intermittently random mixture of successes and failures, reinforcements and non-reinforcements, or gratifications and frustrations than with a background standard based upon consistent success. One might thus tentatively state that courage depends upon having experienced a mixture of failure and success. The empirical problem is finding the proper mixture; and it is, in part, to this issue that Ferster and Skinner (1957) have addressed their investigations of *Schedules of Reinforcement*.

It should be noted that the greater resistance to extinction following an intermittent mixture of reinforcement and non-reinforcement than following consistent reinforcement can readily be made consonant with traditional drive-reduction theory and with other theories as well. Mowrer (1960) has proposed the hypothesis of counter-conditioning wherein repeated encounters with frustrative effects of nonreward then followed by reward makes non-reward a signal for later reward and thereby diminishes the aversiveness of nonreward. From this point of view, increased persistence in the face of consistent nonreward after such experience would be expected.

Lawrence and Festinger (1962) have explained the effects of intermittent reinforcement in terms of Festinger's (1957) theory of cognitive dissonance. From this point of view, the act of striving without reward can only be sensible if the goal is very important. The more failures through which a subject continues to strive, the higher must be the value of his goal and, thus, the greater its resistance to extinction. In this instance the persistence of striving is conceived to reduce the cognitive dissonance. By the same reasoning, increasing effort during acquisition should increase resistance to extinction, and in some cases it does.

The results of several experiments are relevant. Farber (1948) has found that a rat's tendency to go persistently to one goal-box of a T maze for food is increased by shock between the choice-point and the goal-box during acquisition. And this effect of shock on the persistence of response has been found in even more exaggerated form by a study (Salama & Hunt, 1964) in which rats merely reinforced by food persisted for only 2.78 trials once food was omitted from the accustomed goal-box, while rats shocked on the way to the goal-box persisted on the average for 20.68 trials. Similarly, Akhtar (1962) has found that when rats were shocked while lever-pressing to get food during acquisition they lever-pressed longer during extinction than did rats which had encountered an equal number of merely nonrewarded presses during acquisition. Whatever conceptual scheme ultimately best accounts for these experimental phenomena, they are probably not unrelated to the finding that children reared in authoritarian fashion with a good deal of punishment are more persistent in their professions of affection for their parents (Adorno et al., 1950) and more rigid in method of solving problems (Rokeach, 1960) than are children who have been reared more permissively and with less punishment. Frenkel-Brunswik (1949) attributed such evidences of affective rigidity to children's inability to express their emotional ambivalence toward their parents, but perhaps the basic factor is the level of arousal at the time the beliefs, attitudes, and plans were laid down. If this level of arousal has been high, the central processes upon which such standards are based may become highly stable, so that it takes a higher degree of incongruity to effect a modification of the system in the storage, and unadaptive rigidity may be the consequence.

SUMMARY

Theories of motivation have attempted to explain eight factors: instigation, energization, direction-hedonic value, cathexis, choice of response, choice of goal, behavioral change, and persistence of action and belief. In the theory dominant through the first half of this century, it has been assumed that all behavior is motivated by the primary drives of painful stimulation, homeostatic need, and sex, or by acquired drives based on these. This chapter has reviewed the evidence, most of it coming after World War II, showing that play, exploration, manipulation, and interest in novel objects and places all occur in the absence of such motivation. These traditional forms of motivation tend, if anything, to inhibit such behavior. These facts suggest the existence of another kind of motivation, one inherent in the organism's informational interaction with his circumstances.

Recognizing the empirical facts by drive naming, telic-significance naming, and postulating spontaneous behavior are all theoretical blind alleys. Moreover, the change in the conception of the basic functional unit of the nervous system from the reflex to the feedback loop has helped to suggest at least the basic outline of a mechanism for a system of motivation inherent in informational interaction. The instigation question, for instance, can be answered in terms of an incongruity between inputs of the moment and some standard within the organism, the standard fixed by the manner in which the organism is innately structured or established by its past experience. The organism can then be thought to remain active until congruity is reestablished by its action. Evidence has been described to show that emotional arousal is produced when organisms encounter circumstances incongruous with their goal of action or their informational standards. It has been suggested that whether organisms approach or avoid sources of incongruous input is a function of an optimum based upon past experiences—an optimum of either incongruity or arousal, a matter for further investigation.

Motivation inherent in informational interaction functions in the establishment of cathexis or emotional attachments to objects, persons, and places. Recognitive familiarity appears to be an important factor in the acquisition of such emotional attachments. Answers to questions on goal-choice responses have been seen to be a function of value, another form of informational standard derived from experiences of both social communication and direct contact with reality. That organisms seek an optimum of incongruity or arousal has been shown to provide a motivational basis for continual change in behavior. Persistence in attitudes, in beliefs, and in strivings for goals has been seen tentatively as a function of experientially determined standards based upon encounters with mixtures of success and failure and with success only after intensive effort. Pathological rigidity of concepts and beliefs has been attributed tentatively to the level of excitement present when they were first acquired.

5

Intrinsic Motivation and Psychological Development*

J. McV. HUNT

Philosophers of education, ethics, and politics have long given motivation an important role in psychological development. In Western civilization, punishment has been the most widely prescribed form of motivating learning and obedience in the young. The prevalence of this view is evident not only in the history of motivating pupils to learn but also in more recent psychological theorizing. To be sure, there has been a minor strain of philosophers who have suggested that reliance on children's inherent and spontaneous interest in new objects, places, and abilities will achieve the behavior adults desire for their culture. This strain has waxed and waned, and evidence has only recently provided a tentative, empirically based account of the role of intrinsic motivation in psychological development. Before examining this account, it will be well to scan the history.

Motivating the Young in School: Punishment

In the fourteenth, fifteenth, and sixteenth centuries, the developing opposition to the abuses of the authority of the Roman Catholic Church,

* This chapter is in part a revision of work presented earlier (Hunt, 1965a).

131

the invention of the printing press, and Martin Luther's doctrine that salvation must be achieved through direct contact with God's Biblical word combined to increase greatly the importance of reading, especially of reading the Bible (Painter, 1928). Since young children have limited interest in the Bible, teachers all too often had to force their pupils to read by making not learning more painful than learning. Calvin, a native of Geneva, multiplied the zeal for education in the Protestant world with his view of the schools as the way to a theocratic utopia. Moreover, Calvin's emphasis on the notion of the inherent depravity of children (original sin) justified punishment as a motivational tool (see Ariès, 1962; Eby, 1934, p. 118 ff.). During the seventeenth century, the severity of Calvinistic teaching was spread widely by the Reformed church on the European continent and by the Scottish church in the British Isles.

Even so, the sixteenth and seventeenth centuries brought several contrasting conceptions of motivating the young from several sources. Montaigne (see Ulrich, 1954, p. 287 ff.), the French essayist, condemned all violence in education and, from his own personal experience, advocated play, travel, books easy to read, and pleasant tasks. Comenius (see Ulrich, 1954, p. 339), the Moravian prophet of modern educational methods, defined education as "development from within" and concerned himself in his *Great Didactic* with methods of instruction that would be clear, thorough, easy, and pleasant. Samuel Hartlib, the English school-reformer, combined Francis Bacon's notions of inductive logic with the educational ideas of Comenius and invested his fortune in schools. August Herman Franke, the educational leader of German Pietism, tried to make both learning and religion joyful enthusiasms for the young. Although Comenius' writings got wide attention, and although the reforms he and these others advocated were widely discussed, they actually had little influence on practice in the schools. The reasons are many, but ironically, one of them appears to have been the influence of John Locke. Despite Locke's epistemological assumption that the human mind begins as a *tabula rasa* upon which experience writes, he presumed that individuals are motivated only by needs and pain. His essays on education accepted—even advocated—the necessity of punishment to motivate learning.

Early Conceptions of Intrinsic Motivation

It was not until the eighteenth century that Rousseau, another Genevan, instigated a powerful counteraction to the Calvinistic emphasis on punishment. Building upon Francis Bacon's dream of the role of science in society, on the empirical epistemology of John Locke, and perhaps on the ideas of Montaigne and Comenius, Rousseau inverted the moral pessimism of Calvin. In the place of the doctrine of original sin, he claimed "that man is naturally good and that it is these institutions [the contradictions of our social systems] alone which make him bad." Rousseau justified this with the theological argument that "everything is good as it comes from the hands of the Author of nature." In *Emile*, his dissertation on education, Rousseau departed just as radically from other tenets of the widespread Calvinism of that day and argued that teaching need not inculcate religious ideas and proper modes of behavior but should rather supply the child opportunities for functioning natural to each stage of his development. Rousseau also took issue with the tenets of commercialism and introduced the ideal of liberal education by arguing that education should not train a child for a job or role in society. Instead, education should liberate the individual to be himself.

Rousseau's views had continuing influence. In the domain of education, they stimulated Pestalozzi, who founded a school in which children were taught by methods adapted from Rousseau's views. He influenced Herbart, who was perhaps the first of the educational psychologists. Pestalozzi influenced Froebel who authored the kindergarten movement. Pestalozzi, Herbart, and Froebel influenced such architects of universal education in America as Henry Barnard, DeWitt Clinton, and Horace Mann. Although Rousseau's influence fell very far short of eradicating the use of punishment to motivate scholastic learning in the young, he introduced the notion that spontaneous interest in learning exists within children and he stimulated the establishment of schools whose teaching methods were designed accordingly.

This principle appears to have had quite an independent origin in the observations and empirical work on teaching of Itard and Séguin, which led Montessori to presume a spontaneous interest in learning and to build upon it her system of education, so popular from 1910 to 1915 and now regaining popularity (see J. McV. Hunt, 1964).

Formal Theorizing: Reflexes and Instincts

Contemporaneously, the vogue of explaining behavior in terms of reflexes and instincts was growing. The concept of reflex and its historical development from Descartes, and from Bell and Magendie, through Marshall Hall and Sechenov to Pavlov, is discussed in Chapter 4. The concept of the instinct has its modern beginnings in the theories of Darwin. Where Descartes had distinguished sharply between lower animals and men, Darwin sought to establish a continuity. Where Descartes had seen animals moved by stimuli from the external world and men moved by their souls, Darwin and Herbert Spencer found a basis for continuity in the concept of the instinct, defined as compound reflex action. This conception emphasized complex unlearned activities.

W. McDougall later (1908) attributed cognitive and affective aspects to instincts in addition to their active or conative aspect, so providing action with its affective quality and making a place for learning. From the standpoint of such instinct theorizing, McDougall saw maturation and learning to have successive roles in psychological development. The unlearned instinctive repertoire of behavior patterns was presumed to emerge automatically with the maturation of the anatomical structures which provide its basis; once these unlearned patterns had emerged, they could be modified by learning.

McDougall (1908) saw four kinds of learning:

1. Stimulus substitution, or conditioning, wherein instinctive reactions come to be elicited not only by perceptions of objects which directly excite the disposition, but by perceptions of associated objects as well
2. Modifications and complications of the bodily movements in which the instinct finds expression
3. Blending of instincts through the complexity of ideas which can bring several instincts into play simultaneously
4. Dramatic organization of instinctive tendencies into sentiments about certain objects or ideas

Although McDougall's theories were popular with some educators and social scientists for a time, they had relatively little impact on practice in either child rearing or education. What effect they did have tended to reduce somewhat the role of punishment and to prompt teachers to try to associate lesson materials with instincts in order to motivate the child to learn.

McDougall's contemporary, G. Stanley Hall, also took his lead from Darwin's theory of evolution. Although he was less explicit about motivation, he and his Child-Study movement had far greater impact than McDougall and the other instinct theorists on child-rearing and educational practices in the schools. Hall's basic thesis, perhaps borrowed from Herbert Spencer, was the notion of recapitulation: the development of the individual passes through the same phases as the evolution of the race. This notion of recapitulation implies that the development of the individual is predetermined. In practice, Hall's influence stressed *readiness* for learning. Readiness was conceived as a stage of genetically predetermined maturation: the child could not be expected to learn any given thing until he had matured to a point where he was ready for it. The result was a new emphasis on what Hall termed the child-centered school in the place of what he characterized as school centeredness.

Hall also warned against interfering with the natural development of the child. This he illustrated with his favorite parable of the tadpole's tail: if a tadpole's tail is left alone, it is gradually absorbed and disappears; but if it is cut off, the grown tadpole will be a frog with no back legs. That is, the appearance and later disappearance of the tadpole's tail appeared essential for morphological development. Hall generalized his parable to behavioral development. The behavior of each phase was thereby considered essential to the appropriate development of the behavioral patterns of later phases. Here Hall showed a strong appreciation of the epigenetic character of the development of children's behavior and thought. On the motivational side, his influence strengthened the case against punishment, but, because he presumed a predeterminism in development, it also fostered a laissez-faire approach to child rearing and education and minimized the role of early experience in psychological development.

A third strain of motivation theory, stemming almost contemporaneously with those of McDougall and Hall from the evolutionary writings of Darwin and Spencer, came from William James. Through James's influence on E. L. Thorndike and on John Dewey, and through their subsequent influence on many others, this strain became the dominant theory of motivation synopsized in Chapter 4.

James (1890) accepted both reflexes and instincts as the original biological motivators. He claimed that man has more of these than other mammals (p. 393). James, however, considered the instincts as highly modifiable. Once modified through repetitive action, they were conceived to become the habits that determine social and personal character. According to James, as the details of living become habituated, the higher powers of the individual's "stream of thought" are freed to sift the raw data of experience and to choose what he attends to, what he perceives, what he acts upon, and what he becomes. The task of the schools and the teachers was to "make automatic and habitual, as early as possible, as many useful actions as we can" (James, 1899, p. 57). Unfortunately, James's maxims of habit formation, while helpful for mature students trying to learn for themselves, gave teachers little to guide their efforts to motivate young children to learn. Unfortunately also, James showed little appreciation of the epigenetic change in the structure of children's behavior and thought.

E. L. Thorndike discovered psychology in William James's *Principles*. Moreover, he made his early studies of animal problem solving and learning in the basement of the James home. Like James, Thorndike accepted the notions of reflexes and instincts as the "original tendencies" exploitable for good or bad, depending upon what learning takes place (Thorndike, 1913, Vol. 1, chap. 17). Thorndike changed the conception of learning, however, and welded it to the conception of motivation. Where earlier theories had emphasized practice as repetition of association, Thorndike emphasized the success or failure of acts. He found it useful to have his animal subjects hungry when put into the puzzle box, where their activities displayed what Thorndike (1898), following C. Lloyd Morgan, called "trial and error." In subsequent trials, the number of the animals' unsuccessful actions decreased, as did the time between their introduction to the box and their successful responses that led to escape from the box and to food; Thorndike saw this learning process as the establishment of a bond between the stimulus of the situation and the response that brought reward. He also (1898) thought he saw an immediate application of these animal findings to teaching children. He argued that when explanations and imitation failed, "a pupil, if somehow enticed to do the thing, even without comprehension of what it means, even without any real knowledge of what he is doing, will finally get hold of it" (p. 104). Thorndike saw little of value in the changing structure of behavior noted by G. Stanley Hall, and he disagreed sharply with Hall's emphasis on recapitulation, arguing that "we ought to make an effort . . . to omit the useless and antiquated and to get to the best and most useful as soon as possible; we ought to change what *is* to what *ought to be,* as far as we can" (1898, p. 105). It was this view that routines become habits—a view deriving partly from Thorndike and partly from Watson, who is discussed on pp. 137–138 that prompted the writers of child-rearing bulletins from the U.S. Children's Bureau to urge scheduled feeding and early toilet training.

James's *Principles* inspired John Dewey to shift from philosophizing to psychologizing (see Cremin, 1962, p. 116). Not long afterward, Dewey was invited to the University of Chicago (1894) to head the Departments of Philosophy, Psychology, and Pedagogy. There he organized his "laboratory school" and formulated views which came to be called "functional psychology." In many ways, Dewey's psychologizing resembles the educational psychologizing of Rousseau's followers. In some ways, it foreshadows the conceptions of psychological development of intrinsic motivation proposed here. As a psychologist, however, Dewey remained a philosopher in method: his "evidence" was illustration, and although he described his shift as "from absolutism to experimentalism" (Dewey, 1930), he almost never confronted his hypotheses with genuinely experimental data. His was the role of a theorizer—an innovator of conceptions about psychological development, about motivation, and especially about the role of education in society.

Dewey accepted the notion of man's original instinctive nature, but he took sharp exception to the concept of reflexes (Dewey, 1896). Reflexes were too elementary; he preferred to think of the *act* as the unit of psychological functioning. Dewey clearly appreciated the epigenetic character of psychological development. Although he conceived the acts of infants and children to serve instinctive ends, he saw great plasticity or modifiability in both the instrumental acts and the instinctive ends; through experience, he thought, instinctive ends ultimately become critical and rational purposes. It was Dewey's belief in the plasticity of original, instinctive human nature that provided a basis for his faith that the schools could aid progress toward "a larger society which is worthy, lovely, and harmonious" (Dewey, 1900, p. 29; 1916).

CONCEPTUAL AND THEORETICAL DEVELOPMENTS
IN PSYCHOLOGY

Behaviorism

The functional psychology that developed under Dewey at the University of Chicago spawned behaviorism in the sense that Dewey encouraged the founding of the first laboratory of comparative psychology —the laboratory in which J. B. Watson later earned his doctorate. When Watson (1907) discovered that once rats learned to run a maze, they could run it accurately even when cues from the eyes, the ears, and the sense of smell were eliminated, he presumed that kinesthetic memory, which he could not eliminate, might adequately explain such behavior. This prompted him to emphasize the motor aspect of those acts which Dewey had seen as complex sensorimotor organizations. When the early work of Pavlov and Bekhterev came to his attention, Watson (1913) thought he saw the way to eliminate consciousness and much of the perceptual side from psychology. Sensation and perception he reinterpreted as discriminatory response; association he made equivalent to the conditioned reflex; imagery he denied; feelings of pleasantness and unpleasantness he referred to tumescence and detumescence of the genital organs; and thought he gave a peripheral locus as subvocal speech.

Watson (1916) gave the conditioned reflex a central place in his psychology. Conditioning provided a way of investigating behavior change, and Watson and Raynor (1920) proceeded to condition the emotional reactions of infants. Much was gained methodologically, for the fact is that one can observe only the situation in which a subject acts and the characteristics of his action. But the methodological gain was counteracted by a regression in the conceptualization of both psychological development and motivation. Any appreciation of the epigenetic character of behavioral development, and any central concern for motivation were lost. When Watson (1928) concerned himself with child rearing, he advocated leaving the child alone as much as possible during the first year or two, until maturation brought forth the response repertoire then shapeable with conditioning and chaining of reflexive responses. For Watson, motivation was merely a matter of stimuli that evoked responses before conditioning took place.

Physiological Basis of Drive

It was largely from the studies of learning and problem solving in animal subjects and from the studies of physiological regulation—the latter stemming from Claude Bernard (1859), through the research and theorizing of Walter B. Cannon (1915) and the investigations of hunger, thirst, and sex in animal behavior by Richter (1922, 1927)—that the dominant conception of motivation was formed (see Chapter 4). It was no easy matter to control the behavior of animal subjects without submitting them to strong painful stimuli like electric shock, making them hungry or thirsty (as Thorndike did), or arousing them with sexual objects. In this climate, Woodworth (1918) introduced the concept of a central energizing force in behavior which he termed *drive* and which he and others saw as based on painful stimuli, homeostatic needs, and sex.

Psychoanalysis and Freud's Theory of Psychosexual Development

Freud's theorizing took a similar course. Although his evidence came from the talk of his patients, he too was influenced by the evolutionary thought of Darwin and the physiological thought stemming from Claude Bernard. Moreover, Freud appears to have been heavily influenced by Schopenhauer's view of reality as blind unconscious striving toward existence. At any rate, motivation took a central position in his theorizing, and his dynamic instincts were energizers (Freud, 1905, 1915). It was the German word *Trieb* that A. A. Brill, Freud's first translator, rendered as *instinct,* and Holt (1915, 1931) soon identified the Freudian dynamic motivational principle with animal drive as a basis for the learning process.

Freud (1915)—like such later neobehaviorists as Hull (1943), Miller and Dollard (1941), and Mowrer (1950, 1960)—saw the function of all action and thought as drive reduction. In this sense, he, like they, deemphasized the perceptual and cognitive aspects of functioning, or what one may characterize as the informational interaction of organisms with circumstances. Nevertheless, unlike the students of animal behavior, Freud depicted psychological development in epigenetic terms and emphasized a developmental role for experience from birth on. In his theory of psychosexual development, Freud (1905) saw the locus of the erogenous drive changing from the mouth, to the anus and urethra, to the genitals. He saw the infant's first year as preoccupied with sucking, and the theme of the first phase of psychosexual development is the infant at the breast. The frustration of weaning presumably brings on the second phase during which Freud saw the infant as preoccupied with elimination, and the experiential theme is the infant on the toilet. The frustration of toilet training shifts the focus of libidinal concern to the genitalia in the form of infantile masturbation and of curiosity about the anatomical differences between the sexes and about where babies come from. With a combination of castration threats and Oedipal fears, the child's concerns are repressed and the child is pushed into the latency phase which terminates with the maturation of the gonads and puberty. This brings a return of the repressed genital interests and of Oedipal desires, which can then be transformed into love for members of the opposite sex.

According to this psychosexual theory of Freud's, the experience at each phase might produce fixations from either too little or too much gratification, too little or too much frustration. These fixations consist of generalized trait-like attitudinal consequences based on what has been called the "organ language." In the "organ language," prolonged nursing was seen to produce an attitude of passive acceptance, as if the individual fixated at the oral stage viewed the world as an ever flowing breast; interference with the libidinal pleasure of passing and retaining of bowel movements during the second and third years was seen to produce what Freud called the "anal character" with qualities of parsimony, pedantry, and petulance; and the outcome of the Oedipal crisis was seen to be central to the development of neurosis and to later adult capacity for happiness in love and marriage. Thus, the fate of the instinctual drives was presumed to determine the emotional and temperamental characteristics of the adult individual.

Since Freud's theory of psychosexual development had its observational basis in the psychoanalytic treatment of neurotic persons, the theory attempted to explain psychoneurotic and psychotic patterns and ultimately to provide a way to avoid their development. Thus, English and Pearson (1945), for instance, subtitled their book "Avoiding the Neurotic Patterns." They and others have formulated a series of rules for parental management of infantile feeding, toilet training, and masturbation (see Benedek, 1952; English & Pearson, 1945; Mowrer & Kluckhohn, 1944; Ribble, 1944). These rules called for (1) breast feeding rather than bottle feeding, (2) feeding the infant on self-demand rather than on a predetermined schedule, (3) gradual and late rather than

abrupt and early weaning, (4) late and lenient bowel and bladder
training geared to evidence of the infant's capacity for sphincter control
and his recognition of need to eliminate, rather than early toilet training
forced by punishment, and (5) leniency and understanding in the management of both aggression and masturbation. Although earlier reviewers of the clinical and statistical studies aiming to test these principles—
very loosely derived from the theory of psychosexual development—found
the evidence essentially confirmatory (J. McV. Hunt, 1946; Mowrer &
Kluckhohn, 1944; R. R. Sears, 1943), later reviewers of evidence other
than clinical observations found essentially no support for these rules
(see Caldwell, 1964; Orlansky, 1949; Yarrow, 1961).

Psychoanalytic Theories of Ego Development

Psychoanalytic dissatisfaction with the notion that the fate of instinctual drive explains ego development came fairly early. Freud himself, in his book on *Inhibitions, Symptoms, and Anxiety* (1926), took
issue with his own earlier (1923) formulation that the ego is weak and
dependent upon the id for its power, and he came to see the ego's power
deriving from recognition of previously experienced sources of painful
stimulation. Hartmann (1939) took up Freud's revisions and suggested
that the ego's power originates in psychological development quite independent of the instinctual drives. Moreover, he suggested that ego
development yields an intrinsic pleasure of its own and that it largely
takes place outside the domain of the conflict between sexuality and
aggression. Later, however, Hartmann et al. (1946) appear to have
given up the notion of an independent motivational system for the ego,
for they espouse the earlier conception of an ego that somehow utilizes
the energies of sexuality and aggression.

Other psychoanalytic writers have reverted to views resembling Hartmann's. Impressed by the evidence of joy in children acquiring new
skills, Hendrick (1942, 1943) attributed this joy to an "instinct to master."
The same kind of evidence led Mittelmann (1954) to propose an "urge
to be active," and he suggested that the period of motor activity so
prominent during the second and third years of infancy be called "motor
level of ego and libidinal development" instead of the anal stage. In
another theory of the development of the ego, Erikson (1950) retained
the epigenesis theory of the libidinal zones but changed the emphasis in
each. He considered the first, renamed "oral sensory" phase, to include,
along with satisfaction from stimulation of the mouth, concern with all
kinds of receptor input and to be dominated by what he called the "in-
corporative mode," a tendency to take in everything encountered. He
also observed the prevalence of motor and manipulative activity during

the second phase, which he renamed the "muscular-anal stage" and which he considered to be dominated by the "retentive and eliminative modes" manifest in grasping and in letting go and throwing away. Similarly, he changed the term for the third stage to the "locomotor-genital stage," and he considered it to be dominated by the "intrusive mode" manifest in "the intrusion in the bodies by physical attacks; the intrusion into other people's ears and minds by aggressive talking; and the intrusion into space by vigorous locomotion, and the intrusion into the unknown by consuming curiosity" (Erikson, 1950, p. 83). While Erikson's formulation is fascinating, his conception of *modes* is hardly more than a fine set of analogies suggested by the "organ language"; nor do his ego-psychological reformulations clearly suggest any relationships between observable situations encountered in infancy and consequent observable behavior characteristics that will permit empirical verification.

Synthesis of Psychoanalysis and Behaviorism

In order to specify more explicitly the relationships between the antecedent circumstances encountered by infants and the consequent behavioral characteristics of children and adults, the developmental principles of psychoanalysis were recast in behavioristic terms. This synthesis of psychoanalysis and behaviorism began with Hull's psychoanalytic seminar at Yale in the mid-thirties. The result was the formulation of drive-reduction learning theory in its most elegant and explicit form. For nearly thirty years, this theoretical synthesis has been the dominant guide of the investigations of both animal learning and child rearing (see Dollard et al., 1939; Dollard & Miller, 1950; Hull, 1943; J. McV. Hunt, 1941; Miller & Dollard, 1941; Mowrer, 1939, 1950; Mowrer & Kluckhohn, 1944; P. S. Sears, 1951; Spence, 1956).

As employed in the investigations of child rearing, this theoretical synthesis accepted the instinctual stages of psychoanalysis but reformulated them as (1) eating and weaning, (2) toilet training, (3) sex training, (4) dependency training, and (5) aggression training (see R. R. Sears et al., 1953, 1957; Whiting & Child, 1953). The emphasis on training focused upon habit rather than instinct and emphasized the various ways in which parents either rewarded or extinguished those activities of their infants associated with the various instinctual drives. The consequents of these antecedent infantile experiences were seen in terms of the later behavioral characteristics of the individuals concerned, as children, adolescents, or adults.

This reformulation and the evidence it generated produced some changed beliefs about what is important in early experience. The importance attributed to adequate opportunities for oral gratification through sucking (Freud, 1905; Levy, 1934, 1939), for instance, turned out to be misplaced when Sears and Wise (1950) found that children who had been cup-fed from birth, or from two weeks of age, showed less emotional distress at going on to the cup and were somewhat less likely to suck their thumbs than children who had been breast- or bottle-fed for several months (see also Davis et al., 1948; and Yarrow, 1954). Further evidence of this misplaced emphasis came when the intensity of sucking was found to increase with breast-feeding but to decrease with cup-feeding during the eight days following birth (Brodbeck, 1950).

Seldom has it seemed feasible, however, to observe the management of activities associated with feeding, elimination, nudity, sex, dependency, and aggression during infancy and then later to measure the behavioral characteristics of the same infants as adults, or even as children or adolescents. In fact, these early studies of infantile sucking and their almost immediate consequences are the only ones of this kind known to the writer.

An alternate test of these hypothetical relationships has been to assess the degree to which parents of different cultures either indulgently reinforce or frustrate and punish certain instinctual drives and then to relate these assessments to the use of the drive-related activities in coping with disease (Whiting & Child, 1953). According to the reinforcement principle of behavior theory, indulgence of the activities related to an instinctual drive would be associated with their use in therapy, while frustration and punishment of the activities would be associated with their being considered a cause of disease. Whiting and Child (1953) found that societies which manage infant feeding severely and wean children abruptly usually explain disease as a function of things eaten; that societies which severely inhibit infantile sexual behavior tend to produce guilty and fearful members; that societies which severely discourage dependency behavior tend to isolate the ill; and that societies which severely discourage aggressive behavior tend to explain illness as a function of aggression. While such cross-cultural relationships partially support the notion that the rewarding indulgence or the punishing inhibition/frustration of infant instinctual drives has specific consequences, it should be noted that cultures which are indulgent about feeding tend to be indulgent about dependency behaviors, that societies which severely control elimination tend to be severe in their control of sexual behavior, and that cultures which severely control sexual behavior tend to control aggression severely. Although the findings of Whiting and Child do indicate considerable specificity between a society's treatment of behavior associated with various instinctive drives and its members' consequent behavior, the consequences may result less from the fate of instinctual drives than from the manner in which adults treat the children's intentional acts (see Hunt, 1965).

Another alternative approach has been retrospective in nature. The investigators have started with assessments of consequent behavioral characteristics and tried to relate them to the ways in which the various subjects were fed and weaned, toilet trained, etc. The existing or consequent behavioral characteristics have been assessed with doll-play techniques (P. S. Sears, 1951), with personality tests (Sewell, 1952; Sewell & Mussen, 1952; Sewell et al., 1955), with teachers' ratings (Sears et al., 1953), and in court procedures (Bandura & Walters, 1959). The presumed antecedents of these consequents have been sought in parental reports of their child-rearing practices. While the greater theoretical clarity of this psychoanalytic-behavioristic synthesis has better directed the questions asked parents, the parents' retrospective, memorial assessments of their practices must inevitably be highly fallible, as fallible as the reports of patients in therapy, and perhaps even more fallible than generally recognized by the investigators employing them (see Robbins, 1963; Wenar & Coulter, 1962; Yarrow, 1963). Nevertheless, the impact of these investigations has been to diminish faith in the importance of the experiences associated with instinctual drives.

In the most ambitious and extensive of these retrospective studies of child-rearing practices, Sears et al. (1957) found that children's characteristics, as reported by their mothers, showed no relationship to the mothers' reports of their feeding and weaning practices. They found that mothers who were highly anxious about sex started toilet training earlier than mothers more relaxed about sex. They also found that the more severe the toilet training, the more upset the child became about it, and the less successful the training. It appeared to be less the toilet training alone that was important in forming the child's later behavioral characteristics than the mother's general relationship with her child. Mothers who indicated an accepting and tolerant attitude toward their children's dependency were also likely to be affectionately warm toward them, gentle in toilet training, high in sexual permissiveness, unlikely to punish dependent behavior, and likely to be tolerant of aggressiveness. Those who described their children as most dependent expressed the most irritation toward dependent demand, but they recognized that they eventually gave in to their children's demand, thereby rewarding strong forms of dependent demands. One group of mothers who described their children as highly aggressive also expressed strong disapproval of aggression and admitted to punishing aggression by means of aggressive threats or by physical aggression of their own. Although such punishing tended to work for the moment, it appeared also to generate chronic hostility in their children. Moreover, as Sears et al. (1957) pointed out, the use of physical punishment by mothers and fathers provided their children with a model of aggressive, destructive behavior that the children were all too likely to copy. Another group of mothers reporting aggressive children admitted being highly permissive of their children's outbursts, in which cases the aggressive behavior apparently became habitual. Mothers who described their children as tractable reported using firm but gentle disapproval rather than physical punishment to stop aggressive behavior.

In general, all these reports provide little evidence for the psychoanalytic notions that indulging dependency encourages it, or that permitting aggressive behavior allows it to drain off the hostile feeling. Rather, they suggest that when parents keep open the channels of communication with their children, respond quickly to their instinctive needs, take their intentional goals into account, and supply them with a consistent informational standard of what is expected, their children respond both with affection and with behavior that meets the standard. It appears to be more a matter of the kinds of behavior reinforced by maternal attention and of the character of the informational relationship between mothers and children than a matter of the fate of children's instinctual drives that determines their later behavioral characteristics.

Such a formulation of antecedent–consequent relationships receives further support from earlier studies by Baldwin and his collaborators (Baldwin, 1948, 1949; Baldwin et al., 1945, 1949). Intelligence as well as personality characteristics appears to be affected by early child-rearing practices. Children reared under democratic discipline, especially warm democratic discipline, were found to gain an average of some eight points in I.Q. between the ages of four and seven years, whereas children reared in homes where parents were either passively neglectful or actively hostile and demanding of obedience by fiat tended to slip downward in I.Q. (Baldwin et al., 1945). Here, democratic discipline meant that parents discussed policies and decisions with their children and explained their reasons and their conceptions of the consequences of decisions and actions. Warmth had to do with a show of affection, approval of the child as a person, and a concern for his intentions and wishes. Such evidence suggests that informational interaction between parents and their children may have more definite and sustained consequences in behavior and abilities than the fate of instinctive drives—at least at the levels of drive intensity found in middle-class society.

Functional Analysis in Terms of Empirical Reinforcement

Another theoretical orientation coming into prominence is based upon Skinner's (1953a) empirical approach to the analysis of behavior in terms of classical conditioning and shaping operant responses with reinforcement. From the standpoint of this orientation, psychological development is viewed as a sequence of operant responses shaped by reinforcement (Bijou, 1964; Bijou & Baer, 1961, 1963; Gewirtz, 1961). No attempt is made to define the organismic nature of reinforcement. As Bijou (1964) has noted, "reinforcement is not thought of as a kind of reinforcement theory . . . it is viewed as a significant statement concerning the temporal relationships between certain classes of stimuli and responses" (p. 217). In this radically empirical point of view, as Skinner (1953a) has put it, "The only way to tell whether or not a given event is reinforcing to a given organism under given conditions is to make a direct test" (pp. 72–73).

One consequence of this empirical approach has been a recognition of the reinforcing characteristics of kinds of inputs—particularly informational inputs through the eyes and ears—which have not heretofore been conceived to have motivational significance. This has had the value of helping to free the conception of motivation in development from what had become almost a theoretical dogma of drive reduction.

This attempt to see all psychological development in terms of classical conditioning and operant conditioning, however, leaves quite out of account several kinds of effects of experience (J. McV. Hunt, 1966a). First, this attempt omits any consideration of behavior changes which result from encounters with information, changes epitomized in the social psychological studies of the effects of informational input on attitudes and beliefs (see Festinger, 1957; Hovland et al., 1953; Rosenberg et al., 1960). Here the temporal order of events is the opposite of that in operant conditioning. In operant conditioning, the response occurs, and the reward follows; the learning consists in an increase in the rate of emitting the rewarded response. In the studies of attitude change, an input of information is followed directly by a change in the attitude or belief. Since attitudes and beliefs must be turned into behavior to be investigated, the investigative order typically consists of a behavioral assessment of the subject's attitude or belief, then the introduction of a message which has informational import differing from the attitude or belief, and then another assessment of the attitude or belief.

Second, this attempt to see all development in terms of classical conditioning and operant conditioning omits the role of perceptual encounters with objects, persons, and places in cathexis or emotional attachment. Such cathexis or emotional attachment is illustrated in the phenomenon of imprinting in birds (Lorenz, 1937) wherein newly hatched birds come to follow and to become attached to the objects that they encounter perceptually during their first day outside the egg shell (see also Hess, 1959; Moltz, 1963). Such cathexis is also illustrated by the beginnings of intentional efforts of human infants to retain or regain perceptual contact with spectacles made interesting through repeated encounters (see J. McV. Hunt, 1963b; Hunt & Uzgiris, 1968; Piaget, 1936).

Third, this attempt to see all psychological development in terms of classical and operant conditioning leaves out of account the evidence that experience can modify anatomical maturation itself. Experiential modification of maturation has been illustrated by the fact that the retina and other aspects of the visual system fail to develop when animals are reared in the dark (Brattgård, 1952; Liberman, 1962; Rasch et al., 1961; Weiskrantz, 1958), by the fact that living in a complex environment results in thickening of the cerebral cortex and in greater total acetylcholinesterase activity than living in the simple environment of closed cages (Bennett et al., 1964), and by the fact that learning to climb a nylon cord to get to food increases the RNA production of nerve cells in the vestibular nucleus of rats (Hyden & Egyhazi, 1962).

Fourth, this attempt to see all development in terms of classical and operant conditioning omits any consideration of the cumulative effect of encountering and coping with problems of a given kind. Such cumulative effects have been subsumed by Harlow (1949) under the conception of "learning sets" and, as will be seen below, appear to be ubiquitous in psychological development.

Thus, while there is no doubt that both classical and operant conditioning are to be found in psychological development, and that operant conditioning provides a powerful tool for changing behavior, they are not the whole story by far.

Effectance Motivation and Competence

In yet another theory of motivation in psychological development, one which partially resembles the theory of intrinsic motivation to be presented here, R. W. White (1959, 1960) has focused on the behavioral evidences of joy infants manifest as they develop new activities (the same evidence that suggested Hendrick's "instinct to master" and Mittelmann's "motility urge"; see p. 93 above). White (1960) continues the traditional emphasis on the motor side of sensorimotor organization. He focuses on such activities as exploration, manipulation, and play which he considers aspects of "competence" and attributes to a motive called "effectance," a term chosen because the most characteristic feature of these activities is the production of effects upon the environment, accompanied by a joyous "feeling of efficacy." The motive of effectance, as White views it, can be mobilized alone. Typically, however, it is mobilized in close connection with other motive systems. From it emerges not only actual competence, but also "a sense of competence" arising as "the cumulative product of one's history of efficacies and in-efficacies" and gradually coming to operate in new behavior as a kind of set or generalized attitude.

White's formulation pays homage to the modifications of the theory of psychosexual development in the writings of Hartmann (1939), Hendrick (1942, 1943), Erikson (1950), and Mittelmann (1954), but he also takes leave of the psychoanalytic claim that patterns of behavior in psychosexual stages of development can be completely explained by the transformations of the basic instinctual drives of sexuality and aggression. White contends, instead, that the observable behaviors also imply the "motive of efficacy" and the growing sense of competence basic to an effective ego psychology. The difficulty with White's account, however, is that it omits the primacy of receptor function, out of which intentions and the later interest in novel inputs appear to emerge.

APPARENT DEVELOPMENTAL EPIGENESIS OF INTRINSIC MOTIVATION

Even though Piaget concerned himself with intelligence and the construction of reality rather than with motivation, his observations of the psychological development of his own three children have suggested the outline of a developmental epigenesis for intrinsic motivation (see J. McV. Hunt, 1963b, 1965a, 1966b). From Piaget's accounts of his observations, one can glean evidence of roughly three successive stages of intrinsic motivation during the first two years of human life. It may well be that these stages are artifacts in the sense that once the child is born, he encounters a variety of objects, persons, places, and events at approximately the same rate of repetition; perhaps, also, these stages are no more than phases in the course of an infant's encounters with any given kind of change in or pattern of receptor input. Even so, during the first stage an infant is responsive to changes in on-going input. During the second phase, he manifests an interest in maintaining or regaining perceptual contact with sources of input which have been repeatedly encountered and which are presumably becoming recognized. At the third stage, he becomes interested in novelty, and the principle of optimal incongruity, described in Chapter 4, clearly becomes operative.

Stage One of Intrinsic Motivation

Even when newborn, the human child is responsive, not only to painful stimuli and to such homeostatic needs as hunger (see Pratt, 1954) but also to changes in on-going input through his various receptors. Piaget's (1936) observations indicate that an infant's reactions to changes in on-going input consist, almost from birth, of cessation of activity and alertness. Such reactions are comparable to the "orienting reflexes" studied by the Russians (see Berlyne, 1960; Maltzman & Raskin, 1965, Razran, 1961; Sokolov, 1960, 1963).

The Russian studies of the "orienting response" have radically altered the traditional design of classical conditioning experiments. Instead of pairing a single innocuous stimulus (CS) with another stimulus immediately effective in evoking some response (US), they have used a wide variety of response indicators to measure the results of their subjects' repeated exposures to a stimulus that is a change in ongoing input. The response indicators of the "orienting reflex" include dilated pupils and photochemical changes in the retina, arrest of activity (as Piaget observed), increased muscle tonus, and such indicators of arousal as increased palmar conductance (as measured by the galvanic skin response—GSR), increased heart rate (as measured by the electrocardiogram—EKG), increased blood pressure, decreased volume of peripheral blood vessels (as measured by the plethysmograph; see Maltzman & Raskin, 1965; Sokolov, 1963).

The Russian work found that as subjects continuously encounter a given input, the indicators of the "orienting response" decrease. Similarly, as subjects repeatedly encounter a given change of input, the indicators of the "orienting response" decrease in amplitude and are gradually extinguished. The "extinction" of the orienting response has been called both *adaptation* (Helson, 1947, 1964) and *habituation* (Thompson & Spencer, 1966); and the Russian investigations have found marked differences in the readiness with which various species show such extinction to specific kinds of change in input. For instance, rabbits are exceedingly slow to extinguish the orienting reflex to the rustle of grass on grass, whereas dogs show extinction to such an input very rapidly. It was also found that an extinguished orienting response returns immediately when the input to which the subject has become adapted is changed in any way (e.g., Sharpless & Jasper, 1956).

Some of the Russian work has employed very young human infants as subjects. Bronshtein et al. (1958) have reported that repeated administrations of a tone or an odor, which initially serves to interrupt the sucking response, will gradually lose the power. Recovery of the power, however, occurs immediately if the stimulus is changed sufficiently to be discriminated, and Bronshtein and his colleagues have used this fact to investigate the discriminative abilities of infants of various ages. Several studies have confirmed the fact that human neonates show quite rapid extinction of such responses as increases in heart rate, breathing, and bodily activities with repeated encounters either of auditory stimuli (Bartoshuk, 1962a, 1962b; Bridger, 1961) or of olfactory stimuli such as anise or asafoetida (Engen & Lipsitt, 1965; Engen et al., 1963). These same investigators have shown that once bodily movement, interference with respiration, and increased heart rate have been extinguished in the course of repeated encounters, they come back in full force if the nature of the input is changed in any way. Engen and Lipsitt (1965) found that these responses are reinstated by presenting alone such olfactory stimulation as amylacetate even after the infant has already been adapted to this substance repeatedly presented in combination with diethylphthalate and heptanal. This implies that extinction of the orienting reflex can hardly be a matter of peripheral sensory adaptation but must be ascribed to the extinction of habituation of central processes within the brain.

Responsiveness to change in on-going input and to change in characteristics of repeatedly encountered inputs appears to be the earliest form of the motivation inherent in information processing. Although central processes are clearly involved in the recovery of the orienting reflex, the central standard that serves as the basis for the *Test* in the TOTE unit is so dependent upon either on-going input or immediately preceding input that one might say that this initial standard, unlike those of later stages, is effectively outside the organism.

Hypothetical Functions of the Orienting Reflex in Psychological Development

Piaget (1936) has contended that sucking, grasping, looking, listening, vocalizing, and body motility at birth appear to be relatively independent sensorimotor systems or, to use his word, *schemata*. During what Piaget has called the second stage of sensorimotor development, these relatively independent systems become coordinated. A coordination between listening and looking, for instance, occurs when "things heard repeatedly become things to look at." Such a coordination appears to be motivated when changes in auditory input, of such degree and suddenness as to evoke the orienting reflex, are followed repeatedly by changes in visual input, also of such degree and suddenness as to evoke the orienting reflex. A similar coordination between looking and grasping occurs when "things seen become something to reach for and grasp." Another appears between grasping and sucking when "things grasped become something to suck."

Coordination of looking with listening resembles the classical conditioning of Pavlov (1927) except that both looking and listening are channels of input. Changes in auditory input become occasions, or conditional stimuli, for looking, which could originally be evoked only by changed characteristics of illumination. Thus, coordinating looking with listening constitutes more nearly what Hebb (1949) has called *sensory–sensory* association or what Riesen (1958) has termed a *stimulus–stimulus* relationship. The terms *stimulus* and *response* are both equivocal; traditionally they have meant receptor input and its decoding, and motor response, respectively. While looking may involve some motor elements in eye control, this motor output is minimal, and the coordination seems more accurately described as one between the orienting reflex from a change in auditory input and the orienting reflex from a change in visual input. Studies reported by Maltzman and Raskin (1965) indicate that, even in classical conditioning, the orienting reflex elements of alertness, or arousal, and attention must be present if the conditional connection is to be formed.

The fact that evidences of alertness in changes of heart rate and of attention in vascular responses must be present for the stimulus-substitution of classical conditioning to occur suggests why variations in receptor inputs are so important for early psychological development. Without such changes of receptor input, the orienting reflexes are extinguished and apathy ensues. This fact also suggests why homogeneity of receptor input and lack of redundant sequences of sound changes followed by light-pattern changes are so conducive to retardation.

It has long been noted that infants who live in orphanages from birth are typically both apathetic and retarded. The degree of the retardation which can result from orphanage rearing has been dramatized by the findings of Dennis (1960) at an orphanage in Teheran. Of those infants in their second year, approximately 60 per cent were still not sitting up, and of those in their fourth year, 85 per cent were still not walking. Although Dennis attributed this retardation to a lack of opportunity to learn motor and locomotor skills, it seems very likely that the chief factor was the restricted variation in perceptual inputs. For although the infants in this Teheran orphanage had light adequate in amount, their view was of the homogeneous off-whiteness of the ceiling and the sheets around their cribs. And although they heard a great deal of noise, because the orphanage was located in a portion of the city where the intensity of auditory input was high, changes in auditory input were few.

So long as it was assumed that psychological development is genetically predetermined, apathy and retardation were attributed to the genotype. Only genotypically inferior infants were supposed to have got into and remained in orphanages. Then Skeels and Dye (1939) found that I.Q.'s were markedly increased when apathetic and retarded infants were moved from an orphanage to a ward in an institution for the feeble-minded where "the older and brighter girls in the ward became very much attached to the children and would play with them during most of their waking hours," Their discovery at first met with derision (Goodenough, 1939). But Spitz (1945, 1946) helped dispose of the hereditary interpretation with the finding that infants' developmental quotients (D.Q.'s) dropped with time in the "Foundling Home" where the infants were deprived of that maternal contact through which —according to my interpretation—variety of input is most commonly obtained, whereas infants' D.Q.'s actually increased with time in the "Nursery," where mothers had daily contact with their infants.

Changing the circumstances of such apathetic and retarded infants will, at least under some conditions, reverse the developmental trend. The degree of irreversibility for apathy and retardation appears to be largely a function of the duration that the inducing circumstances persist. For instance, while Carmichael (1926) detected no influence of chloretone immersion for eight days on the development of tadpoles' swimming, Matthews and Detwiler (1926) found swimming permanently impaired when tadpoles remained in the chloretone solution for 13 days. And while Cruze (1935) found the capacity to learn pecking undamaged by keeping newly hatched chicks in the dark for as long as five days, Padilla (1935) found that keeping such chicks in the dark for eight or more days left them unable to peck at all. At the human level, Skeels and Dye (1939) found retardation in infants transferred during their second year from an orphanage to a school for the feeble-minded largely overcome within a year or so; but the control infants with originally higher I.Q.'s who remained in the orphanage showed progressive retardation. When Skeels (1965) recently conducted a follow-up of these individuals, the 13 children transferred to the school for the feeble-minded and later adopted all proved to be self-supporting with a median educational level of twelfth grade, while of the 12 who remained as controls in the orphanage, five have been continual wards of the state, and six of the remaining seven are either unemployed or unskilled laborers. On the other hand, the reversibility of circumstantial retardation during the first two or three years has been repeatedly demonstrated, by Sayegh and Dennis (1965), by Dennis and Najarian (1957), and by White and Held (1966). In fact, by means of enriched experience, particularly of visual input, White and Held (1966) have reduced the ages at which fisted swiping at seen objects and visually directed reaching appear from medians of 65 days and 145 days of age, respectively, to ages of 55 days and 85 days, respectively. This is indeed a dramatic effect.

When human infants do encounter a wide variety of changes of receptor inputs during the first months after birth, they are kept alert, and they develop psychologically at a rapid rate. In the course of time, the nature of their intrinsic motivation appears to undergo an epigenetic transformation.

Stage Two of Intrinsic Motivation

A second stage in the developmental epigenesis of intrinsic motivation apparently occurs when infants begin acting to maintain or regain perceptual contact with sources of receptor input. Because such activity implies anticipation of the outcome, Piaget (1936) has considered this transformation evidence of a shift from responsiveness to intentionality. The phenomenon is familiar to anyone who has ever dandled an infant on his knee: when the dandler stops his jouncing motion, the infant takes it up in what appears to be an effort to resume the game. Piaget (1936) observed various such primordially intentional activities: Lucianne shaking her legs to move the dolls hanging from the hood of her bassinet; Laurent waving his arms against strings to move the celluloid balls attached to the hood of his bassinet; Laurent again, at first surprised by the noise of his new rattle, shaking it and getting the noise several times, then devoting himself with delight to the shaking and with each cessation of the noise looking at the rattle as if in anticipation as he resumed the shaking; Jacqueline shaking a little bell to get pappa Jean to continue his imitation of the mewing of a cat; and Laurent shaking his legs to get pappa Jean back to the business of blowing smoke rings.

When such activities appear, the human infant is no longer merely responsive. The fact that the infant apparently anticipates the goal of his action and acts in the absence of some experienced event implies more than the mere attention to input changes that characterizes the first stage of intrinsic motivation.

Piaget (1936) observed the initial appearance of primordially intentional activities in his children between four and five months of age, the age at which operant behavior has been supposed to make its initial appearance (see Lipsitt, 1963). Intentional activities, however, appear to have a basis quite different from that of the typical Skinnerian operants. The operants appear to be motor activities—like sucking, squirming, etc.—which are part of the infant's general repertoire. When such an activity leads to palatable food, to soft contact, or perhaps merely to changed receptor input eliciting the orienting response, the frequency with which the operant response is emitted increases.

Operant conditioning will occur under optimal circumstances much earlier than traditionally supposed. Lipsitt et al. (1966) have found that the rate at which infants less than a week old will suck on a rubber tube can be increased by giving them a dextrose-and-water solution through the tube after the first 10 seconds of sucking. The rate of sucking will show extinction when no solution is given, and will increase again (reconditioning) when the solution is given again.

It may well be that even such operant conditioning involves something akin to noting the contingency between the act and the change in receptor input. The writer has observed an instance of the obverse of operant conditioning in a six-week-old infant which suggests the contingency hypothesis. This infant was fussy when picked up. Holding him in the burping position while paddling his bottom and singing stopped his yummering and squirming. When the paddling and singing stopped, the yummering and squirming began in about half a minute. In seven successive trials, in which the paddling more effectively stopped the yummering and squirming than the singing, the time between the cessation of the paddling and the infant's resumption of the yummering and squirming decreased from approximately half a minute to less than 10 seconds. In the course of another five successive trials, however, the time between the cessation of paddling and the resumption of yummering and squirming began to increase again until the infant went to sleep. In subsequent weeks, this observation was repeated several times. At each session, the time between cessation of paddling and the infant's resumption of yummering and/or squirming on the first trial was much shorter than the original half minute, decreased with successive trials to the order of two or three seconds, and then increased as the infant became drowsy until he finally went to sleep. Here the paddling appears to have reinforced the active inhibition of a response, and the frequency of the inhibition increased with reinforcement until drowsiness altered the course of events.

The "intentional" activities Piaget noted, however, apparently start with the goal of maintaining or regaining perceptual contact with the source of input. Piaget described them as "efforts to make interesting spectacles last." They can be described as "intentional" in the sense that instigation of the action appears to imply anticipation of a perceptual goal. Unlike the Skinnerian operants which tend to be fairly stereotyped patterns of motor action, the infant's activities to regain perceptual contact with his interesting spectacle tend to vary from moment to moment. They have a groping or trial-and-error quality until one of them serves adequately.

These efforts "to make interesting spectacles last" resemble the imprinting of newly hatched birds (Lorenz, 1937). While later, as in Laurent's discovery that he could make noise with the rattle, relatively unfamiliar inputs can become "interesting spectacles," the earliest spectacles appear to interest because they have been encountered repeatedly. That objects, persons, and places tend to become attractive with repeated perceptual encounters suggests that emerging recognitive familiarity is one basis for cathexis or emotional attachment.

To test this hypothesis (see J. McV. Hunt, 1963b), Uzgiris has suspended patterns over the cribs of month-old infants. These patterns, of three kinds, were hung within 12 inches of the infant's eyes. After a pattern had been in position about four weeks, it was removed for 24 hours and, then, paired with a strange pattern, re-presented, to see which the infant would prefer to look at. At the first test, the infants looked longer at the familiar patterns. As Fantz (1963) has reported, some patterns are intrinsically more attractive than others; but at this point, preference for the familiar was evident (Hunt & Uzgiris, 1968). At a test a month later, however, when a pattern had been over the crib for about eight weeks, the unfamiliar pattern was clearly preferred (see also Fantz, 1964). At least tentatively, these results support the hypothesis.

The hypothetical attachment to objects with newfound familiarity apparently leads not only to efforts to regain or obtain perceptual contact, but also to such expressions of delight as the smile and to expressions of distress when the perceptual contact cannot be regained. Spitz and Wolfe (1946) have contended that smiling is strictly a social response, that the infant registers delight at witnessing the facial constellation associated with previous satisfaction of hunger and discomfort. Piaget, however, has reported that his children smiled at many things other than faces. They smiled when the dolls hanging from the hood of the bassinet moved, even though no person was in view. They smiled when familiar objects were hung from the hood. They smiled at the sight of their own hands coming before their eyes, and Laurent smiled on finding his nose with his fingers after repeatedly having made such contact. In these instances, the smile appeared only after the infant had repeatedly encountered the circumstances, from which Piaget gathered that the smile is the sign of recognition. The writer has observed smiles of his own children in similar circumstances. Presumably, once an infant has encountered a circumstance enough times to have established within his brain a central process which provides a coded representation of an object or event, this representative central process provides the basis for recognition through the coded pattern of input derived from previous perceptual contact. These observations suggest that such recognition is a source of joy and of cathexis for the recognized object, person, or place.

The similarities between a human infant's intentional efforts to maintain or regain perceptual contact with what has just acquired recognitive familiarity and the tendency of infant birds to follow imprinted objects needs further comment. One may see the human infant's intentional efforts as functionally equivalent to the "following response" that Heinroth (1910) and Lorenz (1937) observed in such fowls as geese after merely an hour or two of perceptual contact with a human being or with a bird of another species. A wired-in preference appears to exist in some species of newly hatched fowls for the pattern corresponding to the female adult of that species, but chickens, goslings, and infant birds of most other domestic species readily become attached to and follow adult females of other species (see Hess, 1959, 1962; Moltz, 1963). Fowls have been imprinted on such diverse objects as a football (Ramsey, 1951), cardboard cubes of various colors (Moltz et al., 1959), and a flickering light (H. James, 1959). Moreover, Hess (1962) reports that following responses have been shown to occur after a period of perceptual contact in a variety of fish and in mammalian species where the young are mobile shortly after birth and have both their eyes and their ears open.

It would also appear that the duration of perceptual contact required to yield the hypothetical recognitive basis for cathexis increases up the phylogenetic scale. For instance, in ducks and geese, the duration of perceptual contract required to produce the following response appears to be no more than a few minutes, or, at most, two or three hours (see Thorpe, 1956, pp. 357 ff.). In such ungulates as buffalo (Hediger, 1950), deer (Darling, 1938), and sheep (Scott, 1945), the required duration appears to be but two or three days, and lambs prevented perceptual contact with adult sheep for as long as two weeks become chronic loners, lacking that gregarious attachment to the herd by which ungulates survive in the wild (Scott, 1945). These durations of perceptual contact are substantially less than those required by infant primates and human beings to discriminate their mothers from others— a discrimination evidenced by approaches to the mother, fear of strangers, and separation stress. Monkeys require some ten days or two weeks of perceptual contact (Harlow, personal communication); chimpanzees, about two months (Riesen, 1958); and human infants, about five or six months. Although these times are only rough estimates from uncontrolled observation, and although objects hung over the cribs of human infants appeared to acquire recognitive familiarity within a month, it would appear that up the phylogenetic scale, with the increasing ratio of intrinsic portions of the brain to extrinsic portions (Hebb's A/S ratio, 1949, p. 124 ff.), there is an appreciable increase in the duration of perceptual contact required to establish that hypothetical basis for recognitive familiarity and for emotional attachment to objects and to the mother figure. This suggests that the time required to develop the central processes underlying recognitive familiarity and such attachments is substantially longer in brains where the intrinsic portion is relatively large.

Functions of Recognitive Cathexis in Psychological Development

Perhaps the attractiveness of newly familiar objects motivates those responses which Dennis (1941) has characterized as autogenic. One of these, babbling, appears to be an ear–vocal coordination in which the child manages to gain auditory control of his own voice by making the sounds which he hears when he vocalizes. The repetitive element in this vocalization, probably first remarked upon by J. M. Baldwin (1895), has been puzzling and has produced various attempts at explanation. Baldwin's suggestion, based on the concepts of the reflex circle and the neural groove, was that making the sound utilizes a neural pathway and also stimulates the infant; the pathway just used presumably has the least resistance, so the stimulation evokes the same vocal motor response, and, thus, the repetition. Holt (1931) similarly explained the temporal contiguity between hearing a sound and making it. Miller and Dollard (1941) approached the problem from the point of view of drive theory. They suggested that vocal products acquired secondary reward-value from the child's hearing his mother's voice at the time of feeding. In a similar vein, Mowrer (1950) suggested that birds' talking comes about through association of voice sounds with hunger-satisfaction. One may also suggest that repetitive babbling derives from the attractiveness of sounds made recognizable through repeated hearing. It may be very important that when Mowrer trained birds to talk, he kept their cages covered except for the period of vocal contact when he gave them their only food; the mere opportunity to hear vocalizing after such homogeneous input and the resulting intensity of the orienting reflex may well be more important in establishing value for the voice sounds than their association with food. This hypothesis that repeatedly hearing vocal patterns makes them attractive suggests— an interesting experiment—that infants who have repeatedly heard voice sounds from a tape recorder will tend to vocalize more than infants who have not had such an opportunity.

A similar mechanism may motivate hand-watching and foot-watching, autogenic items characteristic of four-month-old infants on scales of infant psychological development (Bühler & Hetzer, 1927; Cattell, 1940). Such movements may provide the infant both with attractive visual input, once the hands are visually recognized, and with changes in view contingent upon his self-initiated movements. The hand-watching game, moreover, appears to provide a built-in source of practice in eye–hand coordination.

Pseudo-imitation of familiar vocalizations and gestures may have a similar motivational basis. Piaget (1936) and others have noted that the first imitations of human infants are observed in connection with activities already within their repertoires. For instance, if one holds a three- to five-month-old infant, looks at him, and talks in adult fashion, the infant typically shows no special interest, although his eyes may seek his holder's. But if one discovers the characteristics of the infant's babbling vocalizations and then approximates these, the infant's response typically shows a radical change: his eyes widen, he is likely to move his mouth, and sometimes he will vocalize the sound in return, and a give-and-take resembling conversation can be established. This is the pseudo-imitation of familiar schemata, and it too appears to be motivated, at least in part, by the interest and delight that the infant must get from hearing an adult make the sounds in his own repertoire.

Finally, it may well be that repeated encounters with a variety of different objects, persons, and places gradually lead to something akin to one of Harlow's (1949) "learning sets." Learning sets emerge from repeatedly encountering and coping with a given class of situations. This particular learning set can be described as a generalization that "things heard and seen should be recognizable," and the set may take on the character of a task or a "plan," to use the term of G. A. Miller et al. (1960). Such an habitual set to recognize objects clearly, corresponds to what Woodworth (1947) described as the goal or "will to perceive" manifested in movements of fixation, focusing, and convergence, in order to find out "what is there."

Such a task-set to recognize apparently marks the transition from Piaget's third and fourth sensorimotor stages to his fifth, wherein interest in novelty appears. If this be true, Piaget's stages may well be products of the infant's informational interaction with his circumstances, artifacts of the particular systems of sights, sounds, and contacts that the infant has encountered—at approximately the same rate—in a given set of circumstances. A difference in the rate at which the systems are encountered is illustrated by the infants of the Tewksbury orphanage, whose visually directed reaching was much advanced by the enrichment programs of White and Held (1966), but whose (unenriched) recognition of vocal patterns and vocalizing remained quite retarded.

The phenomenon of the learning set appears to be ubiquitous in psychological development. Two other learning sets, more involved with action than with information processing, may well appear at approximately this same phase of infant development. First, repeated efforts to regain perceptual contact with interesting spectacles may gradually lead to a kind of generalized set that "if you act, you can make interesting things happen." It is instructive in this connection to return to the findings of such investigators as R. R. Sears et al. (1957), findings which suggest to this writer that the effectiveness of the mother–child relationship depends upon the accuracy with which the mother discerns her infant's intentional goals. White's (1959, 1960) "competence" may well derive from having achieved intentional goals a proper proportion of the time. If the effects of partial reinforcement (Jenkins & Stanley, 1950) can be generalized to infant behavior, it is probably important for an infant to succeed fairly regularly in achieving his goals as they first emerge and then, later, to achieve them only with considerable groping effort. The shaping noted by Skinner (1954) will occur spontaneously in the course of an infant's early groping toward his own intentional goals—if the situation is such that the infant can achieve them a fair portion of the time. If caretakers are alert to the child's goals, it is not difficult, for instance, to help the struggling infant to turn over by disentangling his foot from a blanket, or to help him reach a desired toy by pushing it within the limits of his gropings.

Another learning set may emerge as a consequence of repeated operant conditionings. Ironically, this learning set, which develops from the infant's encounters with unanticipated consequences of his actions, may take the form of a generalized preparation to notice contingencies between actions and consequences. It would not be surprising, for instance, if infants who had had a number of operant activities systematically conditioned during their earliest months would learn a new set of contingencies more readily than infants without such experience.

Receptor Primacy Versus Motor Primacy

If the earliest intentional goals of infantile action are to maintain or regain perceptual contact with newly recognized objects, this has important implications for our theorizing about psychological development. It calls into question the notion that the semiautonomous brain processes mediating behavioral organizations and constituting thought are primarily residues of motor action. As noted above, the notion of motor-primacy has been traditional from the days of William James (1890), G. Stanley Hall (e.g., his aphorism that "the mind of man is hand-made"; see Pruette, 1926), and Dewey (who saw knowledge as the by-product of action, 1899), through Watson (for whom thought was subvocal speech, 1919) and Miller and Dollard (who wrote of response-produced cues and response-produced drive stimuli, 1941), to the present days of Osgood (1952) and Skinner (1953b). Piaget (1936, pp. 159 ff.) apparently missed the fact that his own observations implied the primacy of receptor function. Rather, his interpretations stressed outlined acts as the basis for recognition and from these interpretations

Bruner (1964) apparently generalized that representational processes are first "enactive," then "iconic," and finally "symbolic." But Piaget's observations, on the other hand, suggest that representational processes are first at least crudely iconic and, like Hebb's (1949) "cell assemblies," acquired through looking, listening, and perhaps feeling and even smelling. Later they presumably become iconic and enactive in combination. The differentiation of actions, which are based on intentional goals deriving from information processing, from information processing per se may well occur at this second stage in the developmental epigenesis of intrinsic motivation.

The first action schema Piaget observed to become an end or goal was prehension. In this case, moreover, attractiveness of the seen object apparently motivates the reaching and attempts at prehension. As a consequence, "something to look at becomes something to grasp," in Piaget's aphoristic terms. Even so, the infant apparently intends to grasp the object, and anticipates this goal, because if it remains beyond his grasp, he resorts to other schemata. He may wave his arms, shake himself, shake his legs, roll, or vocalize in complaining fashion. All such alternative activities cease when he grasps the object. This indicates that the goal-standard of the infant's activity was indeed grasping the object, since congruity with this standard stops the striving. Note that except for the feeding bottle, these prehensive goals seldom have any association with relief from pain, hunger, or thirst. At first, the interesting objects appear to be those which have acquired attractiveness through recognitive familiarity with repeated encounters. Only later do the interesting objects become those which are novel.

Such a conception of this second phase or stage in the development of intrinsic motivation provides a kind of hypothetical explanation for Piaget's aphorism that "the more a child has seen [and heard], the more he wants to see [and hear]."

Stage Three of Intrinsic Motivation

A third stage in the developmental epigenesis of intrinsic motivation appears with the emergence of an infant's interest in things novel. According to Piaget's observations, this second "reversal transformation" —this one from an interest in the familiar to an interest in the novel— begins in the latter portion of the fourth developmental stage of sensorimotor intelligence with interest in and attempts to imitate novel vocal patterns. His nine-month-old Jacqueline, for instance, reacted to a new vocalization ("gaga") with such sustained and varied vocalizing as "mama," "aha," "dada," "vava," and finally "papa" (Piaget, 1945, p. 46). Piaget thought the infant's interest in the novel to arise out of a conflict between the attractiveness of the familiar aspect of the new pattern, which prompts an effort at imitative reproduction, and the discrepancy between the new and the familiar, which blocks the effort. He (1945) spoke of imagery as internalized imitation, a view in which imagery corresponds to the "enactive" representational processes Bruner (1964) considered to be first. Piaget contended that "the image is the result of a construction akin to that which produces the schemata of intelligence, but which takes its material from the 'world of sensation' but we must add that this material is motor as well as sensorial . . . the image is as if it were the draft of words to come in the interiorization of acquired exterior language" (1945, p. 70).

Here again appears the issue of the relative primacy of inputs and information processing on the one hand, and of motor action on the other. Here it arises even after the separation of goals from means within intrinsic motivation. Even at this stage, a relative primacy of receptor inputs and information processing appears to show in two ways. First, according to Piaget's own interpretive analysis, interest in the novel apparently derives from the attractiveness of the familiar. Jacqueline's interest in the new "gaga" seemed to derive from the familiar aspects of the vocal pattern. That the rhythm of a double *ah* is common to the instigating pattern and to each of her efforts to reproduce it makes this look like a special case of the stimulus generalization of behavior theory. Second, the discrepancy Piaget mentions is between Jacqueline's immediate memory of the instigating "gaga" pattern and her hearing her own efforts at vocal imitation. According to Piaget's own analysis, it is this perceptual discrepancy which presumably frustrated Jacqueline's intention to reproduce the instigating model. Thus, her groping search through a series of double *ahs* combined with several items from her established repertoire of consonants.

The learning-sets view described above suggests another interpretive analysis. First, repeated encounters with fairly familiar objects gradually become "old stuff," as any adult can demonstrate for himself by rereading a detective story several times, and as the various evidence of perceptual adaptation or habituation attests (see Thompson & Spencer, 1966). For sequentially organized patterns, Hebb (1949) has attributed this *ennui* with repeated encounters to the fact that the semiautonomous brain processes run off more rapidly than the sequence of inputs. Thus, the mismatched timing wherein a sequence's inputs follow its central runoff is the basis for unpleasant boredom. If this be true, it also favors the relative primacy of receptor input. No such phenomenon occurs on the motor side: rather, when a skill like walking is mastered, it ceases to be an intentional concern; it no longer requires attention and self-instruction, but instead of becoming boring, it becomes an automatic activity which frees an individual to attend to other things while utilizing the skill as a component of more complex behavioral organizations. Interest in novel receptor input, however, may well reside in effort to shift the timing of the discrepancy between inputs and central processes so that receptor inputs come before the centrally organized sequence. This very tentative hypothesis may help explain the hedonic value of the novel.

Second, if it be true that infants develop a generalized learning-set that things should be recognizable, this set has an implicit task-like goal. When new patterns of input are not recognized, the resultant frustration motivates continued looking, as adults and older children look at modern paintings of barely recognizable objects. In such instances, persistent looking is no longer attributable to hedonic pleasure but is motivated to "find out 'what is there'" (Woodworth, 1947). In photographic investigations of the eye movements of adults and children examining pictures in which the objects are hard to recognize, Mackworth and Bruner (1965) have found that visual fixations tend to occur on those parts of the display where variations in contour provide maximal information. Adults show greater skill than children in finding these areas of high informational density by fixating them successively over a wider portion of the display, by exhibiting eye movements with larger leaps, and by persisting longer in the search. During such examinations, a sophisticated observer may well call up a series of representational processes, or images, in his effort at recognition (see J. McV. Hunt, 1935). Should he accept one that badly matches the objects, this may interfere with the retrieval of the proper image when the quality of receptor input has cleared. Evidence of such a principle comes from the work of Bruner and his collaborators with the "ambiguiter" (see Bruner & Potter, 1964). The principle is also illustrated historically by the fact that preformationists using the newly invented compound microscope saw homunculi in sperm cells (J. McV. Hunt, 1961, p. 39).

Thus it seems likely that interest in the novel derives from both of these sources: one hedonic and the other an action-goal based on the learning-set that things should be recognizable. In either case, it appears that receptor processes have relative primacy in this transformation from interest in the familiar to interest in the novel or strange.

Once interest in the novel appears, the principle of optimal incongruity (see Chapter 4) comes into play. While the nature of the standards—both informational on the side of information processing, and goal-wise on the side of action—changes continually and progressively, interest in the novel and the principle of optimal incongruity appear to operate through development from the time of their appearance late in the first year to the end of life.

The three epigenetic stages of intrinsic motivation discussed above may possibly be manifest in every organism's informational interaction with every set of circumstances it encounters. More likely, however, the behavioral transformations from responsiveness to intentional effort to regain a familiar contact and from interest in the familiar to interest in the novel represent acquisition of learning-sets through repeated encounters and copings with various classes of circumstances. It is highly unlikely that these learning-sets are as broadly general as Piaget's stages, which are probably artifacts of the fact that his children encountered several varieties of circumstances at about the same rate. Were variations in auditory input increased and variations in visual input decreased, behavior indicating interest in novel auditory patterns might well become quite general even before the appearance of efforts to gain or regain visual contact with familiar scenes. Again, the observations of White and Held (1966) are illustrative; here, of a converse advance in the visual domain and retardation in the auditory. It is interesting in this connection to consider that rats deprived of early visual experience tend to lose races for food to litter mates deprived of auditory experience when the starting signals are visual, and vice versa (Gauron and Becker, 1959; Wolf, 1943). Perhaps such modifications of early experience of human infants, if of sufficient duration, might result in relatively consistent preferences for getting information via spoken speech in the visually deprived or via reading in the case of the aurally deprived.

However, such issues are settled when the evidence is available. Once a child learns that things should be recognizable aurally and visually, and perhaps tactually, and once he becomes interested in novel objects which are not immediately recognizable, he appears to have achieved a final stage in at least one aspect of intrinsic motivation. Thereafter, any epigenetic changes occur in the structure of the standards which serve as the basis for his TOTE-unit tests.

With the development of general interest in the novel, "the problem of the match" (J. McV. Hunt, 1961, pp. 267 ff.) takes on a motivational, as well as intellectual, aspect. On the side of information processing, the principle of optimal incongruity calls for a proper degree of discrepancy or mismatch between the information of the moment and the informational standards already established. On the side of action, effort continues until the input matches perfectly that anticipated in the standard of the task-goal. It must be remembered, moreover, that the intrinsic motivation of both information processing and action interact continuously with other motivational systems: pain avoidance, homeostatic needs, sex, sleep, or rest.

Some Early Developmental Consequences
of Interest and Novelty

Interest in novelty appears to provide motivation for both (1) a number of developmental transitions typically occurring toward the end of the first year and through the second, third, and fourth years, and (2) the continuing process of psychological growth and self-realization (see Chapter 4).

One of the earliest developmental transitions is the shift of attention from perceived spectacles and action schemas per se to objects and what objects do if the infant drops them, throws them, or manipulates them. Piaget (1936) observed this transition in the familiar throwing schema often distressing to mothers proud of their orderly homes. He observed this throwing schema to begin with the emerging new means, "letting go," which the traditional predeterministic conception of development has seen as behavior unfolding automatically with anatomical maturation. To what degree the onset of "letting go" can be speeded or slowed by enrichment or deprivation of previous perceptual and manipulative encounters with objects has not yet been studied. Infants do appear to "discover" this schema of "letting go" quite suddenly. When they discover it, they use it; they delight in dropping things. Their attention soon shifts from the newfound action schema of "letting go" to the object that falls, from relatively passive "dropping" to active intentional "throwing" with eyes focused on the object's trajectory. Infants apparently so learn something about the relationship between the object, its trajectory, and their own efforts. Even though such throwing can play havoc with the order of a home, it may be important to permit infants up to about a year old ample opportunity to throw; this may be a case in which G. Stanley Hall's parable of the tadpole's tail applies.

Dropping and throwing, of course, constitute only two of the infant's manipulative schemata. Others include rolling, striking, sliding, pressing, and mauling objects; with their appearance, the representative central processes mediating object permanency show rapid growth. Presumably, the rate at which information gets into the storage increases markedly with motivation to pursue the novel through manipulation. The increasing stability of the representative central processes mediating object permanency shows in the infant's developing ability to follow an object through sequential displacements instead of looking for it where it was first found (see Hunt, 1961, p. 164 ff.). While information processing may have relative primacy in the development of imagery, Piaget is undoubtedly correct about the importance of action, which appears to increase the angles from which an object is viewed and to increase, per unit of time, the impressions of the object received through various modalities.

A second transition motivated by interest in novelty is the shift from relatively stereotyped action schemas to a tendency to experiment actively. During the interest in the familiar, the action schemata tend to be fixed and repetitive. When infants begin to manifest intentional efforts to retain interesting perceptual spectacles, they may shift from one schema to another, but the execution of each of the schemas in the infant's repertoire tends to be stereotyped. When the infant is handed a new object, he tries out one of the schemas he has employed on other objects. With the development of interest in novelty, these action schemas come to show modification, implying a constructive, creative aspect of the infant's actions.

An early example of this creative aspect was observed by Piaget (1936, Obs. #48) in connection with "the schema of the support." His son Laurent had not understood the relation "placed upon"; only occasionally and accidentally had he drawn a cushion toward him in order to grasp from it a box with which he had previously played. At age 11 months and 16 days, however, Laurent appeared to discover the relation between support and box. Papa Jean immediately tested the generality of Laurent's comprehensions: he put his watch out of Laurent's reach, on a red cushion directly in front of him. After trying to reach the watch directly, and after shaking his legs, Laurent grabbed the cushion and drew it toward him as before. Papa Jean tried this with several other objects which interested Laurent and with several other kinds of support; Laurent immediately grasped each support and drew it toward him. Apparently, Laurent had solved this problem, or, perhaps one should say, had acquired a new "learning-set" for this category of problems, at each problem modifying his motor action to suit the circumstances of the support and of his task-goal.

Other constructively creative actions included the accommodative groping to bring an object within reach with a stick and to bring a stick through the bars of a play pen. Each led to similar groping modifications of behavior as Piaget's children sought to achieve their task-goals. The opportunity to encounter repeatedly a wide variety of problems is very likely essential to what White (1959, 1960) has termed "competence" and the "feeling of competence," particularly if the problems are such that the infant must persist in his accommodative groping to achieve his ends, but such that he can ultimately succeed. Repeated success after persistent and concentrated effort is very probably the kind of experience that leads not only to the "feeling of competence" but to "competence" of achievement. So long as only the infant's own intentional goals are concerned in such efforts, it is unlikely that damage to personality and character can be done; pathological concern for given goals as epitomized in Ahab's obsession with Moby Dick probably develops only when homeostatic needs, punishment, and the acceptance of other people have been made contingent upon an infant's obtaining his goals.

A third transition from interest in novelty brings the child to genuine imitation of actions, gestures, and vocalizations new to him from his pseudo-imitation of actions, gestures, and vocalizations already within his repertoire.

Imitation deserves comment. Along with sympathy and suggestion, it has long been seen to have a central role in socialization (see G. W. Allport, 1954) and to be one of the principal bases for behavioral conformity in savage societies, for fads, fashions, and cultural diffusion, and for empathy and role theory (Mead, 1934b, 1936), as well as for the mental development of children (Baldwin, 1895). Imitation has been defined psychologically in various ways: as an instinct (W. James, 1890), as a "non-specific innate tendency" (McDougall, 1908), as an "echo" of action progress (F. H. Allport, 1924; Holt, 1931), as a generalized instrumental habit of matching one's behavior to a model's to get extrinsic rewards, as an acquired drive wherein being different has acquired drive-value (Miller & Dollard, 1941), and as behavior based upon comprehension of a means–end relationship (Köhler, 1924; Ashby, 1952, chap. 16).

Baldwin's (1895) view of imitation in the psychological development of infants came from observing his own children, as did Piaget's. Baldwin noted both "automatic" (nondeliberate) and "deliberate" imitation in children and adults but not in infants. Like Piaget, Baldwin discerned stages in the course of infant development. In the first, which he called the *projective* stage, receptive perception apparently predominates, infants receiving impressions of the model as photographic plates receive images. In the second, *subjective* stage, infants appear to assume the movements, strains, and attitudes of the model and to become thereby "veritable copying machines." In the third *ejective* stage, young children recognize that they are acting like others, gleaning from the way they feel about their own imitative actions how others must feel about their own situation. It was this *ejective* stage of imitation, in which Baldwin saw the basis for empathy, that George Herbert Mead (1934b) later elaborated into the first formulation of role theory, which has become the dominant theoretical scheme of social psychology.

Although Baldwin's (1895) descriptions of his observations are less clear than Piaget's, his *projective* stage appears to correspond roughly to the pseudo-imitation of familiar objects that Piaget found characteristic of his third and fourth stages of sensorimotor development and to what has here been considered the second stage of intrinsic motivation.

Moreover, from the fact that the models there can hardly have been familiar, one also gleans that Baldwin's *subjective* stage corresponds to the imitation of novel patterns that Piaget considered characteristic of his fifth and sixth stages of sensorimotor development. Perhaps also worth noting is that this imitation of novel actions, gestures, and verbal phones corresponds descriptively to the psychoanalytic conception of "incorporation" motivated by defensive "identification" with the threatening Oedipal father figure or mother figure (Fenichel, 1945, pp. 147 ff. and 164 ff.).

The theorizing of Piaget and of this writer attributes the chief motivation for imitation of novel patterns to the infant's intrinsic interest in novelty, an interest presumably providing the infant's task-goal. Moreover, achievement of that task-goal, as typical of all goal achievements, appears to bring the kind of joy White (1959, 1960) emphasized in connection with his *effectance* motive. As of now, this view and White's (1959, 1960) are but alternative interpretations. This one suggests that increasing the variety of receptor inputs during the first half of the first year should hasten development. Should this prediction receive support from investigation, it would mean that this view has the merit of suggesting a fruitful line of investigation that the competence theory apparently does not.

SOME LATER DEVELOPMENTS INTRINSICALLY MOTIVATED

With interest in novelty, the epigenesis of intrinsic motivation per se ends, and the motivational principle of optimal incongruity comes into play. Seeking an optimum level of incongruity between circumstances encountered and standards already established within the storage serves to motivate an on-going development (see Chapter 4, p. 110 ff.). Developmental changes in the standards of the TOTE-unit tests continue to have an epigenetic character. Within the domain of action, the task-goal standards show a series of developmental transformations. Within the domain of information processing, aesthetic standards and interest standards show radical transformations. Attempting to describe these is beyond the scope of this discussion, but certain later developmental consequences that appear to be motivated by interest in novelty should be synopsized.

Cathexis of Significant Persons and Familiar Places

It is precisely at the stage of development when interest in the novel appears that both chimpanzee and human infants begin to manifest serious and persistent attachments to familiar persons and places. This attachment is attested by the fact that "fear of the strange" (Hebb, 1946; Hebb & Riesen, 1943; Riesen, 1958) and "separation grief" (A. Freud & Burlingham, 1944) appear toward the end of an infant's first year and become most persistent and intense during the second year. Such fear and grief depend upon recognitive differentiation of the objects, persons, and places to which the infant becomes attached.

That such evidence of strong emotional attachment appears when interest in the novel is becoming prevalent is puzzling. The principle of optimal incongruity may be a factor in distress, but it can hardly be the whole story. Infants are attracted by new toys which appear to be quite different perceptually from their familiar toys, but they withdraw from strangers who are perceptually very little different from familiar persons. The infant's strong cathexis of significant objects, persons, and places probably represents an instance in which the effects of intrinsic motivation are combined with the effects from other motivational systems. The role, for instance, of contact comfort as a factor in cathexis has been indicated by the fact that Harlow's (1958, 1961) infant monkeys turned for solace to padded surrogate mothers rather than to the wire-covered mothers on which they nursed.

On the other hand, objects are cathected partially through association with homeostatic gratification, as is attested by the finding of Igel and Calvin (1960) that puppies prefer surrogate mothers providing both lactation and contact comfort to surrogates providing only contact comfort. The participation of familiar persons and places in an infant's intentional efforts to achieve his task-goals probably strengthens cathexis also, as attested by the longitudinal studies of Schaffer and Emerson (1964) which found infants' strongest attachments going to those most responsive to their demands for attention rather than to those caretakers who feed them, etc. Other evidence comes from the observation that infants prefer mobiles which move in response to their shaking themselves over unresponsive mobiles which are merely recognitively familiar (J. McV. Hunt & Uzgiris, 1968). Even the pain-avoidance system may be involved in the identification of an infant's emotional attachment to objects, persons, and places. For, as Festinger (1957) has noted, members value clubs more effortful or painful to join than clubs easy to join. Similarly, rats more persistently continue to seek now-empty chambers where they have once been fed if they have been shocked on the way there than they do if they have merely had their hunger gratified there (Farber, 1948; Salama & Hunt, 1964). Thus, although recognitive familiarity and discrimination are central for cathexis, the resulting attachment is likely to have little firmness and to be readily subject to change with interest in novelty unless it has been strengthened by the effects of other motivational systems.

Of central importance in both appearance and persistence of separation grief is the development of those representative central processes giving objects their permanence. These central processes are the basis for images. Precisely when objects begin to show permanence—in that infants will search with their hands for disappeared objects—does separation grief appear (A. Freud & Burlingham, 1944). Moreover, separation grief increases in both persistence and intensity during infants' second year (Freud & Burlingham, 1944), precisely when imagery is becoming highly stable in that children will follow objects through hidden displacements (Piaget, 1936; Uzgiris & Hunt, 1966). Separation grief decreases during the third year as a child begins to acquire language and with it an extended appreciation of time. A three-year-old can be meaningfully told that parents will come back "after he has gone to bed and got up and played through the day and gone to bed again a few times." The crucial importance of the construction, in representative central processes, of a persisting reality of objects, persons, and places for intense and persistent separation grief or homesickness attests again the central role of receptor and storage processes for such emotional and motivational phenomena.

Language Development

The roles of interest in novelty and of imitation in the development of language deserve special comment because of the tremendous importance of language in socialization.

Language has two quite separate aspects; one motor, the other informational. On the motor side is vocalization: the production of sound patterns. On the side of information, these vocal–motor productions of sound come to symbolize objects, actions, the attributes of objects, adverbial relationships, and conceptions. These two aspects of language appear to have quite separate courses of early development and both appear to be intrinsically motivated.

The role of interest in the familiar in motivating the pseudo-imitation of speech sounds has already been noted above. Interest in novelty appears to be especially important in motivating the development of the motor aspect of language. Just as an infant's interest in novelty motivates his imitation of novel gestures and actions, it also motivates his imitation of novel vocal patterns. An infant's repertoire of vocal phones may be observed to increase rapidly following onset of imitative interest in the novel vocalizations.

Such a conception of the development of the vocal repertoire differs sharply from traditional theory. The development of the vocal repertoire has been conceived to follow the predetermined maturational rules for motor development in general, phones unfolding automatically with anatomical physiological maturation. Some observational studies have appeared to support such a conception (see McCarthy, 1954). Vowel sounds, which require little if any articulation, predominate at first, occurring five times as frequently as consonants during early infancy. Consonant frequency has been observed to equal vowel frequency only after children are about two and a half years of age. According to Irwin's (1941) observational findings, vowel development proceeds from the front to the back of the oral cavity, *i.e.*, from the *e*-sound of the word *lea* through the long *a* of *take*, the short *a* of *at*, the short *o* of *cot*, the long *o* of *coat*, the long *u*-sound of *true*, to the short *u* of *cut*. Contrariwise, the consonants, which result from the fine control of tongue, throat, and lip movements, have been supposed to progress from the gutturals at the back of the oral cavity toward the front. In the course of such maturation, each child has been presumed to unfold within his own vocal repertoire all of the phones of all languages (see Bean, 1932; Grègoire, 1937, 1947; Irwin, 1947; Latif, 1934; Lewis, 1951). According to this traditionally dominant view, socialization has been supposed to select from the infant's presumably abundant repertoire those phones used in the language of the adult culture-bearers. It has been supposed that this selection is achieved, quite unwittingly, by the adult culture-bearers through reinforcement, with facial expressions and vocalizations of approval and interest, of those phones which sound like those of their language.

Some observers of language development have questioned this traditionally dominant view. Lynip (1951) has argued that the early cooing and crying utterances of infants cannot properly be represented with phonetic symbols. Moreover, various investigators (Champneys, 1881; C. Bühler, 1930; M. Shirley, 1933) other than Piaget (1936, 1945) have observed infants imitating novel phones made by others. The conception that an interest in novel vocal sounds can motivate an infant's attempt to make phones new to him is quite consonant with such observations. Moreover, it makes unnecessary the presumption that an infant must unfold a vocal repertoire of all the phones of all languages and that social reinforcement must select those to persist in the child's repertoire.

The vocal products of the motor side of language have, at first, little or no meaning. They stand for nothing. They are not symbols. While there may be a kind of exception to this statement in the same sense that the vocal cries of animals have communication value, this is hardly a genuine exception, for cries are not signs. They are part of the response to distress. Vocal productions become signs first for objects or events, and this only after imagery develops. Both phylogenetic and ontogenetic evidence exists for this statement. In the phylogenetic domain, Hebb and Thompson (1954) have indicated that chimpanzees have imagery, as shown by their skill in dissembling intention. By acting attractive and friendly, a chimpanzee, usually a female, may attract a person or another chimpanzee to come to her. During this acting, she manages to hide her mouthful of water. Once the target person or chimp comes within range, he gets the mouthful of water spit at him. Yet, chimpanzees do not speak. Their vocalizations have no more symbolic significance than those to be found in the emotional cries of other mammals. On the ontogenetic side, Piaget's (1945) observations indicate that even vocalizations comprising pseudo-words, with highly idiosyncratic meanings, came only after his children had shown established imagery by following objects through hidden displacements, imitatively playing with models no longer present, and inventing new means through mental combinations.

The first pseudo-words typically consist on the vocal side of garbled approximations of words. On the informational side, these pseudo-words appear to stand for highly idiosyncratic images. Thus, one of the first words spoken by one of the writer's children was "maia-ma," a corruption of "mail man." At about 11 months of age, when she was learning to walk, her mother permitted her to go through the living room to the front door when the mail man rang twice. "Maia-ma," the infant's garblization of her mother's "mail man," seemed to signify the following: the doorbell ringing, a noise on the front porch, a piece of white paper, a newspaper or a magazine, and the intentional goal of being walked to the front door. Seeing any of these objects might evoke an utterance of "maia-ma." In the case of the goal of being walked, the infant would raise her hands to the writer and say excitedly, "maia-ma, maia-ma." This meant: "Take my hands and walk me to the front door and back," as could be determined by increasing loudness of the vocalizing with hesitation, and cessation of the vocalizing when her hands were taken.

Following acquisition of a number of such pseudo-words, each going through a process of correction from culture-bearing adults, a rather abrupt change typically takes place in language development. At this point, the course of development on the motor side becomes coordinated with the course of development on the informational side that has resulted in imagery. This coordination appears to come in the form of a learning-set that "things have names." This transition in language development was brought to light in the course of Helen Keller's learning to use tactual signs (1911). As is well known, Helen had been both deaf and blind for several years following an illness early in her third year of life. "Teacher" (Anne Sullivan) attempted to develop a set of tactual signs, but Helen did not hit upon the set that "things have names" until the critical water-pump incident in her eighth year, after tedious months of training during which Teacher repeatedly associated the forms of the touch alphabet with objects. But one day while getting a drink, Helen suddenly discriminated, with Teacher's help, the signs of the water flowing onto her hand from the signs of the cup that she held in her hand and from the signs for the act of drinking. The result was the learning-set that prompted Helen almost immediately to touch object after object while putting her hand out for Teacher to spell out the signs. Sudden increments in rate of vocabulary building have similarly been observed with the beginning of children's "What's that?" questions, questions which indicate a new learning-set.

After the task-set that "things have names" come other task-sets: "actions have names" (verbs); "positional relationships have names" (adverbs); "qualities of objects have names" (adjectives); "things come in classes"; and "statements have a syntax." The nature and developmental order of the linguistic learning-sets, from the child's establishment of imagery to his full control of language, remain to be thoroughly investigated. While vocal behavior and the central representational processes that become images appear to be separate streams of development until infants acquire the learning-set that "things have names," thereafter language and thought appear to become increasingly similar. Language for positional relationships and for classes appears to sharpen discrimination and to increase its tranferability, especially where the perceived patterns are complex (Ellis & Muller, 1964; Ranken, 1963). The syntactical skills of language appear to be important not only in facilitating communication but also in facilitating thought (Luria & Yudovich, 1956) and such later thought forms as seriation and the conservation of number and quantity. Syntactical skills also appear important later for learning to read (Bernstein, 1960; Deutsch, 1963; Deutsch & Brown, 1964). Interestingly, teaching procedures based on what teachers of foreign languages call "pattern drill," wherein children learn basic statement patterns and how to answer fundamental questions about them with the answers implicit in the patterns, appear to efficiently overcome the lack of syntactical skill typical of children reared in lower-class homes (Bereiter et al., 1966).

Not all language acquisition is motivated intrinsically. As Skinner (1957) has emphasized, verbal behavior serves to communicate, and it is reinforced by inducing others to provide desired satisfactions. The vocal system has this function almost from birth: the infant's cries bring his mother to minister unto his wants. At first these cries indicate only an undifferentiated wanting, but they become somewhat differentiated so that a certain quality of crying means "I am hungry," another appears to mean "I am alone, and I want company," and yet another that "I hurt," and caretakers soon learn what ministrations will stop which cries. This crying communicates without signifying anything; the cries are part of the nature of the infant's discomfort. Often, too, the infant vocalizes for long periods of time apparently just to keep perceptual contact with his own familiar voice, and this vocalizing has yet another quality without semantic value. But once the child learns that "things have names," the specificity and the precision of his demands increase markedly. At this point, class differences in reinforcement patterns enter the picture: middle-class parents typically delay response to the infant's demands until he correctly vocalizes what he wants; lower-class parents commonly neglect such extrinsic reinforcement. Middle-class parents provide models of and reinforce standard language, but lower-class parents not only provide models of non-standard dialects, but sometimes punish their children's use of standard pronunciation and syntactical forms. For instance, a young woman reared in the hills of eastern Kentucky recalls that imitations of her teacher's "isn't" brought from an older sister: "Isn't, isn't; tryin' ta git above yer rearin', haint ya?" Moreover, the endless verbal questioning, "Show me your nose; show me your eyes; show me the window," etc., that goes on in middle-class families is much less common in lower-class homes. There can be no doubt of the instrumental character of much language, but much is intrinsically motivated too, and it is likely that much, if not most, learning occurs under intrinsic motivation. Incidentally, it is worth noting that the difference between this view of language acquisition and Skinner's (1957), is more than one of motivational emphasis. Skinner's valiant and interesting effort to keep his discourse on language limited to the observables of the situation and to the speaker's vocal utterances would appear to be utterly in vain. While it is valuable to make and keep the observable very clear, so that one knows when and why he is inventing unobservable constructs for explanatory purposes, the human infant appears never to acquire vocal signs for things until he has established central processes that give those objects permanence as images. Although Skinner (1957) is unconcerned with the early acquisition of language, his analysis of language behavior meets serious difficulty when he discusses (1) the relation of words heard to words used in speech (1957, p. 195), (2) "pre-overt self-editing" (1957, pp. 370 ff.), and (3) *"thinking."* In each of these instances, he fails in his attempt to treat language in terms of the conditions for particular verbal responses. In the first instance, of words heard and used, Skinner admits, while discussing bilingualism, that "verbal behavior in one language may give rise to private events within the individual which he may then describe in another language" (1957, p. 198). This statement and the "covert *nonverbal* behavior [which] often occurs in solving problems" mentioned in the next sentence appear to be recognitions of this failure. Similarly, in the instance of "pre-overt self-editing," Skinner (1957, p. 370) says that "Subvocal behavior can, of course, be revoked before it has been emitted audibly . . ."; then he admits that "the subject is a difficult one because it has all the disadvantages of private stimulation" (p. 371). And in the third instance, of *thinking,* he writes: "In a sense verbal behavior which cannot be observed by others is not properly our field. It is tempting to avoid the problems . . . but there would then be certain embarrassing gaps in our account" (1957, p. 434). Skinner falls back upon "inferring covert events," and why not? Students of linguistics find it impossible to find rules that take one from speech to writing, or vice versa, but "both speech and writing are *perfectly regular* (*i.e.,* derivable by rules) and *completely arbitrary* representations of [an inferred construct that we call] language" (Reed, 1965). At first, spoken words can signify only a child's images of things, but later the syntax of his language can be said to shape his thought-language, and language and thought approach isomorphism.

Once young children have acquired language not only as a technique of controlling others but also as a way of coding and storing information, they come into the existential situation of all persons. They have then two main channels of informational input: one—that with which they started—through direct perception of objects, persons, places, and events; the other through linguistic communication. The information acquired through these two sources need not be congruent, and often is not, particularly when it is about the self. When information from observation is inconsistent with conceptions or beliefs acquired through communication—especially in the case of communicated information about the self which is all too likely to come in interpersonal situations strongly tinged with emotion—anxiety is a common consequence, as clinical observation indicated to Kelly (1955) and Rogers (1951).

Encountering communications dissonant with established beliefs will sometimes change the beliefs (Hovland, 1954; Hovland et al. 1957a). At other times, such encounters will prompt defensive discrediting of the communication (Festinger, 1957) and may instigate many of the defensive mechanisms which Anna Freud (1936) described. What kind of effect dissonant information will have depends in part upon how dissonant it is, but it also depends on how firmly the existing beliefs are held and on how the communication is introduced.

Strongly held beliefs not only discredit dissonant information; they may also shape perception. Such shaping may be illustrated by the clinical use of such projective methods as the Rorschach Ink Blot Test and the Thematic Apperception Test, by the studies of the role of social norms in perception (Sherif, 1936), and by items from the history of science like the "observations" of homunculi in ova and spermatozoa under the newly invented compound microscope (Hartsoeker, 1964; J. McV. Hunt, 1961, p. 39). Children do not acquire strongly held beliefs in the course of intrinsically motivated behavior. Beliefs become strong only when they are strongly reinforced, when another much-wanted thing is contingent upon holding them, or when they are part of a plan to which the individual is strongly committed. Attitudes and beliefs acquired through communication and extrinsic reinforcement can seldom be changed with information alone, but require counterconditioning with stronger motivation.

How a communication is introduced has been studied by Ewing (1942). He has found that a message will more likely change a hearer's belief if it opens with a sentence implying that what follows is consonant, rather than dissonant, with the hearer's ready-made beliefs. This was the artifice that Shakespeare had Mark Anthony use when he came "to bury Caesar, not to praise him." It is an artifice that skillful practitioners of the traditional art of psychotherapy have employed in their interpretations. It is one that parents might well utilize in their disciplinary attempts to alter unwanted attitudes in their young.

Some Later Developmental Consequences of the Interest in Novelty

A positive interest in a moderate level of incongruity or novelty appears to persist throughout life. It is commonly termed "curiosity" (see Berlyne, 1960). It leads to interaction with new aspects of the environment and with such cultural products as art and music, which in turn results in new learning-sets and in plans that, in their turn, motivate achievement. Such a cycle appears to go on endlessly, with interest and moderate joy as its emotional concomitants, at least when such extrinsic motivation systems as complying with institutional standards or meeting the demands and expectations of others do not complicate life too much.

Intrinsic motivation—a combination of interest in novelty with task-standards acquired through repeated encounters with problems—appears to lead gradually to acquisition of those flexible, reversible processes of thought in which Piaget (1947) found the properties of operational logic, and to the childish conceptions of causality, quantity, number, space, time, etc. (Piaget, 1947). Each of these operations and conceptions probably comes as a generalized learning-set derived from coping with various kinds of concrete situations and kinds of materials (Uzgiris, 1964). Whether such learning-sets can arise in the absence of fairly elaborate syntactical skills remains to be determined, but they are at least sharpened when represented in the vocal signs of language.

During the primary grades, interest in novelty appears to underlie the child's delight in and preoccupation with phenomena that surprise him and call for explanation (see Charlesworth, 1964; Suchman, 1960a, 1960b). Once skill in reading has been acquired, interest in novelty apparently underlies the child's pleasure in reading about adventure, geographic anomalies, etc. During the years of junior and senior high school, interest in novelty and surprise apparently motivate the use of language to deal with observed phenomena, a use which gradually leads to a linguistic facility which permits logical operations with propositions. That is, whereas observation has previously directed thought, at this point thought comes to direct and dominate observation (Inhelder and Piaget, 1955). Out of this process come interest patterns which help develop personal ambitions and decisions about identity and profession. Throughout adulthood, and even into old age, interest in novelty is manifest in artists' experimentation in new forms and in viewers' appreciation of new techniques; in the musician's play with technique and his listeners' fascination with new compositions; in the bridge expert's captivation with the continually varied combination in hands and with new systems of play, etc. As curiosity, interest in novelty and delight in new achievements appear to persist even after professional ambition and interest in sex have waned.

Individual differences in curiosity are marked. In all likelihood, these are partly based in genotypic constitution, but they are also likely to be a function of the variety of things on which the individual has cultivated loosely held attitudinal and belief standards and in which he has achieved some skill. Perhaps it is again appropriate to cite Piaget's aphorism that "the more a child has seen and heard the more he wants to see and hear," for it appears to be as true for adolescents, adults, and senior citizens as it is for toddlers. Conversely, individual differences in curiosity or interest in the novel may also be a function of the level of commitment to attitudes and beliefs: the stronger the commitment, the less the curiosity. Moreover, as already noted, commitment may well be a function of the degree to which attitudes and beliefs have been strengthened by reinforcement with extrinsic motor systems such as homeostatic need and pain avoidance, and of the degree to which they are involved in an individual's plans.

SUMMARY AND CONCLUSIONS

Although, historically, few people concerned with child rearing and education have been willing to trust the acquisition of educational skills and social conformity to intrinsic motivation, intrinsic motivation does appear to have a major role in the concept of psychological development.

Moreover, until recently, intrinsic motivation has been viewed by motivation theorists with the same incredulity as perpetual motion.

Intrinsic motivation appears to be a reality, however, and to go through a three-stage epigenesis during the first two years of the individual's life.

The first stage, beginning at birth with the orienting response of attention and arousal to changed characteristics of on-going input through the eyes and the ears, motivates coordination of the relatively independent systems of sucking, grasping, looking, listening, vocalizing, or wiggling.

The second stage appears when repeated encounters with given kinds of input have led to recognition. At this point, objects, persons, and places which have become recognitively familiar appear to become motivationally attractive, and the attractiveness of the familiar and of certain innately attractive patterns appears to motivate intentional efforts to retain or regain perceptual contact with them. Recognitive familiarity appears to have a part in motivating such autogenic activities as babbling and hand watching, in pseudo-imitation, and in the learning-set that "things should be recognized." This learning set seems to become an habitual task-standard which makes recognition the goal of perceptual activity. At this point the task-goals of action operate to produce congruity with standards from information processing per se.

The third stage occurs with the transformation of interest in the familiar to interest in the novel and new in an otherwise recognitively familiar situation. This interest in novelty appears to derive from the familiar becoming "old stuff" and from the task-goal implied in the learning-set that "objects should be recognizable." The interest in the novel shifts attention from some action schemata to the objects acted upon, and every action schema may become a goal or a means to a goal interchangeably. When interest in novelty appears, infants begin to manifest a groping modification of their various action schemas and to imitate novel actions, gestures, and vocal patterns. Imitation plays a major role in socialization: it is important in the acquisition of images, of the vocal patterns that constitute the motor side of language, and perhaps of the various learning-sets that underlie syntax. Finally, it is interest in the novel that provides a motive for psychological growth throughout life.

This hypothetical conception of psychological development and of the role of intrinsic motivation in it differs substantially from several of the older theories as well as from more recent ones. Here the role of the environment is much less static than that implied in Froebel's (1826) metaphor of "the soil in which the child-plant grows." This conception is more like the one Dewey (1902) described in his plan for a primary curriculum, except that this one gives primacy to receptor function and less emphasis to extrinsic motives in the shaping of action. This approach differs obviously from Freud's (1905) conception of psychosexual development by placing greater emphasis on the child's informational interaction through the distance receptors and on the fate of his intentions, and less emphasis on sexuality and aggression. It differs radically from the ideas of Gesell et al. (1940) in that it views psychological development and even anatomical maturation as less predetermined and inevitable and more as a function of the informational interaction of infants with their circumstances. Our conception also differs from the approach synthesizing psychoanalytic theory with Hull's learning theory, which has dominated research in personality development and socialization since the late 1930's. We emphasize what appears to be a largely independent motive system inherent in informational encounters and intentional actions with things and people, rather than emphasizing the roles of an acquired dependency drive and the molding of aggressive actions. The analysis presented here also differs markedly from that based on Skinner's (1953b) behavior theory in emphasizing receptor processes and in giving a major behavioral role to the inferred central processes whose structures change with experience. Motivational development as described in this chapter has much in common with White's (1959, 1960), but it gives a greater role to receptor processes. This conception is also similar to that upon which Montessori (1909) based her system of pedagogy, in that both emphasize the role of the receptor side and of the child's spontaneous interest in learning.

6

Cognitive Structures in Personality

JAMES BIERI

In the face of the ubiquitous complexities, uncertainties, and inconsistencies we observe in our personal, social, and political worlds, one may wonder how we do so remarkably well in preserving a sense of order, meaning, and structure in understanding the events around us. How do personality theorists attempt to explain such relative certainty or structure in behavior despite so much informational variation and confusion impinging upon us? One approach which is gaining increasing attention has been to posit that man learns relatively fixed patterns for experiencing his world—patterns which we may refer to as *cognitive structures*. Not that the cognitive theorist has a special insight into this problem, which has fascinated American psychologists since the time of William James. But the cognitive theorist, perhaps because of his own thought patterns, prefers to avoid such time-honored intervening variables as *habit* to explain the more regulated, controlled, and structured features of behavior.

In place of such mediational concepts as habit in behavioral learning theory, the cognitive theorist has a predilection for terms such as *structure, schema, style, system, control, plan,* or *program*. And here we tend to have more than just a semantic distinction, for the cognitive theorist accepts as a basic assumption that a *process* of stimulus or information *transformation* mediates any antecedent–consequent relation in behavior. This is at once both the major distinction between cognitive theories, especially those emphasizing "information processing," and learning theories, as well as the major conceptual ambiguity in cognitive theories. For the cognitive theorist is deeply concerned with the problem of defining the "objective" stimulus as it is "subjectively" experienced or transformed by the person. Such inside-the-head, "black box," "silent" processes of transformation become, then, the hallmark of cognitive theories of personality. Now the cognitive theorist takes this assumption one step further. What is also basic, he holds, is that these structures of transformation are the content of what is learned, not a series of terminal responses built upon a substructure of habits and drives. Essentially, a person is considered to learn strategies, programs, or other transformation operations, the characteristics of which may be termed *cognitive structures*.

FUNCTIONS OF STRUCTURES IN PERSONALITY

To gain a clearer picture of the nature of cognitive structures, a number of processes may be isolated which involve their operation in behavior. These include the *selective* function which cognitive structures serve in filtering, as it were, only certain limited information or stimuli from a complex input. Related to this is the *organizing* function of cognitive structures, in which those aspects of the effective stimulus are patterned or integrated in some characteristic fashion. Further, we may consider the role of cognitive structures in *moderating* or *controlling* motives and affect in the behavior of the individual. Finally, cognitive structures function in relation to *adapting* to situational constraints imposed by the nature of a given task. This set of important and complicated functions obviously imposes a great deal (if not an excess) of theoretical load on the concept of cognitive structure. Let us look at each of these functions in more detail.

The selective role of cognitive structures in processing information can be approached most readily by recourse to the "noisy channel" notion in information theory. In its simplest terms, such a notion reflects the idea that the person acts as a transducer through which any given input must pass and emerge in his behavior somewhat *attenuated* in quality and quantity. We see such information reduction most clearly in studies of the discriminability of physical (sensory) and social stimuli (G. A. Miller, 1956; Bieri et al., 1966). Here we are interested in those aspects of the mediating structure which serve to limit or reduce the ability of the person to discriminate among the stimuli presented. The results of such research indicate that there are rather circumscribed capacities of the individual in discriminating among stimuli along either a sensory or a social continuum. Such limiting selectivity may be considered to be mediated by rather basic, perhaps genetically determined, structures for discriminating among stimuli. The adaptive feature of such structures is evident in allowing the person to respond selectively to certain aspects of the complex environment and not others. At the same time, the limitations imposed on our ability to process information can be a source of constraint and possible frustration when the attempt to recall or recognize a stimulus, as in a memory for digits task, exceeds our ability.

In contrast to the limits placed upon our ability to discriminate among alternative stimuli, the organizing function of cognitive structures may be considered a more complicated issue. Certainly, in research to date, it has proved to be more refractory to systematic empirical analysis than the selective discrimination function of cognitive structures. Consider, for example, the clinician who is provided with a number of test scores and is asked to judge whether a patient is psychotic or not. Here we have an organizing process of information processing inasmuch as the judge must condense or consolidate in some integral fashion a variety of inputs into a binary decision. It is plausible that the information processing here depends upon structures different from those invoked in the discrimination problem we discussed above. For example, the judge may use a structure of linear weighting for each test score and simply combine these weights in arriving at his judgment. Such "strategies" of cue combination could reflect then the operation of cognitive structures appropriate to this type of task. Another possibility is that the task demands a divergent or generative mode of organizing information. We see this perhaps most clearly in clinical inferences in which the clinician generates a variety of different hypotheses concerning a given aspect of behavior in a client. Such open-ended "creative" hypothecation would seem to depend upon structures which allow for freer evocation of response alternatives, perhaps a type of information processing characteristic of more "pre-decisional" phases of cognitive activity or problem solving.

It would be a mistake, however, to construe the prime functions of cognitive structures as being selective information processing and organization. Rather, we must take cognizance of the types of information with which personality theorists are concerned, and these of course are strongly tinged with emotional, motivational, and affective meaning for the individual. Thus, it is apparent that cognitive structures do have commerce with these more drive-oriented personality dispositions. Indeed, the history of personality theory is replete with attempts to reconcile the control over drives and motives which "higher" cognitive organizations may assume. This systematic integration of cognitive and motivational variables in personality theory is as yet an unrealized objective. For example, various dysfunctions in cognitive performance have long been considered to be diagnostic signs for different types of emotional disturbances ranging from mild situational anxiety to acute schizophrenic reactions. Yet, little apparent agreement is evident in the formulation of *specific* hypotheses concerning the interaction of motivational variables and cognitive variables in behavior. We shall have occasion to examine the potential value of several of the approaches to cognitive structure in coping with this important systematic problem.

A further function of cognitive structures in personality concerns the adaptation to *situational* constraints within which any behavior may occur. Such situational factors are the complement, conceptually, to the motivational variables mentioned above. It is not easy to specify what we mean by "situational" influences upon behavior, an observation which may have something to do with psychologists' long history of concern with these influences. However, one approach with some merit is to consider situational factors as merely a detailed specification of stimulus and response variables in any given task. Thus, a specification of all relevant factors in the stimulus yields an analysis which can be situational in nature. Different cognitive structures may be engaged as a function of the particular stimulus conditions of each task. Such stimulus variables as the domain of stimulation (e.g., physical or social), the dimensionality of the stimulus, and the sequential nature of stimulation all may influence the engagement of one or more structures. It may well be, for example, that certain structures are engaged in relation to social stimuli but not in relation to physical stimuli. Further, such cognitive concepts as rigidity, flexibility, impermeability, and constriction are intended to reflect variation in the ability to attend to or incorporate sequential information.

Response factors also assume importance in the analysis of situational constraints in any given task. Such factors as whether fixed alternatives are provided or not, the modality of responding (e.g., verbal or motor), and the type of judgment demanded all may influence the cognitive structure engaged. It is likely that variation in such task characteristics can account in part for failure of different investigators to confirm each other's findings, and that attention to the systematic analysis of the situation will lead to greater clarification of the relative generality or specificity of various cognitive structures.

TYPES OF COGNITIVE STRUCTURES

Having considered briefly the general nature and function of cognitive structures, we can next turn to a discussion of the types of structures which have been conceptualized in personality theory. It is necessary, in this regard, to focus on only a few such conceptions, the selection being dictated as somewhat representative rather than comprehensive.

It was suggested above that one may categorize structures in terms of their relative generality–specificity in personality, much in the same way as general and specific traits have been considered. That is, for some theorists, a central or "core" structure is thought to mediate major aspects of personality functioning, and its influence is detected in a wide variety of behaviors or tasks. An excellent example of this type of structure is Witkin's construct of global–analytic cognitive functioning. As we shall see, Witkin considers differences among individuals in the ability to articulate aspects of their environment to be a basic structural variable in personality with ramifications in a variety of modes of behavior such as body image, dependency behavior, psychopathology, and aspects of intellectual functioning. Such a "grand" conception of cognitive structure carries with it strengths and liabilities, as we shall note, but it does indicate the scope with which structures may be invoked to subsume major functions in personality.

A more specific conception of structure can be found in the work of Klein (1958) and Gardner (1953) on cognitive controls. They assume that there may be a number of structures (controls) which function concurrently, and attempt to isolate such controls by means of factor analysis. The conception of a number of specific structures rather than an overall "master" structure has an inherent face validity akin to considering personality as containing a number of discrete motivations rather than one master motive. More than most theorists in this area, Klein and Gardner emphasize the *control* functions of cognitive structures in relation to human motivation.

A third approach to cognitive structure which we will consider in detail is that concerned with cognitive complexity–simplicity (Bieri, 1961). This is also a more specific conception than is Witkin's, and refers to structural differences in processing information concerning the behavior of others (Bieri et al., 1966). Having its conceptual antecedents in the cognitive personality theory of G. A. Kelly (1955), the concept of cognitive complexity is derived from the notion of *differentiation*, which, we shall see, has a long tradition in personality theory. Before undertaking a more detailed consideration of these three approaches to cognitive structure, let us turn to some necessary theoretical background which will place the ensuing discussion in the proper historical and systematic perspective.

THEORETICAL CONTEXTS FOR COGNITIVE STRUCTURES

The impetus for the increasing viability of cognitive structural concepts in personality theory has come from a variety of sources. The

notion that human behavior may be conceptualized in terms of an intervening variable concerned with a restructuring of stimulus information
is certainly not a recent concept in cognitive theory (Mandler and
Mandler, 1964). For our present purposes, we can identify and discuss
four important tributaries of this stream of endeavor, each of which has
continuing influence in the contemporary theoretical scene.

Psychoanalytic Ego Psychology

With the increasing emphasis in orthodox psychoanalytic theory upon
ego functioning (Hartmann, 1958), there has been an attempt to specify
in greater detail the aspects of the ego, much as earlier classical psychoanalytic theory focused on motivational roots of behavior. As Rapaport
(1959) has shown, an important concern in the newer ego psychology
has been the delineation of the nature of ego *structures,* both as to their
source or development and to their functioning in the personality. These
structures are assumed to be of two chief types, *primary* ego structures
and *secondary* ego structures. The latter are the more familiar *defensive*
structures of the ego which arise from conflicts experienced in the development of the individual, as discussed, for example, by Anna Freud
(1946). These defensive structures may, over time, become relatively
independent of the sources of conflict with which they developed and,
as a result of this change in function, can be identified as *structures of
secondary autonomy.* Such an idea of a shift in function had earlier
been developed by Allport in his conception of *functional autonomy*
(G. W. Allport, 1937).

Primary ego structures are considered to be *given* in personality, i.e.,
inherited or invariably associated with behavior on some constitutional
basis. These cognitive structures may be considered to represent the
functions of sensation, perception, memory, and such processes familiarly
of concern to the psychologist. Such structures of *primary autonomy*
may also partake of defensive energy and may have a supply of energy
of their own, such as neutralized libido or aggression, but the emphasis
in their functioning is upon their relative independence or autonomy
from drive systems. It seems evident that cognitive structures have
gained an important conceptual foothold upon contemporary psychoanalytic theorizing (Rapaport, 1957, 1959), even though the conceptualization is unresolved in terms of how and to what degree these structures
interact with motives and drives of the individual. In the discussion
below of cognitive controls in the work of Klein, Holzman, Gardner, and
others, we shall return to the psychoanalytic interpretation of cognitive
structures. What can be emphasized here is that the lack of clear conceptual resolution of the nature of the interactions between motivational

systems and cognitive systems in personality theory is a key theoretical concern in psychoanalytic ego psychology. Indeed, to date, psychoanalytic theory may have brought this issue closer to a clearer resolution than have other approaches.

Field Theory

A second major source of influence in theories of cognitive structures arises from those systematic positions which emphasize the organism's *cognitive representation* of the psychological environment as a key mediational variable in behavior. Lewin is perhaps the outstanding influence in this regard, although the conceptions put forth by Tolman were also of moment. The prime theoretical precursor of the field theoretical approach was Gestalt psychology, a systematic position which stressed the *organized* nature of perception. Such an organizational emphasis persists in many contemporary interpretations of cognitive structure, although there is perhaps more emphasis currently upon the learned nature of cognitive structures than the Gestalt position itself would have provided. Indeed, both Lewin and Tolman have been considered "learning theorists" (Hilgard, 1956). In discussing the nature of "cognitive maps," Tolman (1948) stressed the learning of mediational representations of the environment, and considered how motivational states could affect the learning of narrow or broad maps. Lewin (1951), in the realm of personality theory, considered that learning as a "change in knowledge" was a problem of the cognitive structure of the person. In specifying how previously unstructured areas of the *life space* became more cognitively structured, Lewin relied heavily upon the concept of *differentiation,* apparently attracted by the biological analog of this concept as well as the relative facility with which it can be represented mathematically (1951, p. 72). While Lewin considered that increasing differentiation was not the only reflection of learned changes in cognitive structures, it is clearly one aspect of the problem of structures on which he placed a major emphasis.

Basically, Lewin considered differentiation to occur when an increased number of regions or cells were generated in the cognitive structure of the individual. Lewin was impressed by the apparent increase in differentiation of the child's life space as development proceeded. The older child's greater behavioral versatility in the motor, intellectual, and social realms was considered strong presumptive evidence for this increased differentiation. At the same time, Lewin was careful to point to other aspects of the cognitive structure of the person which changed with age. In particular, he stressed the change in *simple dependence* among the parts of the structure. That is, for the younger child, a change in one region of the structure is more likely to influence other regions than in the older child. In developing this notion of simple dependence, we are aware of Lewin's concern to specify both the relative complexity of units of structure as well as their organization or interrelation. He carried this further by explicating a more sophisticated type of organization in the structure, in which *hierarchical* relationships are implicated. In general, he desired to keep the degree of hierarchical organization distinct from the differentiation and simple dependence of the structure.

In a commentary upon these ideas (Bieri, 1961), the writer noted that in wrestling with the relations of differentiation and organization of parts of a cognitive structure Lewin, in 1941, had touched upon an important conceptual issue still in need of further articulation. While this need for theoretical development currently exists, it is apparent that Lewin's fertile mind has laid a groundwork which subsequent workers should not ignore. Further, the fact that Lewin developed his notions of cognitive structure within the context of developmental analyses of regression and retrogression (1951, chap. 5) indicated the pervasive importance he attached to these structures in personality functioning. Indeed, it is noteworthy that Tolman also presented in his best known exposition of cognitive structures (1948) a discussion of their import in forms of defensive behavior.

Schema Theories

A third systematic basis for contemporary theories of cognitive structure arises from a set of independent developments in the rather disparate fields of child development and the social psychology of memory. We refer to the schema theories of a Swiss (Piaget) and an Englishman (Bartlett), both of whom were concerned with how experience became organized in some integrated fashion. For both theorists, this process of integration was facilitated by the learning of *schemata*, whose functions were inferred from observations and experiment.

Bartlett's conceptions of cognitive structures as schemata derived in part from Head's work in neurology, in which Head (1920) introduced the concept of schemata as ". . . organised models of ourselves which modify the impression produced by incoming sensory impulses. . . ." While he did not particularly care for the term "schema," Bartlett adapted it to explain how particular learning experiences of the person became organized in such a fashion as to influence the nature of his perceptions and memories of the physical and social environment (Bartlett, 1932). He considered a schema to be ". . . an active organisation of past reactions . . ." which influence ". . . incoming impulses of a certain kind, or mode, to go together to build up an active, organised setting. . . ." Two facets of Bartlett's analyses are worth emphasis here. First, he considered schemata to be *constructive* in character. That is, any given memory is not merely a literal reproduction of an earlier experience, but is elaborated and given idiosyncratic meaning in terms of the person's cognitive structure. Second, the person develops an *attitude* toward this organized past experience (schema) and the affect associated with this attitude assumes a major determining role in the reconstruction process of memory. We see, then, that Bartlett was impressed by the role of affect and feeling in the function of cognitive structures, and outlined a conception bearing striking similarities to psychoanalytic formulations of cognitive structure (Rapaport, 1957).

Piaget, another seminal theorist who invoked the concept of schema, used this notion as a focal construct in elaborating the nature of cognitive development. Piaget considered schemata to be defined by the types of behavior engaged in by the child, such as sucking, sight, and prehension. Like Lewin, Piaget emphasized the progressive differentiation of new structures throughout development: ". . . one sees how each new behavior pattern is formed by differentiation and adaptation of the preceding ones. One can follow the particular history of each schema through the successive stages of development, as the formation of structures cannot be dissociated from the historical development of experience" (Piaget, 1936). Noting the similarity of his idea of schema to that of a "Gestalt," Piaget was careful to point out essential differences between the two conceptions. First, he emphasized that schemata are learned and have a history of development. Further, a schema can be generalized to a much broader class of events than a "Gestalt." In common with a number of conceptions of cognitive structure, Piaget considers schemata to ". . . consist of mobile frames successively applied to various contents . . . ," whereas "Gestalten" are predetermined and are "imposed" upon the situation in a more obtrusive, immediately given manner. Thus, for Piaget, schemata are cognitive structures with plastic qualities, derived from assimilation of external stimuli but continually reorganizing into new schemata through "progressive differentiation."

The reader should consult Piaget (1936) as well as an exposition of his ideas by Flavell (1963). It is clear that Piaget stressed the dual role of differentiation and organization of cognitive structures in emphasizing how they may at once become more specific to certain behaviors but at the same time become organized within a broader network of interrelated structures. Later in this chapter, we shall return to these ideas in an attempt to project future developments in theories of cognitive structures.

Cognitive Personality Theories

The development of field theories and schema theories of cognitive structure was a precursor for the more pervasive transfer of structural notions to other major domains of theorizing. Hebb (1949), in his neuropsychological theory of behavior, reflected his structural bent in the title of his book *Organization of Behavior*. Starting from a neurological base, he evolved a scheme for a general theory of behavior which emphasized the organization of parts of a hypothetical neural structure into *assemblies*. These structures are further organized into phase sequences which, when they attain ". . . a certain degree of complexity . . . ," may be identified with states of consciousness. While Hebb considered in some detail the ramifications of his ideas of structure to certain areas of clinical psychology and personality, we may turn to other recent theorists for whom personality theory within a cognitive framework has been a major preoccupation.

Two major forms of cognitive personality theory can be identified as being conceptually akin to analyses of cognitive structure. One type which we shall mention briefly may be called "self" theories, in that the organizing structure for the personality is the self-concept of the individual. Rogers (1951) in particular exemplifies a theorist for whom experience was mediated by the self-regarding sentiments of the person (to use McDougall's phrase). Such a master structure of the self could be analyzed as having both cognitive and motivational properties, the latter leading to such ethereal drives as self-realization and self-actualization.

A more purely cognitive personality theory in which structural concepts assume a major role is Kelly's *psychology of personal constructs* (1955). Here the major premise is that behavior is channeled by the personal constructs of the individual. These constructs may be considered as miniature cognitive structures or subsystems which in turn are organized in an overall personal construct system. Kelly's use of the term *construct* is in part the reflection of a desire, like Bartlett's, to emphasize the *constructive* nature of our perception of the social world, or what Murray (1938) terms *apperception*. Each construct, however, has a bipolar quality, being a dimension along which the person construes the behavior of others, or of himself. If we consider each construct dimension as a structure within a larger cognitive system, then we can characterize types of substructures, and this is what Kelly has done. He speaks, for example, of *impermeable* constructs which admit no new elements, of *pre-emptive* constructs which are exclusive in nature, and of *constellatory* constructs which define members by a fixed set of attributes.

Constructs in turn are organized into a larger system, although these organizational principles are not easy to specify. Like Lewin, Kelly considers the subordinate–superordinate relation a particularly important principle of hierarchical organization. One unique aspect of Kelly's approach is the development of a method to assess the person's personal constructs, the Role Construct Repertory Test, or Rep Test. In a later section the use of this procedure to measure cognitive complexity as a structural variable will be discussed. For the present, it is sufficient to note that Kelly's framework places cognitive structure squarely in the center of a personality theory and represents, in a sense, an attempt to use such a concept as a major explanatory variable in behavior.

COGNITIVE CONTROLS

As was mentioned earlier, the work of Klein (1958), Holzman (1954), and Gardner (1953) represents the most distinctive attempt to develop a framework for conceptualizing cognitive structures within a psychoanalytic framework. More exactly, perhaps, their work reflects a delineation of cognitive structures as behavioral mechanisms against the *backdrop* of psychoanalysis. In their approach we may identify two major concerns. The first of these is the analysis of how cognitive structures modulate drives—hence the term cognitive controls. The second emphasis is upon the specification of the number and nature of cognitive controls in behavior.

Controls, Drives, and Defenses

In his discussion of "cognitive control and motivation," Klein (1958) has emphasized that cognitive structures serve to regulate the expression of drives so as to bring these drives into realistic accommodation to the perceived demands of the situation at hand. He states:

> Cognitive structures are indispensable to this general accommodative effort involving action and an informational return from objects. . . . [structures] are provided with means of imposing an order upon receptor events which will accord with the relatively constant attributes of objects and events. (Klein, 1958, p. 93.)

It is clear from the above that cognitive controls (previously called cognitive attitudes) serve an adaptive function by steering, as it were, goal-oriented behavior into appropriate channels determined by the nature of the task or situation facing the individual. Klein, in common with contemporary psychoanalytic ego-psychology (Gill, 1959), thus provides cognitive structures with the status of independent variables in behavior which exert a controlling function over the specific forms which drive-induced behavior may assume. He states (Klein, 1958, p. 99): "The idea of drive as a *meaning-including* field of activity implemented by *accommodative structures* makes it easier to use the concept of drive to account for behavior." In terms of psychoanalytic theory cognitive structures act as controls which bring the primary process functioning into the secondary process mode of functioning. In this sense, then, Klein considers drives and cognitive controls as inextricably linked, and one cannot be studied without the other.

Two questions arise at this point. Do different drives have associated with them different types of controls or structures? How many types of controls are normally operative in behavior? Delaying the answer to the second question for the moment, we may say in relation to the first that in general different drives are not associated with specific cognitive structures. Rather, the invocation of a particular cognitive structure is more dependent upon the nature of the *adaptive task* confronting the individual and, in common with other conceptions of cognitive structure, it is assumed that a limited number of structures can be identified to meet a variety of task requirements.

On the other hand, certain ways in which any particular structure or control is developed *may* be related to the *form of conflict* generated by particular drives. For example, characterological traits generated by anal conflicts in the obsessive–compulsive syndrome may be associated with a more pronounced tendency to develop *sharpening* mechanisms in perceptual discrimination tasks which elicit the leveling–sharpening control principle. Later in the chapter we shall turn to a consideration of these developmental factors in the acquisition of cognitive structures.

An empirical example of the interaction of drive and cognitive structure in behavior is provided by the experiment reported by Klein (1954). A control principle of *constricted–flexible* was invoked on the basis of performance on Stroop's color-naming task. This technique requires the individual to read the names of colors printed in incongruous color names such that the flexible control subject has less difficulty in reading the colors quickly than does the constricted person. Both the constricted and the flexible groups of subjects were assigned to either a thirsty experimental treatment (spicy, tempting meal without water) or the same meal with water (sated condition). Subjects then performed in four cognitive tasks, one of which (size reproduction) concerns us here. In adjusting a variable circle to a standard disc containing thirst-related or neutral symbols, it was found that flexible control subjects overestimated the size of the standard while underestimation was characteristic of the constricted subjects. More importantly, these differences were more marked for the thirsty than for the sated subjects, indicating that the drive served only to exaggerate differences in coping styles which were already in evidence under the sated condition. While other details of this study dictate caution in generalizing these results, this research is noteworthy for its simultaneous activation of motivational and cognitive structural variables in studying their joint effect in behavior.

As Gardner et al. (1959) have noted, the study outlined above has merely broached the problem of the specific interactive relations of drives, defenses, and cognitive structures. They point out that while controls may share similar functions to defenses in terms of modulating drive-discharge processes so as to accord with the established modes of adapting to situational demands, defenses and controls must be considered as somewhat separate processes. Rapaport (1957, 1959), for example, makes it clear that controls may have certain structural bases in personality *prior to* and *independent of* the development of defenses. For example, individual differences in perceptual, motor, and memorial functioning may be important precursors to the development of more elaborate forms of information processing. In psychoanalytic theory, these bases of cognitive structures are considered to reside in *primary* autonomous ego functioning. At the same time, however, the development of defensive strategies can also lead to various forms of cognitive structures. These structures may become relatively independent of the drives which generated the original defenses, in a manner akin to G. W. Allport's functional autonomy (1937) and Lewin's ossification (1951). These sources of controls from *secondary* autonomous ego functions pose several major conceptual problems still facing adequate resolution. Foremost, we must ask, how do these primary and secondary sources of controls interact in producing specific structures? Are different structures associated with defensive sources of controls than are associated with primary sources of controls? To date, little conceptual or empirical progress has been made in this direction.

Number and Types of Controls

Perhaps the most systematic effort to conceptually define and empirically isolate *types* of cognitive controls is found in the work of Gardner et al. (1959). These workers were concerned with the more precise empirical analysis of a number of cognitive controls as well as the study of the organization of these controls into superordinate structures, defined earlier by Klein (1958) as *cognitive styles*. They write:

Cognitive controls are . . . slow-changing, developmentally stabilized structures . . . relatively invariant across a given class of situations and intentions. . . . Cognitive controls refer to a level of organization that is more general than the specific structural components underlying perception, recall, and judgment. The invariant which defines a control has to do with the manner of coordination between a class of adaptive intentions and a class of environmental situations. (Gardner et al., 1959, pp. 5–6.)

Two considerations are important in the above definition of controls. First, controls have a range of *generality* across tasks, so that more than one empirical measure can be developed for each control principle. Second, the intention of the subject in a task is a key aspect of the control under study. Thus, in the same task, the subject could be set either to *recall* a series of stimuli or to *discriminate* among a series of stimuli. To the extent that generality of task requirements implies overlap among controls, and to the extent that intentions are shared among diverse tasks, it is evident that interrelations among controls will be found. The parallel case is found in the factor-analytic approach to the identification of so-called primary mental abilities, each of which has some orthogonal status but at the same time shares varying degrees of overlap with the other intellectual abilities. Indeed, Gardner et al. (1959) used factor analysis in their effort to analyze the varieties of control principles.

Five basic controls were analyzed by these researchers. The first of these, leveling–sharpening, was measured by the schematizing test and a kinesthetic time-error test. Tolerance for unrealistic experience, a second control principle, was assessed from behavior on an apparent movement task and indices derived from reactions to aniseikonic lenses. To measure the third control variable, equivalence range, behavior on an object-sorting test and a size constancy task was used. Focusing control was measured by a size estimation procedure and by a picture-sorting task. The fifth control principle, constricted–flexible, referred to above in the work by Klein (1954), was assessed by the Stroop color-word test, as well as by tasks involving incidental recall, size estimation, and free association. In addition, measures designed to assess Witkin's cognitive structural variable of field dependence–independence (rod and frame test and embedded figures test) were given to the subjects.

Using scores derived from these tasks, intercorrelations were factor-analyzed separatedly for the 30 men and 30 women in the study. While each of the five controls appeared in the obtained factors of either men or women, some variability between sexes was found. For example, both leveling–sharpening and equivalence range were represented in factors for women but not for men. In contrast, tolerance for unrealistic experience and scanning (focusing control) were found in the factor structure of males but not for females. Gardner et al. regard these sex differences as possible accidents of sampling, although as we shall see later in this chapter, sex differences in cognitive structures may provide one avenue for the further understanding of the development of structures.

To explore the possibility that controls may be organized into more unitary aggregates called cognitive styles, Gardner et al. used the obtained factor dimensions to *cluster* individuals with common combinations of factor scores. If these clusters do represent an emergent, superordinate level of cognitive structure, more consensus in the response to other tasks should be found for individuals sharing a common cluster than for individuals with extreme scores on the constituent factors. To examine this possibility, responses to an inventory of 234 quite diverse behavioral items were analyzed. Support for the greater behavioral consistency of clusters (styles) than for individual controls was found in women but not in men. The authors indicate that these findings tend to argue against assuming there is a sharpening *type*, or an extensive scanning type, as do the findings that the same control may appear in two clearly distinguishable combinations or clusters. However, they recognise that the greater predictive utility of the style hypothesis awaits more explicit empirical test.

Controls and Personality

The work of Klein, Gardner, and their colleagues points toward the potential integration of cognitive controls into the more extensive matrix of personality functioning involving drives, conflicts, and defenses. To date, we may assess the progress as improving delineation of the initial theoretical formulations and the mapping of tentative empirical characteristics of controls as cognitive structures. While we may evaluate the results to date as promising, particularly in the attempt to conceptualize controls in the context of *total* personality functioning, more sophisticated and extensive empirical analysis of the relations between controls and both drives and defenses remains a major task for future research. For example, Holzman and Gardner (1959) have attempted to relate leveling tendencies and repression. They predicted that those who tend to make assimilative errors (levelers) in a perceptual discrimination task (schematizing test) involving size judgments of squares use repression as a more characteristic defense than those who manifest sharpening tendencies. Even though a small number of subjects was used, and the adequacy of the sole use of the Rorschach as a criterion of repression may be questioned, some support for their expectation was found.

Again, it can be maintained that such isolated empirical morsels should serve to whet our research appetites for more intensive analysis of these problems of control mechanisms in personality functioning.

ANALYTIC–GLOBAL STRUCTURES

In contrast to the efforts of Gardner, Klein, and others to isolate the functioning of a number of cognitive controls, Witkin has, since the early forties, been concerned with elucidating the operation of a single, major dimension of cognitive functioning which he has referred to variously as the global–analytic dimension, the field dependent–independent dimension, or the dimension of degree of differentiation. His productive research has yielded numerous publications and two books, *Personality Through Perception* (Witkin et al., 1954) and *Psychological Differentiation* (Witkin et al., 1962). We have here perhaps the most extensive program of investigation concerning the operation of cognitive structures in personality.

Theoretical Background

Analysis of Witkin's work indicates he has not proceeded from a fixed theoretical base upon which his research program was built. Rather, he has proceeded systematically to explore and refine the measurement of his basic construct of field dependence–independence, and to demonstrate its empirical relationship to a number of aspects of behavior and personality functioning. This empirical nexus has led him to induce certain systematic principles concerning the nature of field dependent–independent personalities and to explore further relationships consistent with these principles. This interweaving of empirical and theoretical activity might give the impression that Witkin has not as yet lifted his work from the empirical to the theoretical plane (Zigler, 1963), but it is perhaps more accurate to say that Witkin has opted to elaborate the empirical position of a *single* theoretical construct so as to demonstrate its pervasive role in personality functioning.

Witkin's concept of field dependence stresses the ability or inability of an individual to articulate perceptually the various aspects of his experience. Specifically, he states:

> The person with a more field-dependent way of perceiving tends to experience his surroundings in a relatively global fashion, passively conforming to the influence of the prevailing field or context. (Witkin et al., 1962, p. 35.)

The field-independent person possesses a more differentiated, analytical approach to his world and can better discriminate between figure and ground in his perceptual behavior. It is important to realize that such distinctions are meant to imply a deep-seated, basic stylistic difference among persons in their cognitive functioning in a wide variety of important behaviors.

Measurement of Field Dependence

From a wider array of methods, Witkin has evolved a basic battery of three experimental techniques which in the aggregate yield an index of global–analytic perceptual functioning. The most elaborate of these is the *tilting room task*, in which the subject must adjust his body position to the upright when surrounded by a room which has been rotated to one side or the other. The *rod-and-frame test* is a second method, and consists of a square frame which is rotated off center. Again, the task of the subject is to adjust a rod superimposed on the frame to a vertical or upright position. The third technique, the *embedded figures test* (EFT), has been used most commonly because of its relative technical simplicity and ease of administration. Patterned after the figures used by Gottschaldt, the task of the subject is to locate a simple geometric figure embedded in a more complex design or pattern. Versions of this test suitable for administration to younger children, as well as forms for group administration, have been devised.

Witkin et al. (1962) report moderate intercorrelations among these three indices of field dependence. However, while these correlations are significant, usually ranging from .30 to .50, they are not of such a high magnitude as to allow one to consider the tests as unequivocally interchangeable.

Developmental and Personality Correlates

In their initial volume, Witkin et al. (1954) report rather consistent changes in these various measures of field dependence as a function of age. It was observed, for example, that a progressive decrease in field dependence occurred from ages eight to fifteen, especially in relation to performance on the tilting room task and the EFT. Witkin et al. (1962) interpret these findings as reflecting the increasing ability of the child to *differentiate* his environment. This process of *differentiation* is assumed to proceed from an initial base of discriminating the self from the environment, and includes the progressive articulation of a body image as well as a more refined differentiation of the external environment.[1] This analysis of the "sense of separate identity" is related to a

---

[1] D. E. Hunt (1965) has advanced a similar conception stemming from a conceptual systems analysis of personality development (Harvey et al., 1961).

variety of empirical studies of the relation of field dependency to such phenomena as dependency upon others (Gordon, 1953; Bell, 1955), conformity to group pressure (Linton, 1952; Linton & Graham, 1959), and such dispositions as authoritarianism (Bieri, 1960; Rudin & Stagner, 1958) and need for approval (Konstadt & Forman, 1965). In his own work, Witkin has emphasized the evaluation of children's analytic and structuring tendencies in such areas of performance as TAT productions, Rorschach, interview behavior, and figure drawing (Witkin et al., 1962). This last type of behavior is assumed by Witkin to reflect the child's articulation of his body concept, and has been studied by comparing the figure drawings of children of varying ages with indices of field dependency. Using a "sophistication scale" as an index for evaluating children's articulation of body concept in drawings, Witkin et al. (1962) report correlations of substantial magnitude with perceptual indices of field dependence, although, as we shall note below, comparable correlations were also found between the sophistication index and children's I.Q. on the Wechsler Intelligence Scale (WISC).

Sex Differences and Intelligence

It has long been noted that many cognitive variables of interest to the personality theorist are often associated with sex differences and intellectual functioning (Maccoby, 1966), and perceptual indices of field dependence are no exception in this regard. Following Witkin's initial report (1949) of sex differences in field dependence–independence, a number of other studies have indicated that females are more field-dependent than males. These studies have ranged from children at the eight-year level (Witkin et al., 1959) to college-age populations (Bieri et al., 1958). The nature of the bases for this sex difference has not been adequately resolved, and various alternatives have been advanced, including experimental factors such as sex-role learning and constitutional factors associated with biological differences between the sexes (Witkin et al., 1962).

Possibly closely linked to sex differences in field dependence is the role of intellectual factors. The work of Witkin and his associates, as well as that of others, makes it clear that certain intelligence measures and indices of field dependence are often substantially correlated. Witkin et al. (1962) report that among ten-year-olds, an aggregate score of the block-design, picture-completion, and object-assembly subtests of the WISC correlated +.66 with the perceptual index, while the correlation with such verbal subtests as vocabulary and comprehension was much lower and nonsignificant. Using college subjects, Bieri et al. (1958) also found verbal measures of academic aptitude to be less correlated with EFT performance than an index of quantitative aptitude.

Such findings have been reported rather frequently and have led some to assert that differences in the cognitive structure of field dependence are "merely" intellectual differences. It certainly does not clarify the situation, however, to assert that "intelligence" explains such differences, particularly when the nature of intelligence is itself an unsettled proposition. Indeed, Witkin et al. (1962) believe many intellectual measures incorporate aspects of cognitive structures, and state that the reported association between field dependence and intelligence test scores is due to the fact that many portions of such tests require analytical functioning. Again, as in the case of sex differences, the association between field dependence and nonverbal intelligence measures awaits fuller conceptual clarification. It is intriguing, as a base for such clarification, to consider that males often tend to do better than females on tests of quantitative ability, males are more field-independent, and field independence is more closely associated with quantitative ability than with verbal abilities. It is possible that an adequate understanding of the bases of these interrelations will provide increased conceptual richness to the role of cognitive structural functioning in such diverse realms of personality as intelligence and sex-role behavior.

Overview of Field Dependence

It is apparent from the above review that Witkin has conceptualized field dependence–independence as a core construct in personality functioning. He has diligently analyzed its relation to a wide variety of behaviors, and indeed has explored its relationship to various forms of pathological behavior. Karp et al. (1965) have discussed its possible involvement in alcoholism, for example, and in more extended form Witkin (1965) has discussed the possible role of this cognitive structural principle in pathology generally. It seems evident that if we assume such a central role for field dependence, the complexity of phenomena we wish to explain demands that additional mediating variables be invoked in the network of theoretical constructs. Even if one delimits the theoretical generality of field dependence, we have seen that further conceptual growth is necessary if one is to understand its relation to intellectual functioning, for example.

Fortunately, one possible avenue for this conceptual growth is seen in Witkin's work and in the research of others to be mentioned later in this chapter. This pathway is the emphasis on *developmental* studies of cognitive structures. At present we are barely more than on the threshold of this work, although as we have noted, the contributions of Lewin and Piaget provide an important background for this effort. Such a developmental strategy would seem to offer at once a more simple organism for study as well as the opportunity to examine more precisely the relation of cognitive structures to such integral psychological processes as language formation, sex-role learning, identification, and intellectual development.

COGNITIVE COMPLEXITY–SIMPLICITY

The central focus of the structure of cognitive complexity is upon the ability of the individual to differentiate the behavior of others. Such a structure is intended to have a more limited range of generality than some of those discussed previously in that it deals exclusively with the processing of information about the *social* world. The more cognitively complex individual is assumed to have available a greater number of dimensions with which to construe the behavior of others than the less cognitively complex person. This conception of relative differentiation of the social environment, while it has antecedents—as we have seen in the work of Lewin, among others—springs most directly from the systematic framework of G. A. Kelly's *Psychology of Personal Constructs* (1955). In his exposition of the differentiation of the individual's personal construct *system*, and more particularly in his presentation of the empirical analysis of the structural characteristics of this system, Kelly employed a variant of factor analysis. Subsequently, Bieri (1955) introduced the concept of cognitive complexity–simplicity, based upon a different analytic method, but intending to reflect the idea that the cognitively complex person has available more construct dimensions than does the cognitively simple individual.

Measurement of Cognitive Complexity

Perhaps the most common method for assessing degree of cognitive complexity has been the row-matching technique first reported by Bieri (1955) and subsequently modified in more recent research (Bieri et al., 1966, chap. 7). Essentially, the subject is presented with a matrix or grid across the top of which he is asked to write in the names of specified persons from his personal life, including parents, relatives, and friends. The rows of the grid represent personal constructs or bipolar trait dimensions, such as outgoing–shy, and adjusted–maladjusted. The subject is asked to rate all of the persons in turn on each of the construct dimensions, using a six-category rating scale. The similarity of the ratings in each row to the ratings in every other row is compared and a numerical index is generated as indicative of relative cognitive complexity.

Further details on this procedure can be found in Bieri (1965) and Bieri et al. (1966).

Types of Empirical Studies

Such a cognitive structure would appear to have explanatory power in a variety of behavioral situations, and it is undoubtedly this feature which has led to the large number of empirical studies of cognitive complexity. In an earlier review of the research and theoretical issues surrounding this concept, Bieri (1961) pointed out that problems of measurement and conceptualization remain to be clarified in the study of cognitive complexity. In his more recent review focused on the assessment issues, Bieri (1965) notes a continuing need for such clarification, although significant steps in resolving measurement problems can be seen. A number of sources present detailed analyses of the variety of empirical work using this concept (Bieri et al., 1966; Bonarius, 1965; Crockett, 1965), and the interested reader is referred to these sources for more detailed reports of research which cannot be presented here. We can, however, indicate the variety of topics which have been studied in relation to cognitive complexity in the past ten years.

Accuracy of Judgment. Because the more cognitively complex person has available more dimensions with which to construe his social world, the assumption is reasonable that he should be more "accurate" in his perceptions of others. Such an hypothesis was studied by Bieri (1955) who found that more complex judges tended to perceive *differences* between the self and others more accurately, but this relation did not hold for the accurate judgment of similarities between self and others. Such a tendency for complex judges to perceive differences more accurately was also noted by Leventhal (1957). It is of interest to speculate on the characterological correlates of this possible disposition for more complex judges to predict differences accurately, including perhaps more compulsive defenses, isolation tendencies, and mild paranoid trends. As we shall note below, only scant evidence on personality correlates of cognitive complexity is available at present. Sechrest and Jackson (1961) also analyzed in some detail the relation of cognitive complexity (which they construed within the broader context of "social intelligence") and judgmental accuracy, and generally found little association. It seems clear that given the difficulties of obtaining unambiguous measures of global accuracy, future research might more reasonably focus on directional tendencies or biases in predictions by high and low cognitively complex judges, as in the work cited above on perceived similarities and differences.

Behavior Change. The relation of cognitive complexity to the processing of *sequential* information has been of concern in a number of investigations. Leventhal (1957) found that with increasing amounts of information, gain in accuracy of predictions about another was more marked in cognitively less complex judges than in more complex judges. It is interesting that in this type of task one could consider the more complex judge as more "rigid" in the sense that he may display less tendency to shift hypotheses about another with the availability of new information. That such a formulation cannot stand without further elaboration is indicated by the study of Lundy and Berkowitz (1957) in the attitude realm. These researchers studied the effects of persuasive information upon attitude change and observed that the low complex judges changed least while the most complex judges responded with a boomerang effect in that they increased the intensity of their initial attitudes.

Inconsistent Information. An important tactic in analyzing the relation of cognitive complexity to information processing is the specification of the nature of the information being judged. One such parameter is the relative consistency or, as it is sometimes referred to, univalence of the information. Bieri (1968) has summarized the research in the area of information inconsistency and cognitive complexity which has been of interest to a number of investigators. Mayo and Crockett (1964) presented contradictory sequential information by first presenting behavior about another that was positive in nature, for example, and then presenting negative behavioral information. Judgments were made after each presentation. It was found that low complex judges attempted to form a more univalent impression by changing their initial judgments toward the most recent (contradictory) information. High complex judges, on the other hand, retained both types of information in their impression, producing ambivalent judgments of the other. Crockett (1965) has recently reported two similar unpublished investigations by Rosenkrantz and by Supnick. Similar effects were obtained for males but not for females by the former investigator, while the latter found inconsistent relationships between cognitive complexity and impressions. Leventhal and Singer (1964) also studied the resolution of inconsistent information by high, moderate, and low complex judges in an elaborate investigation which included certainty judgments as well. Low complex judges reported initially more clarity about their judgments than did high complex judges and the former group became more uncertain following the presentation of inconsistent information. It should be noted that the Rep Test method of assessing cognitive complexity was not used in all of these studies.

Personality Correlates.   Research which attempts to place the cognitive structure of complexity—simplicity within a broader network of personality functioning has yet to be undertaken in any systematic fashion. Bieri (1965) has discussed several personality variables which would appear to have some relation to cognitive complexity, including indices of personal adjustment, extroversion, social desirability, and intelligence. An overview of a number of studies suggested that general measures of neurotic or anxiety symptomatology relate slightly positively to complexity, i.e., more complex judges tend to be more neurotic. Several suggestive studies have indicated that extroversion, as indexed by the scale developed by Eysenck, may be characteristic of the more cognitively simple individual. These results, while in need of further substantiation, indicate that cognitive complexity does not develop as a function of sheer *amount* of contact with others, assuming that the more extroverted individual comes in contact with a greater number of others than the introvert. Indeed, *quality* of interpersonal relations may be a decisive factor, as suggested in several recent studies in which the positive and negative qualities of others were studied. Miller and Bieri (1965) found, for example, that more negative, socially distant persons were construed more complexly than were more positive persons. Irwin et al. (1967) have also found in two additional studies that scores indicative of higher cognitive complexity are generated when negatively valued persons are judged. Crockett (1965) has reported a study by Supnick which obtained results opposite to these, but it seems likely that differences in method may account for this discrepancy.

Related to the positive or negative quality of the persons being judged is the tendency of the persons to react in a socially desirable manner. Using the Marlowe–Crowne scale, Bieri (1965) has reported that more socially desirable responding is associated with less cognitive complexity. This relationship between social desirability and cognitive complexity can be interpreted by considering the Marlowe–Crowne scale as a measure of need for social approval or conformity (Crowne & Marlowe, 1964). It is plausible that a person who is strongly motivated to obtain approval from others would tend to emphasize similarities between himself and others. Indeed, one might speculate that this could be the origin, developmentally, for pronounced tendencies to perceive similarities between oneself and others. Such an interpretation gains some support from an analysis of sex differences in relation to this problem. Bieri (1965) reported, for example, that in one sample of college students the correlation between social desirability scores and cognitive complexity was less pronounced for males than it was for females. This relationship might be part of a wider picture of general conservatism and conformity among female subjects who are less cognitively complex. For example, in addition to social desirability, it was found among females that both authoritarianism and dogmatism correlated significantly with cognitive complexity scores, while no significant relationships between these variables and complexity were found for males.

In the aggregate, these findings provide a tentative base for hypothesizing about the personality structures associated with high and low complex persons. More cognitively complex individuals may have more introversive, obsessive-neurotic character structure while the less complex person may have more of an extroversive, repressive type of disposition. The introversion–extroversion dichotomy as expounded by Eysenck in more recent years is but one of a number of conceptualizations of defensive structure which may warrant more detailed examination in relation to cognitive complexity. Such concepts as repression–sensitization (Byrne, 1964) and the cognitive structure of leveling–sharpening which we discussed earlier in this chapter also come to mind. Further research, aimed in particular at the developmental aspects of such relations (Bieri, 1966), is needed to develop the more detailed structure of the role of cognitive complexity in personality functioning. An alternative way to conceptualize the relation between cognitive complexity and conflict uses concepts of information theory, to which we shall now turn.

Information Theory and Cognitive Complexity

The use of information theory in judgment research generally, and in personality research specifically, has been presented in some detail recently by Bieri et al. (1966). It is important to realize that information theory may be used in two ways, and the following discussion of research with cognitive complexity will exemplify both possibilities. First, we may use the informational *methods of analysis* classically associated with information theory. Such statistical modes of analysis will be considered in studies of the relation of cognitive complexity to the transmission of information in the judgment of multidimensional stimuli. Second, we may use information theory in a more substantive way. Following the inventive beginning of Garner (1962), we may speak of *structure* as a property of both the task and the person. Let us turn initially to this latter application of information theory.

Perceived Conflict and Certainty. We may assume that the amount of structure, defined in informational terms, residing in the cognitive system of the more complex individual is greater than that of the less complex person. That is, the greater number of alternative dimensions available to the more cognitively complex person is equivalent to a greater degree of internal structure of his system (Garner, 1962). Given this assumption, it is plausible that when asked to interpret an ambiguous social stimulus, as in a Thematic Apperception Test, the more complex judge will project greater structure. Such structure can take the form of conflict, since by definition a more conflicting response has greater structure than does a less conflicting response (Berlyne, 1960). This expectation that the more complex judge will project more conflict into his thematic productions than will a less complex judge can also be linked to the former's greater certainty in judging inconsistent information. That is, inconsistent information possesses greater structure than does consistent information, and one would expect greater confidence when judging information consonant with one's own structure. Such ideas were studied by Tripodi and Bieri (1966), who asked subjects to tell stories about imaginary stimulus persons, a task akin to the TAT. Each subject's stories were scored for degree of interpersonal conflict, and it was found that the more cognitively complex judges did tell stories with significantly more conflict than did the less complex judges. Further, when judges were asked to rate their certainty in judging information which was either consistent or inconsistent in nature, high complex judges were significantly more certain of their judgments of the more inconsistent information than they were of the more consistent information, while low complex judges did not have significantly different certainty estimates with the two types of information.

While the results of this study suggest a cognitive structural basis for the expression of conflict in fantasy behavior, such an influence may either be in lieu of or in addition to any projection of "intrapsychic" conflict. The tendency for more cognitively complex subjects to manifest greater conflict in thematic productions is consistent with the results reported by Leventhal and Singer (1964) who found that in an impression formation task high complex subjects sought information related to inner states such as maladjustment while low complex subjects responded more to surface qualities of behavior. Employing a different conception of cognitive structure, Sieber and Lanzetta (1964) also note a tendency for more "abstract" subjects to entertain more conflicting hypotheses in a problem-solving task.

Of course, it is possible that more complex judges perceive greater conflict as a function of more conflict in their personality structure. As we noted above, the evidence to date suggests only slight relationships between measures related to personal conflict, such as the Taylor Manifest Anxiety Scale, and cognitive complexity. In conclusion, then, we may interpret the results of this study as suggesting that a person's tendency to perceive conflict and his certainty in judging conflicting information are dual aspects of an underlying personality disposition to seek congruency between internal and external structure. The individual may prefer those stimulus situations which provide optimal matching between the internal (cognitive) structure and the external (stimulus) structure.

Information Transmission and Multidimensional Stimuli. The use of informational analysis in studying cognitive behavior has leaned heavily on the concept of *channel capacity*, the notion that there is an upper bound to the amount of information the human observer can process. We are most familiar with this *noisy channel* idea in the realm of sensory judgments. A large number of studies have indicated that the ability to discriminate among an array of sensory stimuli is relatively limited, ranging from approximately five to nine discriminations for simple unitary continua (G. A. Miller, 1956; Attneave, 1959; Garner, 1962; Bieri et al., 1966). As stimuli become more multidimensional, increases in information transmission are commonly observed, and yet until fairly recently the empirical analysis of the capacity of the judge to discriminate more complex social stimuli has been rare. One early attempt to analyze discrimination of clinical stimuli was reported by Miller and Bieri (1963). Using capsule descriptions of client behavior, these writers found that increasing the combination of types of stimuli had little effect on information transmission. Subsequently, an increased number of studies have concentrated on information transmission using both clinical and social stimuli and have been reviewed by Bieri et al. (1966).

It would seem reasonable to assume that judges who are high or low in cognitive complexity should differ in the ability to transmit information about social stimuli which vary in dimensionality. Tripodi and Bieri (1964) have studied this problem using judgments of pathology with three behavioral dimensions: aggression, body anxiety, and social withdrawal. Subjects who were either high or low in cognitive complexity judged stimulus items of behavior which varied from one dimension (e.g., aggression) to two dimensions (aggression + withdrawal) to three dimensions (aggression + withdrawal + anxiety). Further, for some judges, stimulus dimensions were combined in a *consistent* manner while for others an *inconsistent* mode of combining dimensions was used. In this latter condition the judge would receive contradictory information in that, for example, an aggressive stimulus indicating high pathology might be combined with a withdrawal stimulus indicating low pathology.

Overall, it was found that subjects were able to make about four reliable discriminations (two *bits*) in their judgments, with the most apparent increase in information transmission occurring as the number of dimensions involved increased from two to three. However, this increase was significant only for judges who were low in cognitive complexity. These results may be compared with those of Leventhal (1957), who found that low complex judges improved their predictions as a function of increased stimulus information. The results of Tripodi and Bieri do suggest that less cognitively complex judges gain more discriminability with increased dimensionality in the stimulus than more complex judges. However, across most stimulus conditions, it was observed that the more complex judges did discriminate better than did the less cognitively complex judges. In particular, this advantage was observed in relation to the judgment of incongruent or inconsistent information. Judges who were more complex transmitted significantly more information *as a group* than did less complex judges.

An analysis of judges' confidence ratings in this study sheds further light on differences between complexity groups. It was observed that more cognitively complex judges were less confident of their judgments in all stimulus conditions save those in which inconsistent information was presented. In judging these incongruent stimuli, subjects who were more complex tended to be most confident while low complexity subjects were least confident. The reader will note that these results are compatible with those of Tripodi and Bieri (1966) discussed in the previous section as well as with those of Leventhal and Singer (1964) mentioned earlier. We have been able to accrue, then, evidence suggesting that the more cognitively complex person feels more confident in judging conflicting information, has more inclination to discriminate more finely among conflicting stimuli, and in a free response situation is more prone to construct conflicting themes than his less cognitively complex peer.

It is apparent that no simple generalizations are to be drawn at this juncture concerning individual differences in processing information about others as a function of cognitive complexity. However, the results of research to date indicate that a careful specification of the nature of the stimulus, in terms of its relative dimensionality and the degree of consistency it contains, as well as attention to the type of response demanded of the subject, can lead to greater understanding of this cognitive structural variable in personality functioning. Such understanding will probably be most useful if it is obtained by studying the interaction of cognitive complexity with other personality variables, including those discussed in an earlier section. Such a strategy of research, involving more systematic attention to task variables and more complicated interactions with other personality dispositions, would appear to hold most promise for the future.

UNRESOLVED CONCEPTUAL ISSUES IN
COGNITIVE STRUCTURES

It has been pointed out that the problems associated with an adequate conceptualization of cognitive structure bear striking resemblance to those associated with the concept of motive or need. We may ask, for example, *how many* such structures do we need to postulate? It seems likely that no simple answer to this question is possible. Rather, we must attend to the entire array of variables postulated in a conception of personality. The work of Klein, Gardner, and others on cognitive styles, perhaps because it is embedded in the more intricate framework of psychoanalytic theory, has evolved a more numerous list of structural variables than some other approaches. For example, neither Witkin's field dependence variable nor the work with cognitive complexity has generated as yet a systematic set of related constructs which would provide the basis for incorporating coordinating cognitive structures within the framework of personality being evolved.

However, related to this problem is the relative *generality* or *specificity* of those structures which are posited. Just as theories of personality may posit master motives, such as self-actualization, so too is there a proclivity to assume that one cognitive structure has primary control over the processing of information from the environment. Again, the work of Witkin is perhaps the clearest example of this conceptual approach. At the other extreme, the attempt to delineate a number of discrete structures is characteristic of much of the work of Gardner and Klein discussed earlier. What stance should be taken on this matter? It seems likely that some middle ground is most useful. On the one hand, while a single master structure reduces considerably the theoretical intricacy of our explanations of behavior, this parsimony may be bought at the price of more rigorous prediction in specific situations. Extreme specificity, on the other hand, carries one to the position of positing a new cognitive structure for each new task, leading to a proliferation that can be both chaotic and conceptually sterile.

The key to this issue may lie in how one conceptualizes *organization* among cognitive structures. It is feasible that just as a motive or need which is "primary" in character may come to subsume a variety of subordinate needs, so too a fundamental structural disposition such as field dependence may operate to organize a range of less general structures. It should be pointed out, however, that to date success in identifying such organizational linkages in cognitive styles has not been marked. For example, such a concept as "problem-solving rigidity" has yielded a wide variety of subtypes of empirically defined rigidity scales, none of which have been strongly interrelated or organized within a broader measure of rigidity (Scott, 1966). Similarly, in the area of cognitive complexity, it seems likely from the evidence to date that ability to differentiate among social stimuli will differ from stimulus realm to stimulus realm. Versatility in differentiating among dimensions of social behavior, for example, need not imply comparable ability to differentiate among attitudes toward social issues.

We probably must push this analysis one step further, however, and recognize that an adequate understanding of the variety, generality, and organization of cognitive structures in personality is not likely to be attained until more systematic attention is given to *developmental* studies. Some of the issues involved in the developmental analysis of cognitive structures have been discussed elsewhere (Bieri, 1966; Kessen & Kuhlman, 1962; Wright & Kagan, 1963), but it must be recognized that several different conceptual stands can be taken in regard to the problem. One can assume, for example, that a given structure has invariant *continuity* over the period of development, such that the young child manifests field-dependent behavior and continues to display such behavior throughout his life even though this disposition might change in intensity at different developmental periods. A second approach would emphasize the *stage-like* development of a cognitive structure, such that individuals who had previously developed one structure "moved," as it were, into a next stage of structural development. The work of Harvey et al. (1961) in plotting stages of cognitive development from the concrete mode of functioning to the abstract mode is of this sort. And, of course, the work of Piaget places primary emphasis upon such sequential stages of cognitive development. Finally, we may extend this stage conception to a third approach, in which cognitive structures would be assumed to develop as previously discrete processes become organized into a functional system. For example, cognitive complexity depends upon such prior cognitive capacities as the ability to discriminate magnitudes, the ability to categorize discrete individuals, the ability to use language, and so forth. There is probably a point in development at which cognitive structures emerge from the fusion of pre-existing structures, and a conception which emphasizes essential continuity over time or simple stage-like progression could overlook such a course of structural development.

METHODOLOGICAL ISSUES

The student of cognitive structures in personality runs afoul of a goodly crop of methodological thorns, many of which have yet to be eliminated. While detailed analyses of some of these problems have been presented by Bieri (1965; 1966), Bieri et al. (1966), and Scott (1963), several persistent issues can be mentioned here. A major problem arises from the lack of comparability of different measures used to index the same cognitive structure. This measurement problem involves two fundamental decisions facing the investigator. First, he must decide upon a specific *task* with which to obtain the judgments or social perceptions considered central to the structure. This choice may involve one of a number of methods, including paired comparisons, absolute judgments, rank-order judgments, object sorting, concept formation, and so on. Generally our theories of personality are too vague to form the basis for selecting a specific assessment task, and to date we have all too little evidence on the comparability of alternative methods, although Witkin and his colleagues have been particularly active in this regard.

Having selected a particular measurement format, the second decision entails selecting an analytic method or mode of empirical analysis for arriving at scores or indices of structure. Thus, given the same task, such as absolute judgments, a number of different analytic procedures can be applied. For example, in measuring the relative dimensionality of cognitive structure, with the same type of judgments a number of analytic procedures have been used, including matching profile analysis, factor analytic methods, and multidimensional scaling. These varying analytic methods do not necessarily result in comparable measures of cognitive structure and caution is required in equating differing approaches. There is perhaps a too ready tendency for an investigator to *assume* his method is equivalent to another without adequate empirical scrutiny of the problem. The optimum strategy in research would seem to involve the comparison of at least two different task and analytic procedures in the same study, both in terms of equivalence and in terms of their ability to predict a criterion. The study reported by Todd and Rappoport (1964) represents such an approach in cognitive structure research.

FUTURE DEVELOPMENTS IN COGNITIVE STRUCTURES

With the unmistakable emphasis upon cognitive processes in contemporary psychological theory, we may expect the continued development of cognitive structural approaches to personality. As the task of staking out the boundaries of this domain becomes less urgent, we are faced with a variety of new challenges, including, as we have seen, those concerned with developmental problems and methodological issues. However, it is perhaps toward the major theoretical issue of the relation between cognitive structures and motivational variables that our attention will be turned with most promise. And here we come full circle with our initial concern with cognitive structures as information-processing constructs. For we cannot ignore the observation that the primary information which we process as social beings involves the drives, desires, and feelings aroused by our relationships with others. Perhaps it will be the paradoxical contribution of future research in cognitive structures to clarify the nature of motivational processes in behavior. Certainly, as in the work of Klein and his associates, and in the more basic developments of ego psychology in psychoanalytic theory, the vague outlines of such a conceptual *rapprochement* between cognitive structures and drives (or affect) can be perceived.

For it is the case that as yet in general psychological theory, not to mention the more complex field of personality, we do not have an adequate empirical or conceptual base upon which to build an understanding of the mutual relations among cognitive functions and drives. Strong affective arousal certainly can influence, for example, the ability of the individual to accurately discriminate features of his environment or to comprehend a complex stimulus. At the same time, depending upon the nature of the situation, and the cognitive structures invoked, such affective arousal may have a facilitating or grossly debilitating effect. Promising starts have been made, building upon such forebears as the Yerkes–Dodson law, although these efforts have generally not proceeded beyond a statement of a curvilinear relationship between affective or motivational arousal on the one hand, and cue or informational use on the other (Broadhurst, 1957).

It would be too bad if the earlier one-sided emphasis on drives, motives, and affect in personality gave way to an equally one-sided concern with cognitive processes in today's theorizing. Rather, we may hope that the newer and promising concern with cognitive structures will provide a conceptual avenue to lead us toward a more useful and theoretically complete view of man as one whose feelings and drives are part and parcel of his understanding of his world.

7

Homo Patiens

SILVAN TOMKINS

The theme here is *homo patiens*—passionate, suffering, caring, feeling Man. But why does he act; and knowledge for what? In a dimly lit cave one night after the day's work had been done, one of our more reflective forebears wrinkled his forehead, scratched his beard, and, in wonder and perplexity, began the study of human motivation. His answer to the fundamental question—"What do human beings really want?" —was the same answer that was to be given for some few thousand years up to and including Hull and Freud. That answer was, and for not a few still is, that the human animal is *driven* to breathe, to eat, to drink, and to have sex—that the biological drives are the primary sources of motivation of all animals, not excluding man. The clarity and urgency of hunger, of thirst, of anoxia, and of lust provided the basic paradigm that captured the imagination of all theorists. Protests against this paradigm have been perennial, but none of its competitors has had its hardiness.

This is a radical error. The intensity, the urgency, the imperiousness, the "umph" of drives is an illusion. The illusion is created by the mis-identification of the drive signal with its amplifier. Its amplifier is the affective response which is ordinarily recruited to boost the gain of the drive signal.

Consider anoxic deprivation. Almost any interference with normal breathing will immediately arouse the most desperate gasping for breath.

209

Is there any motivational claim more urgent than the demand of one who is drowning or choking to death for want of air? And yet it is not simply the imperious demand for oxygen that we observe under such circumstances. We are also observing the rapidly mounting panic ordinarily recruited whenever the air supply is suddenly jeopardized. The panic amplifies the drive signal and it is the combination of drive signal and panic which we have mistakenly identified as the drive signal. We have only to change the rate of anoxic deprivation to change the nature of the recruited affect which accompanies the anoxic drive signal. Thus, in World War II, those pilots who refused to wear their oxygen masks at 30,000 feet suffered a more gradual anoxic deprivation. They did not panic for want of oxygen. They became euphoric. It was the affect of enjoyment which the more slowly developing anoxic signal recruited. Some of these therefore met their death with a smile on their lips.

Consider next that most imperious, primary drive of sex. Surely the tumescent, erect male is driven. Surely the tumescent sexual organ is the site of both the sexual urge and sexual pleasure. So it is, but just as we misidentify panic and the anoxic signal, so here we have misidentified the tumescence of the sexual drive with the affect of excitement. Excitement is ordinarily recruited as an amplifier of the sexual drive signal. But no one has ever observed an excited penis. One is excited and breathes hard, not in the penis, but in the chest, the esophagus, the face, and in the nose and nostrils. Both the sexual urge and the sexual pleasure of intercourse are ordinarily as amplified by excitement as anoxia is amplified by panic. But the potency of the sexual drive is notoriously vulnerable to the learned recruitment of affect which inhibits sexual satisfaction. If one learns to feel ashamed or afraid of sexuality, tumescence may become impossible, and the potent primary drive becomes impotent. To be fully sexually aroused and satisfied one must be capable of excitement as well as tumescence. The contribution of affect to complete sexual satisfaction is nowhere clearer than for those who report unimpaired sexual pleasure and even orgasm, but nonetheless complain of lack of sexual satisfaction. What can it mean when the genitals are tumescent, yield sexual pleasure from mutual stimulation which produces mutual orgasm, and yet both partners report that they are sexually unfulfilled and dissatisfied? Sexual intercourse repeated with the same partner is vulnerable to such attenuation of satisfaction whenever the decline in novelty of the interpersonal relationship is such that excitement can no longer be sustained. Those who are generally bored with each other may also be unable to become sexually excited even when they are capable of stimulating tumescence and orgasm. Excitement is no more a peculiarly sexual phenomenon than panic is unique to anoxic deprivation.

AFFECT AND NONSPECIFIC AMPLIFICATION

The relationship we have postulated between the drive system and the affect system must also be postulated between both of these and nonspecific amplifying systems, such as the reticular formation. This and other amplifier circuits serve both motivational and nonmotivational systems. The words activation and arousal have tended to confound the distinction between amplification from affects and the nonspecific amplification of any neural message, be it a sensory, motor, drive, or affect message.

Amplification is the preferable, more generic term, since it describes equally well the increase or decrease in gain for any and every kind of message or structure. The terms activation and arousal should be abandoned because of their affective connotations.

It is now clear from the work of Sprague et al. (1961, pp. 172–73) that it is possible by appropriate anatomical lesion to produce a cat who is active by virtue of intact amplifier structures but who shows little affect and, conversely, to produce a cat who is inactive, and drowsy, but who responds readily with affect to mild stimulation. "Thus it appears that after interruption of much of the classical, lemniscal paths at the rostral midbrain, the cat shows . . . little attention and affect, despite the fact that the animal is wakeful and active and has good motor capacity. . . . These cats are characterized by a *lack of affect*, showing little or no defensive and aggressive reaction to noxious and aversive situations and no response to pleasurable stimulation or solicitation of affection by petting. The animals are mute, lack facial expression, and show minimal autonomic responses. . . . Without a patterned afferent input to the forebrain via the lemnisci, the remaining portions of the central nervous system, which include a virtually intact reticular formation, seem incapable of elaborating a large part of the animal's repertoire of adaptive behavior. . . . In contrast to this picture, a large reticulate lesion sparing the lemnisci results in an animal whose general behavior is much like that of a normal cat except for chronic hypokinesia or drowsiness and for strong and easily aroused affect to mild stimulation."

DRIVES AS INFORMATION SYSTEMS

Both drives and affects require nonspecific amplification, but the drives have insufficient strength as motives without concurrent amplification by both the affects and the nonspecific amplifiers. Their critical

role is to provide vital information of time, of place, and of response—
where and when to do what when the body does not know how to otherwise help itself. When the drive signal is activated we learn first when
we must start and stop consummatory activity. We become hungry
long before our tissues are in an emergency state of deficit, and we stop
eating, due to satiety, long before the tissue deficit has been remedied.

But there is also information of place and of response—where to do
what. When the drive is activated it tells us a very specific story—that
the "problem" is in the mouth in the case of hunger, farther back in
the throat in thirst, in the finger or wherever we have hurt ourselves
in the case of pain, in the nose and throat and chest if it is an oxygen
drive, in the urethra if it is the urination drive, at the anal sphincter if
it is the defecation drive. This information has been built into the site
of consummation so the probability of finding the correct consummatory
response is very high. That this information is as vital as the message
when to eat can be easily demonstrated.

Let us suppose that the hunger drive were rewired to be localized
in the urethra, and the sex drive were localized in the palm of the hand.
For sexual satisfaction the individual would first open and close his
hand and then reach for a wide variety of "objects" as possible satisfiers,
cupping and rubbing his hand until orgasm. When he became hungry
he might first release the urethra and urinate to relieve his hunger. If
this did not relieve it, he might use his hands to find objects which might
be put inside the urethra, depending on just how we had rewired the
apparatus. Such an organism would be neither viable nor reproducible.
Such specificity of time and place of the drive system, critical though it
is for viability is, nevertheless, a limitation on its general significance for
the human being.

AFFECTS—THE PRIMARY HUMAN MOTIVES

It is the affects, rather than the drives, which are the primary human
motives. First, because the drives require amplification from the affects,
whereas the affects are sufficient motivators in the absence of drives.
One must be excited to be sexually aroused, but one need not be sexually
aroused to be excited. It is quite sufficient to motivate any man, to arouse
either excitement or joy or terror or anger or shame or contempt or distress or surprise.

Second, in contrast to the specificity of the space–time information
of the drive system, the affect system has those more general properties
which permit it to assume a central position in the motivation of man.
Thus, the affect system has generality of time rather than the rhythmic

specificity of the drive system. Because the drive system is essentially a transport system, taking material in and out of the body, it must impose its specific temporal rhythms, strictly. One cannot breathe only on Tuesday, Thursday, and Saturday, but one *could* be happy on Tuesday, Thursday, and Saturday, and sad on Monday, Wednesday, and Friday.

In contrast to the necessary constraints of a system which enjoys few degrees of freedom in transporting material into and out of the body, there is nothing inherent in the structure of the affect mechanism which limits its activation with respect to time. One can be anxious for just a moment, or for a half hour, or for a day, or for a month, or for a year, or a decade, or a lifetime, or *never*, or only occasionally now though much more frequently some time ago, or conversely.

There are structures in the body which are midway between the drive and affect mechanisms. Thus the pain receptors on the back of my hand are as site-specific as any drive. If I were to place a lit cigarette on the skin of my hand, I would experience pain. But the pain mechanism is similar to the affect mechanism in its time generality. There is nothing in the nature of the pain receptors which requires that they be stimulated rhythmically, or that they ever be stimulated, and nothing which would prevent them from being stimulated whenever I happened to have an accident.

The affect system also permits generality or freedom of object. Although one may satisfy hunger by Chinese, American, or Italian food, it must be some variety of edible object. Not so with any affect. There is literally no kind of object which has not been linked to one or another of the affects. In masochism man has even learned to love pain and death. In Puritanism he has learned to hate pleasure and life. He can invest any and every aspect of existence with the magic of excitement and joy or with the dread of fear or shame or distress.

Affects also are capable of much greater generality of intensity than drives. If I do not eat I become hungrier and and hungrier. As I eat I become less hungry. But I may wake mildly irritable in the morning and remain so for the rest of the day. Or, one day I may not be at all angry until quite suddenly something makes me explode in a rage. I may start the day moderately angry and quickly become interested in some other matter and so dissipate my anger.

Not only are both intensity and duration of affect capable of greater modulation than is possible for drives, but so is their density. By affect density we mean the product of intensity times duration. Most of the drives operate within relatively narrow density tolerances. The consequence of too much variation of density of intake of air is loss of consciousness and possible death. Compared with drives, affects may be either much more casual and low in density or much more monopolistic and high in density. By virtue of the flexibility of this system man is enabled to oscillate between affect finickiness, fickleness of purpose, and obsessive possession by the object of his affective investments. We will return to this, our main theme, presently.

Not only may affects be widely invested and variously invested, but they may also be invested in other affects, may combine with other affects, intensify or modulate them, and suppress or reduce them. Neither hunger nor thirst can be used to reduce the need for air, nor is the converse true. However, a child may be shamed into crying, or may be shamed into stopping crying.

The basic power of the affect system is a consequence of its freedom to combine with a variety of other components in what we have called a central assembly. This is an executive mechanism upon which messages converge from all sources, competing from moment to moment for inclusion in this governing central assembly. The affect system can be evoked by central and peripheral messages from any source and in turn can control the disposition of such messages and their sources.

WHAT AND WHERE ARE THE AFFECTS?

If the affects are our primary motives, what are they and where are they? Affects are sets of muscle and glandular responses located in the face and also widely distributed through the body, which generate sensory feedback which is inherently either "acceptable" or "unacceptable." These organized sets of responses are triggered at subcortical centers where specific "programs" for each distinct affect are stored. These programs are innately endowed and have been genetically inherited. They are capable, when activated, of simultaneously capturing such widely distributed organs as the face, the heart, and the endocrines, and imposing on them a specific pattern of correlated responses. One does not learn to be afraid, or to cry, or to startle, any more than one learns to feel pain or to gasp for air.

Most contemporary investigators have pursued the inner bodily responses, since the James–Lange theory has focused attention on their significance. Important as these undoubtedly are, we regard them as of secondary importance to the expression of emotion through the face. We regard the relationship between the face and the viscera as analogous to that between the fingers and forearm, upper arm, shoulders, and body. The fingers do not "express" what is in the forearm, or shoulder, or trunk. They rather lead than follow the movements in these organs of which they are an extension. Just as the fingers respond both more rapidly and with more precision and complexity than the grosser and slower moving arm to which they are attached, so the face expresses affect both to others and to the self via feedback, which is more rapid and more complex than any stimulation of which the slower moving visceral organs are capable.

There is, further, a division of labor between the face and the inner organs of affective expression similar to that between the fingers and the arm. It is the very gross and slower moving characteristic of the inner organ system which provides the counterpoint for the melody expressed by the facial solo. In short, affect is primarily facial behavior. Secondarily it is bodily behavior, outer skeletal and inner visceral behavior. When we become aware of these facial and/or visceral responses we are aware of our affects. The face is a self-stimulation organ not unlike the genitals in certain respects. In the penis there are receptors which are relatively insensitive when the organ is flaccid. When it is engorged with blood, however, the receptors are moved in such a way that they become exquisitely sensitive and stimulating.

It is our belief that there are similar, as yet unidentified receptors in the face which become more sensitive when the face is either engorged with blood or suddenly emptied of blood. The innate affect program, as we conceive it, first seizes control of breathing and voice and at the same time changes the flow of blood to the face (so that, for example, we become red with anger or white with fear, and at the same time roar in anger or scream or gasp in fear). Immediately thereafter there is a set of muscular responses which massages the face, now rendered uniquely sensitive. In this respect the total affect program may be likened to a masturbatory act, since it includes the muscular stimulation of the sensitized organ. In addition to special, as yet unidentified sensory receptors there are the heat and cold receptors which are sensitive to changes in blood flow, producing the sensations of hot anger and blushes, cold clammy sensations of fear, as well as the warm relaxation induced by alcohol or joy. The total affect experience therefore includes a sound (such as a roar, or a cry of distress), a feeling of cold or warmth, an awareness of change in blood flow in the face, an awareness of altered breathing, and characteristic changes in muscular responses of the face (such as a smile or a sneer). It is the totality of these components which is the innate full-blooded affective response.

It is always possible for different components to be suppressed and so alter the innate response. Indeed we rarely see or experience such responses because almost all societies demand modulation of the innate response. Thus the individual whose jaws are tightly clenched and whose eyes are like slits is often misidentified (both by himself and by others) as being angry, when in fact he is trying *not* to express his anger, by keeping his mouth tightly closed. If he were to express his anger his mouth would be open, emitting the roar of anger. Such a response is relatively self-limiting. In contrast the attempt *not* to roar in anger feeds on itself and may grow indefinitely. Many of the supposed characteristics of affects are indeed characteristics of suppressed affects rather than of the innate affects themselves. We may respond with these affects, however, without becoming aware of the feedback from them; e.g., when we are trying to solve a problem our attention may be so focused on the problem that we are relatively unaware of our excitement. Finally, we learn to generate, from memory, images of these same responses which we can become aware of with or without repetition of facial, skeletal, or visceral responses. Just as we may generate visual images by which we play blindfold chess without "seeing," so we may generate affect "images" without facial behavior which nonetheless "feel" the same as if they had come from facial responses.

If we are happy when we smile and sad when we cry, why are we reluctant to agree that this is primarily what it means to be happy or sad? Why should this be regarded as an "expression" of some other, inner state? The reasons are numerous, but not the least of them is a general taboo on sharing this knowledge in interocular intimacy.

The significance of the face in interpersonal relations cannot be exaggerated. It is not only a communication center for the sending and receiving of information of all kinds, but because it is the organ of affect expression and communication, it is necessarily brought under strict social control. There are universal taboos on looking too directly into the eyes of the other because of the likelihood of affect contagion, as well as escalation, because of the unwillingness to express affect promiscuously, and because of concern lest others achieve control through knowledge of one's otherwise private feelings. Man is primarily a voyeuristic animal not only because vision is his most informative sense but because shared interocular interaction is the most intimate relationship possible between human beings, since there is in this way complete mutuality between two selves, each of which simultaneously is aware of the self and the other. Indeed, the intimacy of sexual intercourse is ordinarily attenuated, lest it become too intimate, by being performed in the dark. In the psychoanalytic myth, too, the crime of the son is voyeuristic in the primal scene, and Oedipus is punished, in kind, by blindness.

The taboo on the shared interocular experience is easily exposed. If I were to ask you to turn around and stare directly into the eyes of the other and permit the other to stare at the same time directly into your eyes, you would become aware of the nature of the taboo. Ordinarily we confront each other by my looking at the bridge of your nose and your looking at my cheek bone. If our eyes should happen to meet directly, the confrontation is minimized by glancing down or away, letting the eyes go slightly out of focus, or attenuating the visual datum by making it ground to the sound of the other's voice which is made more figural. The taboo is not only a taboo on looking too intimately, but also on exposing the taboo by too obviously avoiding direct confrontation. These two strategies are taught by shaming the child for staring into the eyes of visitors and then shaming the child a second time for hanging his head in shame before the guest.

Only the young or the young in heart are entirely free of the taboo. Those adults whose eyes are caught by the eyes of the other in the shared interocular intimacy may fall in love on such an occasion or, having fallen in love, thereby express the special intimacy they have recaptured from childhood.

If the affects are primarily facial responses, what are the major affects? We have distinguished eight innate affects. The positive affects are, first, interest or excitement, with eyebrows down, stare fixed or tracking an object. Second, enjoyment or joy, the smiling response. Third, surprise or startle, with eyebrows raised and eyeblink. The negative affects are, first, distress or anguish, the crying response. Second, fear or terror, with eyes frozen open in fixed stare or moving away from the dreaded object to the side, and with skin pale, cold, sweating, trembling, and hair erect. Third, shame or humiliation, with eyes and head lowered. Fourth, contempt, with the upper lip raised in a sneer and disgust, a deeper rejection response with the mouth open as in nausea. Fifth, anger or rage, with a frown, clenched jaw, and red face.

HOW ARE THE AFFECTS ACTIVATED?

If these are innately patterned responses, are there also innate activators of each affect? Inasmuch as we have argued that the affect system is the primary motivational system, it becomes critical to provide a theory of the innate activators of the affect system. Consider the nature of the problem. The innate activators had to include the *drives* as innate activators, but *not be limited* to drives as exclusive activators since the neonate, for example, must respond with innate fear to any difficulty in breathing, but also must be afraid of other objects. Each affect had to be capable of being activated by a *variety* of unlearned stimuli. The child must be able to cry at hunger or loud sound, as well as at a diaper pin stuck in his flesh. Each affect had, therefore, to be activated by some general characteristic of neural stimulation, common to both internal and external stimuli and not, like a releaser, too stimulus-specific. Next the activator had to be correlated with biologically useful information. The young child must fear what is dangerous and smile at what is safe. The activator had to know the address of the subcortical center at which the appropriate affect program is stored—not unlike the problem of how the ear responds correctly to each tone. Next, some of the activators must not habituate, whereas others had to be capable of habituation; otherwise a painful stimulus might too soon cease to be distressing and an exciting stimulus never be capable of being let go—like a deer caught by a bright light. These are some of the characteristics which had to be built into the affect mechanism's activation sensitivity. The most economical assumption on which to proceed is to look for communalities among these varieties of characteristics of the innate alternative activators of each affect. This we have done, and we believe it is possible to account for the major phenomena with a few relatively simple assumptions about the general characteristics of the stimuli which innately activate affect.

DENSITY OF NEURAL FIRING:
THE PRINCIPLE OF INNATE AFFECT ACTIVATION

We would account for the differences in affect activation by three general variants of a single principle—the density of neural firing or stimulation. By density we mean the number of neural firings per unit of time. Our theory posits three discrete classes of activators of affect, each of which further amplifies the sources which activate it. These are stimulation increase, stimulation level, and stimulation decrease. Thus, there are guaranteed three distinct classes of motives—affects about stimulation which is on the increase, stimulation which maintains a steady level of density, and stimulation which is on the decrease. With respect to density of neural firing or stimulation, then, the human being is equipped for affective arousal for every major contingency. If internal or external sources of neural firing suddenly increase, he will startle or become afraid, or become interested, depending on the suddenness of increase of stimulation. If internal or external sources of neural firing reach and maintain a high, constant level of stimulation which deviates in excess of an optimal level of neural firing, he will respond with anger or distress, depending on the level of stimulation. If internal or external sources of neural firing suddenly decrease, he will laugh or smile with enjoyment depending on the suddenness of decrease of stimulation.

The general advantage of affective arousal to such a broad spectrum of levels and changes of levels of neural firing is to make the individual care about quite different states of affairs in different ways. It should be noted that according to our views there are both positive and negative affects (startle, fear, interest) activated by stimulation increase, but that only negative affects are activated by a continuing unrelieved level of stimulation (distress, anger), and only positive affects are activated by stimulation decrease (laughter, joy). This latter, in our theory, is the only remnant of the tension reduction theory of reinforcement. Stimulation increase may, in our view, result in punishing or rewarding affect, depending on whether it is a more or less steep gradient and therefore activates fear or interest. A constantly maintained high level of neural stimulation is invariably punishing inasmuch as it activates the cry of distress or anger, depending on how high above optimal levels of stimulation the particular density of neural firing is. A suddenly reduced density of stimulation is invariably rewarding, whether, it should be noted, the stimulation which is reduced is itself positive or negative in quality. Stated another way, such a set of mechanisms guarantees sensitivity to whatever is new, to whatever continues for any extended period of time, and to whatever is ceasing to happen. In Fig. 7-1 we have graphically represented this theory.

Let us consider first startle, fear, and interest. These differ, with respect to activation, only in the rate at which stimulation or neural firing increases.

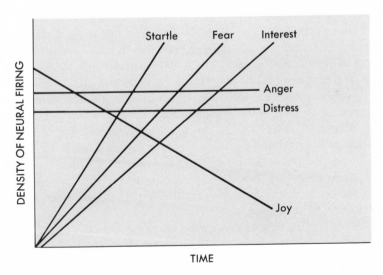

Fig. 7-1. Graphical representation of a theory of innate activators of affect.

Startle

Startle appears to be activated by a critical rate of increase in the density of neural firing. The difference between startle (or in its weaker form, surprise) and interest is a difference in the steepness of the gradient of stimulation. The same stimulus therefore may evoke surprise or interest, depending on the steepness of the rise of stimulation (which in turn depends on numerous factors, prominent among which is the degree of unexpectedness). Thus, a gun shot will evoke startle rather than interest. An unexpected tap on the shoulder by someone who is not seen will also evoke startle rather than interest. In the case of the gun shot, the suddenness of increase of stimulation is primarily in the auditory stimulus itself.

Any auditory stimulus with the physical properties of a square wave might innately activate a startle response. But it should be noted that our theory refers not to the properties of the stimulus but rather to the profile of neural firing. In some cases these will be correlated and in some cases they will not. Otherwise the individual would contrive to be surprised, to be frightened, or to be excited by the same stimulus, no matter how often repeated. Further, the same joke, endlessly repeated, would continue to activate enjoyment and laughter. The gradients of neural firing must not be exclusively identified with the physical properties of the external stimulus for another reason. Consider the startle response activated by an unexpected tap on the shoulder. Although the suddenness of this stimulus might have been sufficient to activate a startle, certainly the density of neural firing is too low to meet the conditions we have specified. We assume that such a stimulus, by virtue of being unexpected, initiates retrieval of information from memory at a rate sufficient to produce the requisite rate of increase of density of neural firing. This mechanism is most obvious in the "double take." Suppose someone with two heads comes into the room. A cursory scanning of such equipment reveals little out of the ordinary. The man is identified as one of the species *homo sapiens*. But then the information still reverberating in immediate memory leads to a second, much more rapid, search through memory for closer identification and at the same time that the head wheels quickly back into position to have a second look, the combined feedback of these secondary responses triggers a startle response.

The general function of the startle response we take to be that of a circuit breaker or interrupter mechanism, which resets the central assembly. This mechanism is similar in design and function to that in a radio or television network which enables special announcements to interrupt any on-going program. It is ancillary to every other affect since it orients the individual to turn his attention away from one thing to another. Whether, having been interrupted, the individual will respond with interest, or fear, or joy, or distress, or disgust, or shame, or anger will depend on the nature of the interrupting stimulus and on the interpretation given to it. The experience of surprise itself is brief and varies from an essentially neutral quality in its milder form to a somewhat negative quality in its more intense form as the startle response. Whatever its quality, positive or negative, it is frequently confused with the affect which immediately follows it. The surprise of seeing an unexpected love object is an overall positive experience. The surprise of seeing a dreaded person is an essentially negative experience. In its intense form it is an involuntary massive contraction of the body as a whole which momentarily renders the individual incapable of either continuing whatever he was doing before the startle or of initiating new activity so long as the startle response is emitted.

Our concept of the central assembly refers to the transmuting mechanism (the mechanism that changes messages in the nervous system into conscious form) and those other components of the nervous system which are functionally linked to the transmuting mechanism at a given moment. Without the startle response, information might not be attended to. But the feedback of the startle response is sufficiently sudden and dense to disassemble the on-going central assembly and to make it possible for the next assembly to be cleared of both the preceding information and the startle feedback and to include in this next central assembly the components of the nervous system which contain the messages which had activated the startle. Surprise or startle, however, is the perpetually unwelcome competitor to any on-going central assembly. It does not favor anything and it is against peaceful coexistence with any visitor to consciousness that has outstayed its welcome. Therefore, as soon as the clamor of the next visitor in the vestibule of the cortex exceeds a critical rate of increase in density of neural firing, the surprise or startle response is activated. The central assembly is now cleared of the unwelcome occupant and attends momentarily to that massive, dense feedback from the startle response, which, since it is momentary in duration, gives way to the rising, dense neural firing of the messages that had activated the startle. This set of messages then reaches the site of the on-going central assembly, which is reassembled to include this new information. Simultaneously the set of messages is transformed into the conscious experience of the specific stimulus which gave rise to surprise.

Fear

If startle, fear, and interest differ with respect to activation only in the rate at which stimulation or neural firing increases, then we can account for the seemingly unstable equilibria among them. First, this explanation would illuminate the familiar sequence of startle, fear, interest. The same object which first causes startle can quickly produce fear, and somewhat less quickly is transformed into interest or excitement. Lorenz (1950) has reported the characteristic sequence of fear and excitement in the raven who, on first encountering anything new, flies up to an elevated perch and stares at the object for hours, after which he gradually approaches the object, still showing considerable fear. As he comes closer, he hops sideways with wings poised for immediate flight. Finally, he strikes one blow at the object and flies right back to his perch. This sequence is repeated until eventually he loses interest in it. Harlow and Zimmerman (1959) have also noted the alternation between escape from and exploration of the feared object when the model mother is present. The infant monkey alternates between clinging to the mother and, when the fear has somewhat abated, exploring the object and then returning to the mother.

With respect to fear, this model would have some of the following consequences. First, there would be a low probability that any stimulus would activate one fear level more than once. The probability would be high that the same stimulus would either activate a more intense fear or no fear. More fear would be activated whenever there was further rapid scanning of the stimulus or further rapid cognition, or both. If there were no further scanning or no further cognition with the requisite neural density the probability would be that there would be no fear upon repetition of the same stimulus. In this respect it would be similar to the intensification of the affect of interest by new scanning or cognition of the same stimulus, and reduction of interest to the same stimulus when there was neither further scanning nor cognition.

Second, fear experience in infancy should have minimal after-effects upon repetition. In support, Levy (1960) found no memory cries of inoculation in the first six months of life. An infant, on seeing the same doctor, in the same setting, about to administer the same needle which had made the baby cry the first time, did not recognize the doctor and did not cry. Even as late as a year of age, if the interval between inoculations exceeded two months, there was no memory cry. There was a rising frequency of memory cries with age, starting with one per cent at six months of age and rising to twenty per cent at twelve months. There is nothing in the visual stimulus of doctor or needle which would innately activate fear, according to our model. Since memory and recognition are primitive in the first year we should expect fear to be limited to only those stimuli which produce the requisite density of neural firing. The pain of the needle does cause crying but the sight of the needle again produces no apparent affect.

Third, we should expect a great variety of sudden internal events to be capable of activating fear. These include the feedback of sudden muscular contractions, as in avoidance responses, the rapidly accelerating retrieval of information from storage, the rapidly accelerating construction of future possibilities via imagery or cognition, the rapid change of rate of any internal organ or system, such as the heart, circulatory system, respiration, endocrine system, and so on. The unexpected complication which arises from this model for the interpretation of fear is that many of the former criteria of fear now appear to be possible activators of fear rather than simply evidences of fear. Thus Schiff, Caviness, and Gibson (1962) have argued that there is an innate looming effect which innately produces fear. They have shown that the increase in the visual mosaic attendant on any object which moves rapidly toward the eye produces fear. We would agree that this happens, but only as a special case of the requisite increase in neural firing. Further, Schiff et al. point to the animal's sudden avoidance response as evidence of the fear produced by the looming stimulus. We do not question the validity of this evidence but present it to show that the criteria of fear will become ambiguous on the second exposure because the feedback of the avoidance response has precisely the same density gradient of neural firing as does the visual stimulation. All of these potential sources of activation of fear illuminate the way in which learning to respond with fear may depend upon the intermediate responses of learning to stimulate oneself through sudden muscular contraction, sudden cognition, sudden remembering. We are suggesting that learning to frighten oneself depends upon learning to produce an internal response whose density of neural firing increases with a particular rising gradient.

Fourth, it follows that any radical change of the internal environment by drugs can either increase or decrease the threshold for fear by increasing or decreasing the general neural rate of firing. We would suggest that the time-honored effect of alcohol on the release of inhibitions is through its relaxation of the skeletal musculature and of the blood vessels lying close to the skin. The muscles relax and the face becomes warm and tingles from vascular relaxation. The combined effect is to reduce radically the possibility of activating fear. A warm bath is similarly disinhibiting and hydrotherapy has been used successfully to control acute anxiety through essentially similar mechanisms. So much for fear.

Interest or Excitement

With respect to interest or excitement, while it is a sufficiently massive motive to amplify and make a difference in such an already intense stimulation as that from sexual intercourse, it is also capable of sufficiently graded, flexible innervation and combination to provide a motive matched to the most subtle cognitive capacities. Rapidly varying perception and thinking is thereby combined with varying shades of interest and excitement, which wax and wane appropriately with the operation of the analyzer mechanisms. The match between excitement and the drives is a different match from that between excitement and cognition. Because the latter is a process which is much more rapid and much more variable in time, it necessarily requires a motivational system which is matched in speed, gradation and flexibility of arousal, combination, and reduction. It must be possible to turn excitement on and off quickly, to grade its intensity, and above all to combine it with ever changing central assemblies. In contrast even with other affects, such as fear and anger, it must have both more and less inertia. It must not necessarily remain activated too long once aroused, but it must also be capable of being sustained indefinitely if the object or activity demands it.

Interest is also a necessary condition for the formation of the perceptual world. In learning to perceive any new object the infant must attack the problem over time. Almost any object is too big a bite to be swallowed whole. If it is swallowed whole it will remain whole until its parts are decomposed, magnified, examined in great detail, and reconstructed into a new more differentiated object. There is thus created a variety of problems in early perception. The object must be perceived in some detail, but it must also be perceived in its unity. Attention must steer a middle course between extreme distractibility passively shifted from one aspect of an object to some other aspect of an adjacent object, on the one hand, and the extreme stickiness of attention on the other hand, as in the cases of a deer caught and immobilized by a light or an animal fascinated by the eyes of a cobra. Attention must stick long enough to achieve detail and then move on to some other aspect of the object, but not to every competing stimulus in the field. In order to make such graded and differential sampling possible, there must be the continuing support of interest or excitement to the *changing* sampling of the object.

Second, not only must there be a perceptual sampling, but there must also be a sampling of the initially slender inner resources of the infant.

In order to achieve full acquaintance with any object one must vary one's perspectives, perceptual and conceptual. One must look at the object now from one angle, now from another. One must watch the object as it moves about in space. One must switch from a perceptual acquaintance to a conceptual orientation, to remembering it and comparing it now with what it was before. One must also have motor traffic with the object. One must touch it and manipulate it and note what happens to it as one moves it, pushes it, squeezes it, puts it in one's mouth (when one is young), and otherwise produces changes in it. To the extent to which such manipulation is guided by hypotheses and suggests new hypotheses, one's acquaintance with the object is enriched and deepened.

In order to shift from one perceptual perspective to another, from the perceptual to the motor orientation and back again, from both the perceptual and the motor to the conceptual level and back again, and from one memory to another, one must at the very least maintain a continuing interest in all of these varying transactions with what is the same object. Without such an underlying continuity of motivational support, there could indeed be no creation of a single object with complex perspectives and with some unity in its variety.

The same affect of interest or excitement must be continually reassembled into each succeeding central assembly as the varying commerce with the object disassembles and reassembles sensory input, memory support, and the varying transformations on both sets of messages.

Interest is also a necessary condition for the physiological support of long-term effort. Excitement lends more than spice to life. Without zest, long-term effort and commitment cannot be sustained, either physiologically or psychologically. What constitutes a clogging of the zest for work can be transformed into a major stasis when the individual through sudden changes in circumstances comes full face with the awareness that he cannot fulfill himself in his work. When the individual knows what he wants but must renounce his central aims, this crisis has dramatic physiological consequences. Alexander and Portis (1944) reported a syndrome they labeled psychosomatic hypoglycemic fatigue. This was found in a group of neurotic patients whose psychological symptoms were accompanied by a specific disturbance of the carbohydrate metabolism—a flat intravenous glucose tolerance curve similar to those found in cases of hypoglycemia.

These patients were not anxious or deeply depressed. Their outstanding problems were apathy—a loss of zest, a general feeling of aimlessness, and a disgust with the routine of everyday life. In addition, they suffered excessive fatigue, either chronic or acute attacks.

The common denominator in the apparent precipitating causes in these cases of excessive fatigue was not any specific personality constellation, but rather a collapse of motivation.

Alexander and Portis found that all of these patients forced them-selves to work hard but at the same time had no enthusiasm for what they were doing. A sense of duty, external necessity, or pride had forced the renunciation of the goals dearest to them. It was after this renun-ciation was finally effected, in fact or in the minds of these patients, that chronic or acute attacks of fatigue overwhelmed them.

Alexander and Portis interpret their findings to mean that the absence of zest and enthusiasm for work produces a "vegetative retreat" charac-teristic of relaxation in which the vagal-insular tonus is preponderant over the sympathetic adrenal tonus. They base this on an extension of Cannon's views on the effects of fear and rage. They argue that interest, enthusiasm, or zest has a sympathicotonic effect which is less intense but more prolonged than that of fear and rage.

The fatigue which these patients suffer, then, is based on lack of preparation of the carbohydrate metabolism for effort. The body is working while the body prepares for rest. Under this vagal prepond-erance hyperinsulinism develops which produces an inability to raise the sugar concentration of the blood—shown in the flat glucose tolerance curve.

Distress

In comparison with startle and fear, the affect of distress appears to be based not on an increase of density of stimulation, but rather on an absolute level of density of stimulation or neural firing, which deviates in excess of an optimal level of neural firing. Thus pain characteristi-cally produces crying in the infant. The suddenness of pain is not the critical feature of the activation of distress. Either sudden or prolonged pain is equally capable of activating distress. Thus, a sudden stab of pain elicits a sudden scream of distress, and prolonged pain ordinarily produces prolonged crying. In contrast to fear, it is the total quantity or density of stimulation over time which further increases the density of stimulation through crying. It is the quantity rather than the quality of stimulation which appears to be critical. The cry or moan of excessive sexual pleasure in intercourse is an example of stimulation which is predominantly pleasurable, nonetheless evoking a cry of distress. If distress is activated by a general continuing level of nonoptimal neural stimulation, then we can account for the fact that such a variety of stimuli, from both internal and external sources, can produce the cry of distress in the infant and the muted distress response in the adult. These range from the low-level pain of fatigue, hunger, cold, wetness, loud sounds, or overly bright lights, to the cry itself as a further stimulus.

The crying response is the first response the human being makes upon being born. The birth cry is a cry of distress. It is not, as Freud supposed, the prototype of anxiety. It is a response of distress at the excessive level of stimulation to which the neonate is suddenly exposed upon being born.

Distress-anguish is a fundamental human affect primarily because of the ubiquity of human suffering. Anxiety, by contrast, is properly an emergency affect. When life and death hang in the balance, most animals have been endowed with the capacity for terror. This is appropriate if life is to be surrendered only very dearly. The cost of terror is so great that the body was not designed for chronic activation of this affect. A human being who responds as if he had reason to be chronically terrorized is properly diagnosed as ill.

It seems very likely that the differentiation of distress from fear was required in part because the coexistence of superior cognitive powers of anticipation with an affect as toxic as fear could have destroyed man if this were the only affect expressing suffering. What was called for was a less toxic, but still negative, affect which would motivate human beings to solve disagreeable problems without too great a physiological cost, without too great a probability of running away from the many problems which confront the human being, and which would permit anticipation of trouble at an optimal psychic and biological cost. Such, we think, is the human cry of distress.

Because trouble is ubiquitous and because anticipation is perennial, man is forever courting suffering. Although the world might be made safe enough to minimize terror, it is inconceivable, given the inherent uncertainty of the world in which we live, that man's existence can be proofed against suffering.

Nor should any theory of personality fail to address itself to this domain. This is because distress is suffered daily by all human beings, as they become tired, as they encounter difficulties in solving problems, as they interact with other human beings in ways which are less than ideal. Distress is as general a negative affect as excitement is a positive one. Between them they account for a major part of the posture of human beings toward themselves, toward each other, toward the world they live in.

Anger

Another affect which is activated by the absolute density level of stimulation is anger. It is our assumption that anger is activated by a higher density level of stimulation than is distress. Hence, if a source of stimulation, say pain, is adequate to activate distress and both of these continue unrelieved for any period of time, the combination of stimulation from pain and distress may reach the level necessary to activate anger. This is also why frustration may lead to anger. Further, either distress alone or pain alone might be sufficiently dense to activate anger. Thus, a slap on the face is likely to arouse anger because of the very high density of receptors on the surface of the face. In contrast, a stab of pain elsewhere in the body may lack both the requisite density and the duration to activate more than a cry of distress. This principle would also account for the irritability produced by continuous loud noise, which would tend to recruit widespread muscle contraction which, added to the distress affect, could raise the density of stimulation to that necessary for anger.

Enjoyment

Finally, in contrast to stimulation increase and stimulation level, there are also affects which operate on the principle of stimulation reduction. The smile of joy and laughter are the primary examples of such a mechanism. The relatively steep reduction of pain or excitement or distress or anger will produce the smile of joy (which represents relief in the case of pain and distress), the smile of triumph in the case of anger, and the smile of familiarity in the case of sudden reduction of excitement.

The smile of joy resulting from the sudden reduction of stimulation accounts for two very disparate phenomena. On the one hand, it accounts for the incremental reward of the sudden cessation of any negative stimulation, such as pain, distress, fear, shame, or aggression. On the other hand, it accounts for the very different phenomenon of the enjoyment of the familiar. If we assume that any unknown but familiar stimulus will first produce interest, with a sudden increase in neural firing from the feedback of this affective response, and then an equally sudden reduction of this stimulation when the familiar stimulus (e.g., the face) is recognized as familiar, then this latter will in our theory activate the smile of joy and so reward the individual for re-establishing contact with a familiar object, personal or impersonal.

This would account for the smiling of the child at the mother, since she moves in and out of view often enough to evoke first excitement by her unexpectedness, and then provokes the smile when the excitement is suddenly reduced because she is recognized. It would also account for Piaget's (1952) observation that his children sometimes smiled at their toys when they were unexpectedly uncovered.

Shame

The same type of mechanism, we believe, operates in the affect of shame, except that stimulation reduction is incomplete compared with joy and appears to be restricted to the reduction of positive affects themselves rather than to the reduction of any kind of stimulation. Hence, any barriers to exploration—whether because one is suddenly looked at by one who is strange, or because one wishes to look at or commune with another person but suddenly cannot because he is strange—which involves an interruption and incomplete reduction of interest or smiling, will activate the lowering of the head and eyes in shame, and thereby reduce further exploration powered either by excitement or joy.

Drives and Affects

This theory would also account for some of the observed differences in types of affect which specific drives recruit as amplifiers. Thus, according to our view the sudden interruption of the air supply activates fear, whereas hunger characteristically first activates interest, because the former produces a denser and steeper gradient of stimulation. As the hunger drive signals gradually increase to a higher and higher level of neural stimulation, interest changes to distress, but not to fear. We should expect on the basis of our theory that variations in metabolic rate between different animals should move the hunger drive between an extreme of steepness of gradient of stimulation, in the case of animals with very high metabolic rate who must eat often to survive, to an extreme of low-level stimulation from the hunger drive signal, with a very gradual gradient of neural firing. For some animals, then, hunger would have effects similar to the interruption of the air supply and would activate fear; for others with a very low metabolic rate, hunger would rarely activate any affect and then only distress, as the level of neural stimulation gradually rose with deprivation.

Further, the characteristic differences between hunger and the need for air on the one hand, and the sex drive on the other, would also be a consequence of differences in gradients and levels of neural firing. In man, sexual stimulation is often sufficiently sudden and peaked in arousal to activate excitement, but not so steep a gradient as to activate fear, as in the interruption of the air supply.

BIOLOGICAL UTILITY OF VARIETY OF AFFECTS

The biological utility of affects with sharply peaked profiles, such as startle, fear, and excitement, to aspects of the environment which themselves may be highly variable, and of the more continuous arousal of distress and aggression by aspects of the inner or outer world which continue to overstimulate the individual, as in constant pain, is evident. No less useful is the decreased probability of becoming aware of affects, such as joy, which are activated by reduction of stimulation, whenever these are in competition either with continuing overstimulation or suddenly rising stimulation which may signify danger or novelty and either startle, frighten, or interest the individual. The joy response is a luxury response when it competes with pain or danger or novelty. The general relationship between the principle of selection of messages for the central assembly (we have assumed that in the competition between messages for inclusion in the central assembly the denser message sets are included and the less dense message sets are excluded) and the principles of the three major types of affect activation guarantee that joy is the most vulnerable to exclusion in competition for consciousness.

It is the innate plasticity of the affect mechanism, we have argued, which permits the investment of any type of affect in any type of activity or object and which makes possible the great varieties of human personalities and societies.

DENSITY OF AFFECT INVESTMENT

We now turn to a closer examination of the phenomenon of density of affect investment. We have defined affect density as the product of intensity times duration. We now introduce a derivative concept: ideo-perceptual-memorial-action-affect density. By this we mean the product of the intensity times the duration of all the capacities for involvement which the individual possesses. At one time his involvement may be primarily ideational; at another time, primarily affective, or primarily overtly behavioral, or primarily perceptual or memorial, or any combination of these. For purposes of brevity we henceforth refer to this as ideo-affective density and use the term ideation to refer to the variety of nonaffective cognitions as well as to action. We do not mean by this to imply in any way that we regard action as a type of thinking, or to blur in any way the differences among perception, memory, and thinking. We will use the term simply as a convenient abbreviation for the density of involvement of all of the critical subsystems which together constitute a human being. Bearing in mind this special usage of the word *ideo-* and the word *ideation,* we will now define ideo-affective density as the product of the intensity and duration of affect and the concurrent ideation about the object of the affect. Low ideo-affective density refers to those experiences which generate little or no affect, and little or no ideation, or in which, if the affect and ideation are intense, they do not last long. High density occurs whenever the individual has both intense feelings and ideation which continue at a high level over long periods of time. In such a case there is a monopolistic capture of the individual's awareness and concern. Low and high densities represent two ends of a continuum of organizations of motive, thought, and behavior which are critical for the understanding of commitment.

We wish to distinguish two gross segments of an ideo-affect density continuum—the low- and high-density segments. Further, we will examine some characteristic examples of each end of this continuum, so that commitment may be seen in its larger context.

LOW IDEO-AFFECTIVE DENSITY

Let us first consider the low end of the continuum. We distinguish two different kinds of organizations, both of which are characteristically low-density organizations. Further, each type of organization may be primarily positive or negative in affect. One organization is *transient* and *casual* and the other is *recurrent* and *habitual*.

Consider first a transitory positive low-density ideo-affective organization. Such would be the laughter in response to a joke. The experience might be extremely enjoyable but nonetheless of very low density, because it recruits no continuing ideation or affect beyond the momentary experience. An example of a transitory negative low-density ideo-affective organization would be a cut while shaving, which occasions a brief stab of pain and distress but no further thought or feeling beyond this isolated experience. Each individual's lifetime contains thousands of such relatively casual, transient encounters. Collectively they may sum to a not inconsiderable segment of the life span. Nonetheless they constitute an aggregate of isolated components without substantial impact on the personality of the individual.

The recurrent, habitual types of low-density ideo-affective organizations characteristically begin with considerable intensity of affect and ideation but end with minimal involvement. Consider first the negative recurrent, habitual case. Everyone learns to cross streets with minimal ideation and affect. We learn to act *as if* we were afraid, but we do not in fact experience any fear once we have learned how to cope successfully with such contingencies. Despite the fact that we know there is real danger involved daily in walking across intersections and that many pedestrians are in fact killed, we exercise normal caution with minimal attention and no fear. The activity remains a low-density ideo-affective organization, despite daily repetition over a lifetime. Successful avoidance strategies remain low-density organizations because they do not generalize or spread; they do not spread just because they are successful. It should be noted that though we have called these organizations recurrent and habitual, they are far from being simple motor habits. They are small programs for processing information with relatively simple strategies, but one may nonetheless never repeat precisely the same avoidance behaviors twice in crossing the street. These simple programs generate appropriate avoidant strategies for dealing with a variety of such situations, and caution is nicely matched to the varying demands of this class of situations, with a minimum of attention and affect. Every individual including the psychotic possesses hundreds of such low-density avoidance and escape organizations. It is always a great surprise on first exposure to psychotic patients to discover that schizophrenics when eating soup for lunch do not put the soup into their eye!

We are not saying that crossing the street was always a low-density ideo-affective organization. The earliest such experiences may well have been high adventures for the daring child, or they may have been the occasion of severe punishment at the hands of an anxious parent terrified at the sight of his toddler walking in front of a speeding automobile. Neither the excitement nor the pain, distress, or fear which might have been suffered at the hands of a parent continues for long. Children quickly learn some caution in this matter and it ceases to claim either much ideation or feeling. Such attenuation of feeling and thought necessarily depends upon the success of problem solutions. Paradoxically human beings are least involved in what they can do best; problems once solved remain solved. Man as a successful problem solver ceases to think and to feel about successful performance and turns ideation and affect to unsolved challenges, continuing or new.

This is so whether the original affect which powered the problem solving was positive or negative. Just as we experience no terror in confronting traffic at the curb, so too with positive low-density ideo-affective organizations: we experience no positive enjoyment or excitement in the daily recurrent performance which once delighted. As I finish my daily shaving I rarely puff with pride and think, "There, I've done it again." I act in this case, as in crossing the street, *as if* I experienced an affect, and had a wish to achieve this goal. I do indeed achieve my intention—to shave—but the positive affect behind this ritual has long ceased to be experienced concurrently with the action. Like the low-density avoidance strategy of crossing the street, it may be done daily with little or no effect on other action, or affect, or memory, or perception. I am in no way deeply engaged by such a daily ritual despite several thousand repetitions during a lifetime.

Two paradoxes arising from the ubiquity of both transients and habitual skills should be noted. Taken together they may constitute a substantial part of any individual's life. To the extent to which this is so the individual may suffer a motivational crisis. This is because transients, by definition, leave no residue and have no further impact on the individual. Since they are not connected or cumulative in any way, their significance is minimal. Habitual skills also yield neither affect nor awareness. The paradox of the habitual skill is that what the individual does *best* he is least proud of—indeed he is hardly aware of it. While the attainment of such skill may at one point have been a moment of glory, it is characteristically a very *brief* moment. Hence *both* those aspects of the world which the individual masters and those aspects over which he has *least control*—those that are transient rather than recurrent—give minimum satisfaction and meaning to his life.

HIGH IDEO-AFFECTIVE DENSITY

What then of the high-density ideo-affective organizations? By definition they can be neither transitory nor recurrent but must be enduring. Whether predominantly positive or negative in tone, they must seize the individual's feelings and thoughts and actions to the exclusion of almost all else. Consider first negative monopolism of thought and feeling. If successful and continuing problem solution is the necessary condition of the low-density organization, *temporary* problem solution is the necessary condition of the negative high-density organization.

Consider our man on the curb. He is normally cautious but not overly concerned because his solution to the problem has always worked. But suppose that one day a passing motorist loses control of his car and seriously injures our hero. After his return from the hospital he is a bit more apprehensive than before, and now stands back a little farther from the edge of the curb than he used to. He may continue his somewhat excessive caution for some time, and, as he notes a car approaching with what appears a little too much speed, may even begin to wonder with occasional fear whether such an accident might ever happen again. But if all goes well this increase in density of ideation and affect will pass and before long he will be indistinguishable from any other casual pedestrian. But in our tragedy all does not go well. Uncannily a drunken driver pursues our hero and he is hit again. This time it is more serious and we see the beginnings of a phobia. Our hero stations himself inside of a building peering up and down the street before he will venture out to dare to negotiate the crossing. By now his preoccupation with and fear of the deadly vehicle has grown to invade his consciousness even when he is far from the scene of potential danger. In the last act of this drama it is a bulldozer which penetrates his apparent fortress. What next? Will he be safe in the hospital? His ideation and affect have now reached a point of no return. He will henceforth generate possibilities which no reasonable man would entertain and these fantasies will evoke affects proportional to their extremity. He will now begin negative ideo-affective creativity.

Such a high-density ideo-affective organization is capable of providing a lifetime of suffering and of resisting reduction through new evidence. This happens if, and only if, there has occurred a sequence of events of this type: threat, successful defense, breakdown of defense and reemergence of threat, second successful new defense, second breakdown of defense and re-emergence of threat, third successful new defense, third breakdown of defense and re-emergence of threat, and so on, until an expectation is generated that no matter how successful a defense against a dread contingency may seem, it will prove unavailing and require yet another new defense, ad infinitum. Not only is there generated the conviction that successful defense can be successful only temporarily, but also as new and more effective defenses are generated the magnitude of the danger is inflated in the imagination of the harried one.

We have defined this dynamic as a circular incremental magnification. It is circular and incremental since each new threat requires a more desperate defense and the successive breakdown of each newly improved defense generates a magnification of the nature of the threat and the concurrent affect which it evokes. We have defined such a circular incremental magnification series as a set of − + − triads in which negative affect is defended against and replaced by positive affect, but then breaks down and again produces negative affect. In comparison with the analogous low-density organization, it is the continuing uncertainty of permanent problem solution which is critical in monopolizing the individual's ideation and affect. Paradoxically it is just the fact that the individual is *not* entirely helpless in dealing with a given situation which continually magnifies both the apparent nature of the threat and his skill in coping with it. In this respect the individual may be likened to a tennis player who is first defeated by a poor opponent and who then practices sufficiently to defeat that opponent. But his triumph proves short-lived since his opponent now also improves and in turn defeats him. This then leads our hero to improve his skill so that once again he defeats his adversary, but this leads to yet another defeat when the latter improves his own skill, and so on and on.

Let us now examine the structure of the positive high-density ideo-affective organization. Instead of a series of − + − triads, a series of + − + triads is responsible for the circular incremental magnification. Instead of increasing concern with warding off a threat, the magnification of a positive affect and the ideation about its object are involved.

Although there is negative affect sandwiched in between two positive affects in this type of triad, the individual is primarily concerned with attaining the object of positive affect. Let us consider two types of such positive ideo-affective organizations.

First, consider what we will define as the psychological addiction. The addicted cigarette smoker will serve as an example. Individual A enjoys smoking a cigar or cigarette after dinner. This is an unadulterated reward. At other times of the day he is unaware both of the enjoyments of smoking and of any suffering because he is not smoking. Individual B does not enjoy smoking per se, but rather uses cigarettes as a pacifier or sedative whenever he becomes distressed or anxious. Smoking at such times reduces his suffering and makes him feel better. It it not only that the function of smoking is here limited to the reduction of negative affect, but also that such negative affect arises from some source other than smoking. He is *not* disturbed simply because he is not smoking, but rather because something else went wrong in his life. So, when everything goes well for B, he does not miss smoking, because the only function smoking serves is to reduce other kinds of suffering. B does not think of smoking when he is not smoking—except on those occasions when he is disturbed. If he is not disturbed he has concerns other than smoking.

Individual C is an addicted smoker. Like A he too enjoys smoking and like B he uses smoking to reduce all types of suffering. But here the resemblances end. First of all, whenever C is not smoking, he is *always* aware of not smoking. Second, he always responds to this awareness with negative affect which continues to increase in intensity until he can smoke. Third, he will always drop all competitors for his attention and try to get a cigarette; and fourth, upon getting a cigarette and beginning to smoke he will respond with intense enjoyment at the reduction of his suffering. Like A he enjoys smoking, and like B he reduces his suffering by smoking, but the suffering which he *must* reduce is the suffering he experiences (and has created) just because he is *not* smoking. No matter how well his life goes, he is unable to be unaware of not smoking, whenever this occurs. Contrary to B he may be able to tolerate many other types of suffering without resort to sedation by smoking. So long as he has a cigarette in hand he may be quite courageous in confronting innumerable problems other than that of not smoking. B in similar circumstances might have had resort to smoking to leave the field, to sedate himself into comfort rather than to confront his problem.

In addiction, too, there is circular incremental magnification produced by an ever accelerating suffering in the absence of a cigarette and an ever increasing rewarding experience of positive affect upon the reduction of the suffering of negative affect. The hold of cigarette smoking or any other high-density addiction arises from the intolerability of the ever mounting negative affect which is experienced whenever the addict attempts to break his addiction. As his suffering mounts, he becomes more and more unable to tolerate the absence of smoking. He extrapolates into the future a vision of increasingly intolerable suffering till in panic at this prospect he succumbs to his longing. It is a series of painful longings reduced by smoking which increases both the suffering of negative affect and the intensity of positive affect while smoking, in an accelerating circular incremental magnification.

Psychologically this process is similar to the mourning experience of the bereaved. The lost love object is magnified in value because of the conjoint suffering and longing which makes vivid to the bereaved his hitherto not entirely appreciated dependence on the lost love object. It is the barrier to enjoying ever again the presence of the beloved which not only reveals but actually *creates* a new appreciation. Although a process similar to addiction is thereby heightened in mourning, and though longing and suffering may be intensified to the point of intolerability, the mourner ultimately is freed from his heightened dependence. This occurs because he is forced to endure suffering his abstinence until it no longer increases in intensity and then until it begins slowly to decline in intensity. Finally, there is minimal suffering and no *awareness* that the lost love object has been lost. In this respect the mourner is returned to the state of someone who has been able to overcome his addiction to smoking. The addicted cigarette smoker will not willingly suffer through such abstinence, because it seems to him, as to the bereaved, that he will never be able to tolerate the loss of the love object. In addiction, it should be noted, we are dealing with the lure of the familiar; the positive affect involved is enjoyment. It is the return to the familiar, heightened in value by the suffering of separation, which creates the magic of reunion, be that reunion with an old friend, an old place, or an old activity such as smoking. In contrast to commitment, as we will presently see, there is here much less involvement of exploration, of novelty, and of creative challenge.

In commitment, the positive high-density ideo-affective organization also involves the reward of the positive affect of enjoyment, but in addition the positive affect of excitement becomes prominent. Let us consider two examples of commitment, one a characteristically abortive commitment which ends either by transformation into an addiction at somewhat less than maximal density, or ends in disenchantment, and the other a high-density commitment which for some people extends over the entire life span. We refer in the first instance to romantic love and in the second to the committed artist or scientist.

Consider first the romantic lover who intends to commit himself for life to his beloved. Like our cigarette smokers, A, B, and C, we may distinguish A in this domain as one who very much enjoys his contacts with his lady friend, but who does not miss her when he is otherwise occupied. B has a lady friend he does not miss when all goes well. But he always turns to her for comfort when he becomes disturbed. She does in fact always bring him tranquility. Having been mothered back into peace of mind, he is prepared again to pick up his life. For the time being, he leaves his benefactress, with gratitude but no regret. Not so with C, the romantic lover. He is forever aware of the absence of his beloved, and of their enforced separation, to which he responds with intense suffering and longing. Every time he is separated, he dies a little. Thereby, like the true mourner, he comes to appreciate more and more his dependence upon the beloved who grows increasingly desirable in her absence. Upon reunion with the beloved, the intensity of his enjoyment and excitement is proportional to his prior suffering and there is begun a circular incremental magnification. If the beloved becomes more valuable when she brings to an end the intolerable suffering and longing which preceded reunion, so much the greater will the next suffering of separation become since the beloved has by now become even more wonderful than before. Just as the nature of the threat is magnified in the negative high-density series of $- + -$ triads, so is the nature of the positive object magnified in the series of $+ - +$ triads. In contrast to the ever increasing negative threat, the beloved does not necessarily continue to support indefinite magnification of her magical qualities. Romantic love imposes separation and uncertainty, which increases the period of time over which longing for the love object can occur; but with the transition to the honeymoon and marriage, the prolonged intimacy and mutual exploration eventually produce a sufficient reduction in novelty and uncertainty so that excitement can no longer be indefinitely maintained. When under these conditions of continuing contact the beloved will no longer support the indefinite magnification of wonder and excitement, there may appear disenchantment or boredom, or an ideo-affective organization of reduced intensity and duration with excitement replaced by the enjoyment of the familiar and deepening relationship. But the husband will no longer miss his wife throughout the working day even though he deeply enjoys his daily reunion with her at each day's end. We have traced this potential high-density ideo-affective organization which may be short circuited by marriage, better to illuminate the nature of enduring high-density commitment.

Consider next the varieties of committed scientists and those who are interested but not committed. Scientist A enjoys tremendously both the discovery of truth and the search for truth. He likes to putter around the laboratory. He likes to run experiments. He enjoys it when they succeed. But he is a nine-to-five scientist. When he goes home it is to another world. He does not take his scientific troubles home with him. Indeed he experiences a minimum of suffering in his role as scientist. He is in this respect like the person who loves to smoke after dinner or the person who enjoys the company of his lady friend; like them he does not miss their enjoyment or suffer in the interim periods. Individual B, on the other hand, uses science as a sedative. Whenever he becomes depressed he turns to reading science of watching TV programs concerning the latest advances in science. However, as soon as his life becomes more rewarding, his interest in science flags, like the person who smokes to comfort himself, and like the individual who seeks out his lady friend to ease his suffering, but once mothered back into peace of mind, forgets his benefactress.

Scientist C is committed for a lifetime to the pursuit of truth. Like the addicted smoker he is always aware of the absence of his longed-for ideal object—ultimate, permanent Truth. Like individual A, he too enjoys the scientific way of life. He enjoys puttering with laboratory equipment and running experiments. But underlying all his enjoyment is a continuing unrest and suffering over the possibilities of error and the possibility of missing the main chance. When everything works as planned he is deeply excited and enjoys briefly the fruits of his labor. But his contact with truth is ordinarily as brief as it is sweet. Truth is a mistress who never gives herself completely or permanently. She will not tolerate a marriage no matter how committed her scientific lover. She must be wooed and won arduously and painfully in each encounter. With each encounter she deepens both the scientist's suffering and his reward. It is a love affair which is never entirely and deeply consummated. Immediately following each conquest of Nature the victory is always discovered to have been less than it appeared and the investigation must now be pursued with more skill and energy than before. The set of triads $+ - +$ is in some respects similar to the negative set of triads $- + -$. In both triads, skill must constantly be improved and the effectiveness of achieved skill is only temporary. The difference is that in the negative high-density ideo-affective organization the individual is pursued by a threat, whereas in positive commitment he pursues an object of ever increasing attractiveness. In both cases circular incremental magnification is responsible for the *creation* of an idealized object. The magic of Truth exists in such a magnified form only in the mind of one who will pursue Truth despite increasing suffering so that each encounter becomes both more bitter and more sweet. There is minimal uncertainty in the familiar object of addiction, and there is a finite uncertainty in the romantic love affair which is almost entirely explored during the honeymoon. In scientific commitment, however, there is sufficient continuing uncertainty so that endless circular incremental magnification of the $+ - +$ triad can be sustained indefinitely if the individual has become committed. Thus a scientist who has made a major discovery and thereafter elects to rest on his laurels has ceased to be a committed scientist with high density of ideation and affect about science. It is a critical feature of high-density commitment that there can be no *enduring* positive affect in having attained the pursued finite object. Rather the object is continually redefined so that a newer version of the quest can be mounted. The same dynamic appears in the pursuit of money or power. These are also capable of committing the individual to an endless, insatiable quest for an object which is put out of reach almost at the instant it is attained.

8

Conceptual Complexity and Personality Organization

HAROLD M. SCHRODER

In this chapter personality is viewed as the style a person uses in processing information about a given domain of stimuli, e.g., interpersonal, political, or religious stimuli. The focus is not upon the content of the information used; rather, it is on the number and connectedness of conceptual or "integrating" rules used for organizing such information in thinking, judging, and valuing. That is, the focus is strictly on the processes involved. It is maintained that in much human thought conceptual structures for combining information items are involved. These structures will be referred to as integrative conceptual rules. The number of different ways an individual learns to combine and relate a set of information items is referred to as the level of conceptual complexity.

The central notion, which represents a basic variable for understanding personality, is that different levels of integrative complexity define different ways of processing information. At the present time these different levels or kinds of information processing models are quite loosely defined and measured. They are also much more complex than the information processing models described by Stone in Chapter 3. Stone states that the representation of "integration" between items of information in a model creates a system which is more complex than any man has built. However, it is highly conceivable that psychological development involves the learning of conceptual rules for selecting, storing, and organizing items of information, which can then act directly as the basic information processing units. It is in this way that everyday thought can be viewed as a relatively simple process based on a set of conceptual rules which represent the summation of a history of complex "program" development. At this stage, the information processing models proposed should be viewed as possibilities, which help formulate process hypotheses. As they become more higly specified, research will shape their modification or lead to their abandonment in favor of a different type of model.

Interest in organizational properties increased with the Gestalt influence, but traditional psychology continued to emphasize the response or performance and paid little attention to the processes generating responses. More recently a number of writers have been stressing the significance of organizational factors for understanding a broad range of psychological problems. The more immediate antecedents to the development of conceptual complexity as a generic personality variable include Adorno et al. (1950), Bruner et al. (1956), Cantril and Livingston (1963), Hebb (1955), Kelly (1955), Lewin (1935), Miller et al. (1960), Piaget (1932, 1950), Rotter (1954), and Sherif and Cantril (1947). Although closely related to the concept of flexibility (see Chapter 1), the first book which attempted to develop conceptual complexity as a personality variable appeared in 1961 (Harvey et al.). Since then, it has been explored and developed in a large number of research studies and research contexts. See, for example, the work of Harvey (1964, 1966) and Harvey and Schroder (1963) on motivation and the development and functioning of social attitudes; D. E. Hunt (1968) on interaction training models; Streufert and Schroder (1965) on the interaction between environmental factors and level of conceptual complexity; Suedfeld and Vernon (1966) on the effects of restricted environments on conceptual complexity; C. C. Anderson (1968) on conceptual complexity and administration; Schroder et al. (1967) on complex problem solving and social interaction; and Karlins (1967) on creativity.

While there are definitional differences in the work described under conceptual complexity, the studies may be grouped together because of their common focus on the study of an "organizational" variable in personality. The aim of this chapter is not to summarize this research but rather to describe various information processing structures differing in complexity and show their effects on social functioning.

DEFINITIONS AND OPERATIONS

Units of Information

In perceiving, judging, and evaluating, individuals extract various kinds or attributes of information from a given class of stimuli. It can be shown, for example, that in judging a series of tones, people (who are not tone deaf in the ranges presented) extract the attributes of both intensity and pitch. Similarly, when presented with an array of colors most people are capable of "reading" three different kinds of information—hue, saturation, and brightness. In this section we will focus on the nature of these basic units of information—the building blocks for thinking and judging.

In the above examples, the sensory apparatus for discriminating along dimensions such as loudness, pitch, and brightness is built into the organism before birth. However, one of the major characteristics of psychological development is increasing differentiation: the learning of new categories, scales, or dimensions along which given sets of stimuli take on additional meanings (Lewin, 1935). For example, in early development the concept of "doggy" or the dimension of "dogness" first permits the child to differentiate a certain set of stimuli from others. Later, depending upon the child's reinforcement history, he might be capable of perceiving or judging this class of stimuli along many dimensions including speed of running, aggressiveness, intelligence, and so on.

Viewed from the perspective of information processing, the initial problem in the study of personality is the discovery of the number of different kinds of information a person "reads," receives, or extracts from a given situation. For example, in evaluating or making judgments about a set of people (interpersonal domain) person A might perceive information about intelligence and friendliness and person B about friendliness, wealth, helpfulness, and reliability. In considering national governments, person A might extract information about democracy–autocracy and military strength and person B about democracy–autocracy, capitalism–socialism, and military strength. The initial problem is to identify these units of information involved in information processing, or specifically, to discover the number and nature of dimensions along which a person scales a given set of stimuli.

The parameters required for describing the units of information processing, in any domain, are as follows.

Differentiation. This refers to the number of categories or kinds of information extracted from a given domain of stimuli. In both examples above, person A is less differentiated than person B. This assumes that the information categories are functionally unique or unrelated—for example, that ratings of a set of stimulus persons by person A on friendliness and intelligence are substantially unrelated (that is, the ratings are neither positively nor negatively correlated).

Differentiation or "the number of different kinds of information perceived" refers to different principles of stimulus ordering. New information or meaning implies that a set of stimulus objects can be ordered or scaled in a new or independent way. The way individuals scale or order stimuli along any single dimension varies enormously. In the simplest case, differentiation may refer merely to a principle of assignment to a category (inclusion–exclusion). Being able to categorize people only into two groups—friendly and not friendly—exemplifies this level. At the other extreme, another person might be capable of making judgments in terms of a sophisticated ratio scale, making fine and reliable discriminations among all members of a set of stimulus persons along a scale of friendliness. Regardless of the sophistication of scaling, we refer to unique kinds of information (whether categorical or discriminative) as dimensions of information. Stimuli are represented by a scale value—whether crude or sophisticated—on each dimension or in each category used by a person in regard to a given set of stimuli. This means that a dimension of "friendliness," for a given person, consists of people arranged from low to high on perceived degree of friendliness. Persons (stimuli) rated high on this dimension may be described as a high scale value on this dimension. These scale values are the units of meaning or information.

Labeling: The Nature of Dimensions. In order to communicate we must provide labels or names for the different ways we order stimuli. The labels for many dimensions (principles of ordering) are highly communicable because of the degree of consensus regarding the operations for scaling, e.g., brightness, length, weight, volume. However, many dimensions which act as foundations for our thinking and judging are relatively unique. The degree of idiosyncrasy is an outcome of the diversity of the reinforcement history in development in any stimulus domain. We are all familiar with situations in which two persons use the same words to connote different meanings. This is well documented in the interpersonal domain by clinical observations, by results obtained using the Role Construct Repertory Test (Kelly, 1955), and by the work on impression formation. However, it is equally apparent, if less studied, in other areas such as in the political domain. One of the major tasks of psychology is the identification: (a) of all ordering principles (categories or dimensions) used by a person in a stimulus domain and (b) of the labels people apply to their ordering schemes. The ordering scheme defines the label, which is so important in communication.

The Measurement of Dimensions. The aim of measurement is the identification of the number and nature of dimensions used by an individual in evaluating or judging an array of stimuli under given situational conditions. In personality and attitude measurement, many investigators impose dimensionality. For example, respondents may be asked to rate nations on degree of autocracy or to rate people on degree of dependency. In such cases, even if we assume that the respondent can make such ratings reliably, we do not know whether he actually uses such dimensions in choice behavior. One of the requirements of measurement is the identification of the particular dimensions an individual uses: it is not sufficient to know all the possible ways of ordering an individual can comprehend.

The introduction of projective techniques, concept formation, and sorting procedures was an important methodological innovation. In open-ended responses the person is free to select or attribute classes of meaning to any set of stimuli. For example, in the Thematic Apperception Test interpersonal stimuli are presented via a set of pictures and the respondent's stories may be scored in terms of the characteristic dimensions along which he orders these stimuli. Common dimensions found include dependency, achievement, aggression, and affiliation (Mc-Clelland et al., 1963; Rotter, 1954; Tomkins, 1962). Here dimensions are measured at the individual level and the technique permits the discovery of the range of dimensions a person uses. Concept formation and sorting procedures (Kelly, 1955; Scott, 1963) have similar advantages. In these situations, dimensions of meaning are divulged by the way a respondent selects, groups, or orders the stimuli (e.g., people, nations, blocks). Scale values of stimuli can be obtained in all cases by having the respondent rate each stimulus on *each* dimension discovered.

Unfortunately, projective and sorting procedures have many disadvantages, particularly in regard to their use in research. While it is possible to train skilled and reliable scorers, it is time-consuming, judgments are subjective, and there is no precise way to assess the relative importance of dimensions and, consequently, the number of effective dimensions to include.

Recently, in the study of personality, a number of more objective procedures for measuring dimensionality have been introduced. The Interpersonal Discrimination Test developed by Bieri (1961) is a modification of Kelly's Role Concept Repertory Test (1955). In this test individuals are asked to rate a number of stimulus persons along ten dimensions such as decisiveness, ascendance, independence. The ratings are used to calculate the number of unique concepts or dimensions each individual uses in his ratings. For example, the more a set of stimulus persons is rated or ordered in a similar way along different dimensions, the lower the differentiation score.

In multidimensional scaling, persons are asked to rank order stimuli or make judgments about the degree of dissimilarity between all pairs of stimuli in a domain. In this geometric model a set of stimuli is viewed as points lying in some multidimensional space (Gulliksen, 1964; Kruskal, 1964; Shepard, 1962; Torgerson, 1958; Tucker & Messick, 1963).

The basic notion is that judged psychological similarity between pairs of objects may be likened to a "distance" between the points representing these objects in space. With a set of objects which may vary along an unknown number of perceptual dimensions, multidimensional scaling (MDS) attempts to determine the location of points in a space of minimum dimensionality such that the distances between points in this space correspond closely to the judgments of similarity or dissimilarity among the objects. The goal of this procedure is to provide a description of the set of objects in terms of empirically discovered dimensions which in some sense represent the "true" underlying aspects of the stimuli (Friendly, 1968).

While there are many conceptual difficulties in the use of this technique for discovering the number and weighting of dimensions involved in judgment, it has been validated in a number of studies (Helm & Tucker, 1962). However, experimental evidence suggests that:

(a) The multidimensional scaling model provides a reasonably accurate representation of the dimensions underlying perception and judgment when such perception involves a single rule by which all dimensions are weighted for judging all stimuli. A single fixed combinatory rule is exemplified by the combination of hue, saturation, and brightness in the perception of color.

(b) The method fails to uncover basic dimensions: (i) when all stimuli are not judged against the same dimensions—for example, when some stimuli are scaled along dimensions A and B and others along dimensions B and C (Schroder & Blackmann, 1965); (ii) when more complex information processing structures are involved—for example, when two different weighting systems are used to combine scale values (Faletti, 1968).

Another approach to the measurement of differentiation in personality research is the method of categorization (Triandis, 1964) or Free Adjective Description (Torbert, 1968; Warr et al., 1969). In the latter procedure, an individual is merely asked to respond to each member of a stimulus set (e.g., person A) with as many relevant descriptive adjectives or short descriptive phrases as he can. A dictionary is then constructed which defines and labels single categories into which all adjectives judged to have similar meanings are placed. The dictionary can be used to translate a set of free adjective descriptions into a set of dimensions—each judged to represent a different meaning or a unique category.

In a recent experimental study (Faletti, 1968) it was shown that all three methods yield valid information about the dimensional units underlying a person's perception of a set of stimuli. A simulated personnel selection situation was used in which subjects studied the "case folders" of eight applicants to fill four managerial positions. The "case folders" were prepared so that in the process of learning about the applicants the subjects came to view the applicants along certain dimensions. In one group the folders provided two independent dimensions along which applicants could be ordered: "strategic thinking" and "social reciprocity." In a second group, the "case histories," while similar in all other respects, provided information which permitted subjects to order applicants along a third dimension of "orderliness." In the training phase, subjects were required to reach criterion, meaning that in the first group applicants were correctly perceived and ordered along only two dimensions and in the second group they were all perceived along the three relevant dimensions and ordered accurately along each.

Subjects were then asked to consider the dimensional scale values of each applicant (either two or three values, depending on the treatment group) and to combine these into an overall impression which might characterize each applicant in the managerial situation. Then subjects were trained to think of applicants in this global sense as we do in everyday judgment. When this was accomplished, when subjects could immediately evaluate applicants in terms of their overall concept, the testing procedures were introduced.

The three tests outlined above were administered to determine their ability to uncover the number and nature of dimensions used in global judgments about the eight applicants. In the Bieri test subjects scaled all eight applicants on ten dimensions, in multidimensional scaling. Subjects were instructed to rate the degree of dissimilarity between all pairs of applicants and descriptive adjectives were recorded for each applicant in the free adjective description test. In all cases the dimensionality scores on these tests were significantly lower for the group trained to use two (as opposed to three) dimensions in perceiving the applicants. It was possible to uncover the number of relevant dimensions by all three methods and to arrive at the appropriate label by the Bieri and adjective tests. It is important to note that all subjects in the two- and three-dimension groups were trained to combine scale values using a single combinatory rule.

The Development of Dimensions. In all learning, via classical conditioning, instrumental conditioning, modeling, or insight, the individual is attributing new or additional meaning to a certain range of stimuli. In a black–white discrimination situation, the rat is learning to scale objects in terms of their "whiteness" or "darkness." A dimension of meaning is developing along which objects can be scaled. The generalization patterns or the degree of discrimination of objects from black through grey to white will also be a function of the degree and range of reinforcement experience.

The type of scale the animal or person learns has received comparatively little attention in learning experiments where the traditional emphasis has been on the response. The transposition experiments are directly related to this question. In these experiments the problem can be posed in the following way: suppose we train an animal or a child to select the black side in a black–white discrimination problem; will he now attribute the learned meaning to the darker of any two stimuli regardless of the absolute shade of the pair? Does he learn that black is positive or does he learn a relationship, that the darker side of any pair is positive?

If we view learning as the acquisition of dimensions, the same problem can be posed as follows: under what conditions will a categorical scale emerge? In the extreme case, with categorical scales, stimuli would be lumped at each end—black at one end and all others (dark, grey, and white) at the other. The acquisition of such a scale would lead us to believe that the child learned to lump a set of stimuli into a category and to respond to these stimuli in a bifurcated, absolutistic way. We would ask, under what conditions will a ratio scale emerge? The acquisition of such a scale, in which degrees are discriminated, implies that meaning is less stimulus-bound and that the child can respond in terms of the relationship between stimuli in a given set.

The kinds of dimensions which children learn and the conditions which produce more categorical and discriminative scales are neglected topics. For example, most children develop scales along which people are perceived. For some, a very restricted set of people is positive and the remainder are lumped together in a categorical fashion as "strangers" to be avoided. For other children a more graded response is apparent. The developmental conditions underlying this "latitude of acceptance" and its relationship to discrimination along all parts of dimensions will be brought more clearly into focus in studies in learning and development if we adopt the acquisition of dimensions as well as responses as a criterion for learning.

Another important component for study in regard to the acquisition of scales is the emergence of the affective component. In many of the dimensional organizations which are present at birth, the approach (positive) and avoidant (negative) properties are built in. For example, an intense noise, a sudden fall, and a bitter taste represent the negative end of each dimension. In general, however, the reinforcement history determines which end of the dimension is negative and which is positive —as when white stimuli take on positive meaning when associated with food or when selected behaviors or choices of the child are approved by a valued source (Bandura and Walters, 1959).

The work of Osgood et al. (1957) shows that, for people in general, evaluation is the chief dimension of meaning. That is, most dimensions along which people learn to order stimuli are evaluative in the sense that the stimuli at one end are approached and are more positive than stimuli at the other end. However, individuals differ in the ways they order stimuli. They use different dimensions, and consequently differ in their evaluation of particular sets of stimuli. In judging a range of stimuli, individuals also differ in the number of dimensions used and in the strength of the correlation between these dimensions and the overall evaluative ordering.

In a recent study of the dimensions people use to judge national governments, it was shown that the first dimension extracted by multi-dimensional scaling or by the free adjective response method was highly related to the evaluative ordering for nearly everyone, but the correlation with evaluation was much lower and even zero for many of the remaining significant dimensions used by individual subjects (Warr et al., 1969). Evidently the more dimensions a person is capable of using in order to scale a set of stimuli—that is, the higher the differentiation in any domain—the more thinking and judging are based on information which is increasingly nonevaluative. Studies of social development indicate that the process is one of movement from a gross evaluative ordering to a more differentiated informational orientation (Mead, 1934b; Piaget, 1954; Werner, 1957). In a study using simulated nations as stimuli, Driver found that the number of dimensions used to scale nations increased and became less evaluative with interaction experience, and decreased and became more evaluative under stress and intense conflict (Schroder et al., 1967).

Organization of Dimensional Scale Values of Information

Our understanding of the learning process and personality development encompasses both the acquisition of dimensions and the organization of dimensional scale values of information. As the Gestalt psychologists so effectively argued, we perceive "wholes" or "organizations." Stimuli may be organized in regard to a single innate or learned concept (category or dimension); e.g., points in space may be organized in terms of an acquired concept such as degree of "squareness" or "circularity." More complex processes of organization are involved when stimuli are scaled on more than one dimension, e.g., a tone has both pitch and loudness, a color has hue, saturation, and brightness, and a person may be perceived as intelligent, stubborn, and compulsive (Asch, 1946). In each case, a stimulus is scaled on two or more dimensions, and except when the two meanings are completely compartmentalized (e.g., as when one reacts to a stimulus person as stubborn on Saturday and intelligent on Sunday), rules for combining these values evolve. *The number of such combinatory rules and the degree of connectedness between these rules define the integrative complexity of conceptual structure* (Schroder et al., 1967).

A simple combinatory rule is illustrated in Fig. 8–1. In this information processing structure, stimulus person A is scaled along three inde-

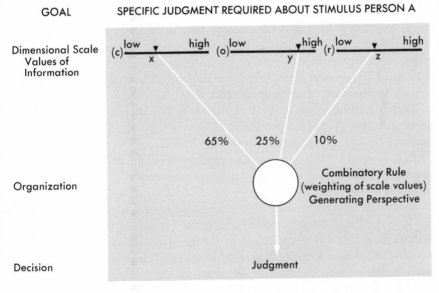

Fig. 8–1. A multidimensional single-rule structure.

pendent dimensions: c (creativity), o (orderliness), and r (reciprocity— the ability to understand another's point of view). Compared to other relevant people, person A is scaled at x, y, and z on the three dimensions respectively, and the scale values, when used in combination, are weighted 65%, 25%, and 10% in decision making. This weighting is expressed by a combinatory rule.

In manipulating the organizational properties of information processing structures, it is necessary to hold differentiation constant and vary the number and connectedness between combinatory rules. In the study described under differentiation (above) the number of dimensions was experimentally manipulated. In this same study (Faletti, 1968), experimental groups were included in which the number of dimensions used to scale applicants was held constant (three dimensions), the scale values of applicants on each dimension were also held constant, but the number of combinatory rules for organizing the scale values of information was varied.

It will be recalled that in this study ego-involved subjects were placed in a simulated personnel selection situation. The multidimensional single rule structure shown in Fig. 8–1 was induced by giving subjects three dimensions of information about each applicant, by presenting the scale value of each applicant on each dimension (for example, his scale position on creativity, orderliness, and reciprocity), and by asking the subject to generate an overall management style for each applicant on the basis of the above information. In arriving at an overall style, we assumed that the subject was combining or organizing the three scale values of information by a rule which weighted the information in various ways. The procedure is similar to that used by Asch (1946) in his studies of impression formation in which subjects were asked to write overall impressions of persons described by three adjectives.

This "combining" or "organizing" process is perhaps one of the most persistent and important problems in psychology. It has been studied particularly in the context of Gestalt psychology, person perception, and clinical judgment, but largely neglected in learning and developmental studies, which, as we indicated earlier, focus almost exclusively on the response as the criterion.

Questions about the judgment process grew out of arguments made by Meehl (1954) in his review of clinical versus statistical prediction. Judgment in these terms referred to the combination of "cues" or "components" on which inferences could be drawn. The question arose as to what mathematical formulae, if any, can we use to describe this clinical judgment process (e.g., in making judgments based on a number of M.M.P.I. profile scores).

According to the linear additive model, a judge consciously or unconsciously computes a weighted sum of the perceived components (the diagnostic judgment). Each component (scale value in the terms used in this chapter) is weighted the same for all patients (stimuli) regardless of their scale value and regardless of the value of any other components. This linear additive model makes surprisingly accurate predictions when compared to clinicians' judgments when the components (dimensions and scale values) are known (N. H. Anderson 1962; Grebstein, 1963; Hammond et al., 1964; P. J. Hoffman, 1960; Lee & Tucker, 1962; Newton, 1965; Oskamp, 1962; Wishner, 1960).

At this point, and in summary, we can state that one model of information processing involving the combination of scale values which actually fits some judgmental processes engaged in human thought, is the multidimensional single rule model. The number of dimensions involved, the scale values of stimuli, their evaluative tone and weighting are empirical matters to be determined for any stimulus domain.

Multiple Principles of Organization

One of the most common and simplistic assumptions in psychology, however, is that persons typically use single combinatory rules in judging, evaluating, and thinking. Much of the work in personality, in attitudes and needs, assumes a single "position," an "own stand." However, it is obvious that persons can generate different perspectives about the same scale values of information by varying the weighting of dimensions. This variation in weighting, the generation of alternate combinatory rules, is common when the situational context changes. But in all complex thinking and judging, people actively generate multiple perspectives and consequently alternative courses of action.

In reacting to the linear additive model in an either/or way, a number of writers have argued for a complex model commonly referred to as the configural model (Meehl, 1950). Basic to this view is the famous work of Asch (1946) in which he asked subjects to make judgments about stimulus persons who were described by a list of three or six adjectives. By manipulating key adjectives in the list, the responses that were given were observed to change radically—far more than we would expect if all six values were contributing in the framework of a single combinatory rule. Anderson (1965) interpreted this to mean that differential weighting of adjectives produced different meanings (perspectives). Configural models have also been proposed by Triandis and Fishbein (1963) and Rokeach and Rothman (1965). Hammond and Summers (1965), in abandoning the "either/or" position, find it more fruitful to look at the situational factors under which people combine cues linearly, configurally, or by both methods. Others stress the significance of set and cognitive factors in generating alternative perspectives (Bieri et al., 1966; Bruner et al., 1968; Kelly, 1955; Restle, 1961; Sarbin et al., 1967; Shranger & Altrocchi, 1964; Tagiuri & Petrullo, 1958; Warr & Knapper, 1968).

The multicombinatory rule model is illustrated in Fig. 8–2. In this information processing structure, as in the multidimensional single rule structures (see Fig. 8–1), the judge perceives three kinds of information relevant to the specific judgment about each stimulus person: creativity, orderliness, and reciprocity. Here, however, the three scale values (at

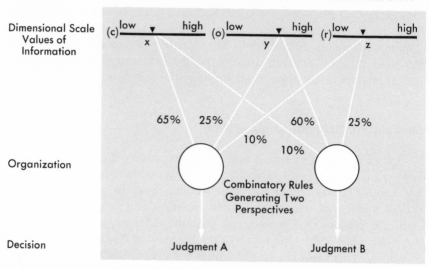

Fig. 8–2. A multidimensional multirule structure.

x, y, and z) are organized by two different combinatory rules generating two perspectives and alternative judgments about each person. Note that the information contained in this model is the same as for the single rule model shown in Fig. 8–1. The only difference is the generation of the additional perspective.

In the study using a simulated personnel selection context, it will be recalled that eight applicants were described in letters of recommendation along the three dimensions shown in Figs. 8–1 and 8–2. Post-testing indicated that the subjects in fact learned to extract three kinds of information and the appropriate scale values for each applicant on each dimension when each applicant was well known to the subject.

The multiple rule model was induced by first having the subject generate a management style for each applicant as described under the single rule structure. That is, the subject combined the three scale values of information according to a rule which weighted each component into an overall impression or perspective. To induce multiple combinatory rules, the subject was then asked to generate an additional or alternative perspective. The instructions for this induction pointed out that managers were generally capable of more than one style and requested the subject to conjure up a different style the applicant was also capable of displaying. Subjects found this to be a realistic request and found no difficulty in using the same three scale values of information to generate two different perspectives.

This ability to generate multiple perspectives by weighting similar dimensional scale values of information differently, represents a critical step in personality development in any stimulus domain. In the interpersonal domain it may be observed as a reduction in absolutistic thinking. It represents the ability to view and understand events from another person's perspective and to arrive at alternative judgments or opinions about people or events. It represents a marked advance in the complexity of thinking, in providing the foundation for an individual to generate conflict and uncertainty for himself. It has been recognized as an important stage in personality development by Piaget (1932) and Kohlberg (1964), and is described under stages of conceptual development by Schroder and Harvey (1963) and Schroder et al. (1967). Its importance in later information processing is obvious.

Connectedness Between Combinatory Rules

A great deal of variation exists in the degree to which the perspectives in a multirule information processing structure are simultaneously present and related during the judgmental process. At the earliest stage in the development of multicombinatory rules the same stimulus may be judged differently in a different situational context because of changes in the dimensions giving meaning to the stimulus. That is, some dimensions are common in both situations, but others are different. Under these conditions, information processing is based strictly on a single rule model but thinking about the stimulus (e.g., a minority group member) is less absolutistic because a different perspective can be generated with certain situational supports.

The less the overlap of common dimensions used in judgment of stimuli in two situations, (a) the more thinking is based on a single rule model, (b) the more compartmentalized the two situational perspectives, and (c) the less they can operate conjointly in thinking and judging. The more the same set of dimensions is used as a foundation for generating multiple perspectives, the greater the relevance of one to the other and the greater the possibility of joint operation in thinking and decision making.

A high degree of connectedness between multiple perspectives represents the most complex model of thinking (see Fig. 8–3). In the induction study, this level of structure was induced by first asking each subject to generate two perspectives. Then he was instructed to use and to practice using both perspectives in arriving at an overall characterization or concept of the applicant.

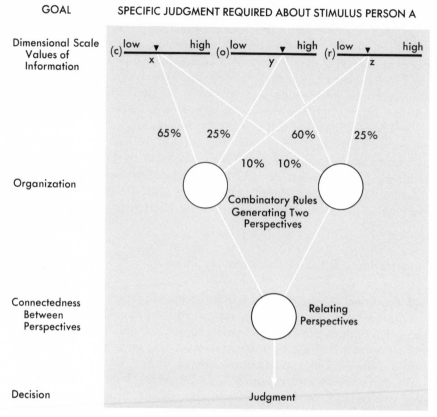

GOAL   SPECIFIC JUDGMENT REQUIRED ABOUT STIMULUS PERSON A

Dimensional Scale
Values of
Information

Organization

Connectedness
Between
Perspectives

Decision

Fig. 8–3. A multidimensional multiconnected rule structure.

MEASUREMENT OF ORGANIZATIONAL PROPERTIES

The history of methods developed for the measurement of the ways individuals reason, think, and generally process information in a given domain is a lengthy one. One set of influences goes back to Asch (1952), Maier (1930), and Duncker (1945). These workers, whose interest grew out of the Würzburg school, were similar to Gibson (1941) and Guilford (1959, 1967) in defining flexibility of thinking in terms of an individual's ability to break away from the *Aufgabe* (his initial set), to engage in many restructurings of his perceptual field, and to reinterpret or redefine information so as to adapt it to new uses.

The "water-jar" problems were designed by Luchins (1949) to measure the degree of rigidity by assessing the subject's ability to change set when meeting new problems. In a similar way Schroder and Rotter (1952) used an object-sorting task in order to train in and measure the degree to which subjects learned a higher level of behavior; namely, "looking for alternative solutions." Rigid behavior was defined as the tendency to approach a given situation with restricted attention to a given set of cues and an expectancy that there is a single pathway to reinforcement or a solution that does not change. The Luchins "water-jar" and the Schroder–Rotter object-sorting tests were primarily designed as paradigms for human learning, much like Harlow's paradigm for "training in" high-level learning sets (1949).

Extreme caution should be observed in generalizing from tests of flexibility of information processing from one stimulus domain to another. The generalization of measures of organizational factors such as flexibility can be empirically observed only when parallel tests can be developed on the basis of an explicit set of operations, in a number of stimulus domains such as the number, interpersonal, political, religious, and work domains. However, all too often, measures of flexibility have been treated as entities as though a person with complex information processing structures in one domain would be capable of the same processes in other domains. According to this overgeneralized view, we would expect a person capable of complex integrative organization of mathematical stimuli to engage similarly complex processes in dealing with religious stimuli. Clearly, this is not necessarily so. If the degree of rigidity is a learned phenomenon (Schroder & Rotter, 1952), then the degree of generalization will depend upon the similarity of the learning conditions across domains.

A further problem is that different workers use different operations to define various organizational terms such as flexibility or cognitive complexity. Commonly, no distinction is made between differentiation and the processes of organization. In an extensive study of a variety of such measures Vannoy (1965) found that scores on the Paragraph Completion Test (P.C.T.) (Phares & Schroder, 1968; Schroder et al., 1967) which was specifically designed to measure organizational processes (the number and connectedness of perspectives), were factorially independent of scores on a cluster of tests including the Bieri Interpersonal Discrimination Test (1966) which measures differentiation. Further evidence for the importance of distinguishing between measures of differentiation and the complexity of integrative factors is provided by Faletti (1968). In this study two effects were demonstrated: (1) As the degree of experimentally induced differentiation was increased, scores on tests of differentiation such as the Interpersonal Discriminations Test (1966) and the Adjective Association Test (Warr et al., 1969) systematically increased, but scores on the P.C.T. remained substantially unchanged. (2) As the degree of experimentally induced organizational complexity was increased, while holding the number of dimensional scale values of information constant, scores on the P.C.T. systematically increased while scores on the tests of differentiation remained substantially the same. In another validity study, Karlins (1967) demonstrated that P.C.T. scores were related to the ability to generate and interrelate new and conflicting information in a complex inductive interpersonal problem while scores on associative flexibility based on the Remote Association Test (Mednick, 1962) were not.

In directly approaching the processes involved in rigid behavior, Frenkel-Brunswik (1949) emphasized the intolerance of emotional, social, and cognitive incongruities, the inability to tolerate the coexistence of positive and negative factors in the same object, and the tendency to engage in black–white solutions. The related work on the authoritarian personality by Adorno et al. (1950) represented a landmark in the theory and measurement of rigid organizational structure. The F test, which grew out of this work, was a measure of authoritarian rigidity in a number of domains—morality, ethnic relations, politics, etc. Apart from the minor methodological problems of acquiescence and response bias which were relatively easy to correct, the test's major problem was its failure to measure structural properties independently of the content of belief. Rigidity was measured via the possession of a conservative ideology and the test ignored the possibility of a rigid authoritarian leftist ideology. Rokeach (1960) stressed the need to define and measure structural properties independently of belief. He developed the Dogmatism Scale on the basis of a comprehensive set of operations for structural rigidity. However, the test to a large extent still relied on the content of political belief as the context for measurement.

The work most directly related to the definition and measurement of organizational factors began with Mead (1934a,b) and Piaget (1932). Piaget was able to distinguish two major stages in conceptual development in the moral domain. The first, moral realism, was characterized by the conception of rules as externally given, as absolute. In the second, that of reciprocity, rules were anchored in "mutual respect"; they could be changed by mutual consent and modified by extenuating circumstances. Moral relativism is similar to the concept of "objectively-principled morality" (Bronfenbrenner, 1962). Clearly in this second stage of Piaget multicombinatory conceptual rules were involved (e.g., self and other perspective).

Like Piaget, Kohlberg (1958) is concerned not so much with the content of moral responses as with the thought structure behind that content. In order to measure organizational properties in the moral domain, Kohlberg developed an interview around stories posing hypothetical moral dilemmas. It was argued that the reasoning used by the child in judging right and wrong in these dilemmas reflected the conceptual properties used to structure the social and moral world (Turiel, 1968). Six stages of development or three levels of conceptual structure were isolated. At the lowest level, duty and rules are external and anchored in obedience and punishment; at the middle level, moral value resides in maintaining the conventional order, in living up to the expectancies of others, in pleasing and helping; and at the highest level, duty is defined in terms of contract, by the avoidance of violating the rights of others and is anchored in principles of logical choice.

The integrative complexity of conceptual structures used in human information processing is another index for defining organizational processes (Schroder et al., 1967). This definition, illustrated in Figs. 8-1, 8-2, and 8-3, refers to precise organizational properties, namely, the number and connectiveness of combinatory conceptual rules. The more different ways the same dimensional scale values of information can be combined and interrelated, the higher the level of integrative complexity. That is, theoretically, conceptual systems at any level of organization can vary in degree of differentiation, in the number of dimensional units of information involved. However, research indicates that the relationship between the number of dimensions of information presented and complexity of information processing is curvilinear (Streufert & Schroder, 1965). In research, the level of differentiation should be held constant when studying the effects of complexity of organizational processes.

This definition embodies many of the operations for flexibility and particularly the processes observed in studying social and moral development. It deals specifically with how (not what) a person thinks in any domain. Some of the major characteristics of information processing at the lowest level (single rule structure) are: a greater tendency toward bifurcated (black–white, good–bad, right–wrong) thinking; absolutistic standards and an apparent dependence on these fixed standards as the only authority; a greater inability to generate conflict or ambiguity and an habitual avoidance of ambiguity—an orientation in which the world is bent to fit the rule; a greater tendency to standardize judgments in a novel situation; a greater inability to interrelate perspectives; a poorer delineation between means and ends; the availability of fewer pathways for achieving ends; a poorer capacity to act "as if" and to understand the other's perspectives; and less potential to perceive the self as a causal agent in interacting with the environment.

The Paragraph Completion Test (P.C.T.) (Schroder et al., 1967) was designed to assess levels of integrative complexity in the "interpersonal-uncertainty" domain. The test presents the subject with six stems representing structure (e.g., Rules . . .), conflict (e.g., When I am criticized . . .), and uncertainty (e.g., When I am in doubt . . .) in the interpersonal area. The subject writes at least three sentences in response to each stem. Completions are scored by judges who are trained to use a manual which focuses exclusively on the structural properties of the response. Responses which could be generated by a single rule (perspective) are given a score of 1, those clearly indicating alternate but unconnected perspectives a score of 3, those indicating a relationship between two perspectives a score of 5, and those indicating multiple relationships a score of 7. Points 2, 4, and 6 represent intermediate judgments between these basic information processing structures.

This test differs from two related measures which were also specifically designed to measure conceptual complexity. Harvey's "This—I—believe" test (T.I.B.) asks the subject to complete in two or three sentences the stem "This I believe about _____," the blank being filled by such referents as myself, friendship, people, etc. Rather than allocate continuous scores, subjects are classfied into four systems (Harvey et al., 1961) which may be roughly ordered along a continuum of conceptual complexity. The main difference, however, between this test and the P.C.T. is that in using Harvey's manual, judges partly focus on the content of completions. In addition to the general referent of absolutism of response, major determinants of a subject's classification include dependency on external authority, on God and/or religion, frequency of normative statements, degree of ethnocentrism, acceptance of socially approved behavior, and concern with interpersonal relationships.

While such operations may indicate lower levels of conceptual structure, the difficulty with using these "secondary" operations is that it may contaminate studies focusing on the relationship between conceptual complexity and the possession of certain beliefs. If dependence on religion, ethnocentrism, and concern with interpersonal relations are by definition indicators of low conceptual complexity, then measures based on these referents cannot be used to investigate relationships between structural properties and the content of belief in these domains. This difficulty in no way affects the use of T.I.B. scores for the general assessment of conceptual complexity in these domains.

The Interpersonal Topical Inventory (I.T.I.) (Tuckman, 1966) is a modification of an earlier test developed by Schroder and Hunt (1959). Here the subject is given the same sentence stems as those used in the Schroder P.C.T. and is asked to choose between alternative completions. Alternative completions represent responses judged, on the basis of the P.C.T. manual, to fall at different places along the continuum of integrative complexity. The assumption here is that more conceptually complex individuals will choose the more conceptually complex completion. A number of studies show a significant low-order positive correlation between the I.T.I. and the P.C.T. Tuckman reports a correlation of .54 between the two tests using 92 naval recruits. Suedfeld et al. found a correlation of .19, with 178 college students (1969). The I.T.I., however, is subject to all the problems of forced-choice objective tests—scores are easily changed by instructions, set, and knowledge. Further, unpublished studies by Hunt and Schroder indicate that the relationship between I.T.I. and the P.C.T. tends to decrease as education increases (see also Tuckman, 1966, *vs.* Suedfeld et al., 1969, above).

Gardiner (1968) has just completed the most extensive study to date on tests of conceptual complexity. This timely factorial study showed that tests such as the P.C.T., T.I.B., and I.T.I. define a factor easily interpreted as level of conceptual complexity, and that this factor is relatively unrelated to measures of differentiation.

The validity of the P.C.T. using the structural manual was experimentally investigated in the Faletti (1968) study. In this study three information processing structures were induced using the simulated personnel selection situation. The information processing structures presented to three matched groups were (A) two-dimensional single combinatory rule, (B) three-dimensional single combinatory rule, and (C) three-dimensional connected multiple combinatory rule. Following the induction, a domain-specific P.C.T., in which the stems refer to applicants, was administered. That is, subjects had been taught to use single or multiple combinatory rules to think about each applicant. If such induced organizational differences affect the structural properties of the paragraph completions, integrative complexity scores should be higher for group C than for groups A and B. The results strongly support the use of the P.C.T. and the manual for assessing the integrative complexity of information processing structures.

Later in the chapter a number of construct validity studies will be presented which provide additional support for use of the P.C.T. manual for measuring structural properties. The problem in using the P.C.T. measure is, of course, the necessity to have trained judges and the amount of time required to train the judges and then score the protocols. Further, our research indicates that the application of traditional objective test items to the measurement of structural properties is inappropriate and all such attempts have failed in cross validation studies. In attempting to overcome this problem, initial studies in the development of a computer procedure for scoring the structural properties of verbal responses are in progress (Carrington, 1968).

A sample of 335 P.C.T. protocols was analyzed by computer to develop an empirical scoring system based on single word frequencies. The analysis indicated different distributions of words for completions judged to differ in integrative complexity score by the hand-scoring procedure. Further, many of the words which discriminated between the high and low scoring groups were judged to be theoretically relevant. When a weighted computer manual based on this sample was cross-validated on a new sample of 121 protocols, the correlation between the computer and hand scores was .62. While a great deal more work is required before this procedure can be used for research purposes, it does appear to show promise. A further advantage is that the procedure will lend itself to scoring all verbal materials, e.g., verbalizations of classroom teachers, parents in interaction with children, political speeches, compositions, etc.

DEVELOPMENT OF ORGANIZATIONAL PROPERTIES

While differentiation and the learning of dimensional properties can be understood in the framework of traditional learning principles, the development of conceptual structures for organizing scale values of information depends upon the nature and extent of "organizational learning." That is, we learn new categories or dimensions via conditioning, the selective operation of rewards and punishments, through observation and language. How we organize scale values of information, already acquired, is a product of the type of environment provided for "organizational" learning.

One type of environment commonly used for organizational learning is characterized by (1) training agent (parent, teacher) determination of combinatory rule and the goal to be reached using the dimensions learned, (2) agent determination of criteria for evaluating child's responses when using the rule, and (3) agent administration of punishments and rewards depending on the degree to which the child's responses match the standards of the agent. This unilateral environment rests on the principles of agent determination of combinatory rule and agent "control of behavior." Training for organizational learning, which falls at the other extreme of this continuum, is characterized by the development of an environment (1) in which the child generates combinatory rules and goals which are relevant to the dimensions or categories previously acquired; (2) which feeds back information relevant to the perspectives, strategies, and goals generated; (3) which is intrinsically interesting and encourages the generation of different uses of the same information. This interdependent environment rests on the principles of the self-generation of combinatory rules and of environmental control.

In unilateral environments the child learns a more or less stable dispositional tendency to look externally for a fixed rule for combining information; he learns to avoid ambiguity and to think by the application and modification of a single perspective. When the child learns to use information in a more interdependent environment he learns to generate combinatory rules, to think by testing the consequences of alternative perspectives, to engage in choice, and to perceive himself as a causal agent.

While there are many gradations between these two extreme environments for learning organizational properties, it will be sufficient in this chapter to summarize evidence which supports this gross distinction. In describing the home environment of rigid authoritarian children, Frenkel-Brunswik (1949) observed that discipline was more traumatic and overpowering, that the environment was characterized by the expectation (on the part of the parent) for the rapid learning of external rigid and superficial rules, and that family role relationships were defined more in terms of dominance and submission. Other investigations do not necessarily stress the punitiveness of the environment; in fact, benevolent unilateral training would also be expected to produce single rule structure. Bronfenbrenner (1962) in outlining five character structures contrasts an adult-oriented training with a more interdependent environment. The latter is characterized by a strong, differentiated family organization with high levels of affection which encourages the child to participate in selected but varied peer group activities both with and without adult supervision. In using dimensions of interpersonal information in this environment the child develops an "objectively-principled" character structure in which morality is based on the individual's capacity to assume, compare, and combine multiple perspectives (resulting in autonomous standards).

In considering the conditions underlying moral development from the egocentric stage of moral realism (single rule structure) to the stage of reciprocity (involving multiple perspectives), Piaget (1950) observes "cooperation alone can shake the child out of its initial state of unconscious egocentrism . . . by forcing the individual to be constantly occupied with the point of view of other people so as to compare it with his own" (p. 190). Similarly, Hoffman (1963a, 1963b) selected children who were (1) conventionals—who tended not to consider the circumstances of transgression but cited fixed principles based on authority and (2) humanists—who considered contextual circumstances and took other human factors into account. The humanist orientation was shown to stem from training practices which minimize frustration, provide explanations, and substitute outlets; which capitalize on the child's potential for empathy; and which permit him to experience the consequences of his acts from another's point of view. These cooperative and inductive training practices exemplify the properties of an interdependent environment.

Experimental studies of organizational learning also support the unilateral-interdependent continuum. In an object-sorting task, Schroder and Rotter (1952) trained one group of subjects to use categories of information in a single fixed way to solve a series of problems. Another group could solve the problems by alternative methods. The group given the opportunity to look for and use alternative solutions was more flexible in a transfer situation. Using the autotelic environment of Anderson and Moore (1960) in conjunction with a "talking typewriter" in teaching reading, children learned to generate and use the principles of phonetics even though such principles had never been taught. This observation is indeed a classic demonstration of the impact of an interdependent environment on organizational learning—in this case the reorganization of learned information into rules of phonetics.

In a more direct study by Lee (1968) single rule and multiconnected rule structures were directly induced using the simulated personnel selection situation. Subjects were trained to use either simple or complex information processing structures to think about eight applicants and make overall judgments as to their suitability for management positions. Dyads of ego-involved subjects who disagreed about the overall effectiveness of applicants were placed in an interaction situation and required to reach a unanimous decision. The question posed here was, "Can such direct short-term induction affect the way individuals use information in a conflicting interpersonal problem situation?" The induction was found to influence significantly the extent to which individuals generate new perspectives in problem solving and in this sense it affected the level of information processing in interaction. In this situation, however, the induction did not influence those characteristics of interaction which imply openness to more complex levels of information processing. These characteristics include the number of times the subject probed the other's perspective, and the extent to which the subject contributed to an atmosphere supportive of reciprocal information processing.

The induction of different information processing structures opens up a direct experimental method for studying the principles of organizational learning and its effects.

SITUATIONAL AND DISPOSITIONAL EFFECTS ON INFORMATION PROCESSING

The less an individual is exposed to organizational training in an inductive interdependent environment, the more conceptual organization becomes arrested at a lower stage of development. Given an optimal interdependent environment, organizational development proceeds through universal stages in any stimulus domain—from categorical single dimensional valuing and thinking through multidimensional single rule structure, multidimensional multirule (unconnected) structure, to multidimensional multiconnected combinatory rule structure. More unilateral, overpowering, or stressful environments lead to arrestation at some lower stage of development.

These long-term training effects in a domain (e.g., in the interpersonal or moral domain) result in the development of more or less stable dispositional information processing structures. Such dispositional tendencies in the interpersonal domain have been measured by applying the structural manual to responses on the Paragraph Completion Test. With the measurement of dispositional conceptual level, it becomes possible to study the interaction between long-term dispositional and short-term situational variables on information processing. The following is a summary of some of the main interactive studies.

Problem Solving

In a series of experiments (Streufert & Castore, 1968; Suedfeld & Streufert, 1966) it has been shown that the interactive effect of dispositional and situational factors on information processing may be expressed as a family of inverted "U" curves (see Fig. 8-4). For any individual, the flexibility of integration involved in information processing will increase as the environment becomes richer (presents more diverse information) until an optimal level of functioning is reached. If the complexity of the environment is increased beyond this point, the level of integration involved in performance begins to decrease. Individuals with higher dispositional levels of conceptual complexity in any domain are capable of higher levels of information processing than low dispositional conceptual level persons in the middle ranges of environmental complexity (see curves in Fig. 8-4). As environmental characteristics become more extreme (increasingly impoverished or complex), organizational properties rapidly deteriorate to a point so low that individual differences cease to exist.

Various forms of a complex problem-solving situation were used to test these hypotheses (Brooks, 1962; Karlins et al., 1965; Lawrence, 1962; Streufert et al., 1965). The situation consisted of a simulated war game in which each team was given the task of making decisions regarding an invasion. Teams were told they were playing against another team; however, all the functions of the opposing team were programmed in order to achieve experimental control over such factors as complexity of feedback and success. Teams of four could issue orders

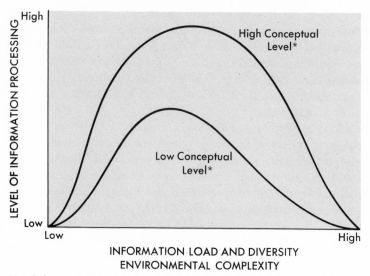

INFORMATION LOAD AND DIVERSITY
ENVIRONMENTAL COMPLEXITY

*Level of conceptual structure is a mediating linkage between environmental factors
and information processing characteristics.

Fig. 8–4. Level of information processing expressed as an interaction between dispositional and situational factors.

and the "programmers" would feed back either "actual" observations which would be made (as a consequence, for example, of reconnaissance) or the "actual" results of actions. Team members could arrive at hypotheses about the enemy and develop strategies on the basis of feedback. One objective index of level of information processing was defined as the number of different connections made between different kinds of feedback and the number of integrations or perspectives generated from a given set of observations in arriving at decisions.

In order to vary the complexity of the environmental input, each team was exposed to seven differing load conditions. During each half-hour game period, teams received either 2, 5, 8, 10, 12, 15, or 25 independent informative statements as feedback from actions taken. The sequential order of load periods was randomized while the amount of success for each period was held constant. Analysis of a rating scale filled out by subjects in various phases of the game indicated that they perceived themselves to be in a moderately favorable position in each period.

The results are presented in Fig. 8–5. The solid line expresses an inverted "U" curve relationship between environmental load and diversity and level of information processing for people in general. In informationally restricted environments, the integrative processes remain unstimulated—simple organizational properties are sufficient to handle the environment. Conceptual properties increase in complexity until reaching an optimal point in the period when information load is ten diverse dimensional units per half-hour period. Further increases in environmental load beyond this point lead to a regressive effect on organizational properties. Using a similar experimental situation, the same relationship has been demonstrated to hold between variations in team success and failure and level of information processing when environmental complexity was held constant (Streufert & Streufert, 1967). This is an important finding since it demonstrates the significance of motivational and affective factors in the environment on conceptual structure. Superoptimal success conditions fail to stimulate organizational processes. Superoptimal success under conditions of involvement has an effect similar to that of superoptimal information load. Both act as stressors, progressively reducing the connectedness and then the number of structures for combining information until the stage of stereotyped single rule functioning is reached. From then on, in this complex strategy game, invalidating feedback quickly leads to retaliatory behavior—the team simply reacts to the actions of the "opponent."

The upper and lower curves in Fig. 8–5 illustrate how different levels of conceptual complexity influence the effect of the environment on information processing. In this experiment, two groups of forty subjects, differing in conceptual level, were selected on the basis of paragraph completions. Individuals in the high conceptual level group used connected multiple rules, while the low conceptual groups were judged to use single or unconnected single rules in responding to the stems in the domain of interpersonal conflict and uncertainty. Groups were matched on SAT verbal and quantitative scores, age, and grade. The results show that differences in dispositional conceptual level may be expressed as a family of "U" curves which define the function relating information load and level of information processing in performance. It was surprising to observe that optimal environmental complexity was the same for both dispositional groups, but in keeping with our expectations, differences in information processing between groups were at a maximum in the central ranges of environmental complexity and decreased as the extremes were approached.

The results of this experiment do not necessarily imply that dispositional organizational properties generalize from the interpersonal domain (Paragraph Completion Test) to problem solving in a complex strategy game. On the contrary, the experiment was designed so as to minimize the intrusion of generalization effects. In setting up four-man teams and in structuring the situation as a team game, the level of information processing in decision making was a direct function of such interpersonal

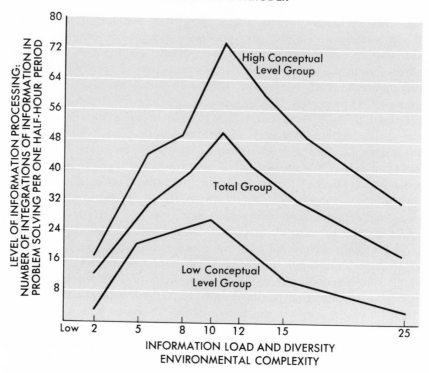

Fig. 8–5. Levels of conceptual structure mediating between environmental complexity and level of information processing.

factors as (1) team members' openness to another's perspectives, (2) the number of perspectives generated, (3) the tendency to study, understand, and use others' perspectives, and (4) the tendency to support others' perspectives. Independent studies support the contention that such tendencies are significantly higher in high dispositional conceptual level teams (Schroder et al., 1964; Lee, 1968). Another experiment (Suedfeld & Hagen, 1966) showed that high conceptual level subjects were better at solving complex verbal problems, but not at solving simple ones.

In related studies using different experimental settings, it has been shown that high dispositional conceptual level teams, as compared to low conceptual level teams, (1) discover more information about competing teams in intergroup, international, and business simulations (Tuckman, 1964; Driver, 1962); (2) exhibit higher levels of information processing under stressful competitive conditions in a simulated internation simulation situation (Driver, 1963); and (3) engage in more complex information processing when presented with conflicting attitudinal information in a stimulus–social deprivation situation (Streufert et al., 1965b; Suedfeld, 1963). Suedfeld (1963, 1964a) also demonstrated that levels of information processing following the presentation of discrepant attitudinal information are lower under conditions of stimulus and social deprivation. This study and others (Suedfeld, 1964b; Suedfeld & Streufert, 1966; Suedfeld & Vernon, 1966) demonstrate the regressive effects of sensory and informational restriction on information processing, and support the "U" curve function mediating between the environment and information processing.

This interactive model has important implications for social development and education. It implies that individuals disposed to process information at a given level will function optimally at a particular level of environmental complexity. In Fig. 8–4, it will be noted that a more structured environment containing fewer degrees of freedom (less complexity) is required to optimize the level of information processing of a dispositionally low conceptual level person.

Some of the most provocative work in moral and educational development using such an interactive model is being done by Grant et al. (1963), D. E. Hunt (1966, 1968), Kelman (1961), Kohlberg (1964), Palmer (1968), and Turiel (1966). These authors, following Piaget (1932) and J. McV. Hunt (1961), are studying the match between the schemata within the organism and characteristics of the environment as the conceptual foundations for understanding development.

Social Attitudes

This approach of looking at attitude as an information processing structure is similar to the work on social judgment (Sherif & Hovland, 1961; Sherif et al., 1965) and to the ideas of Adorno et al. (1950), Katz and Stotland (1959), Rokeach (1960), and Smith et al. (1956). Expressed in structural terms, an attitude may be represented by (1) the number and nature of dimensions engaged in any stimulus domain, and (2) the number and connectedness of conceptual rules used to combine such scale values of information.

If we view attitude in this way, we can expect to find the same "U" curve relationship as shown in Fig. 8–5 for problem solving. Differences in the organizational properties of attitudes may be expressed as a family of "U" curves mediating between situational factors and level of information processing.

A number of studies shows that intensity of involvement in an attitude and the extremity of one's own overall stand on an issue are related to: (1) the exaggeration of the scaled distances between discrepant (pro and con) stimuli. This is strongest for statements highly discrepant from one's own position and is termed contrast. (2) Making more extreme (and fewer neutral) ratings of stimuli in the domain. This is a consequence of the tendency to exaggerate the discrepancies between statements (stimuli) closer to, and more distant from, the "own" position. (3) Greater consistency in ordering attitude-relevant stimuli; and (4) a wider latitude of rejection relative to the latitudes of acceptance (Coffman, 1967; Sherif & Hovland, 1961).

In a related set of studies, Driver (1962) investigated the effect of involvement on information processing performance issuing from attitudes developed in an internation simulation situation. He found that the amount of different and conflicting information integrated in decision making and the number of new dimensions of information generated in interaction (the level of information processing) were highest at a moderate level of involvement. As involvement became either increasingly intense, or decreased from the optimal point, the level of information processing decreased. Evidently, too little involvement fails to stimulate organizational processes and reduces the conceptual properties for structuring stimuli, thus decreasing the consistency of ordering of attitude-relevant stimuli. Too much involvement in an issue can reduce the connectedness between and the number of combinatory rules for organizing stimuli. Increasing stereotypy is a well established concomitant of increasing competitiveness and conflict (Sherif et al., 1961).

In addition to these purely environmental effects on the organizational properties of attitudes, Coffman (1967) also demonstrated the importance of taking dispositional tendencies of information processing into account. Like Berkowitz (1960) and R. Brown (1953), he argued that involvement would manifest itself differently in structurally different personality systems. As expected, he found that (1) the directionality of attitudes toward Negroes was not related to dispositional conceptual level, (2) high involvement led to significant increases in contrast (exaggerating the distance between neutral statements and the subject's own stand) for dispositionally low conceptual level subjects, and (3) such contrast effects were not characteristic of the highly involved dispositionally high conceptual level subjects.

From these results it seems clear that dispositional organizational tendencies, as well as situational factors, must be taken into account in understanding attitudinal functioning. As in the studies on problem solving, a single rule attitude is capable of generating only a single perspective. Such individuals are incapable of simultaneously understanding the issues from other points of view or of taking multiple perspectives into account in thinking in that domain. As involvement or uncertainty increases, thinking becomes more absolutistic, attitude change becomes more black–white (Crutchfield, 1955; Janicki, 1964;

Koslin et al., 1967; Suedfeld, 1964a) and the latitude of acceptance and range of neutral stimuli decrease.

In single rule structure the traditional model, which conceives of attitude as a scale running from pro to con on which we express an individual's "own position," is a reasonably good fit. However, this model is a gross oversimplification for a connected multirule attitude. The integratively complex attitude is more like a set of partially over-lapping circles, each circle representing a somewhat different weighting combination of the same or similar information and each connected to the others. Such attitudes are characterized by many connected "stands." These complex structures are relatively more resistant to the regressive effects of load and involvement (Schroder et al., 1962).

Studies by Schroder and Crano (1965) and Harvey and Ware (1967) illustrate the importance of conceptual system differences in attitude change research. According to many balance models and the dissonance reduction model (Festinger, 1957), information processing induced by dissonance or conflict has as its aim the reduction of the dissonance. Such "reduction" models predict resolution processes which are inter-nally consistent in achieving the goal of conflict reduction. These proc-esses, however, are characteristic of a single rule structure only. In the Schroder and Crano study, six different resolution processes were meas-ured following the presentation of counternorm information: acceptance (movement of attitude toward message), rejection (movement away from message), assimilation (perceive message as being closer to one's position), contrast (exaggeration of differences between message and own position), source approbation (attitude toward source of message becomes more positive), source deprecation (attitude to source becomes more negative). The results show that subjects with more simply struc-tured attitudes either engaged resolution processes in a more internally consistent manner (e.g., rejection with source deprecation and contrast) or utilized processes in a mutually exclusive manner. The more com-plex the attitude structure (the greater the number of discrepant com-binatory rules), the greater the range of processes engaged and the lower the tendency to achieve balance or reduce uncertainty or conflict. Conflict becomes a property of the more complex system. According to a strict interpretation of some proponents of the social judgment theory, increasing involvement is invariably accompanied by increasing bigotry. This is primarily true for dispositionally low conceptual level attitude structures. The goal of social development is the evolvement of conceptual properties which permit the person to be involved in is-sues while engaging high levels of information processing. At higher stages of conceptual development, self-definition is less anchored in terms of the contents (e.g., belief or own stand) and increasingly in the ability to engage in complex information processing.

SOCIAL INTERACTION

Experiments have demonstrated the level of information processing in interpersonal interaction to be a major variable in understanding social organization (Harvey & Schroder, 1963). Like conceptual structure, the level of social structure may be described in terms of (1) the stage of conceptual organization (in the interpersonal domain) of persons making up a group, (2) the degree to which subgroups (combinations of persons) become institutionalized for the purpose of maintaining conflicting perspectives in the system, and (3) the extent to which social procedures evolve for connecting and relating the differing subgroups.

A simple social system may be illustrated by a hierarchical pyramid-like structure in which a single authority is salient. Higher stages of social development are characterized by the utilization of conflict in decision making. The general hypothesis is that dispositional conceptual level of group members and environmental factors interact in group development. The level of information processing of group members sets limits to the level of group development which can be achieved.

In the simulated personnel selection situation (Lee, 1968), half the subjects were taught to use a single combinatory rule structure and the remaining half a connected multicombinatory rule structure (see Figs. 8-1 and 8-3, pp. 249 and 254). Dyads differing in induced conceptual complexity who disagreed about the overall effectiveness of applicants were then placed in interaction and required to arrive at a unanimous ranking. Lee found that those subjects who were given more connected combinatory rules to process information about the applicants generated and used more perspectives in arriving at decisions.

This ability to consider a number of different perspectives in resolving interpersonal conflict is an operation for higher stages of social development. Similar results have been achieved via differential short-term training sequences by Lewin et al. (1939) using authoritarian, laissez-faire, and democratic environments. Experiments by Bandura and McDonald (1963) and Le Furgy and Woloshin (1968) used social reinforcement and social influence in order to modify the level of moral judgment in children. In both of the latter cases, however, a response criterion was used and we cannot be sure that organizational changes did in fact occur.

In addition to the influences of induction, Lee studied the effects of dispositional conceptual level on social interaction. Compared to individuals using single rule structure, individuals judged to use multiple interrelated rules in the Paragraph Completion Test responded to interpersonal conflict by generating more alternative perspectives to arrive at new and different ways to characterize applicants. This orientation was similar to that produced via induction. However, high dispositional conceptual level subjects demonstrated the following characteristics typical of complex social information processing: (1) a stronger tendency to probe the other member in coming to understand his perspectives, (2) a stronger tendency to use and elaborate upon the other's perspectives (not necessarily implying agreement), (3) more frequent support of the other member (via verbal reward or expressions of interest for verbalizing his perspectives), and (4) less tendency to steamroll, interrupt, or reject the other member's attempts to express his alternative views.

Stager (1967) composed teams of four persons to compete against a "programmed" team in a complex strategy war game (see p. 263). The teams differed in terms of the number of dispositionally high conceptual level members in a group. The remaining members were rated as low (single rule) structure on the Paragraph Completion Test. As the percentage of high conceptual level team members increased from 20 per cent through 50 per cent and 75 per cent to 100 per cent, there was a corresponding increase in the tendency for groups to generate and use conflict as the vehicle for making decisions.

In studying task-oriented groups composed of low as opposed to high conceptual level individuals in a range of experimental settings, a persistent observation has been made. The strategy for low conceptual level teams is to reach agreement on the "best" way to view the situation. During this period, interpersonal disagreement may occur—particularly in the early stages before clear status roles develop—but the conflict involves a struggle to have the group adopt a particular schema or hypothesis about the environment. Once the schema is adopted, decisions are more or less deduced from this single rule structure. If feedback requires it, a part of the schema is modified, but characteristically a single rule schema is operative as a basis for decision making and the function of the group is to maintain the most effective plan or theory possible as a basis for action.

High conceptual level teams, on the other hand, are characterized by interaction which supports the evolvement and elaboration of different schemas or perspectives by different team members or combinations of members. This early period involves search and the consideration and isolation of perspectives which have clearly different and conflicting task implications. Decisions are made by testing interrelated implications of each hypothesis which the group considers to be relevant (depending upon the degrees of stress in the environment) and developing the best possible strategy to fit such a range of possibilities. Again, feedback is used to modify, support, or eliminate perspectives, but multiple connected schemas are maintained as the vehicle for adapting.

This same difference between high and low conceptual level functioning has been demonstrated at the individual level in person perception. Studies by Streufert (1966) and Talbot (1968) show that high conceptual level persons change their impressions of others as the situation changes or as new information is added. Talbot utilized a sequence of closed circuit TV interviews to introduce new information to experimental subjects. In both experiments, low conceptual level persons maintained more static and constant impressions of persons as the circumstances changed.

Tuckman (1964) observed that similar patterns of social interaction evolve in homogeneous teams in a simulated competitive business game. In this study, teams were composed of individuals judged to be low, medium low, medium high, and high dispositional conceptual level. The level of social structure which emerged matched the interpersonal conceptual level of members making up the teams. That is, teams composed of low conceptual level persons were more hierarchically organized while high conceptual level teams developed more flexible integratively complex structures. C. C. Anderson (1968) has recently pointed out the implications of such findings for corporate and educational administration. In the studies reported, team members of contrasting groups were matched on verbal and quantitative SAT scores, age, grade, and dominance. Since characteristics of social organization do not emerge clearly until considerable interaction takes place, most studies extended over long periods of time.

Finally, in a study carried out in a natural social interaction setting, Crouse et al. (1968) investigated the relationship between level of interpersonal conceptual organization and patterns of interaction in forty-two married couples. Various aspects of marital interaction including such empathic factors as understanding the other, realization of understanding, correctly feeling understood, and correctly feeling misunderstood, are characteristic of higher levels of information processing. These tendencies were measured via the Interpersonal Perception Method (Laing et al., 1966). The results show that compared to low conceptual level couples, high conceptual level couples are more accurate in their perception of differences and are happier.

SUMMARY

In this chapter, an information processing model was applied to the study of personality. The conceptual properties which generate various levels of information processing were defined as (1) dimensions or categories which determine the number of meanings or scale values of information attributed to any range of stimuli, and (2) combinatory rules which determine the number of and connectedness between different rules for combining (weighting) the same scale values of information.

Levels of organization were described in terms of the number and connectedness of combinatory conceptual rules available for processing information with degree of differentiation held constant. Conceptual level increases from single combinatory rule structure through unconnected multiple rule structure to connected multiple rule structure. Experimental operations for inducing information processing structures at various levels were presented. The experimental induction of such structures provides a method for testing the implications of the model. Evidence was presented to show that more inductive, interdependent developmental environments (as opposed to authoritarian unilateral environments) were associated with the evolvement of higher levels of conceptual structure. This level can vary across domains depending upon the characteristic training environment in each domain. Such long-term factors lead to the development of a more or less stable disposition (dispositional conceptual level) to process information at a particular level over a given range of stimuli.

In a number of studies, it was shown that different dispositional levels of conceptual organization may be expressed as a family of "U" curves mediating differentially between environmental complexity and level of information processing. Information processing characteristics reach a maximum at a moderate level of environmental complexity (information load, diversity, success, and involvement) and decrease as either extreme is approached (e.g., as with too little or too much involvement, or too little or too much stimulation).

This information processing model was then applied to the study of social attitudes, social problem solving, and social interaction. A high level of information processing in these areas does not necessarily define the "best" performance. What is "good" performance depends upon the criterion which one applies. When the situation is more or less static, and when the appropriate interpretation and strategy for achieving a particular goal are known, then single rule (low information processing) can achieve a high level of "success." When the situation is changing, when the task calls for the definition of goals and means, and when alternative perspectives are meaningful, then higher levels of information processing are more effective.

References

ABELSON, R. P. Computer simulation of "hot" cognition. In S. S. Tomkins & S. Messick (Eds.), *Computer simulation of personality.* New York: Wiley, 1963.

ABELSON, R. P. Simulation of social behavior. In G. Lindzey & E. Aronson (Eds.), *Handbook of social psychology.* Vol. 2. (Rev. ed.) Reading, Mass.: Addison–Wesley, 1968. (a)

ABELSON, R. P. When the polls go wrong and why. *Transaction,* 1968, **5,** 20–27. (b)

ABELSON, R. P., ARONSON, E., McGUIRE, W. J., NEWCOMB, T. M., ROSENBERG, M. J., & TANNENBAUM, P. E. (Eds.), *Theories of cognitive consistency: A sourcebook.* Chicago: Rand McNally, 1968.

ABELSON, R. P., & CARROLL, J. D. Computer simulation of individual belief systems. *American Behavioral Scientist,* 1965, **8,** 24–30.

ADORNO, T. W., FRENKEL-BRUNSWIK, E., LEVINSON, D. J., & SANFORD, R. N. *The authoritarian personality.* New York: Harper & Row, 1950.

AKHTAR, M. The role of counterconditioning in intermittent reinforcement. Unpublished doctoral dissertation, University of Illinois, 1962.

ALEXANDER, F., & PORTIS, S. A. Psychosomatic study of hypoglycaemic fatigue. *Psychosomatic Medicine,* 1944, **6,** 191–205.

ALLPORT, F. H. *Social psychology.* Boston: Houghton Mifflin, 1924.

ALLPORT, F. H. *Theories of perception and the concept of structure.* New York: Wiley, 1955.

ALLPORT, G. W. *Personality: A psychological interpretation.* New York: Holt, 1937.

ALLPORT, G. W. The historical background of modern social psychology. In G. Lindzey (Ed.), *Handbook of social psychology.* Vol. 1. Reading, Mass.: Addison–Wesley, 1954.

AMSEL, A. The role of frustrative non-reward in non-continuous reward situations. *Psychological Bulletin,* 1958, **55,** 102–119.

AMSEL, A., & ROUSSEL, J. Motivational properties of frustration: I. Effect on running response of the addition of frustration to the motivational complex. *Journal of Experimental Psychology,* 1952, **43,** 363–368.

ANDERSON, C. C. Technology and education. *Alberta Journal of Educational Research,* 1968, **14,** 5–13.

ANDERSON, N. H. Application of an additive model to impression formation. *Science,* 1962, **138,** 817–818.

ANDERSON, N. H. Primary effects in personality impression formation using a generalized order effect paradigm. *Journal of Personality and Social Psychology,* 1965, **63,** 346–350.

ANDERSON, O. R., & MOORE, O. K. Autotelic folk models. *Sociological Quarterly,* 1960, **1,** 203–216.

APPLETON, L. E. *A comparative study of the play activities of adult savages and civilized children.* Chicago: University of Chicago Press, 1910.

ARIÈS, P. *Centuries of childhood: A social history of family life.* (Trans. R. Baldick.) New York: Knopf, 1962.

ASCH, S. E. Forming impressions of personality. *Journal of Abnormal and Social Psychology,* 1946, **41,** 258–290.

Asch, S. E. Effects of group pressure upon the modification and distortion of judgments. In H. Guetzkow (Ed.), *Groups, leadership and men.* Pittsburgh: Carnegie Press, 1951. (Republished: In E. E. Maccoby, T. M. Newcomb, & E. L. Hartley (Eds.), *Readings in social psychology.* New York: Holt, Rinehart, & Winston, 1958.)

Asch, S. E. *Social psychology.* Englewood Cliffs, N.J.: Prentice-Hall, 1952.

Ashby, W. R. *Design for a brain.* New York: Wiley, 1952.

Attneave, F. Some informational aspects of visual perception. *Psychological Review,* 1954, **61**, 183–193.

Attneave, F. *Applications of information theory to psychology.* New York: Holt, Rinehart, & Winston, 1959.

Baldwin, A. L. Socialization and the parent–child relationship. *Child Development,* 1948, **19**, 127–136.

Baldwin, A. L. The effect of home environment on nursery school behavior. *Child Development,* 1949, **20**, 49–62.

Baldwin, A. L., Kalhorn, J., & Breese, F. H. Patterns of parent behavior. *Psychological Monographs,* 1945, **58**, 1–75.

Baldwin, A. L., Kalhorn, J., & Breese, F. H. The appraisal of parent behavior. *Psychological Monographs,* 1949, **63** (4, Whole No. 299).

Baldwin, J. M. 1895. *Mental development in the child and in the race: Methods and processes.* (3rd ed.) New York: Macmillan, 1906.

Bandura, A., & McDonald, F. J. The influence of social reinforcement and the behavior of models in shaping children's moral judgments. *Journal of Abnormal and Social Psychology,* 1963, **67**, 274–281.

Bandura, A., & Walters, R. H. *Adolescent aggression.* New York: Ronald Press, 1959.

Barber, J. D. *Power in committees.* New York: Rand McNally, 1966.

Bar-Hillel, Y. An examination of information theory. *Philosophy of Science,* 1955, **22**, 86–105.

Barron, F. Complexity-simplicity as a personality dimension. *Journal of Abnormal and Social Psychology,* 1953, **48**, 163–172.

Bartlett, F. C. *Remembering: A study in experimental and social psychology.* Cambridge: Cambridge University Press, 1932.

Bartoshuk, A. K. Human neonatal cardiac acceleration to sound: Habituation and dishabituation. *Perceptual and Motor Skills,* 1962, **15**, 15–27. (a)

Bartoshuk, A. K. Response decrement with repeated elicitation of human neonatal cardiac acceleration to sound. *Journal of Comparative and Physiological Psychology,* 1962, **55**, 9–13. (b)

Batchelder, W. NSF summer institute on computer science in social behavior. Boulder, Colo.: Science Research, 1968.

Bates, F., & Douglas, M. *Programming language one.* Englewood Cliffs, N.J.: Prentice-Hall, 1967.

Bavelas, A. Communication patterns of task-oriented groups. *Journal of the Acoustic Society of America,* 1950, **22**, 725–730.

Beach, F. A. Current concepts of play in animals. *American Naturalist,* 1945, **79**, 523–541.

Beach, F. A. The descent of instinct. *Psychological Review,* 1955, **62**, 401–410.

Beach, F. A. Characteristics of masculine "sex drive." *Nebraska Symposium on Motivation,* 1956, **4**, 1–32. (Lincoln: University of Nebraska Press.)

Bean, C. H. An unusual opportunity to investigate the psychology of language. *Journal of Genetic Psychology,* 1932, **40**, 181–202.

Beck, R. C. On secondary reinforcement and shock termination. *Psychological Bulletin,* 1961, **58**, 28–45.

Bell, C. Idea of a new anatomy of the brain submitted for the observation of his friends. In J. F. Fulton (Ed.), *Selected readings in the history of physiology.* Springfield, Ill.: Charles C Thomas, 1931.

BELL, E. G. Inner-directed and other-directed attitudes. Unpublished doctoral dissertation, Yale University, 1955.

BENEDEK, T. Personality development. In F. Alexander & Helen Ross (Eds.), *Dynamic psychiatry*. Chicago: University of Chicago Press, 1952.

BENNETT, E. L., DIAMOND, M. C., KRECH, D., & ROSENZWEIG, M. R. Chemical and anatomical plasticity of the brain. *Science*, 1964, **146**, 610–619.

BEREITER, C., ENGELMANN, S., OSBORN, J., & REIDFORD, P. A. An academically oriented pre-school for culturally deprived children. In F. M. Hechinger (Ed.), *Pre-school education today*. Garden City, N.Y.: Doubleday, 1966.

BERKOWITZ, L. Leveling tendencies and complexity-simplicity dimension. *Journal of Personality*, 1957, **25**, 743–751.

BERKOWITZ, L. The judgmental process in personality functioning. *Psychological Review*, 1960, **67**, 130–142.

BERLYNE, D. E. Novelty and curiosity as determinants of exploratory behavior. *British Journal of Psychology*, 1950, **41**, 68–80.

BERLYNE, D. E. Attention to change, conditioned inhibition (sIr) and stimulus satiation. *British Journal of Psychology*, 1957, **48**, 138–140. (a)

BERLYNE, D. E. Conflict and information-theory variables as determinants of human perceptual curiosity. *Journal of Experimental Psychology*, 1957, **53**, 399–404. (b)

BERLYNE, D. E. Uncertainty and conflict: A point of contact between information theory and behavior-theory concepts. *Psychological Review*, 1957, **64**, 329–339. (c)

BERLYNE, D. E. The influence of complexity and novelty in visual figures on orienting responses. *Journal of Experimental Psychology*, 1958, **55**, 289–296. (a)

BERLYNE, D. E. Supplementary report: Complexity and orienting responses with longer exposures. *Journal of Experimental Psychology*, 1958, **56**, 183. (b)

BERLYNE, D. E. *Conflict, arousal, and curiosity*. New York: McGraw-Hill, 1960.

BERLYNE, D. E. Motivational problems raised by exploratory and epistemic behavior. In S. Koch (Ed.), *Psychology: A study of a science*. Vol. 5. New York: McGraw-Hill, 1963.

BERLYNE, D. E. *Structure and direction in thinking*. New York: Wiley, 1965.

BERNARD, C. *Leçons sur les propriétés physiologiques et les altérations pathologique des liquides de l'organisme*. Paris: Ballière, 1859. 2 vols.

BERNARD, L. L. *Instinct: A study in social psychology*. New York: Holt, 1924.

BERNSTEIN, B. Language and social class. *British Journal of Sociology*, 1960, **11**, 271–276.

BERRIEN, F. K. *General and social systems*. New Brunswick, N. J.: Rutgers University Press, 1969.

BEXTON, W. H., HERON, W., & SCOTT, T. H. Effects of decreased variation in the sensory environment. *Canadian Journal of Psychology*, 1954, **8**, 70–76.

BIDERMAN, A. D. *March to calumny*. New York: Macmillan, 1963.

BIERI, J. Cognitive complexity-simplicity and predictive behavior. *Journal of Abnormal and Social Psychology*, 1955, **51**, 263–268.

BIERI, J. Parental identification, acceptance of authority, and within-sex differences in cognitive behavior. *Journal of Abnormal and Social Psychology*, 1960, **60**, 76–79.

BIERI, J. Complexity-simplicity as a personality variable in cognitive and preferential behavior. In D. W. Fiske & S. R. Maddi (Eds.), *Functions of varied experience*. Homewood, Ill.: Dorsey Press, 1961.

BIERI, J. Cognitive complexity: Assessment issues in the study of cognitive structure. Paper presented at the meeting of the American Psychological Association, Chicago, September, 1965.

BIERI, J. Cognitive complexity and personality development. In O. J. Harvey (Ed.), *Experience, structure, and adaptability*. New York: Springer, 1966.

BIERI, J. Cognitive complexity and judgment of inconsistent information. In R. P. Abelson, E. Aronson, W. J. McGuire, T. M. Newcomb, M. J. Rosenberg, and P. E. Tannenbaum (Eds.), *Theories of cognitive consistency: A sourcebook*. Chicago: Rand McNally, 1968.

BIERI, J., ATKINS, A. L., BRIAR, S., LEAMAN, R. L., MILLER, H., & TRIPODI, T. *Clinical and social judgment.* New York: Wiley, 1966.

BIERI, J., BRADBURN, W. M., & GALINSKY, M. D. Sex differences in perceptual behavior. *Journal of Personality,* 1958, **26,** 1–12.

BIJOU, S. An empirical concept of reinforcement and a functional analysis of child behavior. *Journal of Genetic Psychology,* 1964, **104,** 215–223.

BIJOU, S., & BAER, D. M. *Child development: A systematic empirical theory.* New York: Appleton-Century-Crofts, 1961.

BIJOU, S., & BAER, D. M. Some methodological contributions from a functional analysis of child development. In L. P. Lipsitt & C. C. Spiker (Eds.), *Advances in child development and behavior.* Vol. 1. New York: Academic Press, 1963.

BINDRA, D. *Motivation: A systematic reinterpretation.* New York: Ronald Press, 1959.

BLAKE, R. R., & RAMSEY, G. V. (Eds.) *Perception: An approach to personality.* New York: Ronald Press, 1951.

BLUM, J. S., CHOW, K. L., & PRIBRAM, K. H. A behavioral analysis of the organization of the parieto-temporo-preoccipital cortex. *Journal of Comparative Neurology,* 1950, **93,** 53–100.

BONARIUS, J. C. J. Research in the personal construct theory of George A. Kelly: Role construct repertory test and basic theory. In B. A. Maher (Ed.), *Progress in experimental personality research.* Vol. 2. New York: Academic Press, 1965.

BOWER, G., & TRABASSO, T. Concept identification. In R. C. Atkinson (Ed.), *Studies in mathematical psychology.* Stanford: Stanford University Press, 1964.

BRATTGÅRD, S. O. The importance of adequate stimulation for the chemical composition of retinal ganglion cells during early post-natal development. *Acta Radiologica* (Stockholm), 1952, Suppl. 96, 1–80.

BRAZIER, M. A. B. The historical development of neurophysiology. In J. Field (Ed. in Chief), *The handbook of physiology.* Sec. 1, Vol. 1. *Neurophysiology.* H. W. Magoun (Ed.) Washington, D. C.: American Physiological Society, 1959.

BRIDGER, W. H. Sensory habituation and discrimination in the human neonate. *American Journal of Psychiatry,* 1961, **117,** 991–996.

BROADBENT, D. E. *Perception and communication.* New York: Pergamon, 1958.

BROADHURST, P. L. Emotionality and the Yerkes–Dodson law. *Journal of Experimental Psychology,* 1957, **54,** 345–352.

BRODBECK, A. J. The effects of three feeding variables on the non-nutritive sucking of newborn infants. *American Psychologist,* 1950, **5,** 292–293.

BRODY, N. Anxiety, induced muscular tension, and the statistical structure of binary response sequences. *Journal of Abnormal and Social Psychology,* 1964, **68,** 540–543.

BRODY, N., PETERSEN, E. A., UPTON, M., & STABILE, R. Anxiety, d-amphetamine, meprobamate, and the variability of word associates. *Psychological Reports,* 1967, **21,** 113–120.

BROEN, W. E., & STORMS, L. H. A reaction potential ceiling and response decrements in complex situations. *Psychological Review,* 1961, **68,** 405–415.

BRONFENBRENNER, U. Soviet methods of character education: Some implications for research. *American Psychologist,* 1962, **17,** 550–564.

BRONSHTEIN, A. I., ANTONOVA, T. G., KAMENETSKAYA, N. H., LUPPOVA, V. A., & SYTOVA, V. A. On the development of the functions of analyzers in infants and some animals at the early stage of ontogenesis. In *Problems of evolution of physiological functions.* U.S.S.R.: Academy of Science (Translation Service, H. E. W., Washington, D. C.), 1958.

BROOKS, S. A. Group composition and satisfaction in group function: The contribution of abstractness of personality structure and ascendance. Unpublished thesis, Princeton University, 1962.

BROVERMAN, D. M. Normative and ipsative measurement in psychology. *Psychological Review,* 1962, **69,** 295–305.

BROWN, J. S. Problems presented by the concept of acquired drives. In M. R. Jones

(Ed.), *Current theory and research in motivation: A symposium.* Lincoln: University of Nebraska Press, 1953.

BROWN, R. A determinant of the relationship between rigidity and authoritarianism. *Journal of Abnormal and Social Psychology,* 1953, **48,** 469–476.

BRUNER, J. S. On perceptual readiness. *Psychological Review,* 1957, **64,** 123–152.

BRUNER, J. S. The course of cognitive growth. *American Psychologist,* 1964, **19,** 1–15.

BRUNER, J. S. *Studies in cognitive growth.* New York: Wiley, 1966.

BRUNER, J. S., GOODNOW, J. J., & AUSTIN, G. A. *A study of thinking.* New York: Wiley, 1956.

BRUNER, J. S., MATTER, J., & PAPANEK, M. L. Breadth of learning as a function of drive level and mechanization. *Psychological Review,* 1955, **62,** 1–10.

BRUNER, J. S., & POTTER, M. C. Interference in visual recognition. *Science,* 1964, **144,** 424–425.

BRUNER, J. S., SHAPIRO, D., & TAGIURI, R. The meaning of traits in isolation and in combination. In R. Tagiuri & L. Petrullo (Eds.), *Person perception and interpersonal behavior.* Stanford: Stanford University Press, 1958.

BRUNER, J. S., & TAJFEL, H. Cognitive risk and environmental change. *Journal of Abnormal and Social Psychology,* 1961, **62,** 231–241.

BÜHLER, C. *The first year of life.* (Trans. P. Greenberg & Rowena Ripin). New York: John Day, 1930.

BÜHLER, C., & HETZER, H. Inventar der Verhaltungsweisen des ersten Lebensjahres. *Quellen und Studien zur Jugendkunde,* 1927, **5,** 125–250.

BÜHLER, K. *Die geistige Entwicklung des Kindes.* Jena: Fischer, 1918.

BÜHLER, K. Displeasure and pleasure in relation to activity. In M. L. Reymert (Ed.), *Feelings and emotions: The Wittenberg Symposium.* Worcester, Mass.: Clark University Press, 1928.

BURSILL, A. E. The restriction of peripheral vision during exposure to hot and humid conditions. *Quarterly Journal of Experimental Psychology,* 1958, **10,** 113–129.

BUTLER, R. A. Discrimination learning by Rhesus monkeys to visual exploration motivation. *Journal of Comparative and Physiological Psychology,* 1953, **46,** 95–98.

BUTLER, R. A. Incentive conditions which influence visual exploration. *Journal of Experimental Psychology,* 1954, **48,** 19–23.

BUTLER, R. A. The differential effect of visual and auditory incentives on the performance of monkeys. *American Journal of Psychology,* 1958, **71,** 591–593.

BYRNE, D. Repression-sensitization as a dimension of personality. In B. A. Maher (Ed.), *Progress in experimental personality research.* Vol. 1. New York: Academic Press, 1964.

CALDWELL, B. The effects of infant care. In *Child Development Research.* Vol. 1. New York: Russell Sage Foundation, 1964.

CANNON, W. B. 1915. *Bodily changes in pain, hunger, fear, and rage.* (2nd ed.) New York: Appleton, 1929.

CANNON, W. B. The physiological basis of thirst. *Proceedings of the Royal Society of London,* 1918, **90B,** 283–301.

CANNON, W. B., & WASHBURN, A. L. An explanation of hunger. *American Journal of Physiology,* 1912, **29,** 441–445.

CANTRIL, H., & LIVINGSTON, W. K. The concept of transaction in psychology and neurology. *Journal of Individual Psychology,* 1963, **19,** 3–16.

CARLTON, P. L. Effects on deprivation and reinforcement—magnitude of response variability. *Journal of the Experimental Analysis of Behavior,* 1962, **5,** 481–486.

CARMICHAEL, L. The development of behavior in vertebrates experimentally removed from influence of external stimulation. *Psychological Review,* 1926, **33,** 51–58.

CARR, H. A. *Psychology, a study of mental activity.* New York: Longmans, 1925.

CARRINGTON, J. H. Computer scoring of structural properties of verbal responses. Unpublished master's thesis, Princeton University, 1968.

CATTELL, P. *The measurement of intelligence in infants and young children.* New York: Psychological Corporation, 1940.

CATTELL, R. B. *Personality.* New York: McGraw-Hill, 1950.

CATTELL, R. B., & SCHEIER, I. H. *The meaning and measure of neuroticism and anxiety.* New York: Ronald, 1961.

CHAMPNEYS, F. H. Notes on an infant. *Mind*, 1881, 6, 104–107.

CHARLESWORTH, W. R. Instigation and maintenance of curiosity behavior as a function of surprise versus novel and familiar stimuli. *Child Development*, 1964, 35, 1169–1186.

CHOW, K. L. Effects of partial extirpations of the posterior association cortex on visually mediated behavior. *Comparative Psychology Monographs*, 1951, 20, 187–217.

CHOW, K. L. Further studies on selective ablation of associative cortex in relation to visually mediated behavior. *Journal of Comparative and Physiological Psychology*, 1952, 45, 109–118.

CHOW, K. L. Behavioral effects following destruction of some thalamic association nuclei in monkeys. *A.M.A. Archives of Neurology and Psychiatry*, 1954, 71, 762–771.

COFFMAN, T. L. Personality structure, involvement, and the consequences of taking a stand. Unpublished doctoral dissertation, Princeton University, 1967.

COHEN, B. P. *Conflict and conformity.* Cambridge: M.I.T. Press, 1963.

COLBY, K. M. Computer simulation of a neurotic process. In S. S. Tomkins & S. Messick (Eds.), *Computer simulation of personality.* New York: Wiley, 1963.

COLBY, K. M. Computer simulation of change in personal belief systems. *Behavioral Science*, 1967, 12, 248–253.

CONANT, J. B. *Science and common sense.* New Haven: Yale University Press, 1951.

CREMIN, L. A. *The transformation of the school: Progressivism in American education, 1876–1957.* New York: Knopf, 1962.

CRESPI, L. P. Quantitative variation of incentive and performance in the white rat. *American Journal of Psychology*, 1942, 55, 467–517.

CROCKETT, W. H. Cognitive complexity and impression formation. In B. A. Maher (Ed.), *Progress in experimental personality research.* Vol. 2. New York: Academic Press, 1965.

CROUSE, B., KARLINS, M., & SCHRODER, H. M. Conceptual complexity and marital happiness. *Journal of Marriage and the Family*, 1968, 30, 643–646.

CROWNE, D. P., & MARLOWE, D. *The approval motive.* New York: Wiley, 1964.

CRUTCHFIELD, R. S. Conformity and character. *American Psychologist*, 1955, 10, 191–198.

CRUZE, W. W. Maturation and learning in chicks. *Journal of Comparative Psychology*, 1935, 20, 371–409.

DARLING, F. F. *Wild country.* Cambridge: Cambridge University Press, 1938. (Cited in Thorpe, 1956.)

DASHIELL, J. F. A quantitative demonstration of animal drive. *Journal of Comparative Psychology*, 1925, 5, 205–208.

DAVIS, H. V., SEARS, R. R., MILLER, H. C., & BRODBECK, A. J. Effects of cup, bottle, and breast feeding on oral activities of newborn infants. *Pediatrics*, 1948, 3, 549–558.

DELGADO, J. M. R. Study of some cerebral structures related to transmission and elaboration of noxious stimulation. *Journal of Neurophysiology*, 1955, 18, 261–275.

DELGADO, J. M. R., ROSVOLD, H. E., & LOONEY, E. Evoking conditioned fear by electrical stimulation of subcortical structures in the monkey brain. *Journal of Comparative and Physiological Psychology*, 1956, 49, 373–380.

DEMBER, W. N. Response by the rat to environmental change. *Journal of Comparative and Physiological Psychology*, 1956, 49, 93–95.

DEMBER, W. N., EARL, R. W., & PARADISE, N. Response by rats to differential stimulus complexity. *Journal of Comparative and Physiological Psychology*, 1957, 50, 514–518.

DENNIS, W. Infant development under conditions of restricted practice and of minimal social stimulation. *Genetic Psychology Monographs,* 1941, **23**, 143–189.

DENNIS, W. Causes of retardation among institutional children: Iran. *Journal of Genetic Psychology,* 1960, **96**, 47–59.

DENNIS, W., & NAJARIAN, P. Infant development under environmental handicap. *Psychological Monographs,* 1957, **71** (7, Whole No. 436).

DENNIS, W., & SAYEGH, Y. The effect of supplementary experiences upon the behavioral development of institutional infants. *Child Development,* 1965, **36**, 81–90.

DESCARTES, R. 1649. *Passions de l'ame.* Amsterdam. (Cited in Brazier, 1959).

DEUTSCH, M. Nursery education: The influence of social programming on early development. *Journal of Nursery Education,* 1963, **19**, 45–67.

DEUTSCH, M., & BROWN, B. Social influences in Negro–White intelligence differences. *Journal of Social Issues,* 1964, **20**, 24–35.

DEVALOIS, R. L. The relation of different levels and kinds of motivation to variability of behavior. *Journal of Experimental Psychology,* 1954, **47**, 392–398.

DEWEY, J. The theory of emotion. *Psychological Review,* 1894, **1**, 553–569, and continued as 1895, **2**, 13–32.

DEWEY, J. The reflex arc concept in psychology. *Psychological Review,* 1896, **3**, 357–370.

DEWEY, J. The school and society. In J. Dewey, *The child and the curriculum, and the school and society.* (2nd ed.) Chicago: University of Chicago Press, 1899. (Republished: Phoenix Books, 1956.)

DEWEY, J. *The school and society.* (3rd ed.) Chicago: University of Chicago Press, 1900. (Republished: Phoenix Books, 1960.)

DEWEY, J. *The child and the curriculum.* Chicago: University of Chicago Press, 1902. (Republished: Phoenix Books, 1960.)

DEWEY, J. *Democracy and education.* New York: Macmillan, 1916.

DEWEY, J. From absolutism to experimentalism. In G. P. Adams & P. Ontague (Eds.), *Contemporary American philosophy.* New York: Macmillan, 1930. 2 vols.

DOLLARD, J., DOOB, L. W., MILLER, N. E., & SEARS, R. R. *Frustration and aggression.* New Haven: Yale University Press, 1939.

DOLLARD, J., & MILLER, N. E. *Personality and psychotherapy: An analysis in terms of learning, thinking, and culture.* New York: McGraw-Hill, 1950.

DRIVER, M. J. Conceptual structure and group processes in an inter-nation simulation. Part one: the perception of simulated nations. *Educational Testing Service Research Bulletin,* RB 62–15, 1962.

DRIVER, M. J. Conceptual structure and group processes in an inter-nation simulation: The performance of simulated nations. Unpublished manuscript, Purdue University, 1963.

DUA, S., & MACLEAN, P. D. Localization for penile erection in medial frontal lobe. *American Journal of Physiology,* 1964, **207**, 1425–1434.

DUNCAN, O. D. Path analysis: Sociological examples. *American Journal of Sociology,* 1966, **72**, 1–12.

DUNCKER, K. On problem solving. *Psychological Monographs,* 1945, **58** (5, Whole No. 270).

DUNLAP, K. Are there any instincts? *Journal of Abnormal and Social Psychology,* 1919, **14**, 307–311.

EARL, R. W. Problem solving and motor skill behaviors under conditions of stimulus complexity. Unpublished doctoral dissertation, University of Michigan, 1957.

EASTERBROOK, J. A. The effect of emotion on cue utilization and the organization of behavior. *Psychological Review,* 1959, **66**, 183–201.

EBY, F. 1934. *The development of modern education.* (2nd ed.) Englewood Cliffs, N. J.: Prentice-Hall, 1952.

ELLIS, H. C., & MULLER, D. G. Transfer in perceptual learning following stimulus predifferentiation. *Journal of Experimental Psychology,* 1964, **68**, 388–395.

ENGEN, T., & LIPSITT, L. P. Decrement and recovery of responses to olfactory stimuli in the human neonate. *Journal of Comparative and Physiological Psychology,* 1965, **59**, 312–316.

ENGEN, T., LIPSITT, L. P., & KAYE, H. Olfactory responses and adaptation in the human neonate. *Journal of Comparative and Physiological Psychology,* 1963, **56,** 73–77.

ENGLISH, O. S., & PEARSON, G. H. S. *Emotional problems of living: Avoiding the neurotic patterns.* New York: Norton, 1945.

ERIKSEN, C. W., & WECHSLER, H. Some effects of experimentally induced anxiety upon discrimination. *Journal of Abnormal and Social Psychology,* 1955, **51,** 458–463.

ERIKSON, E. H. *Childhood and society.* New York: Norton, 1950.

ERNST, G. W., & NEWELL, A. *Generality and GPS.* Pittsburgh: Carnegie Institute of Technology, 1967.

EWING, T. A study of certain factors involved in changes of opinion. *Journal of Social Psychology,* 1942, **16,** 63–88.

FALETTI, M. V. An experimental validation of some measures of cognitive complexity. Unpublished thesis, Princeton University, 1968.

FANTZ, R. L. Form preferences in newly hatched chicks. *Journal of Comparative and Physiological Psychology,* 1957, **50,** 422–430.

FANTZ, R. L. Pattern vision in newborn infants. *Science,* 1963, **140,** 296–297.

FANTZ, R. L. Visual experience in infants: Decreased attention to familiar patterns relative to novel ones. *Science,* 1964, **146,** 668–670.

FARBER, I. E. Response fixation under anxiety and non-anxiety conditions. *Journal of Experimental Psychology,* 1948, **38,** 111–131.

FENICHEL, O. *The psychoanalytic theory of neurosis.* New York: Norton, 1945.

FERSTER, C. B., & SKINNER, B. F. *Schedules of reinforcement.* New York: Appleton-Century-Crofts, 1957.

FESTINGER, L. *A theory of cognitive dissonance.* New York: Harper & Row, 1957.

FILLENBAUM, S. Some stylistic aspects of categorizing behavior. *Journal of Personality,* 1959, **27,** 187–195.

FISHER, D. C. *A Montessori mother.* New York: Holt, 1912.

FISKE, D. W., & MADDI, S. R. *Functions of varied experience.* Homewood, Ill.: Dorsey Press, 1961.

FLAVELL, J. H. *The developmental psychology of Jean Piaget.* Princeton, N. J.: Van Nostrand, 1963.

FOX, S. S. Self-maintained sensory input and sensory deprivation in monkeys: A behavioral and neuropharmacological study. *Journal of Comparative and Physiological Psychology,* 1962, **55,** 438–444.

FREEMAN, G. L. *Introduction to physiological psychology.* New York: Ronald Press, 1934.

FREEMAN, G. L. The relationship between performance level and bodily activity level. *Journal of Experimental Psychology,* 1940, **26,** 602–608.

FRENKEL-BRUNSWIK, E. Intolerance of ambiguity as an emotional and perceptual personality variable. *Journal of Personality,* 1949, **18,** 108–143.

FREUD, A. 1936. *The ego and the mechanisms of defence.* (Trans. Cecil Baines.) New York: International Universities Press, 1946.

FREUD, A., & BURLINGHAM, D. *Infants without families.* New York: International Universities Press, 1944.

FREUD, S. 1900. *The interpretation of dreams.* (Trans. A. A. Brill.) New York: Modern Library, 1950.

FREUD, S. 1905. Three contributions to the theory of sex. (Trans. by A. A. Brill.) New York: Modern Library, 1938.

FREUD, S. 1915. Instincts and their vicissitudes. In *Collected Papers.* Vol. 4. London: Hogarth, 1950.

FREUD, S. 1917. *Introductory lectures on psychoanalysis.* (2nd ed.) (Trans. Joan Riviere.) London: Allen & Unwin, 1940.

FREUD, S. 1920. *Beyond the pleasure principle.* (Trans. C. J. M. Hubback.) New York: Boni & Liveright, 1920.

FREUD, S. 1923. *The ego and the id.* (Trans. Joan Riviere.) London: Hogarth, 1950.

FREUD, S. 1926. *Inhibition, symptom, and anxiety.* (Trans. H. A. Bunker as *The problem of anxiety*). New York: Norton, 1936.

FREUD, S. 1932. *New introductory lectures on psychoanalysis.* (Trans. W. J. H. Sprott). New York: Norton, 1933.

FREUD, S. 1936. *The ego and the mechanisms of defense.* New York: International Universities Press, 1946.

FRIENDLY, M. L. The use of multidimensional scaling and related methods in the analysis of complex psychological judgments. Unpublished manuscript, Princeton University, 1968.

FROEBEL, F. 1826. *The education of man.* (Trans. W. N. Hailman). New York: Appleton, 1892.

FUSTER, J. M. Tachistoscopic perception in monkeys. *Federation Proceedings,* 1957, **16**, 43.

GARDINER, G. S. Some correlates of cognitive complexity. Unpublished master's thesis, University of Alberta, 1968.

GARDNER, R. W. Cognitive styles in categorizing behavior. *Journal of Personality,* 1953, **22**, 214–233.

GARDNER, R. W., HOLZMAN, P. S., KLEIN, G. S., LINTON, H. B., & SPENCE, D. P. Cognitive control: A study of individual consistencies in cognitive behavior. *Psychological Issues,* 1959 (1, Whole No. 4).

GARNER, W. R. *Uncertainty and structure as psychological concepts.* New York: Wiley, 1962.

GAURON, E. F., & BECKER, W. C. The effects of early sensory deprivation on adult rat behavior under competition stress: An attempt at replication of a study by Alexander Wolf. *Journal of Comparative and Physiological Psychology,* 1959, **52**, 689–693.

GESELL, A., HALVERSON, H. M., ILG, F. L., THOMPSON, H., CASTNER, B. M., & AMES, L. B. *The first five years of life.* New York: Harper, 1940.

GEWIRTZ, J. L. A learning analysis of the effects of normal stimulation, privation, and deprivation on the acquisition of social motivation and attachment. In B. M. Foss (Ed.), *Determinants of infant behavior: Proceedings of a Tavistock study group on mother–infant interaction held in the house of the CIBA Foundation.* London: Methuen, 1961.

GIBSON, J. J. A critical review of the concept of set in contemporary experimental psychology. *Psychological Bulletin,* 1941, **38**, 781–817.

GILL, M. M. The present state of psychoanalytic theory. *Journal of Abnormal and Social Psychology,* 1959, **58**, 1–8.

GLANZER, M. Stimulus satiation: An explanation of spontaneous alternation and related phenomena. *Psychological Review,* 1953, **60**, 257–268. (a)

GLANZER, M. The role of stimulus satiation in spontaneous alternation. *Journal of Experimental Psychology,* 1953, **45**, 387–393. (b)

GLIXMAN, A. F. Categorizing behavior as a function of meaning domain. *Journal of Personality and Social Psychology,* 1965, **2**, 370–377.

GOODENOUGH, F. L. A critique of experiments on raising the IQ. *Educational Method,* 1939, **19**, 73–79. (Republished in W. Dennis (Ed.), *Readings in child psychology.* Englewood Cliffs, N. J.: Prentice-Hall, 1951.)

GORDON, B. An experimental study of dependence-independence in a social and laboratory setting. Unpublished doctoral dissertation, University of Southern California, 1953.

GRABOWSKI, U. Prägung eines Jungschafs auf den Menschen. *Zeitschrift für Tierpsychologie,* 1941, **4**, 326–329.

GRANIT, R. *Receptors and sensory perception.* New Haven: Yale University Press, 1955.

GRANT, M. Q., WARREN, M., & TURNER, J. K. Community treatment project: An evaluation of community treatment for delinquents. CTP Research Report No. 3. Sacramento: California Youth Authority, 1963.

GREBSTEIN, L. The relative accuracy of actuarial prediction, experienced clinicians, and graduate students in a clinical judgment task. *Journal of Consulting Psychology*, 1963, **27**, 127–132.

GREGG, L. W., & SIMON, H. A. Process models and stochastic theories of simple concept formation. *Journal of Mathematical Psychology*, 1967, **4**, 246–276.

GRÈGOIRE, A. *L'apprentissage du langage: Les deux premières années.* Paris: Droz, 1937.

GRÈGOIRE, A. *L'apprentissage du langage: II. La troisième année et les années suivant.* Paris: Droz, 1947.

GRINKER, R. R., & SPIEGEL, J. P. *Men under stress.* Philadelphia: Blakiston, 1945.

GROOS, K. 1896. *The play of man.* (Trans. E. L. Baldwin.) New York: Appleton, 1905.

GUETZKOW, H. *Simulation in international relations.* Englewood Cliffs, N. J.: Prentice-Hall, 1963.

GUILFORD, J. P. The structure of intellect. *Psychological Bulletin*, 1956, **53**, 267–293.

GUILFORD, J. P. Three faces of intellect. *American Psychologist*, 1959, **14**, 469–479.

GUILFORD, J. P. Creativity, yesterday, today, and tomorrow? *Journal of Creative Behavior*, 1967, **1**, 3–14.

GULLIKSEN, H. The structure of individual differences in optimality judgments. In M. W. Shelly and G. L. Bryan (Eds.), *Human judgments and optimality.* New York: Wiley, 1964.

GUTHRIE, E. R. *The psychology of human conflict: the clash of motives within the individual.* New York: Harper, 1938.

HABER, R. N. Discrepancy from adaptation level as a source of affect. *Journal of Experimental Psychology*, 1958, **56**, 370–375.

HABER, R. N. (Ed.) *Current research in motivation.* New York: Holt, Rinehart, & Winston, 1966.

HALL, C. S., & LINDZEY, G. *Theories of personality.* New York: Wiley, 1957.

HALL, M. 1843. *New memoire on the nervous system.* London: *Proceedings of the Royal Academy.* (Cited in Brazier, 1959.)

HAMMOND, K. R., HURSCH, C. J., & TODD, F. Analyzing the components of clinical inference. *Psychological Review*, 1964, **71**, 438–456.

HAMMOND, K. R., & SUMMERS, D. A. Cognitive dependence on linear and non-linear cues. *Psychological Review*, 1965, **72**, 215–224.

HARLOW, H. F. The formation of learning sets. *Psychological Review*, 1949, **56**, 51–65.

HARLOW, H. F. Learning and satiation of response in intrinsically motivated complex puzzle performance by monkeys. *Journal of Comparative and Physiological Psychology*, 1950, **43**, 289–294.

HARLOW, H. F. The nature of love. *American Psychologist*, 1958, **13**, 673–685.

HARLOW, H. F. The development of affectional patterns in infant monkeys. In B. M. Foss (Ed.), *Determinants of infant behavior.* New York: Wiley, 1961.

HARLOW, H. F., HARLOW, M. K., & MEYER, D. R. Learning motivated by a manipulation drive. *Journal of Experimental Psychology*, 1950, **40**, 228–234.

HARLOW, H. F., & McCLEARN, G. E. Object discrimination learned by monkeys on the basis of manipulation motives. *Journal of Comparative and Physiological Psychology*, 1954, **47**, 73–76.

HARLOW, H. F., & ZIMMERMAN, R. R. Affectional responses in the infant monkey. *Science*, 1959, **130**, 421–432.

HARPER, R. J. C., ANDERSON, O. C., CHRISTENSEN, C. M., & HUNKA, S. M. (Eds.) *The cognitive processes: Readings.* Englewood Cliffs, N. J.: Prentice-Hall, 1964.

HARTMAN, E. B. The influence of practice and pitch-distance between tones on the absolute identification of pitch. *American Journal of Psychology*, 1954, **67**, 1–14.

HARTMANN, H. Ich-Psychologie und Anpassungsproblem (Ego psychology and the problem of adaptation). *Internationale Zeitschrift für Psychoanalyse und Imago*, 1939, **24**, 62–135. Excerpted in D. Rapaport (Ed.), *Organization and pathology of thought: Selected sources.* New York: Columbia University Press, 1951.

HARTMANN, H. 1939. *Ego psychology and the problem of adaptation.* (Trans. D. Rapaport.) New York: International Universities Press, 1958.

HARTMANN, H., KRIS, E., & LOEWENSTEIN, R. M. Comments on the formation of psychic structure. *The psychoanalytic study of the child.* Vol. 2. New York: International Universities Press, 1946.

HARTSOEKER, N. *Essay de dioptrique.* Paris: 1964. Cited by J. Needham, *A history of embryology.* New York: Abelard-Schuman, 1959.

HARVEY, O. J. Some cognitive determinants of influenceability. *Sociometry,* 1964, **27,** 208–221.

HARVEY, O. J. System structure, flexibility, and creativity. In O. J. Harvey (Ed.), *Experience, structure and adaptability.* New York: Springer, 1966.

HARVEY, O. J., HUNT, D. E., & SCHRODER, H. M. *Conceptual systems and personality organization.* New York: Wiley, 1961.

HARVEY, O. J., & SCHRODER, H. M. Cognitive aspects of self and motivation. In O. J. Harvey (Ed.), *Motivation and social interaction.* New York: Ronald Press, 1963.

HARVEY, O. J., & WARE, R. Personality differences in dissonance resolution. *Journal of Personality and Social Psychology,* 1967, **7,** 227–230.

HAYWOOD, H. C. Relationships among anxiety, seeking of novel stimuli, and level of unassimilated percepts. *Journal of Personality,* 1961, **29,** 105–114.

HAYWOOD, H. C. Novelty-seeking behavior as a function of manifest anxiety and physiological arousal. *Journal of Personality,* 1962, **30,** 63–74.

HAYWOOD, H. C. Differential effects of delayed auditory feedback upon palmar sweating, heart rate, and pulse pressure. *Journal of Speech and Hearing Research,* 1963, **6,** 181–186.

HAYWOOD, H. C., & HUNT, J. McV. Effects of epinephrine upon novelty preference and arousal. *Journal of Abnormal and Social Psychology,* 1963, **67,** 206–213.

HEAD, H. *Studies in neurology.* London: Oxford University Press, 1920.

HEBB, D. O. On the nature of fear. *Psychological Review,* 1946, **53,** 259–276.

HEBB, D. O. *The organization of behavior.* New York: Wiley, 1949.

HEBB, D. O. Drives and the C. N. S. (conceptual nervous system). *Psychological Review,* 1955, **62,** 243–254.

HEBB, D. O., & RIESEN, A. H. The genesis of irrational fears. *Bulletin of the Canadian Psychological Association,* 1943, **3,** 49–50.

HEBB, D. O., & THOMPSON, W. R. The social significance of animal studies. In G. Lindzey (Ed.), *Handbook of social psychology.* Vol. 1. Reading, Mass.: Addison-Wesley, 1954.

HEDIGER, H. *Wild animals in captivity.* (Trans. G. Sircom.) London: Buttersworth, 1950. (Cited in Thorpe, 1956.)

HEIDER, F. *The psychology of interpersonal relations.* New York: McGraw-Hill, 1958.

HEINROTH, O. 1910. Beitrage zur Biologie, namentlich Ethologie und Physiologie der Anatiden. *Verhandlunger des V International Ornithologische Kongress,* 589–702. (Cited in Thorpe, 1956.)

HELM, C. E., & TUCKER, L. R. Individual differences in the structure of color perception. *American Journal of Psychology,* 1962, **75,** 437–444.

HELSON, H. Adaptation-level as frame of reference for prediction of psychophysical data. *American Journal of Psychology,* 1947, **60,** 1–29.

HELSON, H. Adaptation-level theory. In S. Koch (Ed.), *Psychology: a study of a science.* Vol. 1. *Sensory, perceptual, and physiological formulations.* New York: McGraw-Hill, 1959.

HELSON, H. *Adaptation-level theory.* New York: Harper & Row, 1964.

HENDRICK, I. Instinct and the ego during infancy. *Psychoanalytic Quarterly,* 1942, **11,** 33–58.

HENDRICK, I. The discussion of the "instinct to master." *Psychoanalytic Quarterly,* 1943, **12,** 561–565.

HERNANDEZ-PEÓN, R., SCHERRER, H., & JOUVET, M. Modification of electric activity in cochlear nucleus during "attention" in unanesthetized cats. *Science,* 1956, **123,** 331–332.

HERON, W., DOANE, B. K., & SCOTT, T. H. Visual disturbances after prolonged perceptual isolation. *Canadian Journal of Psychology,* 1956, **10,** 13–18.

HESS, E. H. The relationship between imprinting and motivation. *Nebraska Symposium on Motivation,* 1959, **7,** 44–77. Lincoln: University of Nebraska Press.

HESS, E. H. Ethology: An approach toward the complete analysis of behavior. In R. Brown, E. Galanter, E. H. Hess, & G. Mandler (Eds.), *New directions in psychology.* New York: Holt, Rinehart & Winston, 1962.

HILGARD, E. R. Human motives and the concept of self. *American Psychologist,* 1949, **4,** 374–382.

HILGARD, E. R. *Theories of learning.* (2nd ed.) New York: Appleton-Century-Crofts, 1956.

HOFFMAN, M. L. Child-rearing practices and moral development: Generalizations from empirical research. *Child Development,* 1963, **34,** 294–318. (a)

HOFFMAN, M. L. Parent discipline and the child's consideration for others. *Child Development,* 1963, **34,** 573–588. (b)

HOFFMAN, P. J. The paramorphic representation of clinical judgment. *Psychological Bulletin,* 1960, **57,** 116–131.

HOLT, E. B. *The Freudian wish and its place in ethics.* New York: Holt, 1915.

HOLT, E. B. *Animal drive and the learning process.* New York: Holt, 1931.

HOLZMAN, P. S. The relation of assimilation tendencies in visual, auditory, and kinesthetic time-error to cognitive attitudes of leveling and sharpening. *Journal of Personality,* 1954, **22,** 375–394.

HOLZMAN, P. S. Scanning: A principle of reality contact. *Perceptual and Motor Skills,* 1966, **23,** 835–844.

HOLZMAN, P. S., & GARDNER, R. W. Leveling and repression. *Journal of Abnormal and Social Psychology,* 1959, **59,** 151–155.

HOUSTON, J. P., & MEDNICK, S. A. Creativity and the need for novelty. *Journal of Abnormal and Social Psychology,* 1963, **66,** 137–141.

HOVLAND, C. I. Effects of the mass media of communication. In G. Lindzey (Ed.), *Handbook of social psychology.* Vol. 2. Reading, Mass.: Addison-Wesley, 1954.

HOVLAND, C. I., HARVEY, O. J., & SHERIF, M. Assimilation and contrast effects in reactions to communication and attitude change. *Journal of Abnormal and Social Psychology,* 1957, **55,** 244–252. (a)

HOVLAND, C. I., & JANIS, I. L. (Eds.) *Personality and persuasibility.* New Haven: Yale University Press, 1959.

HOVLAND, C. I., JANIS, I. L., & KELLEY, H. H. *Communication and persuasion.* New Haven: Yale University Press, 1953.

HOVLAND, C. I., MANDELL, W., CAMPBELL, E. H., BROCK, T., LUCHINS, A. S., COHEN, A. R., McGUIRE, W. J., JANIS, I. L., FEIERABEND, R. L., & ANDERSON, N. H. *The order of presentation in persuasion.* New Haven: Yale University Press, 1957. (b)

HUGHLINGS-JACKSON, J. Evolution and dissolution of the nervous system. *Lancet,* 1884, **1,** 555–558, 649–652, 739–744.

HULL, C. L. *Principles of behavior: An introduction to behavior theory.* New York: Appleton, 1943.

HULL, C. L. *Essentials of behavior.* New Haven: Yale University Press, 1951.

HULL, C. L. *A behavior system.* New Haven: Yale University Press, 1952.

HUMPHREYS, L. G. The effect of random alternation of reinforcement on the acquisition and extinction of conditioned eyelid reactions. *Journal of Experimental Psychology,* 1939, **25,** 141–158. (a)

HUMPHREYS, L. G. Acquisition and extinction of verbal expectation in a situation analogous to conditioning. *Journal of Experimental Psychology,* 1939, **25,** 294–301. (b)

HUMPHREYS, L. G. Extinction of conditioned psychogalvanic responses following two conditions of reinforcement. *Journal of Experimental Psychology,* 1940, **27,** 71–75.

HUMPHREYS, L. G. The strength of a Thorndikian response as a function of the number of practice trials. *Journal of Comparative Psychology,* 1943, **35,** 101–110.

HUNT, D. E. Conceptual systems assessment in planning differential educational treatment and in measuring developmental change. Paper presented at the meeting of the American Psychological Association, Chicago, September, 1965.

HUNT, D. E. A model for analyzing the training of training agents. *Merrill-Palmer Quarterly*, 1966, **12**, 137–156.

HUNT, D. E. Matching models and moral training. Paper presented at the meeting of the Conference on Moral Education, Ontario Institute for Studies in Education, Toronto, June, 1968.

HUNT, E. B. *Concept learning: An information processing problem.* New York: Wiley, 1962.

HUNT, E. B., MARIN, J., & STONE, P. J. *Experiments in induction.* New York: Academic Press, 1966.

HUNT, J. McV. A functional study of observation. *American Journal of Psychology,* 1935, **47**, 1–39.

HUNT, J. McV. The effects of infantile feeding-frustration upon adult hoarding in the albino rat. *Journal of Abnormal and Social Psychology,* 1941, **36**, 338–360.

HUNT, J. McV. Experimental psychoanalysis. In P. L. Harriman (Ed.), *Encyclopedia of Psychology.* New York: Philosophical Library, 1946.

HUNT, J. McV. Experience and the development of motivation: Some reinterpretations. *Child Development,* 1960, **31**, 489–504.

HUNT, J. McV. *Intelligence and experience.* New York: Ronald Press, 1961.

HUNT, J. McV. Motivation inherent in information processing and action. In O. J. Harvey (Ed.), *Motivation and social interaction: Cognitive determinants.* New York: Ronald Press, 1963. (a)

HUNT, J. McV. Piaget's observations as a source of hypotheses concerning motivation. *Merrill-Palmer Quarterly,* 1963, **9**, 263–275. (b)

HUNT, J. McV. Montessori revisited. Introduction to *The Montessori method.* New York: Schocken Books, 1964.

HUNT, J. McV. Intrinsic motivation and its role in psychological development. In D. Levine (Ed.), *Nebraska Symposium on Motivation,* 1965, **13**, 189–282. (Lincoln: University of Nebraska Press.) (a)

HUNT, J. McV. Traditional personality theory in the light of recent evidence. *American Scientist,* 1965, **53**, 80–96. (b)

HUNT, J. McV. Toward a theory of guided learning in development. In R. H. Ojemann & Karen Pritchett (Eds.), *Giving emphasis to guided learning.* Cleveland, Ohio: Educational Research Council, 1966. (a)

HUNT, J. McV. The epigenesis of intrinsic motivation and early cognitive learning. In R. N. Haber (Ed.), *Current research in motivation.* New York: Holt, Rinehart, & Winston, 1966. (b)

HUNT, J. McV., & QUAY, H. C. Early vibratory experience and the question of innate reinforcement value of vibration and other stimuli: A limitation on the discrepancy (burnt soup) principle in motivation. *Psychological Review,* 1961, **68**, 149–156.

HUNT, J. McV., & UZGIRIS, I. C. Cathexis from recognitive familiarity: An exploratory study. In P. R. Merrifield (Ed.), *Experimental and factor analytic measurement of personality: Contributions by students of J. P. Guilford.* Kent, Ohio: Kent State University Press, 1968.

HYDEN, H., & EGYHAZI, E. Nuclear RNA changes of nerve cells during a learning experiment in rats. *Proceedings of the National Academy of Science,* 1962, **48**, 1366–1373.

IGEL, G. J., & CALVIN, A. D. The development of affectional responses in infant dogs. *Journal of Comparative and Physiological Psychology,* 1960, **53**, 302–306.

INHELDER, B., & PIAGET, J. 1955. *The growth of logical thinking from childhood to adolescence: An essay on the construction of formal operational structures.* (Trans. Anne Parsons & S. Milgram.) New York: Basic Books, 1958.

INSKO, C. A. *Theories of attitude change.* New York: Appleton-Century-Crofts, 1967.

IRWIN, M., TRIPODI, T., & BIERI, J. Affective stimulus value and cognitive complexity. *Journal of Personality and Social Psychology,* 1967, **5**, 444–448.

Irwin, O. C. Research on speech sounds for the first six months of life. *Psychological Bulletin*, 1941, **38**, 277–285.

Irwin, O. C. Development of speech during infancy: Curve of phonemic frequencies. *Journal of Experimental Psychology*, 1947, **37**, 187–193.

Jacobsen, C. F., Wolfe, J. B., & Jackson, T. A. An experimental analysis of the functions of the frontal association areas in primates. *Journal of Nervous and Mental Disease*, 1935, **82**, 1–14.

James, H. Flicker: An unconditioned stimulus for imprinting. *Canadian Journal of Psychology*, 1959, **12**, 59–67.

James, W. *Principles of psychology.* New York: Holt, 1890. 2 vols.

James, W. *Talks to teachers on psychology: And to students on some of life's ideals.* New York: Holt, 1899.

Janicki, W. P. Effect of disposition on resolution of incongruity. *Journal of Abnormal and Social Psychology*, 1964, **69**, 579–584.

Jaynes, J. Imprinting: The interaction of learned and innate behavior. I. Development and generalization. *Journal of Comparative and Physiological Psychology*, 1956, **49**, 201–206.

Jaynes, J. Imprinting: The interaction of learned and innate behavior. II. The critical period. *Journal of Comparative and Physiological Psychology*, 1957, **50**, 6–10.

Jaynes, J. Imprinting: The interaction of learned and innate behavior. III. Practice effects on performance, retention, and fear. *Journal of Comparative and Physiological Psychology*, 1958, **51**, 234–237.

Jenkins, W. O., & Stanley, J. C., Jr. Partial reinforcement: A review and critique. *Psychological Bulletin*, 1950, **47**, 193–234.

Jensen, A. R., & Rohwer, W. D., Jr. The Stroop Color-Word Test: A review. *Acta Psychologica*, 1966, **25**, 36–93.

Jersild, A. T., & Holmes, F. B. Children's fears. *Child Development Monographs*, 1935, **20**. (New York: Columbia University Teachers' College.)

Jones, A. Drive and incentive variables associated with the statistical properties of sequences of stimuli. *Journal of Experimental Psychology*, 1964, **67**, 423–431.

Jones, A. Information deprivation in humans. In B. A. Maher (Ed.), *Progress in experimental personality research.* Vol. 3. New York: Academic Press, 1966.

Jones, A., & McGill, D. W. The homeostatic character of information drive in humans. *Journal of Experimental Research in Personality*, 1967, **2**, 25–31.

Jones, A., Wilkinson, H. J., & Braden, I. Information deprivation as a motivational variable. *Journal of Experimental Psychology*, 1961, **62**, 126–137.

Jones, H. E., & Jones, M. C. A study of fear. *Child Education*, 1928, **5**, 136–143.

Kagan, J., Moss, H. A., & Sigel, I. E. The psychological significance of styles of conceptualization. In J. C. Wright & J. Kagan (Eds.), Basic cognitive processes in children. *Monographs of the Society for Research in Child Development*, 1963, **28**, 73–112.

Karlins, M., Lee, R. E., III, & Schroder, H. M. Creativity and information search in a problem-solving context. *Psychonomic Science*, 1967, **8**, 165–166.

Karlins, M. Conceptual complexity and remote-associative proficiency as creativity variables in a complex problem-solving task. *Journal of Personality and Social Psychology*, 1967, **6**, 264–278.

Karlins, M., & Schroder, H. M. Discovery learning, creativity, and the inductive teaching program. *Psychological Reports*, 1967, **20**, 867–876.

Karlins, M., Schroder, H. M., & Streufert, S. A fixed input program for a tactical war game. Unpublished manuscript, American Documentation Institute, Auxiliary Publications Project, Document No. 8621, 1965.

Karp, S. A., Witkin, H. A., & Goodenough, D. R. Alcoholism and psychological differentiation: Effect of alcohol on field dependence. *Journal of Abnormal Psychology*, 1965, **70**, 262–265.

Karplus, J. P. II. Ein Sympathicuszentrum in Zwischenhira. *Archiv für die gesamte Physiologie, Pflügers*, 1910, **135**, 401–416. (Cited in Pribram, 1960.)

KARPLUS, J. P. III. Sympathicusleitung im Gehira und Halsmark. *Archiv für die gesamte Physiologie, Pflügers*, 1912, **143**, 109–127. (Cited in Pribram, 1960.)

KARPLUS, J. P., & KREIDL, A. Gehirn and Sympathicus. I. Zweischenhirabasis und Halssympathicus. *Archiv für die gesamte Physiologie, Pflügers*, 1909, **129**, 138–144. (Cited in Pribram, 1960.)

KATZ, D. The functional approach to the study of attitude. *Public Opinion Quarterly*, 1960, **24**, 163–204.

KATZ, D., & STOTLAND, E. A preliminary statement to a theory of attitude structure and change. In S. Koch (Ed.), *Psychology: A study of a science*. Vol. 3. New York: McGraw-Hill, 1959.

KELLER, H. A. *The story of my life*. New York: Grosset & Dunlap, 1911.

KELLY, G. A. *The psychology of personal constructs*. New York: Norton, 1955. 2 vols.

KELMAN, H. C. Compliance, identification and internalization: Three processes of attitude change. *Journal of Conflict Resolution*, 1958, **2**, 51–60. (Republished in H. Proshansky & B. Seidenberg, *Basic studies in social psychology*. New York: Holt, Rinehart, & Winston, 1965.)

KELMAN, H. C. Processes of opinion change. *Public Opinion Quarterly*, 1961, **25**, 57–79.

KESSEN, W., & KUHLMAN, C. (Eds.) Thought in the young child. *Monographs of the Society for Research in Child Development*, 1962, **27**, (2), Ser. No. 83.

KIERNAN, C. C. Positive reinforcement by light: Comments on Lockard's article. *Psychological Bulletin*, 1964, **62**, 351–357.

KIVY, P. N., EARL, R. W., & WALKER, E. L. Stimulus context and satiation. *Journal of Comparative and Physiological Psychology*, 1956, **49**, 90–92.

KLEIN, G. S. Need and regulation. In M. R. Jones (Ed.), *Nebraska Symposium on Motivation*. Vol. 2. Lincoln: University of Nebraska Press, 1954.

KLEIN, G. S. Cognitive control and motivation. In G. Lindzey (Ed.), *Assessment of human motives*. New York: Rinehart, 1958.

KLEMMER, E. T., & FRICK, F. C. Assimilation of information from dot and matrix patterns. *Journal of Experimental Psychology*, 1953, **45**, 15–19.

KLÜVER, H. Visual functions after removal of the occipital lobes. *Journal of Psychology*, 1941, **11**, 23–45.

KOGAN, N., & WALLACH, M. A. *Risk taking: A study in cognition and personality*. New York: Holt, Rinehart, and Winston, 1964.

KOHLBERG, L. The development of modes of moral thinking in the years ten to sixteen. Unpublished doctoral dissertation, University of Chicago, 1958.

KOHLBERG, L. Development of moral character and moral ideology. In J. Hoffman and L. Hoffman (Eds.), *Review of child development research*. Vol. 1. New York: Russell Sage Foundation, 1964.

KÖHLER, W. 1924. *The mentality of apes*. (Trans. Ella Winter.) New York: Vintage Books, 1959.

KONSTADT, N., & FORMAN, E. Field dependence and external directedness. *Journal of Personality and Social Psychology*, 1965, **1**, 490–493.

KOSLIN, B. L., SUEDFELD, P., & PARGAMENT, R. The induction of belief instability and opinion change. Unpublished manuscript, Princeton University, 1967.

KRUSKAL, J. B. Nonmetric multidimensional scaling: A numerical method. *Psychometrika*, 1964, **29**, 115–129.

LAING, R. D., PHILLIPSON, H., & LEE, A. R. *Interpersonal perception: a theory and method of research*. New York: Springer, 1966.

LANE, R. *Political ideology*. New York: Free Press, 1962.

LANSING, R. W., SCHWARTZ, E., & LINDSLEY, D. B. Reaction time and EEG activation. *American Psychologist*, 1956, **11**, 433.

LASHLEY, K. S. The accuracy of movement in the absence of excitation from the moving organ. *American Journal of Physiology*, 1917, **43**, 169–194.

LATIF, I. The physiological basis of linguistic development and of the ontogeny of meaning: I and II. *Psychological Review*, 1934, **41**, 55–85 and 153–170.

LAWRENCE, D. H., & FESTINGER, L. *Deterrents and reinforcement: The psychology of insufficient reward.* Stanford: Stanford University Press, 1962.

LAWRENCE, E. A. An investigation of some relationships between personality structure and group functioning. Unpublished thesis, Princeton University, 1962.

LEARY, T. *Interpersonal diagnosis of personality.* New York: Ronald Press, 1957.

LEATON, R. N., SYMMES, D., & BARRY, H. Familiarization with the test apparatus as a factor in the reinforcing effect of change in illumination. *Journal of Psychology,* 1963, **55**, 145–151.

LEE, J. C., & TUCKER, R. B. An investigation of clinical judgment: A study in method. *Journal of Abnormal and Social Psychology,* 1962, **64**, 272–280.

LEE, R. E., III. Dispositional and induced information processing structures. Technical Report No. 18, 1968, Princeton University, Office of Naval Research.

LE FURGY, W. G., & WOLOSHIN, G. W. The modification of children's moral judgments through experimentally induced social influence. Unpublished manuscript, Princeton University, 1968.

LEUBA, C. Toward some integration of learning theories: The concept of optimal stimulation. *Psychological Reports,* 1955, **1**, 27–33.

LEVENTHAL, H. Cognitive processes and interpersonal predictions. *Journal of Abnormal and Social Psychology,* 1957, **55**, 176–180.

LEVENTHAL, H., & SINGER, D. L. Cognitive complexity, impression formation, and impression change. *Journal of Personality,* 1964, **32**, 210–226.

LEVIN, J., & BRODY, N. Information deprivation and creativity. Paper presented at the meeting of the Eastern Psychological Association, New York, April, 1966.

LEVY, D. M. Experiments on the sucking reflex and social behavior in dogs. *American Journal of Orthopsychiatry,* 1934, **4**, 203–224.

LEVY, D. M. Release therapy. *American Journal of Orthopsychiatry,* 1939, **9**, 713–736.

LEVY, D. M. The infant's earliest memory of innoculation: a contribution to public health procedures. *Journal of General Psychology,* 1960, **96**, 3–46.

LEWIN, K. *A dynamic theory of personality: Selected papers.* New York: McGraw-Hill, 1935.

LEWIN, K. *Principles of topological psychology.* New York: McGraw-Hill, 1936.

LEWIN, K. *Field theory in social science.* New York: Harper, 1951.

LEWIN, K., LIPPIT, R., & WHITE, R. Patterns of aggressive behavior in experimentally designed social climates. *Journal of Social Psychology,* 1939, **10**, 271–299.

LEWIS, M. M. *Infant speech: A study of the beginnings of language.* (2nd ed.) New York: Humanities Press, 1951.

LIBERMAN, R. Retinal cholinesterase and glycolysis in rats raised in darkness. *Science,* 1962, **135**, 372–373.

LINDSLEY, D. B. Physiological psychology. *Annual Review of Psychology,* 1956, **7**, 323–348.

LINDSLEY, D. B. Psychophysiology and motivation. In M. R. Jones (Ed.), *Nebraska Symposium on Motivation.* Lincoln: University of Nebraska Press, 1957.

LINTON, H. Relations between mode of perception and tendency to conform. Unpublished doctoral dissertation, Yale University, 1952.

LINTON, H., & GRAHAM, E. Personality correlates of persuasibility. In I. L. Janis et al. (Eds.), *Personality and persuasibility.* New Haven: Yale University Press, 1959.

LIPSITT, L. P. Learning in the first year. In L. P. Lipsitt & C. C. Spiker (Eds.), *Advances in child development and behavior.* Vol. 1. New York: Academic Press, 1963.

LIPSITT, L. P., & KAYE, H. Conditioned sucking in the human newborn. *Psychonomic Science,* 1965, **2**, 221–222.

LIPSITT, L. P., KAYE, H., & BOSACK, T. Enhancement of neonatal sucking through reinforcement. *Journal of Experimental Child Psychology,* 1966, **4**, 163–168.

LOCKARD, R. B. Some effects of light upon the behavior of rodents. *Psychological Bulletin,* 1963, **60**, 509–529.

LOEB, J. 1890. *Der Heliotropismus der Thiere und seine Übereinstimmung mit dem Heliotropismus der Pflanzen.* Würzberg: Hertz. (Cited in Loeb, 1918.)

LOEB, J. 1899. *Comparative physiology of the brain and comparative psychology.* New York: Putnam, 1900.

LOEB, J. *Forced movements, tropisms and animal conduct.* Philadelphia: Lippincott, 1918.

LOEHLIN, J. C. *Computer models of personality.* New York: Random House, 1968.

LORENZ, K. The companion in the bird's world. *Auk,* 1937, **54,** 245–273.

LORENZ, K. The comparative method in studying innate behavior patterns. *Society for Experimental Biology Symposia,* 1950, **4,** 221–268.

LUCHINS, A. S. Rigidity and ethnocentrism: A critique. *Journal of Personality,* 1949, **17,** 449–466.

LUNDIN, R. W. *An objective psychology of music.* New York: Ronald Press, 1953.

LUNDY, R. M., & BERKOWITZ, L. Cognitive complexity and assimilative projection in attitude change. *Journal of Abnormal and Social Psychology,* 1957, **55,** 34–37.

LURIA, A. R., & YUDOVICH, F. 1956. *Speech and the development of mental processes in the child.* (Tran. Joan Simon.) London: Staples Press, 1959.

LYNIP, A. W. The use of devices in the collection and analyses of the preverbal utterances of an infant. *Genetic Psychology Monographs,* 1951, **44,** 221–262.

MACCOBY, E. (Ed.) *The development of sex differences.* Stanford: Stanford University Press, 1966.

MACKWORTH, N. H., & BRUNER, J. S. Selecting visual information during recognition by adults and children. Cambridge: Harvard Center for Cognitive Studies (mimeographed), 1965.

MAGENDIE, F. Experiences sur les functions des racines des nerfs rachidiens. *Journal of Physiological Experiences and Pathology,* 1822, **2,** 276. Cited in Brasier, 1959.

MAIER, N. R. F. Reasoning in humans: I. On direction. *Journal of Comparative Psychology,* 1930, **10,** 115–144.

MALTZMAN, I., & RASKIN, D. C. Effects of individual differences in the orienting reflex on conditioning and complex processes. *Journal of Experimental Research in Personality,* 1965, **1,** 1–16.

MANDLER, J. M., & MANDLER, G. *Thinking: From association to Gestalt.* New York: Wiley, 1964.

MARRS, C. L. Categorizing behavior as elicited by a variety of stimuli. Unpublished master's thesis, University of Kansas, 1955. (Cited in Gardner et al., 1959.)

MASLOW, A. H. A dynamic theory of human motivation. *Psychological Review,* 1943, **50,** 370–396.

MASLOW, A. H. *Motivation and personality.* New York: Harper, 1954.

MASSERMAN, J. H. *Behavior and neurosis.* Chicago: University of Chicago Press, 1943.

MATTHEWS, S. A., & DETWILER, S. R. The reaction of Amblystoma embryos following prolonged treatment with chloretone. *Journal of Experimental Zoology,* 1926, **45,** 279–292.

MAYO, C. W., & CROCKETT, W. H. Cognitive complexity and primacy-recency effects in impression formation. *Journal of Abnormal and Social Personality,* 1964, **68,** 335–338.

McCALL, R. B. Stimulus change in light-contingent bar-pressing. *Journal of Comparative and Physiological Psychology,* 1965, **59,** 258–262.

McCALL, R. B. Initial-consequent-change surface in light-contingent bar-pressing. *Journal of Comparative and Physiological Psychology,* 1966, **62,** 35–42.

McCARTHY, D. Language development in children. In L. Carmichael (Ed.), *Manual of child psychology.* (2nd ed.) New York: Wiley, 1954.

McCLELLAND, D. C., ATKINSON, J. W., CLARK, R. W., & LOWELL, E. L. *The achievement motive.* New York: Appleton-Century-Crofts, 1953.

McDOUGALL, W. *Social psychology.* Boston: Luce, 1908.

McDOUGALL, W. *Outline of psychology.* New York: Scribner, 1923.

McGILL, W. J. Multivariate information transmission. *Psychometrika*, 1954, **19**, 97–116.

McGINNIES, E. Emotionality and perceptual defense. *Psychological Review*, 1949, **56**, 244–251.

MEAD, G. H. *The social psychology of George Herbert Mead.* Chicago: University of Chicago Press, 1934. (a)

MEAD, G. H. *Mind, self and society.* C. M. Morris (Ed.) Chicago: University of Chicago Press, 1934. (b)

MEDNICK, S. A. The associative basis of the creative process. *Psychological Review*, 1962, **69**, 220–232.

MEEHL, P. E. Configural scoring. *Journal of Consulting Psychology*, 1950, **14**, 165–171.

MEEHL, P. E. *Clinical versus statistical prediction.* Minneapolis: University of Minnesota Press, 1954.

MEIER, G. W., FOSHEE, D. P., WITTRIG, J. J., PEELER, D. F., & HUFF, F. W. Helson's residual factor versus innate S–R relations. *Psychological Reports*, 1960, **6**, 61–62.

MELTON, A. W. Learning. In W. S. Munroe (Ed.), *Encyclopedia of educational research.* New York: Macmillan, 1941.

MILLER, G. A. What is information measurement? *American Psychologist*, 1953, **8**, 3–11.

MILLER, G. A. The magical number seven, plus or minus two: Some limits on our capacity for processing information. *Psychological Review*, 1956, **63**, 81–97.

MILLER, G. A., GALANTER, E., & PRIBRAM, K. H. *Plans and the structure of behavior.* New York: Holt, Rinehart, & Winston, 1960.

MILLER, H., & BIERI, J. An informational analysis of clinical judgment. *Journal of Abnormal and Social Psychology*, 1963, **67**, 317–325.

MILLER, H., & BIERI, J. Cognitive complexity as a function of the significance of the stimulus object being judged. *Psychological Reports*, 1965, **16**, 1203–1204.

MILLER, J. G. Toward a general theory for the behavioral sciences. *American Psychologist*, 1955, **10**, 513–531.

MILLER, N. E. Experimental studies of conflict. In J. McV. Hunt (Ed.), *Personality and the behavior disorders.* New York: Ronald Press, 1944.

MILLER, N. E. Learnable drives and rewards. In S. S. Stevens (Ed.), *Handbook of experimental psychology.* New York: Wiley, 1951.

MILLER, N. E. Central stimulation and other new approaches to motivation and reward. *American Psychologist*, 1958, **13**, 100–108.

MILLER, N. E., & DOLLARD, J. *Social learning and imitation.* New Haven: Yale University Press, 1941.

MISHKIN, M. Visual discrimination performance following partial ablations of the temporal lobe: II. Ventral surface vs. hippocampus. *Journal of Comparative and Physiological Psychology*, 1954, **47**, 187–193.

MISHKIN, M., & PRIBRAM, K. H. Visual discrimination performance following partial ablations of the temporal lobe: I. Ventral vs. lateral. *Journal of Comparative and Physiological Psychology*, 1954, **47**, 14–20.

MITTELMANN, B. Motility in infants, children, and adults. *Psychoanalytic Study of the Child*, 1954, **9**, 142–177.

MOLTZ, H. Imprinting: Empirical basis and theoretical significance. *Psychological Bulletin*, 1960, **57**, 291–314.

MOLTZ, H. Imprinting: An epigenetic approach. *Psychological Review*, 1963, **70**, 123–138.

MOLTZ, H., ROSENBLUM, L. A., & HALIKAS, N. Imprinting and level of anxiety. *Journal of Comparative and Physiological Psychology*, 1959, **52**, 240–244.

MONTESSORI, M. 1909. *The Montessori method: Scientific pedagogy as applied to child education in "The Children's Houses," with additions and revisions.* (Trans. Anne E. George with Introduction by J. McV. Hunt.) New York: Schocken Books, 1964.

MONTGOMERY, K. C. A test of two explanations of spontaneous alteration. *Journal of Comparative and Physiological Psychology*, 1952, **45**, 287–293.

MONTGOMERY, K. C. Exploratory behavior as a function of "similarity" of stimulus situations. *Journal of Comparative and Physiological Psychology*, 1953, **46**, 129–133.

MONTGOMERY, K. C. The role of exploratory drive in learning. *Journal of Comparative and Physiological Psychology*, 1954, **47**, 60–64.

MONTGOMERY, K. C., & SEGALL, M. Discrimination learning based upon the exploratory drive. *Journal of Comparative and Physiological Psychology*, 1955, **48**, 225–228.

MOORE, H. T. The genetic aspect of consonance and dissonance. *Psychological Review*, 1914, **17** (2, Whole No. 73), 1–68.

MORRIS, C. *Signs, language and behavior.* Englewood Cliffs, N. J.: Prentice-Hall, 1946.

MOTE, F. A., & FINGER, F. W. Exploratory drive and secondary reinforcement in the acquisition and extinction of a simple running response. *Journal of Experimental Psychology*, 1942, **31**, 57–69.

MOWRER, O. H. A stimulus–response analysis of anxiety and its role as a reinforcing agent. *Psychological Review*, 1939, **46**, 553–566.

MOWRER, O. H. On the psychology of "talking birds"—a contribution to language and personality theory. In O. H. Mowrer, *Learning theory and personality dynamics.* New York: Ronald Press, 1950.

MOWRER, O. H. *Learning theory and behavior.* New York: Wiley, 1960.

MOWRER, O. H., & KLUCKHOHN, C. Dynamic theory of personality. In J. McV. Hunt (Ed.), *Personality and the behavior disorders.* New York: Ronald Press, 1944.

MUNSINGER, H., & KESSEN, W. Uncertainty, structure, and preference. *Psychological Monographs*, 1964, **78** (9, Whole No. 586), 1–24.

MUNSINGER, H., & KESSEN, W. Stimulus variability and cognitive change. *Psychological Review*, 1966, **73**, 164–178.

MUNSINGER, H., KESSEN, W., & KESSEN, M. L. Age and uncertainty: Developmental variation in preference for variability. *Journal of Experimental Child Psychology*, 1964, **1**, 1–15.

MURPHY, G. *Historical introduction to modern psychology.* (Rev. ed.) New York: Harcourt, Brace, 1949.

MURRAY, H. A. *Explorations in personality.* New York: Oxford University Press, 1938.

MYERS, A. K., & MILLER, N. E. Failure to find learned drive based on hunger: Evidence for learning motivated by "exploration." *Journal of Comparative and Physiological Psychology*, 1954, **47**, 428–436.

NEEDHAM, J. *A history of embryology.* New York: Abelard-Schuman, 1959.

NEISSER, U. *Cognitive psychology.* New York: Appleton-Century-Crofts, 1967.

NEWELL, A., SHAW, J. C., & SIMON, H. A. Elements of a theory of human problem solving. *Psychological Review*, 1958, **65**, 151–166.

NEWELL, A., & SIMON, H. A. Computer simulation of human thinking. *Science*, 1961, **134**, 2011–2017.

NEWTON, J. R. Judgment and feedback in a quasi-clinical situation. *Journal of Personality and Social Psychology*, 1965, **1**, 336–342.

NICHOLS, I., & HUNT, J. McV. A case of partial bilateral frontal lobectomy: A psychopathological study. *American Journal of Psychiatry*, 1940, **96**, 1063–1083.

NISSEN, H. W. A study of exploratory behavior in the white rat by means of the obstruction method. *Journal of Genetic Psychology*, 1930, **37**, 361–378.

NISSEN, H. W. The nature of drive as innate determinant of behavioral organization. In M. R. Jones (Ed.), *Nebraska Symposium on Motivation.* Lincoln: University of Nebraska Press, 1954.

OLDS, J. Physiological mechanisms of reward. In M. R. Jones (Ed.), *Nebraska Symposium on Motivation.* Lincoln: University of Nebraska Press, 1955.

OLDS, J. Approach-avoidance dissociation in the rat brain. *American Journal of Physiology*, 1960, **199**, 965–968.

OLDS, J., & MILNER, P. Positive reinforcement produced by electrical stimulation of the septal area and other regions of the rat brain. *Journal of Comparative and Physiological Psychology*, 1954, **61**, 59–72.

ORLANSKY, H. Infant care and personality. *Psychological Bulletin*, 1949, **46**, 1–48.

OSGOOD, C. E. The nature and measurement of meaning. *Psychological Bulletin*, 1952, **49**, 197–237.

OSGOOD, C. E. Language universals and psycholinguistics. In J. H. Greenberg (Ed.), *Universals of language*. Cambridge: M.I.T. Press, 1963.

OSGOOD, C. E., SAPORTA, S., & NUNNALLY, J. Evaluative assertion analysis. *Litera*, 1956, 3, 47–102.

OSGOOD, C. E., SUCI, G. J., & TANNENBAUM, P. H. *The measurement of meaning*. Urbana: University of Illinois Press, 1957.

OSKAMP, S. How clinicians make decisions from the MMPI: An empirical study. *American Psychologist*, 1962, **17**, 316 (abstract).

PADILLA, S. G. Further studies on the delayed pecking of chicks. *Journal of Comparative Psychology*, 1935, **20**, 413–443.

PAINTER, F. V. N. *Luther on education*. St. Louis: Concordia Publishing House, 1928.

PALMER, T. B. An overview of matching in the community treatment project. Paper presented at the meeting of the Western Psychological Association, San Diego, March, 1968.

PAVLOV, I. P. *Conditioned reflexes*. (Trans. G. V. Anrep.) London: Oxford University Press, 1927.

PAVLOV, I. P. *Lectures on conditioned reflexes*. (Trans. W. H. Gantt.) New York: International Publishers, 1928.

PETRIE, A., COLLINS, W., & SOLOMON, P. Pain sensitivity, sensory deprivation, and susceptibility to satiation. *Science*, 1958, **128**, 1431–1433.

PETTIGREW, T. F. The measurement and correlates of category width as a cognitive variable. *Journal of Personality*, 1958, **26**, 532–544.

PHARES, J. O., & SCHRODER, H. M. Self-scoring manual for Paragraph Completion Test. Technical Report No. 2, Princeton University, Office of Naval Research, 1968.

PIAGET, J. *The moral judgment of the child*. New York: The Free Press, 1932.

PIAGET, J. 1936. *The origins of intelligence in children*. (Trans. Margaret Cook.) New York: International Universities Press, 1952.

PIAGET, J. 1945. *Play, dreams, and imitation in childhood*. (Trans. C. Gattegno & F. M. Hodgson.) New York: Norton, 1951.

PIAGET, J. 1947. *The psychology of intelligence*. (Trans. Malcolm Piercy & D. E. Berlyne.) London: Routledge and Kegan Paul, 1959.

PIAGET, J. *Psychology of intelligence*. Totowa, N. J.: Littlefield, Adams Co., 1950.

PIAGET, J. *The construction of reality in the child*. New York: Basic Books, 1954.

PLATT, J. R. *The step to man*. New York: Wiley, 1966.

POLYA, G. *How to solve it*. Princeton, N. J.: Princeton University Press, 1945.

POOL, I., ABELSON, R. P., & POPKIN, S. L. *Candidates, issues, and strategies*. Cambridge: M.I.T. Press, 1964.

PRATT, K. C. The neonate. In L. Carmichael (Ed.), *Manual of child psychology*. New York: Wiley, 1954.

PRIBRAM, K. H. Neocortical function in behavior. In H. F. Harlow & C. N. Woolsey (Eds.), *Biological and biochemical bases of behavior*. Madison: University of Wisconsin Press, 1958.

PRIBRAM, K. H. A review of theory in physiological psychology. *Annual Review of Psychology*, 1960, **11**, 1–40.

PRUETTE, L. *G. Stanley Hall: A biography of a mind*. New York: Appleton, 1926.

QUILLIAN, M. R. Word concepts: A theory and simulation of some basic semantic capabilities. *Behavioral Science*, 1967, **12**, 410–430.

RAMÓN Y CAJAL, S. *Textura del sisteme nervioso del hombre y de los vertebrados.* Madrid: 1904.

RAMSEY, A. O. Familial recognition in domestic birds. *Auk,* 1951, **58,** 57–58.

RANKEN, H. B. Effects of name learning on serial learning, position learning and recognition learning with random shapes. *Psychological Reports,* 1963, **13,** 663–678.

RAPAPORT, D. Toward a theory of thinking. In D. Rapaport (Ed.), *Organization and pathology of thought: Selected sources.* New York: Columbia University Press, 1951.

RAPAPORT, D. Cognitive structures. In J. S. Bruner *et al., Contemporary approaches to cognition: A Symposium at the University of Colorado.* Cambridge: Harvard University Press, 1957.

RAPAPORT, D. The theory of ego autonomy: A generalization. *Bulletin of the Menninger Clinic,* 1958, **22,** 13–35.

RAPAPORT, D. The structure of psychoanalytic theory: A systematizing attempt. In S. Koch (Ed.), *Psychology: A study of a science.* Vol. 3. New York: McGraw-Hill, 1959.

RASCH, E. R., SWIFT, H., RIESEN, A. H., & CHOW, K. L. Altered structure and composition of retinal cells in dark-reared mammals. *Experimental Cellular Research,* 1961, **25,** 348–363.

RAZRAN, G. The observable unconscious and the inferable conscious in current Soviet psychophysiology: Interoceptive conditioning, semantic conditioning, and the orienting reflex. *Psychological Review,* 1961, **68,** 81–147.

REED, D. W. A theory of language, speech, and writing. *Elementary English,* 1965, **42,** 845–851.

REITMAN, W. R. Heuristic programs, computer simulations, and higher mental processes. *Behavioral Science,* 1959, **4,** 330–335.

REITMAN, W. R. *Cognition and thought: An information processing approach.* New York: Wiley, 1965.

RESTLE, F. *Psychology of judgment and choice: A theoretical essay.* New York: Wiley, 1961.

RESTLE, F. The selection of strategies in cue learning. *Psychological Review,* 1962, **69,** 329–343.

RIBBLE, M. A. Infantile experience in relation to personality development. In J. McV. Hunt (Ed.), *Personality and the behavior disorders.* Vol. 2. New York: Ronald Press, 1944.

RICHTER, C. P. A behavioristic study of the activity of the rat. *Comparative Psychological Monographs,* 1922, **1** (2).

RICHTER, C. P. Animal behavior and internal drives. *Quarterly Review of Biology,* 1927, **2,** 307–343.

RICKERS-OVSIANKINA, M. Die Wiederaufnahme von unterbrochener Handlungen. *Psychologische Forschung,* 1928, **11,** 302–375.

RIESEN, A. H. The development of visual perception in man and chimpanzee. *Science,* 1947, **106,** 107–108.

RIESEN, A. H. Plasticity of behavior: Psychological aspects. In H. F. Harlow & C. N. Woolsey (Eds.), *Biological and biochemical bases of behavior.* Madison: University of Wisconsin Press, 1958.

ROBBINS, L. C. The accuracy of parental recall of aspects of child development and of child-rearing practices. *Journal of Abnormal and Social Psychology,* 1963, **66,** 261–270.

ROGERS, C. R. *Client-centered therapy.* Boston: Houghton Mifflin, 1951.

ROKEACH, M. *The open and closed mind.* New York: Basic Books, 1960.

ROKEACH, M., & ROTHMAN, G. The principle of belief congruence and the congruity principle as models of cognitive interaction. *Psychological Review,* 1965, **72,** 128–142.

ROMANES, G. J. *Animal intelligence.* New York: Appleton, 1883.

Rose, J. E., & Woolsey, C. N. The relations of thalamic connections, cellular structure and evocable electrical activity in the auditory region of the cat. *Journal of Comparative Neurology,* 1949, **91,** 441–466.

Rosenberg, M. J., Hovland, C. I., McGuire, W. J., Abelson, R. P., & Brehm, J. W. *Attitude organization and change.* New Haven: Yale University Press, 1960.

Rotter, J. B. *Social learning and clinical psychology.* Englewood Cliffs, N. J.: Prentice-Hall, 1954.

Rotter, J. B., Seeman, M., & Liverant, S. Internal versus external control of reinforcement: A major variable in behavior theory. In N. Washburne (Ed.), *Decisions, values, and groups.* Vol. 2. New York: Pergamon, 1962.

Rudin, S. A., & Stagner, R. Figure-ground phenomena in the perception of physical and social stimuli. *Journal of Psychology,* 1958, **45,** 213–225.

Ryan, T. A. *Intentional behavior.* New York: Ronald, 1970.

Salama, A. A., & Hunt, J. McV. "Fixation" in the rat as a function of infantile shocking, handling, and gentling. *Journal of Genetic Psychology,* 1964, **105,** 131–162.

Sarbin, T. R., Taft, R., & Bailey, D. E. *Clinical inference and cognitive theory.* New York: Holt, Rinehart, & Winston, 1967.

Sargent, S. S. *Social psychology.* (3rd ed.) New York: Ronald, 1966.

Sayegh, Y., & Dennis, W. The effect of supplementary experiences upon the behavioral development of infants in institutions. *Child Development,* 1965, **36,** 81–90.

Schachter, S., & Singer, J. E. Cognitive, social and physiological determinants of emotional state. *Psychological Review,* 1962, **69,** 379–399.

Schachter, S., & Wheeler, L. Epinephrine, chlorpromazine, and amusement. *Journal of Abnormal and Social Psychology,* 1962, **65,** 121–128.

Schaffer, H. R., & Emerson, P. E. The development of social attachments in infancy. *Monographs of the Society for Research in Child Development,* 1964, **29** (3, Whole No. 94).

Schiff, W., Caviness, J. A., & Gibson, J. J. Persistent fear responses in Rhesus monkeys to the optical stimulus of "looming." *Science,* 1962, **136,** 982–983.

Schlesinger, H. J. Cognitive attitudes in relation to susceptibility to interference. *Journal of Personality,* 1954, **22,** 354–374.

Schlosberg, H., & Stanley, W. C. A simple test of the normality of twenty-four distributions of electrical skin resistance. *Science,* 1953, **117,** 35–37.

Schneidman, E. S. Psycho-logic: A personality approach to patterns of thinking. In J. Kagan & G. Lesser (Eds.), *Contemporary issues in thematic apperception methods.* Springfield: Charles C Thomas, 1961.

Schneirla, T. C. An evolutionary and developmental theory of biphasic processes underlying approach and withdrawal. In M. R. Jones (Ed.), *Nebraska Symposium on Motivation.* Lincoln: University of Nebraska Press, 1959.

Schneirla, T. C. Aspects of stimulation and organization in approach/withdrawal processes underlying vertebrate behavioral development. In D. H. Lehrman, R. Hinde, and E. Shaw (Eds.), *Advances in the study of behavior.* New York: Academic Press, 1964.

Schroder, H. M., & Blackman, S. The measurement of conceptual dimensions. Technical Report No. 16, Princeton University, Office of Naval Research, 1965.

Schroder, H. M., & Crano, W. D. Complexity of attitude structure and processes of conflict resolution. Unpublished manuscript, Princeton University, 1965.

Schroder, H. M., Driver, M. J., & Streufert, S. *Human information processing.* New York: Holt, Rinehart, & Winston, 1967.

Schroder, H. M., & Harvey, O. J. Conceptual organization and group structure. In O. J. Harvey (Ed.), *Motivation and social interaction: Cognitive determinants.* New York: Ronald Press, 1963.

Schroder, H. M., Harvey, O. J., Hunt, D. E., & Koslin, B. L. Component assessment in Peace Corps trainees. Peace Corps Technical Report, Princeton University, 1965.

SCHRODER, H. M., & HUNT, D. E. The role of three processes in determining responses to interpersonal disagreement. Joint Progress Report: Office of Naval Research, Contract Nonr-171-055 and U.S. Public Health Service, Project No. M-955, 1959.

SCHRODER, H. M., & ROTTER, J. B. Rigidity as learned behavior. *Journal of Experimental Psychology,* 1952, **44**, 141–150.

SCHRODER, H. M., STREUFERT, S., & ALLEN, P. A. The effects of instructional variation and stress on the perception of aniseikonic distortion. Unpublished manuscript, Princeton University, 1962.

SCHRODER, H. M., STREUFERT, S., & WEEDEN, D. The effect of structural abstractness in interpersonal stimuli on the leadership role. Technical Report No. 3, Princeton University, Office of Naval Research, 1964.

SCHULTE, R. H. The effect of drugs and experience on preference for stimulus variability. Unpublished doctoral dissertation, University of Illinois, 1964.

SCOTT, J. P. Social behavior, organization, and leadership in a small flock of domestic sheep. *Comparative Psychology Monographs,* 1945, **18** (4, Whole No. 96), 1–29.

SCOTT, W. A. Conceptualizing and measuring structural properties of cognition. In O. J. Harvey (Ed.), *Motivation and social interaction: Cognitive determinants.* New York: Ronald Press, 1963.

SCOTT, W. A. Flexibility, rigidity, and adaptation: Toward clarification of constructs. In O. J. Harvey (Ed.), *Experience, structure and adaptability.* New York: Springer, 1966.

SEARS, P. S. Doll-play aggression in normal young children: Influence of sex, age, sibling status, father's absence. *Psychological Monographs,* 1951, **65** (6, Whole No. 323).

SEARS, R. R. *Survey of objective studies of psychoanalytic concepts.* Social Science Research Council Bulletin No. 51, 1943.

SEARS, R. R., MACCOBY, E. E., & LEVIN, H. *Patterns of child rearing.* Evanston, Ill.: Row, Peterson, 1957.

SEARS, R. R., WHITING, J. W. M., NOWLIS, V., & SEARS, P. S. Some child-rearing antecedents of aggression and dependency in young children. *Genetic Psychology Monographs,* 1953, **47**, 135–234.

SEARS, R. R., & WISE, G. W. Relation of cup feeding in infancy to thumb-sucking and the oral drive. *American Journal of Orthopsychiatry,* 1950, **20**, 123–138.

SECHENOV, I. M. 1863. Reflexes of the brain. Medizinsky Vestnik. English translation in *Sechenov's Selected Works.* Moscow-Leningrad: State Publications House, 1935, p. 263. (Cited by Brazier, 1959.)

SECHREST, L. B., & JACKSON, D. N. Social intelligence and accuracy of interpersonal predictions. *Journal of Personality,* 1961, **29**, 167–181.

SELFRIDGE, O. G. Pattern recognition and modern computers. *Proceedings of the Western Joint Computer Conference,* 1955, **7**, 91–93.

SEWELL, W. H. Infant training and the personality of the child. *American Journal of Sociology,* 1952, **58**, 150–159.

SEWELL, W. H., & MUSSEN, P. H. The effects of feeding, weaning, and scheduling procedures on childhood adjustment and the formation of oral symptoms. *Child Development,* 1952, **23**, 185–191.

SEWELL, W. H., MUSSEN, P. H., & HARRIS, C. W. Relationships among child training practices. *American Sociological Review,* 1955, **20**, 137–148.

SHANNON, C. E., & WEAVER, W. *The mathematical theory of communication.* Urbana: University of Illinois Press, 1949.

SHARPLESS, S., & JASPER, H. H. Habituation of the arousal reaction. *Brain,* 1956, **79**, 655–680.

SHEPARD, R. N. The analysis of proximities: Multidimensional scaling with an unknown distance function. *Psychometrika,* 1962, **27**, 125–140.

SHELDON, A. B. Preference for familiar or novel stimulation as a function of the novelty of the environment. Unpublished doctoral dissertation, George Washington University, 1967.

SHERIF, C. W., SHERIF, M., & NEBERGALL, R. E. *Attitude and attitude change.* Philadelphia: Saunders, 1965.

SHERIF, M. *The psychology of social norms.* New York: Harper, 1936.

SHERIF, M., & CANTRIL, H. *The psychology of ego involvements.* New York: Wiley, 1947.

SHERIF, M., & HOVLAND, C. I. *Social judgment: Assimilation and contrast effects in communication and attitude change.* New Haven: Yale University Press, 1961.

SHERRINGTON, C. S. *The integrative action of the nervous system.* New York: Scribner's, 1906. (Republished: Cambridge: Cambridge University Press, 1947.)

SHIRLEY, M. The first two years: A study of 25 babies: Vol. II, Intellectual development. *Institute of Child Welfare Monograph Series,* No. 7. Minneapolis: University of Minnesota Press, 1933.

SHRANGER, S., & ALTROCCHI, J. The personality of the perceiver as a factor in person perception. *Psychological Bulletin,* 1964, **62,** 289–308.

SIEBER, J. E., & LANZETTA, J. T. Conflict and conceptual structure as determinants of decision-making behavior. *Journal of Personality,* 1964, **32,** 622–641.

SIMON, H. Motivational and emotional controls of cognitions. *Psychological Review,* 1967, **7,** 29–39.

SIMON, H., & GUETZKOW, H. A model of short and long run mechanisms involved in pressures toward uniformity in groups. *Psychological Review,* 1955, **62,** 56–68.

SKEELS, H. M. Some preliminary findings of three follow-up studies on the effects of adoption on children from institutions. *Children,* 1965, **12,** 33–34.

SKEELS, H. M., & DYE, H. B. A study of the effects of differential stimulation of mentally retarded children. *Proceedings of the American Association on Mental Deficiency,* 1939, **44,** 114–136.

SKINNER, B. F. On the rate of extinction of a conditioned reflex. *Journal of Genetic Psychology,* 1933, **8,** 114–129.

SKINNER, B. F. Are theories of learning necessary? *Psychological Review,* 1950, **57,** 193–216.

SKINNER, B. F. *Science and human behavior.* New York: Macmillan, 1953. (a)

SKINNER, B. F. Some contributions of an experimental analysis of behavior to psychology as a whole. *American Psychologist,* 1953, **8,** 69–78. (b)

SKINNER, B. F. The science of learning and the art of teaching. *Harvard Educational Review,* 1954, **24,** 86–97. (Republished in A. A. Lumsdaine & R. Glaser (Eds.), *Teaching machines and programmed learning.* Washington, D. C.: National Education Association, 1960.)

SKINNER, B. F. The experimental analysis of behavior. *American Scientist,* 1957, **45,** 343–371. (a)

SKINNER, B. F. *Verbal behavior.* New York: Appleton-Century-Crofts, 1957. (b)

SKINNER, B. F. Reinforcement today. *American Psychologist,* 1958, **13,** 94–99.

SMEDSLUND, J. Mental processes involved in rapid logical reasoning. *Scandinavian Journal of Psychology,* 1968, **9,** 187–205.

SMITH, M. B., BRUNER, J. S., & WHITE, R. W. *Opinions and personality.* New York: Wiley, 1956.

SOKOLOV, E. N. Neuronal models and the orienting reflex. In M. A. B. Brazier (Ed.), *The central nervous system and behavior.* New York: Josiah J. Macy Foundation, 1960.

SOKOLOV, E. N. Higher nervous functions: The orienting reflex. *Annual Review of Physiology,* 1963, **25,** 545–580.

SPALDING, D. A. Instinct with original observations on young animals. *Macmillan's Magazine,* 1873, **27,** 282–293.

SPENCE, K. W. The role of secondary reinforcement in delayed reward learning. *Psychological Review,* 1947, **54,** 1–8.

SPENCE, K. W. *Behavior theory and conditioning.* New Haven: Yale University Press, 1956.

SPITZ, R. A. Hospitalism: An inquiry into the genesis of psychiatric conditions in early childhood. *Psychoanalytic Study of the Child,* 1945, **1,** 53–74.

SPITZ, R. A. Hospitalism: A follow-up report. *Psychoanalytic Study of the Child*, 1946, **2**, 113–117.

SPITZ, R. A., & WOLFE, K. M. The smiling response: A contribution to the ontogenesis of social relations. *Genetic Psychology Monographs*, 1946, 34, 57–125.

SPRAGUE, J. M., CHAMBERS, W. W., & STELLAR, E. Attentive, affective, and adaptive behavior in the cat. *Science*, 1961, 133, 165-173.

STAGER, D. P. Conceptual level as a composition variable in small-group decision making. *Journal of Personality and Social Psychology*, 1967, **5**, 152–161.

STAPLES, R. The responses of infants to color. *Journal of Experimental Psychology*, 1932, **15**, 119–141.

STEFFLRE, V. Simulations of people's behavior towards new objects and events. *American Behavioral Scientist*, 1965, 8, 12–15.

STEVENS, S. S. Mathematics, measurement, and psychophysics. In S. S. Stevens (Ed.), *Handbook of experimental psychology*. New York: Wiley, 1951.

STIRNIMANN, F. Ueber das Farbenfinden Neugeborener. *Annales de Pediatrie, La Semaine des Hopitaux*, 1944, **163**, 1–25.

STONE, P. J. *Monitoring and influencing of public opinion: Implications for a democratic society*. New York: Basic Books, 1970.

STONE, P. J., SMITH, M., DYRPHY, D., KELLY, E., CHANG, K., & SPEER, T. Improved quality of content analysis categories: Computerized disambiguation rules for high frequency English words. In G. Gerbner, O. Holsti, W. Paisley, & P. J. Stone (Eds.), *Content in communications*. New York: Wiley, 1969.

STREUFERT, S. Attitude generalization in social triads as a function of personality structure and availability of social support. Unpublished doctoral dissertation, Princeton University, 1962.

STREUFERT, S. Conceptual structure, communication importance and interpersonal attitudes towards conforming and deviant group members. *Journal of Personality and Social Psychology*, 1966, **4**, 100–103.

STREUFERT, S. Increasing failure and response rate in complex decision making. Technical Report No. 12, Rutgers—The State University, Office of Naval Research, 1968.

STREUFERT, S., & CASTORE, C. H. Effects of increasing success and failure on perceived information quality. *Psychonomic Science*, 1968, **11**, 63–64.

STREUFERT, S., CLARDY, M., DRIVER, M. J., KARLINS, M., SCHRODER, H. M., & SUEDFELD, P. A tactical game for the analysis of complex decision making in individuals and groups. *Psychological Reports*, 1965, **17**, 723–729. (a)

STREUFERT, S., & SCHRODER, H. M. Conceptual structure, environmental complexity and task performance. *Journal of Experimental Research in Personality*, 1965, **1**, 132–137.

STREUFERT, S., & STREUFERT, S. C. The effects of conceptual structure, failure and success on attribution of causality and interpersonal attitudes. Technical Report No. 7, Rutgers—The State University, Office of Naval Research, 1967.

STREUFERT, S., SUEDFELD, P., & DRIVER, M. J. Conceptual structure, information search, and information utilization. *Journal of Personality and Social Psychology*, 1965, **2**, 736–740. (b)

STROOP, J. R. Studies of interference in serial verbal reactions. *Journal of Experimental Psychology*, 1935, **18**, 643–661.

SUCHMAN, J. R. Inquiry training and science education. In H. Ruchlis (Ed.), *Laboratories in the classroom*. New York: Science Materials Center, 1960. (a)

SUCHMAN, J. R. Inquiry training in the elementary school. *Science Teacher*, **27**, 42–47, 1960. (b)

SUEDFELD, P. Conceptual and environmental complexity as factors in attitude change. Technical Report No. 14, Princeton University, Office of Naval Research, 1963.

SUEDFELD, P. Attitude manipulation in restricted environments: I. Conceptual structure and response to propaganda. *Journal of Abnormal and Social Psychology*, 1964, **68**, 242–246. (a)

SUEDFELD, P. Conceptual structure and subjective stress in sensory deprivation. *Perceptual and Motor Skills*, 1964, 19, 896–898. (b)

SUEDFELD, P. (Chairman) Personality theory *in vivo:* Field research in conceptual structure. Symposium at the meeting of the Eastern Psychological Association, Boston, April, 1967.

SUEDFELD, P., & HAGEN, R. L. Measurement of information complexity: I. Conceptual structure and information pattern as factors in information processing. *Journal of Personality and Social Psychology*, 1966, 4, 233–236.

SUEDFELD, P., & STREUFERT, S. Information search as a function of conceptual and environmental complexity. *Psychonomic Science*, 1966, 4, 351–353.

SUEDFELD, P., & VERNON, J. Attitude manipulation in restricted environments: II. Conceptual structure and the internalization of propaganda received as a reward for compliance. *Journal of Personality and Social Psychology*, 1966, 3, 586–589. (Republished in R. L. Rosnow & E. J. Robinson (Eds.), *Experiments in persuasion.* New York: Academic Press, 1967.)

SUEDFELD, P., TOMKINS, S. S., & TUCKER, W. H. On some relationships between perceptual and cognitive information processing. *Perception & Psychophysics,* 1969, 6, 45–46.

SUGERMAN, A. A., & HARONIAN, F. Body type and sophistication of body concept. *Journal of Personality*, 1964, 32, 380–394.

SUMNER, W. G. 1906. *Folkways.* Boston: Ginn, 1940.

TAGIURI, R., & PETRULLO, I. (Eds.). *Person perception and interpersonal behavior.* Stanford: Stanford University Press, 1958.

TAJFEL, H., EVERSTINE, L., & RICHARDSON, A. Individual judgment consistencies in conditions of risk taking. *Journal of Personality*, 1964, 32, 550–565.

TALBOT, G. T. Dispositional and induced conceptual level in an impression formation task. Unpublished doctoral dissertation, Princeton University, 1968.

TAYLOR, D. W. Toward an information processing theory of motivation. In M. R. Jones (Ed.), *Nebraska Symposium on Motivation.* Lincoln: University of Nebraska Press, 1960.

TESLER, L., ENEA, H., & COLBY, K. M. *A directed graph representation for computer simulation of belief systems.* Stanford: Stanford University, Department of Computer Science, 1967.

THOMPSON, R. F., & SPENCER, W. A. Habituation: A model phenomenon for the study of neuronal substrates of behavior. *Psychological Review*, 1966, 73, 16–43.

THORNDIKE, E. L. Animal intelligence. *Psychological Review*, 1898, 2 (Monogr. Suppl. 8), 1–109.

THORNDIKE, E. L. *Educational Psychology. I. The original nature of man.* New York: Teachers College, Columbia University, 1913.

THORNDIKE, E. L. *Educational Psychology. II. The psychology of learning.* New York: Teachers College, Columbia University, 1913.

THORNTON, D., & JONES, A. The nonspecific character of information drive with respect to sensory modalities. Paper presented at the meeting of the Midwestern Psychological Association, Chicago, April, 1965.

THORPE, W. H. The learning ability of birds. *Ibis,* 1951, 93, 1–52, 252–296.

THORPE, W. H. *Learning and instinct in animals.* London: Methuen, 1956.

TODD, F. J., & RAPPOPORT, L. A cognitive structure approach to person perception: A comparison of two models. *Journal of Abnormal and Social Psychology,* 1964, 68, 469–478.

TOLMAN, E. C. The nature of fundamental drives. *Journal of Abnormal and Social Psychology,* 1926, 20, 349–358.

TOLMAN, E. C. The law of effect. *Psychological Review*, 1938, 45, 165–203.

TOLMAN, E. C. A stimulus-expectancy need-cathexis psychology. *Science,* 1945, 101, 160–166.

TOLMAN, E. C. Cognitive maps in rats and men. *Psychological Review*, 1948, 55, 189–208.

TOLMAN, E. C., & BRUNSWIK, E. The organism and the causal texture of the environment. *Psychological Review*, 1935, 42, 43–77.

TOMKINS, S. S. *Affect, imagery, consciousness.* New York: Springer, 1962 ff. 4 vols.

TOMKINS, S. S. The psychology of commitment. In S. S. Tomkins & C. Izard (Eds.), *Affect, cognition and personality.* New York: Springer, 1965.

TOMKINS, S. S., & MESSICK, S. (Eds.) *Computer simulation of personality.* New York: Wiley, 1963.

TORBERT, V. W., III. Toward a new national character: Discovering the dimensionality of international perception. Unpublished thesis, Princeton University, 1968.

TORGERSON, W. A. *Theory and methods of scaling.* New York: Wiley, 1958.

TRABASSO, T., & BOWER, G. A. *Attention in learning: theory and research.* New York: Wiley, 1968.

TRIANDIS, H. C. Cultural influences upon cognitive processes. In L. Berkowitz (Ed.), *Advances in experimental social psychology.* New York: Academic Press, 1964.

TRIANDIS, H. C., & FISHBEIN, M. Cognitive interaction in person perception. *Journal of Abnormal and Social Psychology,* 1963, **67**, 446–453.

TRIPODI, T., & BIERI, J. Information transmission in clinical judgments as a function of stimulus dimensionality and cognitive complexity. *Journal of Personality,* 1964, **32**, 119–137.

TRIPODI, T., & BIERI, J. Cognitive complexity, perceived conflict, and certainty. *Journal of Personality,* 1966, **34**, 144–153.

TUCKER, L. R., & MESSICK, S. An individual difference model for multidimensional scaling. *Psychometrika,* 1963, **28**, 333–367.

TUCKMAN, B. W. Personality structure, group composition and group functioning. *Sociometry,* 1964, **27**, 269–487.

TUCKMAN, B. W. Integrative complexity: Its measurement and relation to creativity. *Educational and Psychological Measurement,* 1966, **26**, 269–283.

TUKEY, J. W. Analyzing data—sanctification or detective work. Paper presented at the meeting of the American Psychological Association, San Francisco, September, 1968.

TURIEL, E. An experimental test of the sequentiality of developmental stages in the child's moral judgments. *Journal of Personality and Social Psychology,* 1966, **3**, 611–618.

TURIEL, E. Development processes in the child's moral thinking. In P. Mussen, J. Langer, & M. Covington (Eds.), *New directions in developmental psychology.* New York: Holt, Rinehart, & Winston, 1968.

TURING, A. M. Computing machinery and intelligence. *Mind,* 1950, **59**, 433–460.

ULRICH, R. *Three thousand years of educational wisdom.* Cambridge: Harvard University Press, 1954.

UZGIRIS, I. C. Situational generality of conservation. *Child Development,* 1964, **35**, 831–841.

UZGIRIS, I. C., & HUNT, J. McV. A longitudinal study of recognition learning. Paper presented at the meeting of the Society for Research in Child Development, Minneapolis, March, 1965.

UZGIRIS, I. C., & HUNT, J. McV. An instrument for assessing infant psychological development. (Mimeographed.) Urbana: University of Illinois, Psychological Development Laboratory, 1966.

VANNOY, J. S. Generality of cognitive complexity-simplicity as a personality construct. *Journal of Personality and Social Psychology,* 1965, **2**, 385–396.

VINOGRADOVA, O. S. On the dynamics of the orientation reflex in the process of closing conditioned connections. In L. G. Voronin et al. (Eds.), *Orientirovochny refleks i orientirovochnoeissledovatel' skaia deiatelnost'.* (The orienting reflex and exploratory behavior.) Moscow: Akademiia Pedagogicheskikh Nauk RSFSR, 1958.

VOLKART, E. H. *Social behavior and personality: Contributions of W. I. Thomas to theory and social research.* New York: Social Science Research Council, 1951.

WALKER, A. E., & WEAVER, T. A., JR. Ocular movements from the occipital lobe in the monkey. *Journal of Neurophysiology,* 1940, **3**, 353–357.

WALKER, E. L. Psychological complexity as a basis for a theory of motivation and choice. In D. Levine (Ed.), *Nebraska Symposium on Motivation.* Lincoln: University of Nebraska Press, 1964.

WARDEN, C. J. *Animal motivation: Experimental studies on the albino rat.* New York: Columbia University Press, 1931.

WARR, P. W., & KNAPPER, C. *The perception of people and events.* New York: Wiley, 1968.

WARR, P. W., SCHRODER, H. M., & BLACKMAN, S. The structure of political judgment. *British Journal of Social and Clinical Psychology,* 1969, **8**, 32–43.

WARREN, R. P., & PFAFFMANN, C. Early experience and taste aversion. *Journal of Comparative and Physiological Psychology,* 1958, **52**, 263–266.

WATSON, J. B. Kinaesthetic and organic sensations: Their role in the reactions of the white rat to the maze. *Psychological Monographs,* 1907, **8** (2).

WATSON, J. B. Psychology as the behaviorist views it. *Psychological Review,* 1913, **20**, 158–177.

WATSON, J. B. The place of the conditioned reflex in psychology. *Psychological Review,* 1916, **23**, 89–116.

WATSON, J. B. *Psychology from the standpoint of a behaviorist.* Philadelphia: Lippincott, 1919.

WATSON, J. B. *Behaviorism.* New York: Norton, 1924.

WATSON, J. B. *Psychological care of infant and child.* New York: Norton, 1928.

WATSON, J. B., & RAYNOR, R. Conditioned emotional reactions. *Journal of Experimental Psychology,* 1920, 3, 1–14.

WEISKRANTZ, L. Sensory deprivation and the cat's optic nervous system. *Nature,* 1958, **181**, 1047–1050.

WEIZENBAUM, J. Symmetric list processor. *Communications of the ACM,* 1963, **6**, 524–536.

WENAR, C., & COULTER, J. B. A reliability study of developmental histories. *Child Development,* 1962, **33**, 453–462.

WERNER, H. *Comparative psychology of mental development.* (Rev. ed.) New York: International Universities Press, 1957.

WERTHEIMER, M. Figural aftereffect as a measure of metabolic efficiency. *Journal of Personality,* 1955, **24**, 56–73.

WHITE, B. L., & HELD, R. Plasticity of sensorimotor development in the human infant. In J. F. Rosenblith and W. Allinsmith (Eds.), *The causes of behavior: Readings in child development and educational psychology.* (2nd ed.) Boston: Allyn & Bacon, 1966.

WHITE, R. W. Motivation reconsidered: The concept of competence. *Psychological Review,* 1959, **66**, 297–333.

WHITE, R. W. Competence and the psychosexual stages of development. In *Nebraska Symposium on Motivation.* Lincoln: University of Nebraska Press, 1960.

WHITE, R. W. *The abnormal personality.* (3rd ed.) New York: Ronald, 1964.

WHITING, J. W. M., & CHILD, I. L. *Child training and personality: A cross-cultural study.* New Haven: Yale University Press, 1953.

WIENER, N. *Cybernetics.* New York: Wiley, 1948.

WILLIAMS, S. B. Resistance to extinction as a function of the number of reinforcements. *Journal of Experimental Psychology,* 1938, **23**, 506–522.

WILLIS, T. 1672. *De anima brutorum (De scientia seu cognitione brutorum).* London: Davis. (Cited in Brazier, 1959.)

WISHNER, J. A reanalysis of "Impressions of personality." *Psychological Review,* 1960, **67**, 96–112.

WITKIN, H. A. Sex differences in perception. *Transactions of the New York Academy of Science,* 1949, **12**, 22–26.

WITKIN, H. A. Psychological differentiation and forms of pathology. *Journal of Abnormal Psychology,* 1965, **70**, 317–336.

WITKIN, H. A., DYK, R. B., FATERSON, H. F., GOODENOUGH, D. R., & KARP, S. A. *Psychological differentiation.* New York: Wiley, 1962.

WITKIN, H. A., GOODENOUGH, D. R., & KARP, S. A. Developmental changes in perception. Unpublished manuscript, 1959.

WITKIN, H. A., LEWIS, H. B., HERTZMAN, M., MACHOVER, K., MEISSNER, P. B., & WAPNER, S. *Personality through perception.* New York: Harper, 1954.

Wolf, A. The dynamics of the selective inhibition of specific functions in neuroses. *Psychosomatic Medicine*, 1943, **5**, 27–38. (Republished in S. S. Tomkins (Ed.), *Contemporary psychopathology*. Cambridge: Harvard University Press, 1943.)

Woodworth, R. S. *Dynamic psychology*. New York: Columbia University Press, 1918.

Woodworth, R. S. How emotions are identified and classified. In M. L. Reymert (Ed.), *Feelings and emotions: The Wittenberg symposium*. Worcester, Mass.: Clark University Press, 1928.

Woodworth, R. S. Reinforcement of perception. *American Journal of Psychology*, 1947, **60**, 119–124.

Woodworth, R. S., & Sheehan, M. R. *Contemporary schools of psychology*. (3rd ed.) New York: Ronald, 1964.

Wright, J. C., & Kagan, J. (Eds.) Basic cognitive processes in children. *Monographs of the Society for Research in Child Development*, 1963, **28**.

Yarrow, L. J. The relationship between nutritive sucking experienced in infancy and non-nutritive sucking in childhood. *Journal of Genetic Psychology*, 1954, **84**, 149–162.

Yarrow, L. J. Maternal deprivation: Toward an empirical and conceptual re-evaluation. *Psychological Bulletin*, 1961, **58**, 459–490.

Yarrow, M. R. Problems of methods in parent-child research. *Child Development*, 1963, **34**, 215–226.

Yngve, V. H. A model and a hypothesis for language structure. *Proceedings of the American Philosophical Society*, 1960, **104**, 444–466.

Yoshii, N. K., & Tsukiyama, K. EEG studies on conditioned behavior of the white rat. *Japanese Journal of Physiology*, 1952, **2**, 186–193.

Young, P. T. *Motivation of behavior*. New York: Wiley, 1936.

Young, P. T. *Motivation and emotion*. New York: Wiley, 1961.

Zarcone, V., Gulevich, G., Pivik, T., & Dement, W. Partial REM phase deprivation and schizophrenia. *Archives of General Psychiatry*, 1968, **18**, 194–202.

Zeigarnik, B. Über Behalten von erledigten und unerledigten Handlungen. *Psychologische Forschung*, 1927, **9**, 1–85.

Zigler, E. F. A measure in search of a theory. *Contemporary Psychology*, 1963, **8**, 133–135.

Author Index

Subject Index